Connectionism

Connectionism:

Debates on Psychological Explanation, Volume Two

Edited by
Cynthia Macdonald
and Graham Macdonald

BLACKWELL
Oxford UK & Cambridge USA

Copyright © Basil Blackwell Ltd, 1995

First published 1995

Blackwell Publishers Ltd
108 Cowley Road
Oxford OX4 1JF
UK

Blackwell Publishers Inc.
238 Main Street
Cambridge, Massachusetts 02142
USA

BF311
.C6213
1995

i0631197451

British Library Cataloguing in Publication Data

A CIP catalogue record for this book is available from the British Library.

Library of Congress Cataloging-in-Publication Data

Connectionism: debates on psychological explanation/edited by Cynthia
    Macdonald and Graham Macdonald.
        p. cm.
    Includes bibliographical references and index.
    ISBN 0–631–19744–3 (alk. paper). – ISBN 0–631–19745–1 (pbk.: alk.
paper)
    1. Connectionism. 2. Cognition. I. Macdonald, Cynthia, 1951–.
II. Macdonald, Graham.
    BF311.C6213 1995
    153 – dc20   94–31003
                                                                        CIP

Typeset in 10½ on 12 pt Erhardt by Photoprint, Torquay, Devon
Printed in Great Britain by Hartnolls Ltd, Bodmin, Cornwall

This book is printed on acid-free paper.

Contents

List of Figures   vii

List of Contributors   ix

Acknowledgements   xi

Preface   xii

PART I
Subdoxastic Explanation I: Connectionism and Classical Architecture   1

1   Introduction: Classicism *v.* Connectionism
    Cynthia Macdonald   3

2   On the Proper Treatment of Connectionism
    Paul Smolensky   28

3   Connectionism and Cognitive Architecture: A Critical
    Analysis
    Jerry A. Fodor and Zenon W. Pylyshyn   90

4   Connectionism, Constituency and the Language of
    Thought
    Paul Smolensky   164

5   Connectionism and the Problem of Systematicity: Why
    Smolensky's Solution Doesn't Work
    Jerry A. Fodor and Brian P. McLaughlin   199

6   Reply: Constituent Structure and Explanation in an
    Integrated Connectionist/Symbolic Cognitive Architecture
    Paul Smolensky   223

PART II
Subdoxastic Explanation II: Connectionism and Eliminativism 291

7 Introduction: Connectionism and Eliminativism
  Cynthia Macdonald 293

8 Connectionism, Eliminativism and the Future of Folk
  Psychology
  William Ramsey, Stephen Stich and Joseph Garon 311

9 Connectionist Minds
  Andy Clark 339

10 On the Projectable Predicates of Connectionist Psychology:
  A Case for Belief
  Paul Smolensky 357

11 Reply to Clark and Smolensky: Do Connectionist Minds
  Have Beliefs?
  Stephen Stich and Ted Warfield 395

  Index 412

Figures

Figure 1.1   Typical connectionist network with hidden units.   10

Figure 3.1   A connectionist network model illustrating the two stable representations of the Necker cube. (Reproduced with permission from Feldman and Ballard, 1982, p. 221.)   94

Figure 3.2   A possible connectionist network for drawing inferences from A&B to A or to B.   100

Figure 3.3   A possible connectionist network which draws inferences from $P\&Q\&R$ to P and also draws inferences from $P\&Q$ to P.   130

Figure 4.1   Fodor and Pylyshyn's network.   170

Figure 4.2   Representation of cup with coffee.   172

Figure 4.3   Representation of cup without coffee.   173

Figure 4.4   'Representation of coffee'.   173

Figure 4.5   PTC $v.$ implementationalism. (Reprinted with permission of *Behavioral and Brain Sciences*.)   185

Figure 6.1   Extracting S_j from the vector $\mathbf{q}_j = \mathbf{r}_0 S_j + \mathbf{r}_1 K_j$.   277

Figure 8.1   A semantic network representation of memory in the style of Collins and Quillian (1972).   318

Figure 8.2   Semantic network with one proposition removed.   319

Figure 8.3   Typical three-tiered feed-forward network with 16 input units, four hidden units and one output unit.   325

Figure 8.4   Input weights and bias to first hidden node in network with 16 propositions.   326

Figure 8.5   Weights and biases in network with 16 propositions.   326

Figure 8.6   Network's response to the proposition *Dogs have fur*.   327

Figure 8.7   Input weights and bias to first hidden node in network with 17 propositions.   328

Figure 8.8   Weights and biases in network with 17 propositions.   328

Figure 10.1   RSGnet$_0$, a simplification of RS&G's network RSGnet.   366

Figure 10.2   Diagrams of the state space of RSGnet$_0$ in the visualizable, two-dimensional case of two input units ($n = 2$).   367

Figure 10.3   Given the training vectors $\mathbf{p}$, $\mathbf{q}$ representing propositions for which $tr(p) =$ TRUE, $tr(q) =$ FALSE, the solution space is the intersection of the two half-spaces $\mathbf{p}^+$, $\mathbf{q}^-$. One arbitrarily chosen weight vector $\mathbf{w}$ in the solution space is shown.   369

Figure 10.4   RSGnet$_2$, a version of RSGnet with two hidden units and with extraneous input units removed. Excitatory connections are shown with solid lines, inhibitory with broken lines. The 'bias unit' has constant activity value 1.   387

Contributors

Andy Clark is Senior Lecturer in Philosophy at the University of Sussex and Professor of Philosophy at Washington University. He is author of *Microcognition: Philosophy, Cognitive Science, and Parallel Distributed Processing, Associative Engines*, and articles on the philosophy of psychology.

Jerry A. Fodor is Professor of Philosophy at Rutgers University and CUNY Graduate Center. He has written extensively on the philosophy of mind and the philosophy of psychology, and is author of *The Modularity of Mind, Psychosemantics, A Theory of Content*, and co-author with Ernest LePore of *Holism: A Shopper's Guide*.

Joseph Garon is a former graduate student.

Cynthia Macdonald is Senior Lecturer in Philosophy at the University of Manchester. She is author of *Mind-Body Identity Theories*, and has written articles on metaphysics, the philosophy of mind and the philosophy of psychology.

Brian P. McLaughlin is Associate Professor of Philosophy at Rutgers University. He is editor of *Dretske and his Critics*, co-editor with Ernest LePore of *Actions and Events: Perspectives on the Philosophy of Donald Davidson*, co-editor with Amelie Rorty of *Perspectives on Self-deception*, and author of articles on metaphysics and the philosophy of mind.

Zenon W. Pylyshyn is currently Director of the Center for Cognitive Science and Board of Governors Professor of Cognitive Science at Rutgers University. He is past president of the Society for Philosophy and Psychology and the Cognitive Science Society, and is on the editorial board of seven journals on cognitive science and artificial intelligence. He is author of *Computation and Cognition: towards a Foundation for Cognitive Science*, as well as more than 70 contributions to books and journals.

William Ramsey is Assistant Professor of Philosophy at the University of Notre Dame. He is co-editor, with Stephen Stich and David Rumelhart, of *Philosophy and Connectionist Theory*, and author of articles on the philosophy of mind and the philosophy of psychology.

Paul Smolensky is Professor of Cognitive Science at The Johns Hopkins University and Professor of Computer Science at the University of Colorado at Boulder. He is co-author with Alan Prince of *Optimality Theory: Constraint Interaction in Generative Grammar*, co-author, with Geraldine Legendre and Yoshiro Miyata, of *Principles for an Integrated Connectionist/Symbolic Theory of Higher Cognition*, and author of articles on connectionism and other techniques in artificial intelligence.

Stephen Stich is Professor of Philosophy and Cognitive Science at Rutgers University. His works include *From Folk Psychology to Cognitive Science* and *The Fragmentation of Reason*, and articles on the philosophy of language and the philosophy of psychology. He is co-editor, with Ted Warfield, of *Mental Representation: A Reader*.

Ted Warfield is Assistant Professor of Philosophy at the University of Notre Dame. He is co-editor with Stephen Stich of *Mental Representation: A Reader* and author of articles on the philosophy of mind and epistemology, including articles in *Philosophical Studies, Philosophy and Phenomenological Research, Analysis* and *Synthese*.

Acknowledgements

The editors and the publisher wish to acknowledge with thanks permission to reprint the following material, previously published elsewhere, in this volume.

Andy Clark, 'Connectionist Minds', *Proceedings of the Aristotelian Society*, **90**, 1989/90, reprinted by courtesy of the Editor of the Aristotelian Society: 1989/90.

Jerry A. Fodor and Brian P. McLaughlin, 'Connectionism and the Problem of Systematicity: Why Smolensky's Solution Doesn't Work', *Cognition*, **35**, 1990, reprinted by permission of the authors and Elsevier Science Publishers, BV.

Jerry A. Fodor and Zenon W. Pylyshyn, 'Connectionism and Cognitive Architecture: A Critical Analysis', *Cognition*, **28**, 1988, reprinted by permission of the authors and Elsevier Science Publishers, BV.

William Ramsey, Stephen Stich and Joseph Garon, 'Connectionism, Eliminativism and the Future of Folk Psychology', *Philosophical Perspectives*, **4**, 1990, copyright © Ridgeview Publishing Company, reprinted by permission of the authors and Ridgeview Publishing Company.

Paul Smolensky, 'On the Proper Treatment of Connectionism', *Behavioral and Brain Sciences*, **11**, 1988, reprinted by permission of the author and Cambridge University Press.

Paul Smolensky, 'Connectionism, Constituency and the Language of Thought', in B. Loewer and G. Rey (eds), *Meaning in Mind: Fodor and his Critics* (Oxford, Basil Blackwell, 1991), copyright © 1991 Basil Blackwell, reprinted by permission of the author and Basil Blackwell.

Preface

Those involved in the study of human behaviour and cognition have been interested for decades in the question of what an integrated overall psychology might look like. We are all familiar with the kinds of psychological states that common-sense or 'folk' psychology recognizes. On a day-to-day basis, we make sense of, or explain, human behaviour by attributing to people beliefs, desires and the like – states with propositional content. My going to the refrigerator and reaching for a coke is explained by the fact, among others, that I desire a coke and I believe that there is a coke in the fridge; states which jointly cause my behaviour and do so in virtue of their propositional contents. If my belief and desire had had different contents – if, for example, they had concerned, not coke, but cigarettes – I would have behaved differently: rather than go to the refrigerator, I would have headed for my coat pocket.

We know that many 'folk' theories, such as 'folk' physics, are often left behind by the sciences that they found. We also know, however, that beliefs, desires and other propositional states currently figure in explanations in various parts of psychology. For instance, propositional states figure in explanations of various aspects of cognition, for example, memory, and in explanations in behavioural psychology: human behaviour is thereby usefully predicted and explained. This raises the question of what kinds of descriptions a completed psychology will employ in its explanations. Will that science find room for descriptions of beliefs and desires, states with propositional content? And if so, how might these descriptions relate to descriptions of cognitive processes, the psychological mechanisms involved, for example, in information storage and retrieval, and descriptions of the neurophysiological structures and connections in the brain that underlie cognition?

Since the work of David Marr and others, it has become customary for those working in the behavioural sciences to expect that an adequate overall psychology will employ descriptions at many levels of explanation, and that these explanatory levels will supplement rather than compete with one another. In his seminal work, *Vision*, Marr (1982) developed a theory of visual perception that employs three distinct levels of description. The first, *computational*, level describes the function carried out by the visual system, whereas the second, *algorithmic*, level describes how the system carries out that function, how it computes it. The third, *implementational*, level describes the physical means by which the function is carried out, how the function is physically realized.

Consider, for example, an ADDER, a system that takes numbers as arguments and delivers sums as values. We know that there are many types or kinds of physical mechanisms that qualify as ADDERS, even though they are constructed physically very differently. Take the function $z = 3 (x + y)$. An electronic calculator will realize this function physically differently from a human being; but both are capable of carrying out the function. So there is a difference between a description of an ADDER at the computational level and a description of it at the level of physical implementation. But there is another way in which ADDERS can differ, a way that emerges at the algorithmic level of description. Here differences in the *ways* that various ADDERS carry out the same function at the computational level, differences in the algorithms employed by the systems which need not imply differences at the level of physical implementation, may emerge. Two ADDERS may compute the function $z = 3 (x + y)$ differently. The first may compute the function by adding the values of x and y and multiplying the result by 3, whereas the second may multiply each of the values of x and y by 3 and add the results. These different step-by-step procedures are different algorithms.

Marr's three-level model is widely accepted by theorists involved in the study of human behaviour and cognition. The model is a particularly useful one for illustrating how psychology might both accommodate different varieties of description and explanation and show how these varieties relate to and integrate with one another. It naturally suggests a model for human cognition which can integrate descriptions of propositional states at the computational level with descriptions of states at other (cognitive processing and neurophysiological) explanatory levels.

Theories of cognition concern themselves mainly with the first two of Marr's three levels, the computational and the algorithmic levels. Until recently, such theories have been dominated by a particular view of cognition known as the Classical view (see Fodor and McLaughlin in chapter 5 of this volume).[1] This view, which has its source in the work of Alan Turing, construes cognition as symbol manipulation. The idea is that cognitive processes involve manipulating objects that have a syntax and a semantics, and which can be combined and transformed according to fixed rules. Such symbols are also capable of being stored in and retrieved from memory. In short, the Classical view construes thought as language-like in involving the manipulation of symbols, or representations, that have both a syntax and a semantics.

However, in the 1980s another, alternative view of cognition, based on a model known as connectionist, or parallel distributed processing, emerged. A motivating factor in the development of this new conception was to construct a model of cognition that more closely resembles the structure of the human brain, and so is more biologically plausible than classical models. What prompted the conception was the recognition that the brain is a neural network. Whereas classical models of cognition work serially, i.e. by creating, comparing and transforming strings of symbols according to fixed rules which are seen as governing cognition itself, connectionism offers a very different conception of the basic processing involved in cognition. Connectionist models do not work serially but in parallel and interactive ways. The models involve a network of elementary units or nodes, each of which has a degree of activation. These units are connected to each other and the connections are weighted, so that, given the degree of activation of a unit and the weight of its connections to others, it will either excite or inhibit those other units. The behaviour of the system as a whole is determined by the initial degree of activation of the units plus the strengths of the weights connecting them. Crucially, in widely distributed networks, the individual units or nodes are not semantically interpretable, and the semantically interpretable units, if there are any, do not correspond in a one-to-one way with any discrete unit or collection thereof. So these models represent a departure from the Classical view of cognition as symbol manipulation.

The emergence of connectionist models of cognition has created a great deal of controversy among those involved in the study of human behaviour and cognition. Two important debates have emerged from the controversy, which form the subject matter of this second volume of debates on psychological explanation. (The first volume, *Philosophy of Psychology: Debates on Psychological Explanation*, is also published by Basil Blackwell.) The first centres on the assumption that three crucial and essential features of human cognition, or thought, are (a) its productivity, (b) its inferential coherence, and (c) its systematicity; and that any adequate theory of cognition must explain these features. The claim made by opponents of connectionist models is that they do not explain these features; in particular, they do not explain the systematicity of thought. Thoughts, or cognitive capacities, are systematic if and only if they are *intrinsically* connected, according to Jerry Fodor and Zenon Pylyshyn (see chapter 3). Thought is systematic in the sense that the ability to think *aRb* is intrinsically connected to the ability to think *bRa*. Classical models are capable of explaining systematicity because they construe cognitive processes as operating on symbols; constituents that can be moved around and transformed in strings according to rules. But, it is argued, because connectionist models do not conceive of cognition as involving the manipulation of symbols, they do not explain systematicity in this way. This presents connectionists with a challenge: if they cannot explain systematicity in a Classical way, can they explain it at all?

The response is that the proper understanding of connectionism is one according to which, although the individual activation values of units are incapable of semantic interpretation, patterns of activity, or vectors of activity, are capable of such interpretation. The result, it is claimed, is that connectionist models are able to explain the systematicity of thought, albeit in a non-Classical way.

Both sides of this controversy assume that descriptions of propositional states such as beliefs and desires, the states of common-sense psychology, will figure in an overall theory of cognition. The issue is whether connectionism is up to the job of explaining various features of these states. One side argues that propositional states have certain features, connectionist models do not have these features, therefore connectionist models are not adequate to the task of providing an adequate overall theory of cognition.

This way of viewing the first debate in the volume, that between classicism and connectionism, links it to the second, that between connectionism and eliminativism. The core of the first debate centres on the issue of whether connectionism is compatible with common-sense, or propositional attitude, psychology. If not, and if one believes that descriptions of propositional attitudes will figure in an overall theory of cognition, then connectionism is under threat. The second debate too assumes that propositional states have certain features, viz. (a) semantic evaluability, (b) functional discreteness, and (c) causal efficacy. The question that arises, and upon which the debate focuses, is whether the states of certain connectionist models of memory (and other propositional states) have these three features. One side argues that they do not, so that *if* these models are correct, then common-sense psychology is false. It further argues that if common-sense psychology is false, then there are no propositional states (i.e. that eliminativism is true). The response to this argument is that the first conditional in it is false: connectionist models have all, or most, of the features ascribed to the states of common-sense psychology.

Putting these debates side by side raises interesting and important philosophical questions about the nature of propositional states and methodological questions concerning the possible conflict between emerging scientific theories of the mind and common-sense conceptions. The philosophical questions concern the appropriate way to characterize propositional attitudes. It is indicative of the unsettled nature of discussions of the common-sense conception that there is no overlap in the two debates presented in this volume in the features taken to be characteristic of and essential to propositional states. This in itself raises an interesting methodological question about the appropriate way to respond to a potential conflict between common-sense conceptions and emerging scientific paradigms of the mind. The authors in the second debate accept that if there is a conflict between the emerging connectionist paradigm and the common-sense conception of propositional states, it is the common-sense conception that is under threat. The authors in the first debate, on the other hand, accept that if there is a conflict between the connectionist paradigm and the common-sense conception, it is the connectionist paradigm that is under threat. Neither of the two debate questions the conception of propositional states appealed to in the controversy, and so neither exploits the strategy of attempting to reconcile emerging connectionist paradigms with the common-sense conception by questioning the paradigm of the common-sense conception appealed to. However, by appealing to different conceptions of propositional attitudes, and by invoking different methodological strategies, the two debates in volume should stimulate discussion on these important issues.

Connectionist architectures promise to provide novel and important insights into human behaviour and cognition, but the development of the theory of such architectures is still in its infancy. One point that emerges from both debates in the present volume is the unsettled nature of opinion about exactly how connectionist models are to be understood, and in what way they differ from classical models of cognition. The debates should also stimulate discussion on this important issue.

Each debate consists of papers previously published which present seminal views on the relation between connectionist architectures and propositional states, along with entirely new contributions by certain authors which further the debate. Introductions to each debate are also included. These introductions aim to provide assistance to the reader in identifying the central issues in dispute, and make the volume valuable for upper level courses in philosophy of psychology and cognitive science, whether these be in upper-level undergraduate classes or at postgraduate level. Students of cognitive science, psychology and philosophy will stand to benefit from such a course.

We would like to thank all of the contributors to this volume for their co-operation; working with them has been a great pleasure. We would also like to express our thanks to those who have read and commented on our contributions to the volume, and in particular to Stephen Laurence, Graham Bird, Brian McLaughlin and Eve Garrard. We have benefited greatly from their comments. We wish to extend our thanks to Sue Ashton for her very careful work on a difficult manuscript. Acknowledgements to one another and to our children, Ian and Julia, complete our thanks.

CAM
GFM

Note

1 In this volume, we adopt the following stylistic convention regarding Classical/Connectionist theory and classicism/connectionism. All uses of the terms related to the theory employ an upper-case 'C'; all other uses employ a lower-case 'c'.

Reference

Marr, D. (1982) *Vision*. New York, W.H. Freeman.

PART I

Subdoxastic Explanation I: Connectionism and Classical Architecture

1

Introduction: Classicism *v.* Connectionism

Cynthia Macdonald

How can a physical system such as a human being possess semantic properties – how can it represent Bill Clinton, for instance? And how can such a system be rational, in the sense that its physical state transitions preserve semantic properties? Jerry Fodor has given answers to these questions that make use of three views: the Representational Theory of Mind (RTM), the Language of Thought Hypothesis (LOT) and the Computational Theory of Mind (CTM).[1] Roughly, according to RTM, propositional attitudes, such as the belief that Bill Clinton is a Democrat, are relations between subjects and mental representations that express propositions, and mental processes are sequences of tokenings of mental representations. According to LOT, mental processes involve a form of mental representation that has the central features of a language: specifically, mental representation is language-like in having a combinatorial syntax and semantics. And, according to CTM, mental processes are computational processes, processes that have access only to the formal or syntactic properties of mental representations, not to their semantic properties. Fodor appeals to the 'computer metaphor' to support his view that mental representations are internally structurally isomorphic to the propositions they represent; and it is in virtue of the fact that the operations are defined on syntactic properties of those representations that the causal relations that hold between mental processes preserve semantic relations between mental representations.

The view that mental processes are computational processes (CTM), and the 'computer metaphor' itself, have their source in the work of Alan Turing. Turing created the theoretical device known as a Turing machine in order to formalize the notion of computation. One consequence of his formalization was the birth of classical cognitive science. Turing's formalization (a) circumscribed a class of physical mechanisms solely in terms of their formal properties of symbol manipulation, rather than in terms of their physical compositional features: and (b) showed how these physical mechanisms could solve problems that would normally require human intelligence to solve. Since human beings are also physical mechanisms capable of symbol manipulation, Turing's formalization of the notion of computation suggested that machines can imitate the human mind, and it is this that led to the birth of cognitive science.

Turing conceived of an algorithm as operating on symbols in a deterministic way. In order to demonstrate the deterministic nature of the symbol manipulation, he imagined the algorithm being carried out by a deterministic device (a Turing machine) that operates on symbols written linearly on a long tape marked off into squares, each with only one symbol from a finite alphabet written on it. He supposed that this device could read or write only one symbol at a time on this one-dimensional tape, and that at any time it could only scan one of the squares on the tape.

Turing realized that in order to describe such a mechanism, nothing whatever had to be assumed about its physical make-up. But in order to guarantee that the procedures carried out by the machine really were computational, i.e. were algorithms, he did need to assume that it operated according to a fixed set of rules or instructions. To capture this idea, Turing required that his 'machine' could only 'be' in a finite number of states, and that at any given time, it must be in only one of these states.

Turing showed how it was possible for causal transitions from one syntactic state to another to preserve semantic links between those states' contents, and this inspires the 'computer metaphor' of the mind. Computers illustrate how the syntactic properties of symbols might connect with their causal properties, namely via their syntax. The syntactic properties of symbols are purely formal higher-order properties of them in virtue of which they instantiate causal laws. Fodor says that syntactic properties can be conceived of as properties of symbols' shapes. Because of this we can think of the shape of a symbol as determining its causal role. So we can conceive of symbol tokenings interacting causally in virtue of their shape.

Modern logic has demonstrated that the semantic relations between symbols can be 'mimicked' by their purely formal/syntactic ones (this is the first idea of classicism appealed to by Fodor and Pylyshyn in chapter 3). A logic system consists of a set of symbols plus rules or procedures for manipulating them. In propositional logic, these symbols are taken as standing for propositions plus the logical connectives such as 'and' and 'or'. A goal of propositional logic is to specify a set of rules or procedures which will enable users to deductively generate only true propositions from other true ones. A system of such rules is thereby truth-preserving. From the proof-theoretic perspective, all that matters to the evaluation of a pattern of inference are the relations between symbols themselves, construed as syntactic entities. But from the model-theoretic perspective, what matters to the evaluation of a pattern of inference is that symbols are capable of being identified as true or false. It is an important feature of logical systems that they are able to integrate these two perspectives, and they do this by generating proof procedures that are truth-preserving. In this way, the syntactic properties of symbols are integrated with their semantic ones. This encourages the thought that if we could build machines that operate entirely by transforming symbols, producing only changes in their shapes (or syntactic features) by operating on syntactic features of those symbols, then they will produce these changes if and only if the transformations *preserve* the semantic features of the symbols. This would be an example of a system where the syntax of a symbol determines its causal role in a way that matches the semantic role of content (this is the second idea of classicism appealed to by Fodor and Pylyshyn in chapter 3).

For the computer metaphor to work as a model of the mind, one needs *mental symbols*: mental states that have both semantic and syntactic properties. Then it is possible to explain the inferential connections between semantic properties of mental tokenings in terms of the causal roles of their syntactic properties. The computer metaphor is important for two reasons. First, the human body, and, in particular, the human brain, like a computer, is a *syntactically*, rather than a semantically, driven machine. Causal transactions between brain processes have access only to physical features of those processes, so if brains can think – if human beings can think – it can only be by accessing physical features of physical processes. Syntactic properties are higher-order physical properties, and we know that machines that operate only on these properties of entities are capable of semantic descriptions. So the computer metaphor shows us how the human brain, by operating only on syntactic features of physical processes, could be a semantic system. Secondly, the computer metaphor shows how the causal roles of physical processes' syntactic properties could preserve the semantic roles of those processes' contents. So, if the mind is a kind of computer, then the computer metaphor explains how thoughts that are causally connected are also content-connected.

This conception of how mental processing takes place is often referred to as the 'Classical' view of cognition. Fodor and McLaughlin (Chapter 5, p. 202) summarize the view as follows:

(C): if a proposition P can be expressed in a system of mental representation M, then M contains some complex mental representation (a 'mental sentence') S, such that S expresses P and the (Classical) constituents of S express (or refer to) the elements of P.

It is critical to the debate in this volume between classicism and connectionism that, on the Classical view, both the propositions expressed by mental representations *and* the mental processes themselves have internal (or constituent) structure, and the structure of the one corresponds in an appropriate way to that of the other. This is a central thesis of both LOT and CTM.

Until recently, the Classical view of cognition dominated work in cognitive science. However, in the past decade a second approach to cognitive modelling, the Connectionist approach, has emerged. According to at least one proponent of this approach, Paul Smolensky, connectionist models of cognition are properly viewed as alternatives to, rather than implementations of, classical models. While both sorts of models treat mental processes as representational, and while both postulate constituent structure for mental representations, connectionist models work with a notion of 'constituent' which is decidedly non-Classical. This difference is at the core of the classicist/connectionist debate presented in this volume. The debate revolves around the question of whether the non-Classical constituents that connectionists postulate are 'real' in the sense that they can be deployed in an explanation of three features that are characteristic of, and, according to Fodor, Pylyshyn, McLaughlin and Smolensky alike, essential to, cognitive capacities: their systematicity, their inferential coherence and their productivity. According to classicists like Fodor, Pylyshyn and McLaughlin, Connectionist 'constituents' are *not* real in this sense. And according to connectionists like Smolensky, they are.

The classicists and connectionists involved in this debate all agree, on empirical grounds, that any adequate theory of cognition must explain (among other things) the three features of systematicity, inferential coherence, and productivity. But what is it for a cognitive capacity to be systematic, or inferentially coherent, or productive? According to Fodor and Pylyshyn (Chapter 3, p. 120), 'What we mean when we say that linguistic capacities are *systematic* is that the ability to produce/understand some sentences is *intrinsically* connected to the ability to produce/understand certain others.' Likewise, thought is systematic in that the ability to entertain some thoughts is intrinsically connected to the ability to entertain others. For example, anyone capable of thinking that the dog chases the cat is capable of thinking that the cat chases the dog; anyone capable of preferring cheese to beans is capable of preferring beans to cheese; anyone capable of believing that squares are four-sided figures and who possesses the concept of a rectangle is capable of believing that rectangles are four-sided figures. These capacities are related in two ways. First, the intentional states that involve the exercise of them bear content-connections to one another, and, secondly, the states that bear content-connections to one another are in the same intentional mode (e.g. thought, preference, belief).

Cognitive capacities are also inferentially coherent. Thoughts that $p\&q$ tend to cause thoughts that p and thoughts that q. Cognitive systems that infer p from $p\&q\&r$ also as a rule infer p from $p\&q$. Logically similar inferences are 'matched' by similar cognitive capacities.

Finally, although this is a more controversial matter, cognitive capacities are productive. Anyone capable of thinking that England is damp is capable of thinking that England and Florida are damp, that England, Florida and Madeira are damp, and so on. In general, humans are capable of having indefinitely many and indefinitely complex thoughts. There is no fixed bound to this number or complexity. Since humans are finite, they presumably manage to accomplish this by finite means.

Both classicists and connectionists involved in the debate in this part of the volume agree that human cognitive capacities are productive. In fact, Smolensky thinks that classicism's biggest strength is that it is capable of explaining productivity, whereas at present connectionist approaches have no real explanation for it. Inferential coherence is thought by Fodor and Pylyshyn to be of a piece with systematicity, and its explanation as a distinct feature of cognition plays no real role in the debate between classicists Fodor, Pylyshyn and McLaughlin, on the one hand, and Smolensky, on the other. The main focus of discussion thus centres on the feature of systematicity, and it's near relative, compositionality.

Fodor and Pylyshyn say that in order for a cognitive capacity to be systematic, it needs to be compositional. As noted above, systematically related linguistic capacities and systematically related thoughts are so related in part because of the semantic/content-connections that hold between them. The ability to understand 'The cat chases the dog' is intrinsically connected to the ability to understand 'The dog chases the cat' only in so far as the sentences are semantically related. However, for the sentences to be semantically related requires not only that similar constituent structure be discerned in the sentences thus related, but that the syntactic constituents make the *same* semantic contributions in the two sentences. Similarly for the contents of thoughts. That is to say, similar constituent structure *only* accounts for semantic relations if the semantic constituents are *context-independent*. The constituents in classical systems are context-independent.

This raises a number of issues concerning the status of the constituents in conectionist networks. One question, upon which Fodor and Pylyshyn focus, and to which Smolensky's early reply responds, is whether the constituents in connectionist architectures *are* context-independent. It turns out that this issue can be resolved, as Fodor, Pylyshyn and Smolensky resolve it, by distinguishing between 'weak' and 'strong' compositionality and between local and widely distributed networks. Smolensky agrees with Fodor and Pylyshyn that local connectionist networks, which are only weakly compositional, while working with a notion of a constituent, do *not* employ a notion of a context-independent constituent and hence cannot explain system-aticity.

However, Smolensky argues that certain widely distributed connectionist networks do work with a context-independent notion of a con-stituent which is *genuinely* different from that of a Classical constituent and which is capable of explaining the systematicity of language acquisition/understanding and thought. The central question to which Fodor and Pylyshyn, Fodor and McLaughlin, and Smolensky address themselves, therefore, is this: can the compositionally structured representations of certain widely distributed connectionist networks provide a genuinely non-Classical explanation of systematicity, i.e. provide an explanation of systematicity without invoking the idea that connectionist architectures are implementations of classical ones? Fodor and Pylyshyn's, and Fodor and McLaughlin's, answer is *no*: either (1) connectionist architectures are a genuine alternative to classical ones, in which case connectionist models do not have compositionally structured representations, or (2) connectionist archi-tectures do have compositionally structured representations, in which case connectionist models are not a genuine alternative to classical ones. Smolensky rejects both (1) and (2), arguing that (3) connectionist architectures do have compositionally structured representations that are genuinely non-Classical. In his view, the proper understanding of connectionism is of an architecture which does offer an explanation of systematicity by appealing to a genuinely non-Classical notion of a constituent. The new term Smolensky coins for this architecture in his final reply, an *Integrated Connectionist/Symbolic network* (or ICS network), is intended to mark this unique position Smolensky believes should be occupied by connectionist architectures, *properly* understood. In order to appreciate the debate that follows, four issues need to be addressed:

1 How connectionist models differ from classical ones.
2 What the implications are of the refinement/implementation distinction for the debate between classicists and connectionists.
3 How the strong/weak compositionality distinction figures in the debate between classicists and connectionists.
4 What the issue of 'real' constituents amounts to in the classicist/connectionist debate.

Connectionist Models: How do They Differ from Classical Ones?

Connectionist networks were inspired by the recognition that the brain is a network. The main motivation for developing them was to construct a model of cognition that more closely resembles the structure of the brain, thereby being more biologically plausible. Connectionism can be distinguished from classical cognitivism in that it does not construe cognitive processes as involving symbol manipulation. Instead, it offers a very different model of the basic processing involved in cognition. Crudely, this conception involves a network of elementary units or nodes, each of which has a degree of activation. These units are connected to each other, and these connections are weighted, so that, given the degree of activation of a unit and the weight of its connections to others, it will either excite or inhibit those other units. The whole network is conceived of as a dynamic system which, once supplied with initial input to the input units, spreads inhibitions and excitations among its hidden units, eventually exciting certain output units and inhibiting others. The behaviour of the system as a whole is determined by the initial degree of activation of the units plus the strengths of the weights connecting them. Figure 1.1 (taken from chapter 8, p. 325) is an illustration of a typical connectionist network with hidden units.

Unlike classical models, which work serially (i.e. by creating, modifying and comparing strings of symbols in a step-by-step way), connectionist models work in parallel and interactive ways. The power of connectionist networks lies, not in the individual units, but in the connections between them. Because the way in which connectionist systems 'compute' a solution to a problem is so different from the way in

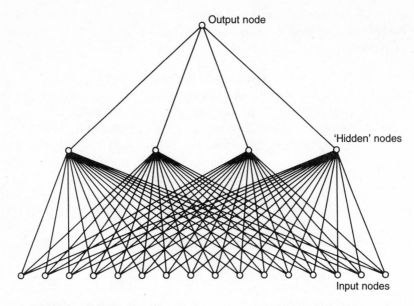

Figure 1.1 Typical connectionist network with hidden units.

which classical ones do, they have a number of interesting features, one of which is that they can be made to 'learn' by altering the weights of the connections as a function of certain sorts of feedback. They are also widely thought to be more neurally plausible and better at pattern recognition than classical systems (although McLaughlin, 1993, disputes this).

Both connectionist and classical models are capable of semantic interpretation. The difference is that, whereas classical models assign semantic content to expressions, i.e. symbols, connectionists assign semantic content to units, or aggregates of units, or, in Smolensky's case, to activity vectors (of units). More precisely, whereas classical systems work with semantically interpretable objects (symbols) that have both causal and structural (syntactic) properties, connectionist systems work with objects (individual units) that have causal properties, plus objects (vectors) that have syntactic (and semantic) properties. More precisely still, the objects that causally interact at the processing level in connectionist networks are not semantically evaluable, and do not have semantically evaluable constituents. What is semantically evaluable in connectionist networks (patterns of activity, or activity vectors) is *not* what does the causal work in those systems: if such systems have semantically evaluable constituents, they are, in Smolensky's words, 'acausally explanatory' (Chapter 6, p. 249).

The Refinement/Implementation Debate

Smolensky argues, in chapter 2, that connectionist architectures are properly understood to be *refinements* of classical ones, rather than implementations of them. In chapter 4, he further elaborates on this point. According to Smolensky, given two accounts of a computational system, one 'higher-level' and the other 'lower-level', 'the lower one is an *implementation* of the higher one if and only if the higher description is a complete, precise, algorithmic account of the behavior of that system' (Chapter 4, p. 167). By this standard, he argues, connectionist systems are *not* implementations of classical ones. In classical architectures, the entities that are semantically evaluable are the *same* entities that are operated on at the algorithmic level. In order for connectionist architectures to implement classical ones, both must work with the same ideas about how semantic content is represented *and* processed. But they do not. Unlike classical systems, connectionist systems involve a 'split-level' architecture: at the level of semantic interpretation, there are constituents, but complete, precise algorithms cannot be defined on them; and at the algorithmic level, complete, precise algorithms can be defined, but on units (constituents) which are not semantically evaluable. In short, connectionist architectures do not work with Classical constituents, constituents which are both semantically evaluable and play a causal role in the behaviour of the system, and Smolensky believes that for this reason they cannot implement classical architectures.

Fodor and Pylyshyn do not see why, for a connectionist architecture to be an implementation of a classical architecture, the entities and structure of the implementing theory must 'match' those of the theory implemented. After all, they point out, theories in biochemistry and quantum mechanics are theories of cognitive implementation, and they work with posits that are likely to differ radically from the posits of theories of cognition. If theories of neural implementation need not constrain theories of cognition in this way, then connectionist models can be viewed as implementations of classical ones (which have their own precise, complete algorithmic accounts) by dropping the semantically evaluable constituents from the account, retaining the activity-unit constituents, and treating the latter, not as the entities on which algorithms are defined, but as the entities that realize classical symbolic algorithms.

However, Smolensky also believes that there is no *need* for classicists to appeal to architectures beyond classical ones, since classical architectures themselves provide precise complete algorithmic accounts of the behaviour of cognitive systems. *A fortiori*, there is no need to appeal to the activity of connectionist units, over which algorithms are defined in connectionist systems, in order to provide such accounts. But Fodor and McLaughlin argue that if the need is to see how brains, which are neural networks, can think, then connectionist systems might serve the very important purpose of illustrating how symbol-manipulating processes can be realized in neural networks. Construed in this way, the debate between classicists and connectionists is no real debate: given that quantum physics implements chemistry, it is like asking whether we should or should not study quantum physics instead of chemistry, or whether the study of quantum phenomena dispenses with the need to study chemistry. The answer is that we need to study both, not that we must choose between them. But then, just as quantum physics is no replacement for chemistry, connectionist models are no replacement for classical ones.

If connectionist models are to be viewed as implementations of classical ones, connectionist algorithms will have no role to play in cognitive modelling. For cognitive modelling is concerned with (a) what cognitive functions are computed; and (b) what algorithms compute these functions. As implementations of cognitive architectures, connectionist architectures will not *compete* with classical architectures, since classical ones alone will provide answers to (a) and (b). Alternatively, Fodor and McLaughlin suggest, connectionists could give up on the idea that connectionist architectures provide an adequate model for cognition generally but argue that they provide an adequate model for certain cognitive processes, such as the drawing of statistical inferences. This would be to opt for a 'mixed model' approach to cognition (to which Fodor and McLaughlin have no objection), but again such an approach would not supplant the Classical approach.

However, this is not the way many connectionists wish to view their project. Smolensky stresses the point that, on a proper understanding of connectionist architectures, they are best viewed as refinements of classical ones, just as quantum mechanics is a refinement of Newtonian. His claim is that, just as Newtonian mechanics is an approximation to quantum mechanics, so too are classical architectures an approximation to connectionists ones. Just as both quantum and Newtonian mechanics are both theories of mechanics and so *compete* with each other, classical and connectionist architectures are both theories of cognition and so compete with each other. The fact that connectionist architectures posit patterns of activity, or activity vectors, that have representational content, and so put themselves forward as models of cognition, is clear evidence of this. And Smolensky himself explicitly rejects the implementation project as one in which connectionists are engaged. Given that classical and connectionist architectures are in competition with one another, and given that both work with a notion of a semantic constituent, the critical question that the debate hinges on is whether connectionist architectures work with a notion of constituent that can explain systematicity, but in a non-classical way.

Weak *v.* Strong Compositional Structure and ICS Systems

It is a central theme of Smolensky's that connectionist architectures assign constituent structure to mental representations. In both chapters 4 and 6, Smolensky introduces the notion of a *vector* as a mental representation, where vectors are patterns of activity over units in Integrated Connectionist/Symbolic (ICS) systems. Smolensky distinguishes between ultra-local and distributed networks, and argues that, while local ones cannot sustain a notion of semantic constituent, distributed ones can. Of these, he distinguishes between weakly compositional networks (the coffee story is intended to illustrate how the notion of a constituent works in these) and strongly compositional networks (where the idea of a tensor product representation is crucial). Smolensky argues that it is in the strongly compositional networks that one finds context-independent constituents, ones which 'can move around and fill any of a number of different roles in different structures' (chapter 4, p. 177). In strongly compositional architectures, mental representations are tensor product representations. Smolensky further explains this notion of a tensor product representation in Chapter 6. Since Smolensky, and Fodor and McLaughlin, are agreed that the weakly compositional architectures do not work with a notion of a constituent that is genuinely semantic, the focus of interest lies in the strongly compositional ones.

Smolensky's aim in his final reply is to show that connectionist architectures, specifically ICS systems, are genuinely symbolic and work with a genuinely semantic notion of a constituent which can explain productivity in a non-Classical way. It is his view that connectionist systems are capable of sharing some important features with classical systems, and his introduction of a new term for his connectionist architecture, 'Integrated Connectionist/Symbolic architecture', is intended to capture this. In particular, the following principles are true of both ICS systems and classical ones:

(3) **Rep**$_{\text{sym}}$: In core parts of higher cognitive domains, representations are symbol structures.

(4) **Sem**$_{\text{sym}}$: The semantic interpretations of these symbolic representations are compositionally derived from their syntactic structure.

(5) **Fun**$_{\text{sym}}$: In core parts of higher cognitive domains, the input/output functions computed by cognitive processes are described by (recursive) symbolic functions. (Chapter 6, p. 224)

The one critical principle of classical systems that is rejected by ICS systems is:

(7) **Alg**$_{\text{sym}}$: Higher cognitive processes are described by symbolic algorithms. (Chapter 6, p. 224)

This is because, as previously noted, ICS systems involve a 'split-level' architecture: the entities (constituents) of representations that are semantically evaluable are not the entities on which algorithms are defined, nor are these constituents implicated in the causal processing of mental representations.

Representations in ICS systems are complex vectors of activity which have as constituents sub-vector representations. These complex representations have syntactic structure in the sense that parse-tree structures can be mapped onto them, and their constituents are 'real' in that they can fill any number of roles in different structures. Smolensky tells us that the formal framework for accounting for this is 'to assume that there is a set of discrete structures S (like parse trees) and a vector space V – a space of activity states of a connectionist network' (chapter 4, p. 178). The structures in S can be mapped onto vectors in the space V by means of tensor product representations, which are constructed in two steps. The first specifies a process whereby discrete structures, such as parse trees, are broken down or decomposed into their constituents, each filling a role in the structure as a whole. This step has nothing specifically to do with connectionist systems: it simply specifies the types of constituents to be represented in those systems. These constituents are role-dependent. The second specifies two connectionist representations, one for the fillers of structural roles, and the other for the roles. Each filler is assigned a vector in the vector space for fillers in the network, and each role is assigned a vector in the vector space for roles in the network. These filler vectors and role vectors are the basic building blocks of tensor product representations.

Each complex representation is a vector generated out of these filler and role constituent vectors, by two operations. The first is the tensor product operation, which multiplies filler vectors and role vectors, i.e. vectors which represent the units that occupy roles and vectors that represent roles that the units occupy, thereby *binding* them, and the vectors that result are 'filled role' vectors. These filled role vectors are tensor product representations, and they realize the constituents of discrete structures, such as parse trees. However, they realize these constituents *in their structural roles*, and so are context-dependent representations. The *true* constituents of tensor product representations in ICS systems are the *filler* vectors, and these are context-independent, unlike the constituents in weakly compositional connectionist architectures. Other complex representations are generated from tensor product ones by the operation of superposition or vector addition. So there are two kinds of complex vectors in ICS systems: tensor product representations, which are generated from filler vectors and role vectors by the tensor product operation, and superposition representations, which are generated from tensor product vectors by vector addition.

Smolensky illustrates how the symbol structure representing the proposition expressed in English as *Sandy loves Kim* is realized in ICS systems. In accordance with the Lisp convention, Smolensky takes the symbol structure representing this proposition to be the binary-branching tree:

(33)

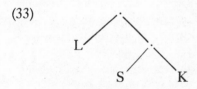

also written as [L, [S, K]] (chapter 6, p. 236). This symbol structure is realized as a complex activity vector, which is decomposable into sub-vectors representing the constituents of the proposition. These sub-vectors realize constituents of the symbol structure (i.e. the atomic symbols L, S, and K, which refer to the predicate and arguments referred to by *loves, Sandy*, and *Kim*) in their roles in the symbol structure. At this level of analysis, the vectors are still complex, since they represent symbols in their roles (e.g. L, in the first syntactic position in the symbol structure). But these vectors can be decomposed still further to vectors that realize symbols (filler vectors), and vectors that realize symbol positions (role vectors). These are the basic building-blocks by which symbolic structures are realized as vectors in ICS systems. Thus, the ICS representation of the symbol structure [L, [S, K]] is

(34) $p = r_0 \otimes L + r_1 \otimes [r_0 \otimes S + r_1 \otimes K]$ (Chapter 6, p. 237)

Just as the symbolic representation [L, [S, K]] of the proposition expressed by *Sandy loves Kim* depends on the association of the predicate 'loves' and the arguments, 'Sandy' and 'Kim', with the symbols L, S, and K, so too in ICS systems the representation of that proposition depends on the association of the predicate 'loves' and the arguments, 'Sandy' and 'Kim', with the activity vectors L, S, and K. Further,

> the symbolic representation [L, [S, K]] of the proposition p depends on an arbitrary association of the propositional arguments Sandy and Kim to the syntactic positions – first and second – of their corresponding symbols S and K in the syntactic structure. Similarly, the ICS representation of p depends on the association of the argument Sandy to a vector r_0 which can be thought of as signifying 'left branch' of a binary-branching tree node; this association is manifest in the part $r_0 \otimes S$ of the ICS representation (34). (Chapter 6, p. 237)

Symbols like $r_0 \otimes S$ are tensor product representations that represent filled roles in symbol structures like [L, [S, K]]. The complex vector that is the representation of the proposition expressed by *Sandy loves Kim* is generated from the vectors that are tensor product representations of its constituents by superimposing, or adding, these vectors.

Similarly, Fodor and McLaughlin illustrate how the account might explain the representation of individual words in the following way:

> consider how a connectionist machine might represent four-letter English words. Words can be decomposed into roles (viz. ordinal positions that letters can occupy) and things that can fill these roles (viz. letters). Correspondingly, the machine might contain activity vectors over units which represent the relevant roles (i.e. over the *role units*) and activity vectors over units which represent the fillers (i.e. over the *filler units*). Finally, it might contain activity vectors over units which represent *filled roles* (i.e. letters in letter positions); these are the *binding units*. The key idea is that the activity vectors over the binding units might be tensor products of activity vectors over the role units and the filler units. The representation of a word would then be a superposition vector over the binding units; that is, a vector that is arrived at by superimposing the tensor product vectors. (Chapter 5, p. 211)

Two features of tensor product representations are critical to their semantic interpretability. One is that tensor products can be recursively embedded: the tensor product, $r \otimes f$ may have constituents which are themselves tensor products, as when $f = a \otimes b$. The second is that, although the vectors of tensor product representations can be decomposed in an infinite number of ways into a sum of vectors, *only* vectors of the form $r_0 \otimes x$ and $r_1 \otimes y$ will be semantically evaluable. Further, Smolensky argues that the fact that r_0 and r_1 are independent vectors makes it impossible for there to be two semantic interpretations of a single vector (so, for any vector of the form $r_0 \otimes x$, there will be a unique semantic interpretation), provided that the vector-space notion of independence is preserved.

Are ICS Constituents Real?

Smolensky claims that superposition representations have constituent syntactic structure in the sense that parse-tree structures can be mapped onto them, and this makes ICS representations symbol structures (Rep_{sym}). He also claims that the semantic interpretation of ICS representations is derived from these symbol structures (Sem_{sym}) and that the input/output functions of ICS systems are described by recursive symbolic functions (Fun_{sym}). However, as Fodor and McLaughlin point out, it does not follow from the fact that Classical tree structures can be mapped onto superposition and tensor product vectors that these vectors have Classical constituent structure, and Smolensky himself explicitly denies that they do have such structure. What Smolensky is concerned to establish is that ICS systems have representations with real constituents, in the sense that they are (a) symbolic, (b) context-independent, (c) semantically evaluable, and (d) involved in the explanation of input/output functions computed by ICS systems. These constituents do not, however, play a causal role in the processes which produce the output of the system. The algorithms of the system are defined on superposition vectors, which are comprised of individual activity values, and the semantically evaluable constituents of these vectors play no causal role in the system. Since Classical constituents are both semantically evaluable and causally implicated in the behaviour of the system, ICS constituents are not Classical.

Smolensky argues that ICS systems' constituent structure can explain productivity, but in a non-Classical way. What makes the explanation non-Classical is that the semantically evaluable constituents (vectors) in ICS systems play no causal role in producing productive behaviour. What does produce such behaviour are individual activity values on which ICS algorithms are defined: such algorithms are non-symbolic, since no single unit, nor any aggregate of units, has a single, fixed, semantic interpretation. Smolensky also claims that neither ICS *nor* classical systems explain compositionality: compositionality is simply assumed in both theories. Further, he claims that, whereas classical systems simply assume systematicity (since they must assume not only that representations are symbol structures in higher cognitive domains, but that these structures form a symbol *system*), ICS systems explain systematicity, albeit in a non-Classical way. Finally, Smolensky acknowledges that the issue of inferential coherence is not currently explicable in ICS systems, whereas it is in classical ones. However, he points out that the Classical assumption that generates an explanation of this feature of cognitive systems on the Classical view, viz.

(81) **Alg$_{sym}$ (Inf)**: Inference is performed by serially applying the symbol manipulation operation of resolution. (Chapter 6, p. 270)

can also be adopted by ICS systems. This would be to view ICS systems as implementing classical ones with regard to inferential coherence. Smolensky's preferred option is to wait and see whether better ICS approaches might become available to explain this feature of cognition.

A number of questions arise out of Smolensky's discussion of ICS systems. One is whether, from the fact that symbol structures and their constituents can be mapped onto superposition vectors and tensor product vectors, it follows that superposition vectors themselves have syntactic structure and tensor product vectors have symbolic constituents. Fodor and McLaughlin point out that it does not follow from the fact that tensor product/superposition representations *represent* entities that have constituent structure that these representations themselves have constituent structure. Fodor and McLaughlin believe that they do not.

> As Smolensky puts it, the activity states of the filler and role units can be 'imaginary' even though the ultimate activity vectors – the ones which do not themselves serve as filler or role components of more complex structures – must be actual activity patterns over units in the machine. Consider again our machine for representing four-letter words. The superposition pattern that represents, say, the word 'John' will be an activity vector actually realized in the machine. However, the activity vector representing 'J' will be merely imaginary, as will the activity vector representing *the first letter position*. Similarly for the tensor product activity vector representing 'J' *in the first letter position*. The only pattern of activity that will be *actually tokened* in the machine is the superposition vector representing 'John'. (Chapter 5, p. 212)

However, Smolensky does not see things in quite the way that Fodor and McLaughlin do. As he sees it, there are two questions concerning the reality of the constituents of tensor product representations. One is whether they are *semantically* real, in the sense that they 'can move around and fill any of a number of roles'. Smolensky believes that the activity vectors over filler units are semantically real.

> Are the constituents of a tensor product representation *really there?* ... Since the individual constituents are superimposed when combined, they certainly do lose their individual identity in an intuitively compelling sense. [However] ... for an intuition that lends some plausibility to the notion of vector constituents, consider superposition of sound waves: the pressure wave encoding *The Sounds of Silence* is, after all, a superposition which mixes up altogether the Simon and the Garfunkel constituents – yet we have no trouble believing that in a meaningful sense those constituents are real. (Chapter 6, p. 241)

The second is whether these activity vectors are *causally* real, in the sense that they play a causal role in the behaviour of the system, i.e. in its state transitions. Smolensky distinguishes these questions because he believes that, in connectionist systems, the entities that are the basic semantic constituents (i.e. activity vectors over filler units) are not the entities that 'drive the machine'. What drives the machine are the individual activity values of weights and units that realize superposition vectors, and these are part of the system's microstructure. So the constituents of tensor product representations are not causally real.

> Are the vector constituents in physical and connectionist systems causally efficacious? It would appear not, since the real mechanism driving the behavior of the system operates oblivious to our descriptive predilection to vector decomposition. It is the numerical values comprising the vector (in the connectionist case, the individual activity values) that really drive the machine. (chapter 4, p. 190)

But why does the fact that the activity values of individual weights and units, 'drive the machine' *preclude* the constituents of activity vectors being causally real? After all, Smolensky tells us that these individual activity values *comprise* the constituents of tensor product representations (chapter 4 p. 190). Perhaps we can understand this better by looking at Smolensky's analogy with the way vectors figure in representing the state of a dynamic system in modern physics, which is the source of his idea of a tensor product representation. In modern physics, the state of a system, such as an atom, is represented by a sum, or a superposition, vector, whose constituents are vectors, each of which represents an electron in its orbital role or position in the atom as a whole. These vectors are themselves tensor products of others. Each electron's representation in its orbital role in the atom is a tensor product of the vector which represents its internal state (its 'spin') and the vector which represents its orbital position.

Are the constituents of vectors which represent the atom as a whole (i.e. those that represent each electron's 'spin' and those that represent each electron's orbital situation) causally efficacious? Smolensky replies,

> The term 'causally efficacious' must be used with some caution. The equations that drive the atom do not work by first figuring out what the component particles are, and then working on each of them separately. The equations take the elements comprising the vector for the whole atom and change them in time. We can *analyze* the system by breaking up the vector for the whole into vectors for the parts, and in general that's a good way to do the analysis; but nature doesn't do that in updating the state of the system from one moment to the next. (chapter 4, p. 196, n. 13)

Similarly, Smolensky claims, for ICS systems. But what exactly does this answer show? Does it show that the constituent vectors of a tensor product representation *aren't* causally efficacious? If so, how? Smolensky says that it is the individual activity values that are 'elements' of vectors that do the real causing in the system. But why does this preclude vectors causing?

These questions cannot be properly answered unless we have a clearer idea of what the relation is between the constituents of tensor product representations and the elements of the 'microstructure', individual activity values that 'drive the machine'. For example, do the latter *realize* the former, in something like the way subvenient base properties realize the properties that supervene on them? From what Smolensky says in many places in chapters 4 and 6, it seems that they do. But his analogy with electrons being constituents of atoms (see the quote above), and his use of the term 'comprise' to describe the relation between individual activity values and tensor product and superposition vectors, suggest that he sees the relation as more of a part-whole, or mereological one.

If either of these two suggestions is correct, then it is unclear why the constituents of tensor product representations are not *thereby* causally efficacious. Why not conclude, for example, that the individual activity values explain *how* the constituents of tensor product representations are causally efficacious? The reason, Smolensky says, is that the individual activity values do their work 'oblivious of our descriptive predilection to vector decomposition'. But how can it matter that there are many ways in which to decompose a vector, either on the realization view or on the mereological view? Does the fact that biological processes – however they are taxonomized – are realized by (or comprised of) physico-chemical ones show that biological processes aren't causally efficacious? Does the fact that physical processes such as snow's melting are realized by (or comprised of) micro-level processes show that snow's melting isn't causally efficacious? And if so, then doesn't the fact that the units of connectionist systems may be realized neurally *also* show that connectionist *units* aren't causally efficacious?

> After all, we get *still more* precision when we go down from unit-sensitive operations to molecule-sensitive operations, and more precision yet when we go down from molecule-sensitive operations to quark-sensitive operations. The moral is not, however, that the causal laws of psychology should be stated in terms of the behavior of quarks. Rather, the moral is that whether you have a level of causal explanation is a question, not just of how much precision you are able to achieve, but also of *what generalizations you are able to express*. Fodor and McLaughin, Chapter 5, pp. 217–18)

So there is a real question here as to whether Smolensky is committed to the view that the constituents of tensor product representations aren't causally efficacious. But suppose that he is. Fodor and McLaughlin clearly believe that these constituents are only 'imaginary' because they are not actually tokened in the system. What is tokened in the system are the superposition vectors of which they are constituents. So semantic constituents play no causal role in the system.

The problem here is not that Smolensky's account leads to epiphenomenalism, the view that mental states are causally inefficacious, since epiphenomenalism is a problem for the Classical view too. On the Classical view, it is the syntactic features of symbols, not the semantic ones, that play a causal role in the production of the behaviour of the system. It is true that, given the computer metaphor, the semantic structure of mental representations can be seen to correspond in an appropriate way to their syntactic structure. But the semantic properties of mental symbols do not do any independent causal work in the production of the system's behaviour. So intentional descriptions, in so far as they cite *semantic* properties, rather than syntactic properties, of classical systems, do not cite features of Classical constituents that make any causal contribution to the production of systematic and productive behaviour. The *entities* that have both semantic and syntactic properties – mental symbols – are causally efficacious in the production of the behaviour of the system, but such symbols are efficacious *in virtue* of their *syntactic* properties, not their semantic ones.

On the other hand, the constituents of classical systems that are capable of semantic evaluation also do causal work. They may do this work because of their syntactic properties rather than their semantic ones, but the entities that have semantic properties play a causal role in the state transitions of the system and in the production of the system's behaviour. In contrast, if Smolensky is right, the symbols that serve as constituents in ICS systems play no causal role *at all* in its state transitions and in the production of systematic and productive behaviour. Not only do the semantic properties of such constituents fail to play a causal role in the system, but their syntactic properties also fail to do any causal work.

So the problem is that ICS systems work with no notion of a constituent which is *both* semantically evaluable and causally efficacious in the system. But how important is this to the question of systematicity? It is true that the semantically evaluable constituents of representations in a classical system that form the 'constitutive bases' (McLaughlin, 1993) of the cognitive capacities that are systematically related are *also* the entities on which the causal operations of the system are defined. And the Classical explanation of systematicity appeals to this fact.

However, there is no reason why an explanation of systematicity *must* appeal to this fact. Nor do Fodor and McLaughlin suppose that it must.

> Thus, for example, since (C) [*editor's note*: see p. 6 above] implies that anyone who can represent a proposition can, *ipso facto*, represent its elements, it implies, in particular, that anyone who can represent the proposition that John loves the girl can, *ipso facto*, represent John, the girl and the two-place relation *loving*. Notice, however, that the proposition that *the girl loves John* is *also* constituted by these same individuals/ relations. So, then, assuming that the processes that integrate the mental representations that express propositions have access to their constituents, it follows that anyone who can represent John's loving the girl can also represent the girl's loving John. (Chapter 5, pp. 202–3)

> The relevant question is whether tensor product representations . . . have the kind of constituent structure to which causal processes can be sensitive, hence the kind of constituent structure to which an explanation of systematicity might appeal. (Chapter 5, pp. 214–15)

The explanation of systematicity seems only to require that there be the same generative bases for those capacities that are systematic, and that there be *some* psychological mechanism in virtue of whose functioning those capacities are systematic. What the mechanism in the system is that enables the system to effect causal transactions from one semantically evaluable state to another is a separate matter. Smolensky clearly has a different story to tell about systematicity, since his story does not appeal to the fact that Classical constituents play a causal role in mental processes at the algorithmic level. So Fodor and McLaughlin's complaint is not that Smolensky's story cannot explain systematicity because the semantically evaluable constituents of ICS systems do no causal work. (This complaint would in any case be question-begging, since it assumes the correctness of the Classical view.) Their complaint is that Smolensky has not provided any alternative to the Classical explanation of systematicity at all. But if an explanation of systematicity does not require that the entities that are semantically evaluable are the entities on which causal operations are defined, then how can the fact (if it is a fact) that the semantically evaluable constituents in Smolensky's ICS systems do not play a causal role in those systems' state transitions matter?

This fact matters because Fodor and McLaughlin do not see how, if the constituents of tensor product representations are not actually realized or tokened in ICS systems, the phenomenon of systematicity can be explained. For the explanation of systematicity requires two things. First, it requires an explanation of the *intrinsic* connections between cognitive abilities such as the ability to think that aRb and the ability to think that bRa. Secondly, it requires an explanation of the psychological mechanism whose functioning is responsible for those intrinsic connections. Fodor and McLaughlin do not see that Smolensky's account has provided an explanation of either of these.

Consider the first. Suppose that two tensor product representations of the structures, *aRb* and *bRa*, are decomposable into constituents that are not only semantically evaluable, but uniquely so, and that these constituents are of shared constituent bases. Would this be enough to explain systematicity? No. Fodor and McLaughlin argue that it is not enough to show that *it is possible* to construct a system which is such that, if it can represent *aRb*, then it can represent *bRa* (and vice versa), i.e. to show that systematic cognitive capacities are possible given the architecture of the system. Since for a cognitive capacity to be systematic is for it to be such that the ability to exercise the one is *intrinsically* connected to the ability to exercise the other, one must show that it is *necessary* that if an organism is able to exercise the one, it is able to exercise the other. However, nothing in Smolensky's account of the workings of ICS systems shows the latter.

No doubt it is possible for Smolensky to wire a network so that it supports a vector that represents *aRb* if and only if it supports a vector that represents *bRa* . . . The trouble is that, although the architecture permits this, it equally permits Smolensky to wire a network so that it supports a vector that represents *aRb* if and only if it supports a vector that represents *zSq*; or, for that matter, if and only if it supports a vector that represents *The Last of the Mohicans*. The architecture would appear to be absolutely indifferent as among these options. (Chapter 5, p. 216).

The Classical view, on the other hand, in building semantically evaluable constituents into the architecture of the system, makes it inevitable that, if an organism is capable of representing aRb, it is thereby capable of representing *bRa*. This is because the representations themselves have shared constituent bases, *and* because an organism cannot token a representation without tokening its constituents.

The problem here is not, as it might seem to be, that there is no unique way to decompose a vector. As Smolensky argues, although this is true, only vectors of the form $r_0 \otimes x$ and $r_1 \otimes y$ will be semantically evaluable, so only certain vectors will be capable of having semantically evaluable constituents. Moreover, Smolensky argues that, provided that the vector-space notion of independence is respected, the independence of vectors r_0 and r_1 makes it impossible for there to be two semantic interpretations of a single vector. Further, he argues that the genuinely combinatorial nature of tensor product representations ensures that any system that is capable of representing *aRb* (or $R(a, b)$) will be capable of representing *bRa* (or $R(b, a)$), since if it contains the vector

$$\mathbf{P} = \mathbf{R} \otimes \mathbf{r_0} + \mathbf{a} \otimes \mathbf{r_0} \otimes \mathbf{r_1} + \mathbf{b} \otimes \mathbf{r_1} \otimes \mathbf{r_1}$$

it will also contain the vector

$$\mathbf{P'} = \mathbf{R} \otimes \mathbf{r_0} + \mathbf{b} \otimes \mathbf{r_0} \otimes \mathbf{r_1} + \mathbf{a} \otimes \mathbf{r_1} \otimes \mathbf{r_1}$$

The procedures for binding and unbinding are essential to the explanation of the combinatorial nature of tensor product representations, and so to the explanation of systematicity. Further, the processes of extraction and construction described in Smolensky's final reply (chapter 6) afford an explanation of how ICS systems compute structure-sensitive functions such as that from the structure [L [S,K]] to the structure [L [K,S]]. The explanation appeals to semantic constituents of tensor product representations, but these constituents do not participate causally in the state transitions from input to output. Rather, superposition vectors as wholes participate in these state transitions.

So Smolensky's ICS systems do seem to be capable of showing that two complex representations, *aRb* and *bRa*, have shared constituent bases. However, if Fodor and McLaughlin are right, this is not sufficient for the explanation of systematicity. One must also show how the architecture of the system supports the *necessary connection* between the ability to represent *aRb* and the ability to represent *bRa*. The problem here, as Fodor and McLaughlin see it, is that the semantic constituents of tensor product representations are not actually tokened in the system. And, given that they are not, there is no explanation of why, if an organism is capable of representing *aRb*, it *cannot but* be capable of representing *bRa*. This is a problem concerning the psychological *mechanism* whose functioning is responsible for systematicity (the second requirement on the explanation of systematicity mentioned above). The Classical view provides an explanation of this by ensuring that mental processes are sensitive to the semantically evaluable constituents of representations (i.e. symbols). However, Smolensky's ICS system account provides no explanation of how cognitive capacities could be systematic if mental processes are *not* sensitive to semantically evaluable constituents.

But is this true? Being tokened in the system matters to cognitive processing, and since the semantically evaluable constituents of tensor product representations are not actually tokened in the system, they cannot be implicated in an explanation of the psychological mechanism responsible for cognitive systematicity. However, if the issue of the systematicity of cognitive capacities is distinct from the issue of the causal efficacy of semantically evaluable constituents, this fact cannot by itself show why Smolensky's tensor product account does not provide an adequate explanation of systematicity. Nor is it as though there is no causal story to tell in the explanation of the psychological mechanism responsible for systematicity, given that the vectors that are semantically evaluable are realized in, or constituted by, individual activity values in the system, which in turn effect state transitions from one semantically evaluable state to another. Everything turns here on the relation between the semantically evaluable constituents of tensor product representations and the individual activity values that comprise them; and, while Smolensky's story here may be incomplete, the fact that algorithms are defined on superposition vectors whose constituents are uniquely semantically evaluable and context-independent does appear to provide a promising basis for the completion of that story.

In so far as this much of the story is incomplete, Fodor and McLaughlin's claim that Smolensky has not provided an explanation of systematicity seems correct. But then, as McLaughlin (1993) also points out, there is much in the Classical story that is incomplete too. In any case, the interesting question is not whether Smolensky's ICS systems account *does* provide an account of the psychological mechanism responsible for intrinsic connections between cognitive abilities, but whether it is *capable* of providing such an account. Why is Smolensky's story not enough to satisfy Fodor and McLaughlin that a complete story might be forthcoming? The answer, perhaps, is that unless the relation between the semantically evaluable constituents and the constituents implicated in the psychological mechanism responsible for cognitive systematicity is *itself* intrinsic or necessary, there is no *guarantee* that the connections between cognitive capacities are preserved (i.e. no guarantee that these connections are intrinsic) in the way that an explanation of systematicity requires. If Fodor and McLaughlin are right, it will not suffice for this explanation that one show how *it is possible* for a system's representation of the proposition, *John loves the girl* to be realized in such a way that the state transitions of the system effect a realization of a representation of the proposition, *the girl loves John*. Since systematicity is no accident, one must show how this could be so as a matter of *law*. However, in the absence of any intrinsic connection between the constraints which govern semantic evaluability at the level of super-position and tensor product vectors and the constraints which govern the causal processing at the algorithmic level, it is difficult to see how the explanation of systematicity that Smolensky offers can meet this requirement.

But is also difficult to see how *any* appropriately similar explanation, i.e. an explanation at the level of causal processes, would do the trick. Fodor and McLaughlin get systematicity by building it into their description of the syntactic level, and by stipulating that the psycho-logical mechanism must conform to the requirements of systematicity. Smolensky could, and in effect does, reply that their 'explanation' of systematicity is the product of theft rather than honest toil: 'the Classical theory gets systematicity by *assuming* it, not by deriving it from more fundamental principles. The necessity of systematicity is not *explained* by the Classical theory in any sense; it is simply *described* by it' (chapter 6, p. 269). The objection will be that once one gets to the level of causal processes, there can be no *guarantee* that systematicity will be produced. In the computer case, we make sure that the causal circuits provide for syntactic processes which are systematic. This need not be the case (for instance, there seems to be no reason to suppose that a von Neumann computer could not be wired in such a way that it fails to be systematic), but in so far as it is, *we* are the guarantors. In the neural case, perhaps the best we can hope for is the guarantee provided by evolution and learning.

Acknowledgement

I am indebted to Stephen Laurence for discussions on issues involved in this debate.

Note

1 The explanation of how a physical system can possess semantic properties actually requires more than this, since it requires an explanation of how mental representations get their meanings. This latter explanation is given by Fodor's theory of content; see, for example, chapter 4 of Fodor (1987) and 'A Theory of Content I' and 'A Theory of Content II' in Fodor (1990).

References

Fodor, J.A. (1987) *Psychosemantics*. Cambridge, Mass., MIT Press.
Fodor, J.A. (1990) *A Theory of Content*. Cambridge, Mass., MIT Press.
McLaughlin, B. (1993) The connectionism/classicism battle to win souls. *Philosophical Studies* 71, 163–90.

2

On the Proper Treatment
of Connectionism

Paul Smolensky

1 Introduction

In the past half-decade the Connectionist approach to cognitive modeling has grown from an obscure cult claiming a few true believers to a movement so vigorous that recent meetings of the Cognitive Science Society have begun to look like connectionist pep rallies. With the rise of the connectionist movement come a number of fundamental questions which are the subject of this chapter. I begin with a brief description of connectionist models.

1.1 Connectionist models

Connectionist models are large networks of simple parallel computing elements, each of which carries a numerical *activation value* which it computes from the values of neighboring elements in the network, using some simple numerical formula. The network elements, or *units*, influence each other's values through connections that carry a numerical strength, or *weight*. The influence of unit i on unit j is the activation value of unit i times the strength of the connection from i to j. Thus, if a unit has a positive activation value, its influence on a neighbor's value is positive if its weight to that neighbor is positive, and negative if the weight is negative. In an obvious neural allusion, connections carrying positive weights are called *excitatory* and those carrying negative weights are *inhibitory*.

In a typical connectionist model, input to the system is provided by imposing activation values on the *input units* of the network; these numerical values represent some encoding, or *representation*, of the input. The activation on the input units propagates along the connections until some set of activation values emerges on the *output units*; these activation values encode the output the system has computed from the input. In between the input and output units there may be other units, often called *hidden units*, that participate in representing neither the input nor the output.

The computation performed by the network in transforming the input pattern of activity to the output pattern depends on the set of connection strengths; these weights are usually regarded as encoding the system's knowledge. In this sense, the connection strengths play the role of the program in a conventional computer. Much of the allure of the connectionist approach is that many connectionist networks *program themselves*, that is, they have autonomous procedures for tuning their weights to eventually perform some specific computation. Such learning procedures often depend on training in which the network is presented with sample input/output pairs from the function it is supposed to compute. In learning networks with hidden units, the network itself 'decides' what computations the hidden units will perform; because these units represent neither inputs nor outputs, they are never 'told' what their values should be, even during training.

In recent years connectionist models have been developed for many tasks, encompassing the areas of vision, language processing, inference, and motor control. Numerous examples can be found in recent proceedings of the meetings of the Cognitive Science Society (Hinton and Anderson, 1981; *Cognitive Science*, 1985; Feldman et al., 1985; McClelland et al., 1986; Rumelhart et al., 1986b; see also Ballard, 1986).

1.2   Goal of this chapter

Given the rapid development in recent years of the connectionist approach to cognitive modelling, it is not yet an appropriate time for definitive assessments of the power and validity of the approach. The time seems right, however, for an attempt to articulate the goals of the approach, the fundamental hypotheses it is testing, and the relations presumed to link it with the other theoretical frameworks of cognitive science. A coherent and plausible articulation of these fundamentals is the goal of this chapter. Such an articulation is a non-trivial task, because the term 'Connectionist' encompasses a number of rather disparate theoretical frameworks, all of them quite undeveloped. The connectionist framework I will articulate departs sufficiently radically from traditional approaches in that its relations to other parts of cognitive science are not simple.

For the moment, let me call the formulation of the Connectionist approach that I will offer PTC. I will not argue the scientific merit of PTC; that some version of connectionism along the lines of PTC constitutes a 'proper description of processing' is argued elsewhere (e.g. in McClelland et al. 1986; Rumelhart et al., 1986b). Leaving aside the scientific merit of connectionist models, I want to argue here that PTC offers a 'Proper Treatment of Connectionism': a coherent formulation of the Connectionist approach that puts it in contact with other theories in cognitive science in a particularly constructive way. PTC is intended as a formulation of Connectionism that is at once strong enough to constitute a major cognitive hypothesis, comprehensive enough to face a number of difficult challenges, and sound enough to resist a number of objections in principle. If PTC succeeds in these goals, it will facilitate the real business at hand: assessing the scientific adequacy of the connectionist approach, that is, determining whether the approach offers computational power adequate for human cognitive competence and appropriate computational mechanisms to accurately model human cognitive performance.

PTC is a response to a number of positions that are being adopted concerning connectionism – pro, con, and blandly ecumenical. These positions, which are frequently expressed orally but rarely set down in print, represent, I believe, failures of supporters and critics of the traditional approach truly to come to grips with each other's views. Advocates of the traditional approach to cognitive modeling and AI (artificial intelligence) are often willing to grant that connectionist systems are useful, perhaps even important, for modeling lower-level processes (e.g. early vision), or for fast and fault-tolerant implementation of conventional AI programs, or for understanding how the brain might happen to implement LISP.

These ecumenical positions, I believe, fail to acknowledge the true challenge that connectionists are posing to the received view of cognition; PTC is an explicit formulation of this challenge.

Other supporters of the traditional approach find the connectionist approach to be fatally flawed because it cannot offer anything new (since universal Turing machine are, after all, 'universal'), or because it cannot offer the kinds of explanations that cognitive science requires. Some dismiss connectionist models on the grounds that they are too neurally unfaithful. PTC has been designed to withstand these attacks.

On the opposite side, most existing connectionist models fail to come to grips with the traditional approach – partly through a neglect intended as benign. It is easy to read into the connectionist literature the claim that there is no role in cognitive science for traditional theoretical constructs such as rules, sequential processing, logic, rationality, and conceptual schemata or frames. PTC undertakes to assign these constructs their proper role in a connectionist paradigm for cognitive modeling. PTC also addresses certain foundational issues concerning mental states.

I see no way of achieving the goals of PTC without adopting certain positions that will be regarded by a number of connectionists as premature or mistaken. These are inevitable consequences of the fact that the connectionist approach is still quite underdeveloped, and that the term 'Connectionist' has come to label a number of approaches that embody significantly conflicting assumptions. PTC is *not* intended to represent a consensus view of what the connectionist approach is or should be.

It will perhaps enhance the clarity of the chapter if I attempt at the outset to make my position clear on the present value of connectionist models and their future potential. This chapter is not intended as a defense of all these views, though I will argue for a number of them, and the remainder have undoubtedly influenced the presentation. On the one hand, I believe that:

(1) (a) It is far from clear whether connectionist models have adequate computational power to perform high-level cognitive tasks: there are serious obstacles that must be overcome before connectionist computation can offer modelers power comparable to that of symbolic computation.

   (b) It is far from clear that connectionist models offer a sound basis for modeling human cognitive performance: the connectionist approach is quite difficult to put into detailed contact with empirical methodologies.

   (c) It is far from clear that connectionist models can contribute to the study of human competence: connectionist models are quite difficult to analyze for the kind of high-level properties required to inform the study of human competence.

   (d) It is far from clear that connectionist models, in something like their present forms, can offer a sound basis for modeling neural computation: as will be explicitly addressed in section 4, there are many serious gaps between connectionist models and current views of important neural properties.

   (e) Even under the most successful scenario for connectionist cognitive science, many of the currently practiced research strategies in cognitive science would remain viable and productive.

On the other hand, I believe that:

(1) (f) It is very likely that the Connectionist approach will contribute significant, long-lasting ideas to the rather impoverished theoretical repertoire of cognitive science.

(g) It is very likely that connectionist models will turn out to offer contributions to the modeling of human cognitive performance on higher-level tasks that are at least as significant as those offered by traditional, symbolic, models.

(h) It is likely that the view of the competence/performance distinction that arises from the connectionist approach will successfully heal a deep and ancient rift in the science and philosophy of mind.

(i) It is likely that connectionist models will offer the most significant progress of the past several millenia on the mind/ body problem.

(j) It is very likely that, given the impoverished theoretical repertoire of computational neuroscience, connectionist models will serve as an excellent stimulus to the development of models of neural computation that are significantly better than both current connectionist models and current neural models.

(k) There is a reasonable chance that connectionist models will lead to the development of new somewhat-general-purpose self-programming, massively parallel analog computers, and a new theory of analog parallel computation: they may possibly even challenge the strong construal of Church's thesis as the claim that the class of well-defined computations is exhausted by those of Turing machines.

1.3   Levels of analysis

Most of the foundational issues surrounding the Connectionist approach turn, in one way or another, on the level of analysis adopted. The terminology, graphics and discussion found in most connectionist papers strongly suggest that connectionist modeling operates at the neural level. I will argue, however, that it is better *not* to construe the principles of cognition being explored in the connectionist approach as the principles of the neural level. Specification of the level of cognitive analysis adopted by PTC is a subtle matter which consumes much of this chapter. To be sure, the level of analysis adopted by PTC is lower than that of the traditional, symbolic paradigm; but, at least for the present, the level of PTC is more explicitly related to the level of the symbolic paradigm than it is to the neural level. For this reason I will call the paradigm for cognitive modeling proposed by PTC the *sub-symbolic* paradigm.

A few comments on terminology. I will refer to the traditional approach to cognitive modeling as the *symbolic paradigm*. Note that I will always use the term 'symbolic paradigm' to refer to the traditional approach to cognitive *modeling*: the development of AI-like computer programs to serve as models of psychological performance. The symbolic paradigm in cognitive modeling has been articulated and defended by Newell and Simon (1976; Newell, 1980), as well as by Fodor (1975, 1987), Pylyshyn (1984), and others. The fundamental hypotheses of this paradigm embrace most of mainstream AI, in addition to AI-based systems that are explicitly offered as models of human performance. The term 'symbolic paradigm' is explicitly *not* intended to encompass competence theories such as the formal theory of grammar; such competence theories bear deep relations to the symbolic paradigm but they are not a focus of attention in this chapter. In particular, much of the work in formal linguistics differs from the symbolic paradigm in cognitive modeling in many of the same ways as the Connectionist approach I will consider; on a number of the dimensions I will use to divide the symbolic and sub-symbolic paradigms, much linguistics research falls on the sub-symbolic side.

I have found it necessary to deal only with a subset of the symbolic and connectionist approaches in order to get beyond superficial, syntactic issues. On the symbolic side, I am limiting consideration to the Newell/Simon Fodor/Pylyshyn view of cognition, and excluding, for example, the view adopted by much of linguistics; on the connectionist side, I will consider only a particular view, the 'sub-symbolic paradigm', and exclude a number of competing connectionist perspectives. The only alternative I see at this point is to characterize the symbolic and connectionist perspectives so diffusely that substantive analysis becomes impossible.

In calling the traditional approach to cognitive modeling the 'symbolic paradigm', I intend to emphasize that in this approach, cognitive descriptions are built of entities that are symbols both in the semantic sense of referring to external objects and in the syntactic sense of being operated upon by symbol manipulation. These manipulations model fundamental psychological processes in this approach to cognitive modeling.

The name 'sub-symbolic paradigm' is intended to suggest cognitive descriptions built up of entities that correspond to *constituents* of the symbols used in the symbolic paradigm; these fine-grained constituents could be called *sub-symbols*, and they are the activities of individual processing units in connectionist networks. Entities that are typically represented in the symbolic paradigm by symbols are typically represented in the sub-symbolic paradigm by a large number of sub-symbols. Along with this semantic distinction comes a syntactic distinction. Sub-symbols are not operated upon by symbol manipulation: they participate in numerical – not symbolic – computation. Operations in the symbolic paradigm that consist of a single discrete operation (e.g a memory fetch) are often achieved in the sub-symbolic paradigm as the result of a large number of much finer-grained (numerical) operations.

Since the level of cognitive analysis adopted by the sub-symbolic paradigm for formulating connectionist models is lower than the level traditionally adopted by the symbolic paradigm, for the purposes of relating these two paradigms, it is often important to analyze connectionist models at a higher level; to amalgamate, so to speak, the sub-symbols into symbols. Although the symbolic and sub-symbolic paradigms each have their preferred level of analysis, the cognitive models they offer can be described at multiple levels. It is therefore useful to have distinct names for the levels: I will call the preferred level of the symbolic paradigm the *conceptual level* and that of the sub-symbolic paradigm the *sub-conceptual level*. These names are not ideal, but will be further motivated in the course of characterizing the levels. A primary goal of this chapter is to articulate a coherent set of hypotheses about the sub-conceptual level: the kind of cognitive descriptions that are used, the computational principles that apply, and the relations between the sub-conceptual and both the symbolic and neural levels.

The choice of level greatly constrains the appropriate formalism for analysis. Probably the most striking feature of the Connectionist approach is the change in formalism relative to the symbolic paradigm. Since the birth of cognitive science, *language* has provided the dominant theoretical model. Formal cognitive models have taken their structure from the syntax of formal languages, and their content from the semantics of natural language. The mind has been taken to be a machine for formal symbol manipulation, and the symbols manipulated have assumed essentially the same semantics as words of English.

The sub-symbolic paradigm challenges both the syntactic and semantic role of language in formal cognitive models. Section 2 formulates this challenge. Alternative fillers are described for the roles language has traditionally played in cognitive science, and the new role left to language is delimited. The fundamental hypotheses defining the sub-symbolic paradigm are formulated, and the challenge that nothing new is being offered is considered. Section 4 considers the relation between the sub-symbolic paradigm and neuroscience; the challenge that connectionist models are too neurally unfaithful is addressed. Section 5 presents the relations between analyses of cognition at the neural, sub-conceptual and conceptual levels. It also previews the remainder of the chapter, which deals with the relations between the sub-conceptual and conceptual levels; the types of explanations of behavior provided by the symbolic and sub-symbolic paradigms are then discussed. Section 6 faces the challenge of accounting for conscious, rule-guided behavior within the sub-symbolic paradigm. Section 7 addresses the challenge of distinguishing cognitive from non-cognitive systems at the sub-conceptual level. Various properties of sub-symbolic mental states, and the issue of rationality, are considered. Section 8 elaborates briefly on the computational principles that apply at the sub-conceptual level. Section 9 discusses how higher, conceptual-level descriptions of sub-symbolic models approximate symbolic models (under their conceptual-level descriptions).

In this chapter I have tried to typographically isolate concise formulations of the main points. Most of these numbered points serve to characterize the sub-symbolic paradigm, but a few define alternative points of view; to avoid confusion, the latter have been explicitly tagged by the phrase, *To be rejected.*

2 Formalization of Knowledge

2.1 *Cultural knowledge and conscious rule interpretation*

What is an appropriate formalization of the knowledge that cognitive agents possess and the means by which they use that knowledge to perform cognitive tasks? As a starting point, we can look to those knowledge formalizations that predate cognitive science. The most formalized knowledge is found in sciences like physics that rest on mathematical principles. Domain knowledge is formalized in linguistic structures such as 'energy is conserved' (or an appropriate encryption), and logic formalizes the use of that knowledge to draw conclusions. Knowledge consists of axioms, and drawing conclusions consists of proving theorems.

This method of formulating knowledge and drawing conclusions has extremely valuable properties:

(2) (a) *Public access*: the knowledge is accessible to many people.

(b) *Reliability*: different people (or the same person at different times) can reliably check whether conclusions have been validly reached.

(c) *Formality, bootstrapping, universality*: the inferential operations require very little experience with the domain to which the symbols refer.

These three properties are important for science because it is a cultural activity. It is of limited social value to have knowledge that resides purely in one individual (2a). It is of questionable social value to have knowledge formulated in such a way that different users draw different conclusions (e.g. can't agree that an experiment falsifies a theory) (2b). For cultural propagation of knowledge, it is helpful if novices with little or no experience of a task can be given a means for performing that task, and thereby a means for acquiring experience (2c).

There are cultural activities other than science that have similar requirements. The laws of a nation and the rules of an organization are also linguistically formalized procedures for effecting action which different people can carry out with reasonable reliability. In all these cases, the goal is to create an abstract decision system that resides outside any single person.

Thus, at the cultural level, the goal is to express knowledge in a form that can be executed reliably by different people, even inexperienced ones. We can view the top-level conscious processor of individual people as a *virtual machine* – the *conscious rule interpreter* – and we can view cultural knowledge as a program that runs on that machine. Linguistic formulations of knowledge are perfect for this purpose. The procedures that different people can reliably execute are explicit, step-by-step linguistic instructions. This is what has been formalized in the theory of *effective procedures* (Turing, 1936). Thanks to property (2c), the top-level conscious human processor can be idealized as universal: capable of executing any effective procedure. The theory of effective procedures – the classical theory of computation (Hopcrof and Ullman, 1979) – is physically manifest in the von Neumann (serial) computer. One can say that the von Neumann computer is a machine for automatically following the kinds of explicit instructions that people can fairly reliably follow – but much faster and with perfect reliability.

Thus we can understand why the production system of computation theory, or more generally the von Neumann computer, has provided a successful model of how people execute instructions (e.g. models of novice physics problem-solving such as that of Larkin et al., 1980). In short, when people (e.g. novices) consciously and sequentially follow rules (such as those they have been taught), their cognitive processing is naturally modeled as the sequential interpretation[1] of a linguistically formalized procedure. The rules being followed are expressed in terms of the consciously accessible concepts with which the task domain is conceptualized. In this sense, the rules are formulated at the conceptual level of analysis.

To sum up:

(3)   (a)   Rules formulated in natural language can provide an effective formalization of cultural knowledge.

  (b)   Conscious rule application can be modeled as sequential interpretation of such rules by a virtual machine called the conscious rule interpreter.

  (c)   These rules are formulated in terms of the concepts consciously used to describe the task domain – they are formulated at the conceptual level.

2.2   *Individual knowledge, skill and intuition in the symbolic paradigm*

The constraints on cultural knowledge formalization are not the same as those on individual knowledge formalization. The intuitive knowledge in a physics expert or a native speaker may demand, for a truly accurate description, a formalism that is not a good one for cultural purposes. After all, the individual knowledge in an expert's head does not possess the properties (2) of cultural knowledge: it is not publically accessible or completely reliable, and it is completely dependent on ample experience. Individual knowledge is a program that runs on a virtual machine that need not be the same as the top-level conscious processor that runs the cultural knowledge. By definition, conclusions reached by intuition do not come from conscious application of rules, and intuitive processing need not have the same character as conscious rule application.

What kinds of programs are responsible for behavior that is not conscious rule application? I will refer to the virtual machine that runs these programs as the *intuitive processor*. It is presumably responsible for all of animal behavior and a huge portion of human behavior: perception, practiced motor behavior, fluent linguistic behavior, intuition in problem-solving and game-playing – in short, practically all skilled performance. The transference of responsibility from the conscious rule interpreter to the intuitive processor during the acquisition of skill is one of the most striking and well-studied phenomena in cognitive science (Anderson, 1981). An analysis of the formalization of knowledge must consider both the knowledge involved in novices' conscious application of rules and the knowledge resident in experts' intuition, as well as their relationship.

An appealing possibility is this:

(4)   (a) The programs running on the intuitive processor consist of linguistically formalized rules that are sequentially interpreted. (*To be rejected.*)

This has traditionally been the assumption of cognitive science. Native speakers are unconsciously interpreting rules, as are physics experts when they are intuiting answers to problems. Artificial intelligence systems for natural language processing and problem-solving are programs written in a formal language for the symbolic description of procedures for manipulating symbols.

To the syntactic hypothesis (4a) a semantic one corresponds:

(4)   (b) The programs running on the intuitive processor are composed of elements, that is, symbols, referring to essentially the same concepts as the ones used to consciously conceptualize the task domain. (*To be rejected.*)

This applies to production system models in which the productions representing expert knowledge are compiled versions of those of the novice (Lewis, 1978, Anderson, 1983) and to the bulk of AI programs.

Hypotheses (4a) and (4b) together comprise:

(4)   The unconscious rule interpretation hypothesis: (*To be rejected.*) The programs running on the intuitive processor have a syntax and semantics comparable to those running on the conscious rule interpreter.

This hypothesis has provided the foundation for the symbolic paradigm for cognitive modeling. Cognitive models of both conscious rule application and intuitive processing have been programs constructed of entities which are *symbols* both in the syntactic sense of being operated on by symbol manipulation and in the semantic sense of (4b). Because these symbols have the conceptual semantics of (4b), I am calling the level of analysis at which these programs provide cognitive models the *conceptual level*.

2.3   The sub-symbolic paradigm and intuition

The hypothesis of unconscious rule interpretation (4) is an attractive possibility which a connectionist approach to cognitive modeling rejects. Since my purpose here is to formulate rather than argue the scientific merits of a connectionist approach, I will not argue against (4) here. I will point out only that in general, connectionists do not casually reject (4). Several of today's leading connectionist researchers were intimately involved with serious and long-standing attempts to make (4) serve the needs of cognitive science.[2] Connectionists tend to reject (4) because they find the consequences that have actually resulted from its acceptance to be quite unsatisfactory, for a number of quite independent reasons, including:

(5)   (a) Actual AI systems built on hypothesis (4) seem too brittle, too inflexible, to model true human expertise.
      (b) The process of articulating expert knowledge in rules seems impractical for many important domains (e.g. common sense).
      (c) Hypothesis (4) has contributed essentially no insight into how knowledge is represented in the brain.

What motivates the pursuit of connectionist alternatives to (4) is a hunch that such alternatives will better serve the goals of cognitive science. Substantial empirical assessment of this hunch is probably at least a decade away. One possible alternative to (4a) is:

(6)   The neural architecture hypothesis: (*To be rejected.*) The intuitive processor for a particular task uses the same architecture that the brain uses for that task.

Whatever appeal this hypothesis might have, it seems incapable in practice of supporting the needs of the vast majority of cognitive models. We simply do not know what architecture the brain uses for performing most cognitive tasks. There may be some exceptions (such as visual and spatial tasks), but for problem-solving, language and many others (6) simply cannot do the necessary work at the present time.

These points and others relating to the neural level will be considered in more detail in section 4. For now the point is simply that characterizing the level of analysis of connectionist modeling is not a matter of simply identifying it with the neural level. While the level of analysis adopted by most connectionist cognitive models is not the conceptual one, it is also not the neural level (see also Anderson, (1987).

The goal now is to formulate a connectionist alternative to (4) that, unlike (6), provides a viable basis for cognitive modeling. A first, crude approximation to this hypothesis is:

(7)   The intuitive processor has a certain kind of connectionist architecture (which abstractly models a few of the most general features of neural networks). (*To be elaborated.*)

Postponing consideration of the neural issues to section 4, we now consider the relevant kind of connectionist architecture.

The view of the connectionist architecture I will adopt is the following (for further treatment of this viewpoint, see Smolensky, 1986b). The numerical activity values of all the processors in the network form a large *state vector*. The interactions of the processors, the equations governing how the activity vector changes over time as processors respond to one another's values, is an *activation evolution equation*. This evolution equation governing the mutual interactions of the processors involves the connection weights: numerical parameters which determine the direction and magnitude of the influence of one activation value on another. The activation equation is a differential equation (usually approximated by the finite difference equation that arises from discrete time slices; the issue of discrete approximation is taken up in section 8.1). In learning systems, the connection weights change during training according to the learning rule, which is another differential equation: the *connection evolution equation*.

Knowledge in a connectionist system lies in its connection strengths. Thus, for the first part of our elaboration on (7) we have the following alternative to (4a):

(8)   (a)   *The connectionist dynamical system hypothesis*: the state of the intuitive processor at any moment is precisely defined by a vector of numerical values (one for each unit). The dynamics of the intuitive processor are governed by a differential equation. The parameters in this equation constitute the processor's program or knowledge. In learning systems, these parameters change according to another differential equation.

This hypothesis states that the intuitive processor is a certain kind of *dynamical system*: like the dynamical systems traditionally studied in physics, the state of the system is a numerical vector evolving in time according to differential evolution equations. The special properties that distinguish this kind of dynamical system – a *connectionist dynamical system* – are only vaguely described in (8a). A much more precise specification is needed. It is premature at this point to commit oneself to such a specification, but one large class of sub-symbolic models is that of quasi-linear dynamical systems, explicity discussed in Smolensky (1986b) and Rumelhart et al. (1986a). Each unit in a quasi-linear system computes its value by first calculating the weighted sum of its inputs from other units and then transforming this sum with a non-linear function. An important goal of the sub-symbolic paradigm is to characterize the computational properties of various kinds of connectionist dynamical systems (such as quasi-linear systems) and thereby determine which kinds provide appropriate models of various types of cognitive processes.

The connectionist dynamical system hypothesis (8a) provides a connectionist alternative to the syntactic hypothesis (4a) of the symbolic paradigm. We now need a semantic hypothesis compatible with (8a) to replace (4b). The question is: what does a unit's value *mean*? The most straightforward possibility is that the semantics of each unit is comparable to that of a word in natural language; each unit represents such a concept, and the connection strengths between units reflect the degree of association between the concepts.

(9) *The conceptual unit hypothesis*: (*To be rejected*.) Individual intuitive processor elements – individual units – have essentially the same semantics as the conscious rule interpreter's elements, namely, words of natural language.

But (8a) and (9) make an infertile couple. Activation of concepts spreading along degree of association links may be adequate for modeling simple aspects of cognition – such as relative times for naming words or the relative probabilities of perceiving letters in various contexts – but it cannot be adequate for complex tasks such as question-answering or grammaticality judgments. The relevant structures cannot even be feasibly represented in such a network, let alone effectively processed.

Great computational power must be present in the intuitive processor to deal with the many cognitive processes that are extremely complex when described at the conceptual level. The symbolic paradigm, based on hypothesis (4), gets its power by allowing highly complex, essentially arbitrary, operations on symbols with conceptual-level semantics: simple semantics, complex operations. If the operations are required to be as simple as those allowed by hypothesis (8a), we cannot get away with a semantics as simple as that of (9).[3] A semantics compatible with (8a) must be more complicated:

(8)   (b) *The sub-conceptual unit hypothesis*: The entities in the intuitive processor with the semantics of conscious concepts of the task domain are complex patterns of activity over many units. Each unit participates in many such patterns.

(See several of the papers in Hinton and Anderson 1981; Hinton et al. 1986; the neural counterpart is associated with Hebb, 1949; Lashley, 1950, about which see Feldman, 1986.) The interactions between *individual units* are simple, but these units do not have conceptual semantics: they are *sub-conceptual*. The interactions between the entities with conceptual semantics, interactions between complex patterns of activity, are not at all simple. Interactions at the level of activity patterns are not directly described by the formal definition of a sub-symbolic model; they must be computed by the analyst. Typically, these interactions can be computed only approximately. In other words, there will generally be no precisely valid, complete, computable formal principles at the conceptual level; such principles exist only at the level of individual units – the *sub-conceptual level*.

(8)   (c) *The sub-conceptual level hypothesis*: Complete, formal and precise descriptions of the intuitive processor are generally tractable not at the conceptual level, but only at the sub-conceptual level.

In (8c), the qualification 'complete, formal and precise' is important: conceptual-level descriptions of the intuitive processor's performance can be derived from the sub-conceptual description, but, unlike the description at the sub-conceptual level, the conceptual-level descriptions will be either incomplete (describing only certain aspects of the processing) or informal (describing complex behaviors in, say, qualitative terms) or imprecise (describing the performance up to certain approximations or idealizations such as 'competence' idealizations away from actual performance). Explicit examples of each of these kinds of conceptual-level descriptions of sub-symbolic systems will be considered in section 9.

Hypotheses (8a-c) can be summarized as:

(8)   The sub-symbolic hypothesis: the intuitive processor is a sub-conceptual connectionist dynamical system that does not admit a complete, formal and precise conceptual-level description.

This hypothesis is the cornerstone of the sub-symbolic paradigm.[4]

2.4   The incompatibility of the symbolic and sub-symbolic paradigms

I will now show that the symbolic and sub-symbolic paradigms, as formulated above, are incompatible – that hypotheses (4) and (8) about the syntax and semantics of the intuitive processor are not mutually consistent. This issue requires care because it is well known that one virtual machine can often be implemented in another, that a program written for one machine can be translated into a program for the other. The attempt to distinguish sub-symbolic and symbolic computation might well be futile if each can simulate the other. After all, a digital computer is in reality some sort of dynamical system simulating a von Neumann automaton and, in turn, digital computers are usually used to simulate connectionist models. Thus it seems possible that the symbolic and sub-symbolic hypotheses (4) and (8) are *both* correct: The intuitive processor can be regarded as a virtual machine for sequentially interpreting rules on one level *and* as a connectionist machine on a lower level.

This possibility fits comfortably within the symbolic paradigm, under a formulation such as:

(10)   Valid connectionist models are merely implementations, for a certain kind of parallel hardware, of symbolic programs that provide exact and complete accounts of behavior at the conceptual level. (*To be rejected.*)

However (10) contradicts hypothesis (8c), and is thus incompatible with the sub-symbolic paradigm. The symbolic programs that (4) hypothesizes for the intuitive processor could indeed be translated for a connectionist machine; but the translated programs would *not* be the kind of sub-symbolic program that (8) hypothesizes. If (10) is correct, (8) is wrong; at the very least, (8c) would have to be removed from the defining hypothesis of the sub-symbolic paradigm, weakening it to the point that connectionist modeling does become mere implementation. Such an outcome would constitute a genuine defeat of a research program that I believe many connectionists are pursuing.

What about the reverse relationship, where a symbolic program is used to implement a sub-symbolic system? Here it is crucial to realize that the symbols in such programs represent the activation values of units and the strengths of connections. By hypothesis (8b), these do not have conceptual semantics, and thus hypothesis (4b) is violated. The sub-symbolic programs that (8) hypothesizes for the intuitive processor can be translated for a von Neumann machine, but the translated programs are *not* the kind of symbolic program that (4) hypothesizes.

These arguments show that unless the hypotheses of the symbolic and sub-symbolic paradigms are formulated with some care, the substance of the scientific issue at stake can easily be missed. It is well known that von Neumann machines and connectionist networks can simulate each other. This fact leads some people to adopt the position that the connectionist approach cannot offer anything fundamentally new because we already have Turing machines and, following Church's thesis, reason to believe that, when it comes to computation, Turing machines are everything. This position, however, mistakes the issue for cognitive science to be the purely syntactic question of whether mental programs are written for Turing/von Neumann machines or connectionist machines. This is a non-issue. If one cavalierly characterizes the two approaches *only syntactically*, using (4a) and (8a) alone, then indeed the issue – Connectionist or not Connectionist – appears to be 'one of AI's wonderful red herrings'.[5]

It is a mistake to claim that the Connectionist approach has nothing new to offer cognitive science. The issue at stake is a central one: does the complete formal account of cognition lie at the conceptual level? The position taken by the sub-symbolic paradigm is: No – it lies at the sub-conceptual level.

3   Representation at the Sub-conceptual Level

Having hypothesized the existence of a sub-conceptual level, we must now consider its nature. Hypothesis (8b) leaves open important questions about the semantics of sub-symbolic systems. What kind of sub-conceptual features do the units in the intuitive processor represent? Which activity patterns actually correspond to particular concepts or elements of the problem domain?

There are no systematic or general answers to these questions at the present time; seeking answers is one of the principal tasks for the sub-symbolic research paradigm. At present, each individual sub-symbolic model adopts particular procedures for relating patterns of activity – activity vectors – to the conceptual-level descriptions of inputs and outputs that define the model's task. The vectors chosen are often values of fine-grained features of the inputs and outputs, based on some pre-existing theoretical analysis of the domain. For example, for the task studied by Rumelhart and McClelland (1986), transforming root phonetic forms of English verbs to their past-tense forms, the input and output phonetic strings are represented as vectors of values for context-dependent binary phonetic features. The task description at the conceptual level involves consciously available concepts such as the words 'go' and 'went', while the sub-conceptual level used by the model involves a very large number of fine-grained features such as 'roundedness preceded by frontalness and followed by backness'. The representation of 'go' is a large pattern of activity over these features.

Substantive progress in sub-symbolic cognitive science requires that systematic commitments be made to vectorial representations for individual cognitive domains. It is important to develop mathematical or empirical methodologies that can adequately constrain these commitments. The vectors chosen to represent inputs and outputs crucially affect a model's predictions, since the generalizations the model makes are largely determined by the similarity structure of the chosen vectors. Unlike symbolic tokens, these vectors lie in a topological space in which some are close together and others far apart.

What kinds of methodologies might be used to constrain the representation at the sub-conceptual level? The methodology used by Rumelhart and McClelland (1986) in the past-tense model is one that has been fairly widely practiced, particularly in models of language processing: representational features are borrowed from existing theoretical analyses of the domain and adapted (generally in somewhat *ad hoc* ways) to meet the needs of connectionist modeling. This methodology clearly renders the sub-symbolic approach dependent on other research paradigms in the cognitive sciences and suggests that, certainly in the short term, the sub-symbolic paradigm cannot *replace* these other research paradigms. (This is a theme I will return to in the conclusion of the chapter.)

A second possible theoretical methodology for studying sub-conceptual representation relates to the learning procedures that can train hidden units in connectionist networks. Hidden units support internal representations of elements of the problem domain, and networks that train their hidden units are in effect learning effective sub-conceptual representations of the domain. If we can analyze the representations that such networks develop, we can perhaps obtain principles of sub-conceptual representation for various problem domains.

A third class of methodology views the task of constraining sub-conceptual models as the calibration of connectionist models to the human cognitive system. The problem is to determine what vectors should be assigned to represent various aspects of the domain so that the resulting behavior of the connectionist model matches human behavior. Powerful mathematical tools are needed for relating the overall behavior of the network to the choice of representational vectors; ideally, these tools should allow us to *invert* the mapping from representations to behavior so that by starting with a mass of data on human performance we can turn a mathematical crank and have representational vectors pop out. An example of this general type of tool is the technique of *multi-dimensional scaling* (Shepard, 1962), which allows data on human judgments of the similarity between pairs of items in some set to be turned into vectors for representing those items (in a sense). The sub-symbolic paradigm needs tools such as a version of multi-dimensional scaling based on a connectionist model of the process of producing similarity judgments.

Each of these methodologies poses serious research challenges. Most of these challenges are currently being pursued, so far with at best modest success. In the first approach, systematic principles must be developed for adapting to the connectionist context the featural analyses of domains that have emerged from traditional, non-Connectionist paradigms. These principles must reflect fundamental properties of connectionist computation, for otherwise, the hypothesis of connectionist computation is doing no work in the study of mental representation. In the second methodology, principles must be discovered for the representations learned by hidden units, and in the third methodology, principles must be worked out for relating choices of representational vectors to overall system behavior. These are challenging mathematical problems on which the ultimate success of the sub-symbolic paradigm rests. Sections 8 and 9 discuss some results related to these mathematical problems, but they are far from strong enough to carry the necessary weight.

The next two sections discuss the relation between the sub-conceptual level and other levels: the relation to the neural levels is addressed in section 4, and the relation to the conceptual level is taken up in section 5.

4   The Sub-conceptual and Neural Levels

The discussion in the preceding section overlooks an obvious methodo-logy for constraining sub-conceptual representations – just look at how the brain does it. This brings us back to the parenthetical comment in (7) and the general issue of the relation between the sub-conceptual and neural levels.[6]

The relation between the sub-conceptual and neural levels can be addressed in both syntactic and semantic terms. The semantic question is the one just raised: how do representations of cognitive domains as patterns of activity over sub-conceptual units in the network models of the sub-symbolic paradigm relate to representations over neurons in the brain? The syntactic question is: how does the processing architecture adopted by networks in the sub-symbolic paradigm relate to the processing architecture of the brain?

There is not really much to say about the semantic question because so little is known about neural representation of higher cognitive domains. When it comes to connectionist modeling of say, language processing, the 'just look at how the brain does it' methodology doesn't take one very far towards the goal of constructing a network that does the task at all. Thus it is unavoidable that, for the time being, in sub-symbolic models of higher processes, the semantics of network units are much more directly related to conceptual level accounts of these processes than to any neural account. Semantically, the sub-conceptual level seems at present rather close to the conceptual level, while we have little ground for believing it to be close to the neural level.

This conclusion is at odds with the commonly held view that connectionist models are neural models. That view presumably reflects a bias against semantic considerations in favor of syntactic ones. If one looks only at processing mechanisms, the computation performed by sub-symbolic models seems much closer to that of the brain than to that of symbolic models. This suggests that syntactically, the sub-conceptual level is closer to the neural level than to the conceptual level.

Let us take then the syntactic question: is the processing architecture adopted by sub-symbolic models (8a) well suited for describing processing at the neural level? Table 2.1 presents some of the relations between the architectures. The left column lists currently plausible features of some of the most general aspects of the neural architecture, considered at the level of neurons (Crick and Asanuma, 1986). The right column lists the corresponding architectural features of the connectionist dynamical systems typically used in sub-symbolic models. In the center column, each hit has been indicated by a + and each miss by a −.

In Table 2.1 the loose correspondence assumed is between neurons and units, between synapses and connections. It is not clear how to make this correspondence precise. Does the activity of a unit correspond to the membrane potential at the cell body? Or the time-averaged firing rate of the neuron? Or the population-averaged firing rate of many neurons? Since the integration of signals between dendritic trees is probably more like the linear integration appearing in quasi-

Table 2.1 Relations between the neural and sub-symbolic architectures

Cerebral cortex		*Connectionist dynamical systems*
State defined by continuous numerical variables (potentials, synaptic areas . . .)	+	State defined by continuous numerical variables (activations, connection strengths)
State variables change continuously in time	+	State variables change continuously in time
Interneuron interaction parameters changeable; seat of knowledge	+	Interunit interaction parameters changeable; seat of knowledge
Huge number of state variables	+	Large number of state variables
High interactional complexity (highly non-homogeneous interactions)	+	High interactional complexity (highly non-homogeneous interactions)
Neurons located in 2+1-d space	–	Units have no spatial location
have dense connectivity to nearby neurons;	–	uniformly dense
have geometrically mapped connectivity to distant neurons	–	connections
Synapses located in 3-d space; locations strongly affect signal interactions	–	Connections have no spatial location
Distal projections between areas have intricate topology	–	Distal projections between node pools have simple topology
Distal interactions mediated by discrete signals	–	All interactions non-discrete
Intricate signal integration at single neuron	–	Signal integration is linear
Numerous signal types	–	Single signal type

linear dynamical systems than is the integration of synaptic signals on a dendrite, would it not be better to view a connection not as an individual synaptic contact but rather as an aggregate contact on an entire dendritic tree?

Given the difficulty of precisely stating the neural counterpart of components of sub-symbolic models, and given the significant number of misses, even in the very general properties considered in table 2.1, it seems advisable to keep the question open of the detailed relation between cognitive descriptions at the sub-conceptual and neural levels.

There seems no denying, however, that the sub-conceptual level is significantly closer to the neural level than is the conceptual level: symbolic models possess even fewer similarities with the brain than those indicated in table 2.1.

The sub-conceptual level ignores a great number of features of the neural level that are probably extremely important to understanding how the brain computes. None the less, the sub-conceptual level does incorporate a number of features of neural computation that are almost certainly extremely important to understanding how the brain computes. The general principles of computation at the sub-conceptual level – computation in high-dimensional, high-complexity dynamical systems – *must* apply to computation in the brain; these principles are likely to be necessary, if not sufficient, to understand neural computation. And while sub-conceptual principles are not unambiguously and immediately applicable to neural systems, they are certainly more readily applicable than the principles of symbolic computation.

In sum:

(11)   The fundamental level of the subsymbolic paradigm, the sub-conceptual level, lies between the neural and conceptual levels.

As stated earlier, on semantic measures, the sub-symbolic level seems closer to the conceptual level, whereas on syntactic measures, it seems closer to the neural level. It remains to be seen whether, as the sub-symbolic paradigm develops, this situation will sort itself out. Mathematical techniques like those discussed in the previous section may yield insights into sub-symbolic representation that will increase the semantic distance between the sub-conceptual and conceptual levels. There are already significant indications that as new insights into sub-symbolic computation are emerging, and additional information-processing power is being added to sub-symbolic models, the syntactic distance between the sub-conceptual and neural levels is increasing. In the drive for more computational power, architectural decisions seem to be driven more and more by mathematical considerations and less and less by neural ones.[7]

Once (11) is accepted, the proper place of sub-symbolic models in cognitive science will be clarified. It is common to hear dismissals of a particular sub-symbolic model because it is not immediately apparent how to implement it precisely in neural hardware, or because certain neural features are absent from the model. We can now identify two fallacies in such a dismissal. First, following (11): sub-symbolic models should not be viewed as neural models. If the sub-symbolic paradigm proves valid, the best sub-symbolic models of a cognitive process should one day be shown to be some reasonable higher-level approximation to the neural system supporting that process. This provides a heuristic that favors sub-symbolic models that seem more likely to be reducible to the neural level. But this heuristic is an extremely weak one given how difficult such a judgment must be with the current confusion about the precise neural correlates of units and connections, and the current state of both empirical and theoretical neuroscience.

The second fallacy in dismissing a particular sub-symbolic model because of neural unfaithfulness rests on a failure to recognize the role of individual models in the sub-symbolic paradigm. A model can make a valuable contribution by providing evidence for general principles that are characteristic of a broad class of sub-symbolic systems. The potential value of 'ablation' studies of the NETtalk text-to-speech system (Sejnowski and Rosenberg, 1986), for example, does not depend entirely on the neural faithfulness of the model, or even on its psychological faithfulness. NETtalk is a sub-symbolic system that performs a complex task. What happens to its performance when internal parts are damaged? This provides a significant clue to the general principles of degradation in *all* complex sub-symbolic systems: principles that will apply to future systems that are more faithful as models.

There are, of course, many neural models that do take many of the constraints of neural organization seriously, and for which the analogue of table 2.1 would show nearly all hits. But we are concerned here with connectionist models for performing cognitive tasks, and these models typically possess the features displayed in table 2.1, with perhaps one or two deviations. The claim is not that neural models don't exist, but rather that they should not be confused with sub-symbolic models.

Why is it that neural models of cognitive processes are, generally speaking, currently not feasible? The problem is not an insufficient quantity of data about the brain. The problem, it seems, is that the data are generally of the wrong kind for cognitive modeling. Our information about the nervous system tends to describe its structure, not its dynamic behavior. Sub-symbolic systems are dynamical systems with certain kinds of differential equations governing their dynamics. If we knew which dynamical variables in the neural system for some cognitive task were the critical ones for performing that task, and what the 'equations of motion' were for those variables, we could use that information to build neurally faithful cognitive models. But generally what we know instead are endless static properties of how the hardware is arranged. Without knowing which (if any) of these structures support relevant dynamical processes, and what equations govern those processes, we are in a position comparable to someone attempting to model the solar system, armed with voluminous data on the colored bands of the planets but with no knowledge of Newton's Laws.

To summarize:

(12)   (a) Unlike the symbolic architecture, the sub-symbolic archi-
           tecture possesses a number of the most general features of
           the neural architecture.
       (b) However, the sub-symbolic architecture lacks a number of
           the more detailed but still quite general features of the neural
           architecture; the sub-conceptual level of analysis is higher
           than the neural level.
       (c) For most cognitive functions, neuroscience cannot provide
           the relevant information to specify a cognitive model at the
           neural level.
       (d) The general cognitive principles of the sub-conceptual level
           will probably be important contributors to future discoveries
           of those specifications of neural computations that we now
           lack.

5   Reduction of Cognition to the Sub-conceptual Level

The previous section considered the relationship between the fundamental level of the sub-symbolic paradigm – the sub-conceptual level –
and the neural level. The remainder of this chapter will focus on
relations between the sub-conceptual and conceptual levels; these have
so far only been touched upon briefly (in 8c). Before proceeding,
however, it is worth summarizing the relationships between the levels,
including those that will be discussed in the remainder of the chapter.

Imagine three physical systems: a brain that is executing some
cognitive process; a massively parallel connectionist computer running a
sub-symbolic model of that process; and a von Neumann computer
running a symbolic model of the same process. The cognitive process
may involve conscious rule application, intuition or a combination of the
two. According to the sub-symbolic paradigm, here are the relationships:

(13)   (a) Describing the brain at the neural level gives a neural model.
       (b) Describing the brain approximately, at a higher level – the
           sub-conceptual level – yields, to a good approximation, the

model running on the connectionist computer, when it too is described at the sub-conceptual level. (At this point, this is a goal for future research. It could turn out that the degree of approximation here is only rough; this would still be consistent with the sub-symbolic paradigm.)

(c) We can try to describe the connectionist computer at a higher level – the conceptual level – by using the patterns of activity that have conceptual semantics. If the cognitive process being executed is conscious rule application, we will be able to carry out this conceptual-level analysis with reasonable precision, and will end up with a description that closely matches the symbolic computer program running on the von Neumann machine.

(d) If the process being executed is an intuitive process, we will be unable to carry out the conceptual-level description of the connectionist machine precisely. None the less, we will be able to produce various approximate conceptual-level descriptions that correspond to the symbolic computer program running on the von Neumann machine in various ways.

For a cognitive process involving both intuition and conscious rule application, (13c) and (13d) will each apply to certain aspects of the process.

The relationships (13a) and (13b) were discussed in the previous section. The relationship (13c) between a sub-symbolic implementation of the conscious rule interpreter and a symbolic implementation is discussed in section 6. The relations (13d) between sub-symbolic and symbolic accounts of intuitive processing are considered in section 9. These relations hinge on certain sub-symbolic computational principles operative at the sub-conceptual level (13b); these are briefly discussed in section 8. These principles are of a new kind for cognitive science, giving rise to the foundational considerations taken up in section 7.

The relationships in (13) can be more clearly understood by reintroducing the concept of 'virtual machine'. If we take one of the three physical systems and describe its processing at a certain level of analysis, we get a virtual machine that I will denote 'system$_{level}$'. Then (13) can be written:

(14) (a) Brain$_{neural}$ = Neural model
      (b) Brain$_{sub-conceptual}$ $\simeq$ Connectionist$_{sub-conceptual}$
      (c) Connectionist$_{conceptual}$ $\simeq$ von Neumann$_{conceptual}$ (conscious rule application)
      (d) Connectionist$_{conceptual}$ $\sim$ von Neumann$_{conceptual}$ (intuition)

Here, the symbol $\simeq$ means 'equals to a good approximation' and $\sim$ means 'equals to a crude approximation'. The two nearly equal virtual machines in (14c) both describe what I have been calling the 'conscious rule interpreter'. The two roughly similar virtual machines in (14d) provide the two paradigms' descriptions of the intuitive processor at the conceptual level.

Table 2.2 indicates these relationships and also the degree of exactness to which each system can be described at each level – the degree of precision to which each virtual machine is defined. The levels included in table 2.2 are those relevant to predicting high-level behavior. Of course, each system can also be described at lower levels, all the way down to elementary particles. However, levels below an exactly describable level can be ignored from the point of view of predicting high-level behavior, since it is possible (in principle) to do the prediction at the highest level that can be exactly described (it is presumably much harder to do the same at lower levels). This is why in the symbolic paradigm any descriptions below the conceptual level are not viewed as significant. For modeling high-level behavior, how the symbol manipulation happens to be implemented can be ignored – it is not a relevant part of the cognitive model. In a sub-symbolic model, exact behavioral prediction must be performed at the sub-conceptual level, but how the units happen to be implemented is not relevant.

The relation between the conceptual level and lower levels is fundamentally different in the sub-symbolic and symbolic paradigms. This leads to important differences in the kind of explanations the paradigms offer of conceptual-level behavior, and the kind of reduction used in these explanations. A symbolic model is a *system* of interacting processes, all with the same conceptual-level semantics as the task

Table 2.2   Three cognitive systems and three levels of description

Level	(Process)	Brain	Sub-symbolic	Symbolic
			Cognitive system	
Conceptual	(Intuition)	?	Rough approximation $\sim$	Exact
	(Conscious rule application)	?	Good approximation $\simeq$	Exact
Sub-conceptual		Good approximation $\simeq$	Exact	
Neural		Exact		

behavior being explained. Adopting the terminology of Haugeland (1978), this *systematic explanation* relies on a *systematic reduction* of the behavior that involves no shift of semantic domain or *dimension*. Thus a game-playing program is composed of sub-programs that generate possible moves, evaluate them, and so on. In the symbolic paradigm, these systematic reductions play the major role in explanation. The lowest-level processes in the systematic reduction, still with the original semantics of the task domain, are then themselves reduced by *intentional instantiation*: they are implemented exactly by other processes with different semantics but the same form. Thus a move-generation sub-program with game semantics is instantiated in a system of programs with list-manipulating semantics. This intentional instantiation typically plays a minor role in the overall explanation, if indeed it is regarded as a cognitively relevant part of the model at all.

Thus cognitive explanations in the symbolic paradigm rely primarily on reductions involving no dimensional shift. This feature is not shared by the sub-symbolic paradigm, where accurate explanations of intuitive behavior require descending to the sub-conceptual level. The elements in this explanation, the units, do *not* have the semantics of the original behavior: that is the content of the sub-conceptual unit hypothesis, (8b). In other words:

(15) Unlike symbolic explanations, sub-symbolic explanations rely crucially on a semantic ('dimensional') shift that accompanies the shift from the conceptual to the sub-conceptual levels.

The overall dispositions of cognitive systems are explained in the sub-symbolic paradigm as approximate higher-level regularities that emerge from quantitative laws operating at a more fundamental level with different semantics. This is the kind of reduction familiar in natural science, exemplified by the explanation of the laws of thermodynamics through a reduction to mechanics that involves shifting the dimension from thermal semantics to molecular semantics. (Section 9 discusses some explicit sub-symbolic reductions of symbolic explanatory constructs.)

Indeed, the sub-symbolic paradigm repeals the other features that Haugeland identified as newly introduced into scientific explanation by the symbolic paradigm. The inputs and outputs of the system are not quasi-linguistic representations but good old-fashioned numerical vectors. These inputs and outputs have semantic interpretations, but these are not constructed recursively from interpretations of embedded constituents. The fundamental laws are good old-fashioned numerical equations.

Haugeland went to considerable effort to legitimize the form of explanation and reduction used in the symbolic paradigm. The explanations and reductions of the sub-symbolic paradigm, by contrast, are of a type well established in natural science.

In summary, let me emphasize that in the sub-symbolic paradigm, the conceptual and sub-conceptual levels are not related as the levels of a von Neumann computer (high-level-language program, compiled low-level program etc.). The relationship between sub-symbolic and symbolic models is more like that between quantum and classical mechanics. Sub-symbolic models accurately describe the microstructure of cognition, whereas symbolic models provide an approximate description of the macrostructure. An important job of sub-symbolic theory is to delineate the situations and the respects in which the symbolic approximation is valid, and to explain why.

6   Conscious Rule Application in the Sub-symbolic Paradigm

In the symbolic paradigm, both conscious rule application and intuition are described at the conceptual level; that is, conscious and unconscious rule interpretation, respectively. In the sub-symbolic paradigm, conscious rule application can be formalized in the conceptual level but intuition must be formalized at the sub-conceptual level. This suggests that a sub-symbolic model of a cognitive process that involves both intuition and conscious rule interpretation would consist of two components using quite different formalisms. While this hybrid formalism might have considerable practical value, there are some theoretical problems with it. How would the two formalisms communicate? How would the hybrid system evolve with experience, reflecting the development of intuition and the subsequent remission of conscious rule application? How would the hybrid system elucidate the fallibility of actual human rule application (e.g. logic)? How would the hybrid system get us closer to understanding how conscious rule application is achieved neurally?

All these problems can be addressed by adopting a unified sub-conceptual-level analysis of both intuition and conscious rule interpretation. The virtual machine that is the conscious rule interpreter is to be implemented in a lower-level virtual machine: the same connectionist dynamical system that models the intuitive processor. How this can, in principle, be achieved is the subject of this section. The relative advantages and disadvantages of implementing the rule interpreter in a connectionist dynamical system, rather than a von Neumann machine, will also be considered.

Section 2.1 described the power of natural language for the propagation of cultural knowledge and the instruction of novices. Someone who has mastered a natural language has a powerful trick available for performing in domains where experience has been insufficient for the development of intuition: verbally expressed rules, whether resident in memory or on paper, can be used to direct a step-by-step course to an answer. Once sub-symbolic models have achieved a sufficient subset of the power to process natural language, they will be able to exploit the same trick. A sub-symbolic system with natural language competence will be able to encode linguistic expressions as patterns of activity; like all other patterns of activity, these can be stored in connectionist memories using standard procedures. If the linguistic expressions stored in memory happen to be rules, the sub-symbolic system can use them to solve problems sequentially in the following way. Suppose, for concreteness, that the rules stored in Memory are production rules of the form 'if *condition* holds, then do *action*'. If the system finds itself in a particular situation where *condition* holds, then the stored production can be retrieved from the connectionist memory via the characteristic *content-addressability* of these memories: of the activity pattern representing the entire production, the sub-part that pertains to *condition* is present, and this then leads to the reinstantiation in the memory of the entire pattern representing the production. The competence of the sub-symbolic system to process natural language must include the ability to take the portion of the reinstantiated pattern that encodes the verbal description of *action*, and actually execute the action it describes; that is, the sub-symbolic system must be able to *interpret*, in the computational sense of the term, the memorized description of *action*. The result is a sub-symbolic implementation of a production system, built purely out of sub-symbolic natural language processing mechanisms. A Connectionist account of natural language processes must eventually be developed as part of the sub-symbolic paradigm, because natural language processes of fluent speakers are intuitive and thus, according to the sub-symbolic hypothesis (8), must be modeled at the sub-conceptual level using sub-symbolic computation.

In summary:

(16)   The competence to represent and process linguistic structures in a native language is a competence of the human intuitive processor; the sub-symbolic paradigm assumes that this com-

petence can be modeled in a sub-conceptual connectionist dynamical system. By combining such linguistic competence with the memory capabilities of connectionist systems, sequential rule interpretation can be implemented.

Now note that our sub-symbolic system can use its stored rules to perform the task. The standard learning procedures of connectionist models now turn this experience of performing the task into a set of weights for going from inputs to outputs. Eventually, after enough experience, the task can be performed directly by these weights. The input activity generates the output activity so quickly that before the relatively slow rule-interpretation process has a chance to reinstantiate the first rule in memory and interpret it, the task is done. With intermediate amounts of experience, some of the weights are well enough in place to prevent some of the rules from having the chance to instantiate, while others are not, enabling other rules to be retrieved and interpreted.

6.1   Rule interpretation, consciousness, and seriality

What about the conscious aspect of rule interpretation? Since consciousness seems to be a quite high-level description of mental activity, it is reasonable to suspect that it reflects the very coarse structure of the cognitive dynamical system. This suggests the following hypothesis:

(17)   The contents of consciousness reflect only the large-scale structure of activity patterns: sub-patterns of activity that are extended over spatially large regions of the network and that are stable for relatively long periods of time.

(See Rumelhart et al., 1986c. Note that (17) hypothesizes a *necessary* – not a *sufficient* – condition for an aspect of the sub-symbolic state to be relevant to the conscious state.) The spatial aspect of this hypothesis has already played a major role in this chapter – it is in fact a restatement of the sub-conceptual unit hypothesis, (8b): concepts that are consciously accessible correspond to patterns over large numbers of units. It is the temporal aspect of hypothesis (17) that is relevant here. The rule interpretation process requires that the retrieved linguistically coded rule be maintained in memory while it is being interpreted. Thus the pattern of activity representing the rule must be stable for a relatively long time. In contrast, after connections have been developed to perform the task directly, there is no correspondingly stable pattern formed during the performance of the task. Thus the loss of conscious phenomenology with expertise can be understood naturally.

On this account, the sequentiality of the rule interpretation process is not built into the architecture; rather, it is linked to our ability to follow only one verbal instruction at a time. Connectionist memories have the ability to retrieve a single stored item, and here this ability is called upon so that the linguistic interpreter is not required to interpret multiple instructions simultaneously.

It is interesting to note that the preceding analysis also applies to non-linguistic rules: any notational system that can be appropriately interpreted will do. For example another type of rule might be a short series of musical pitches; a memorized collection of such rules would allow a musician to play a tune by conscious rule interpretation. With practice, the need for conscious control goes away. Since pianists learn to interpret several notes simultaneously, the present account suggests that a pianist might be able to apply more than one musical rule at a time; if the pianist's memory for these rules can simultaneously recall more than one, it would be possible to generate multiple musical lines simultaneously using conscious rule interpretation. A symbolic account of such a process would involve something like a production system capable of firing multiple productions simultaneously.

Finally, it should be noted that even if the memorized rules are assumed to be linguistically coded, the preceding analysis is uncommitted about the form the encoded rules take in memory: phonological, orthographic, semantic, or whatever.

6.2 Symbolic versus sub-symbolic implementation of rule interpretation

The (approximate) implementation of the conscious rule interpreter in a sub-symbolic system has both advantages and disadvantages relative to an (exact) implementation in a von Neumann machine.

The main disadvantage is that sub-conceptual representation and interpretation of linguistic instructions is very difficult and we are not actually able to do it now. Most existing sub-symbolic systems simply don't use rule interpretation.[8] Thus they miss out on all the advantages listed in (2). They can't take advantage of rules to check the results produced by the intuitive processor. They can't bootstrap their way into a new domain using rules to generate their own experience: they must have a teacher generate it for them.[9]

There are several advantages of a sub-conceptually implemented rule interpreter. The intuitive processor and rule interpreter are highly integrated, with broad-band communication between them. Understanding how this communication works should allow the design of efficient hybrid symbolic/sub-symbolic systems with effective communication between the processors. A principled basis is provided for studying how rule-based knowledge leads to intuitive knowledge. Perhaps most interesting, in a sub-symbolic rule interpreter, the process of rule selection is intuitive! Which rule is reinstantiated in memory at a given time is the result of the associative retrieval process, which has many nice properties. The best match to the productions' conditions is quickly computed, and even if no match is very good, a rule can be retrieved. The selection process can be quite context-sensitive.

An integrated sub-symbolic rule interpreter/intuitive processor in principle offers the advantages of both kinds of processing. Imagine such a system creating a mathematical proof. The intuitive processor would generate goals and steps, and the rule interpreter would verify their validity. The serial search through the space of possible steps, which is necessary in a purely symbolic approach, is replaced by the intuitive generation of possibilities. Yet the precise adherence to strict inference rules that is demanded by the task can be enforced by the rule interpreter; the creativity of intuition can be exploited while its unreliability can be controlled.

6.3   Two kinds of knowledge – one knowledge medium

Most existing sub-symbolic systems perform tasks without serial rule interpretation: patterns of activity representing inputs are directly transformed (possibly through multiple layers of units) into patterns of activity representing outputs. The connections that mediate this transformation represent a form of task knowledge that can be applied with massive parallelism: I will call it *P-knowledge*. For example, the P-knowledge in a native speaker presumably encodes lexical, morphological, syntactic, semantic, and pragmatic constraints in such a form that all these constraints can be satisfied in parallel during comprehension and generation.

The connectionist implementation of sequential rule interpretation described above displays a second form that knowledge can take in a sub-symbolic system. The stored activity patterns that represent rules also constitute task knowledge: call it *S-knowledge*. Like P-knowledge, S-knowledge is embedded in connections: the connections that enable part of a rule to reinstantiate the entire rule. Unlike P-knowledge, S-knowledge cannot be used with massive parallelism. For example, a novice speaker of some language cannot satisfy the constraints contained in two memorized rules simultaneously; they must be serially reinstantiated as patterns of activity and separately interpreted. Of course, the connections responsible for reinstantiating these memories operate in parallel, and indeed these connections contain within them the potential to reinstantiate either of the two memorized rules. But these connections are so arranged that only one rule at a time can be reinstantiated. The retrieval of each rule is a parallel process, but the satisfaction of the constraints contained within the two rules is a serial process. After considerable experience, P-knowledge is created: connections that can simultaneously satisfy the constraints represented by the two rules.

P-knowledge is considerably more difficult to create than S-knowledge. To encode a constraint in connections so that it can be satisfied in parallel with thousands of others is not an easy task. Such an encoding can only be learned through considerable experience in which that constraint has appeared in many different contexts, so that the connections enforcing the constraint can be tuned to operate in parallel with those enforcing a wide variety of other constraints. S-knowledge can be acquired (once the linguistic skills on which it depends have been encoded into P-knowledge, of course) much more rapidly. For example, simply reciting a verbal rule over and over will usually suffice to store it in memory, at least temporarily.

That P-knowledge is so highly context-dependent, while the rules of S-knowledge are essentially context-independent, is an important computational fact underlying many of the psychological explanations offered by sub-symbolic models. Consider, for example, Rumelhart and McClelland's (1986) model of the U-shaped curve for past-tense production in children. The phenomenon striking: a child is observed using *goed* and *wented* when at a much younger age *went* was reliably used. This is surprising because we are prone to think that such linguistic abilities rest on knowledge that is encoded in some context-independent form such as 'the past tense of *go* is *went.*' Why should a child *lose* such a rule once acquired? A traditional answer invokes the acquisition of a different context-independent rule, such as 'the past tense of x is $x \times ed$' which, for one reason or another, takes precedence. The point here, however, is that there is nothing at all surprising about the phenomenon when the underlying knowledge is assumed to be context-dependent and not context-independent. The young child has a small vocabulary of largely irregular verbs. The connections that implement this P-knowledge are reliable in producing the large pattern of activity representing *went*, as well as those representing a small number of other past-tense forms. Informally we can say that the connections producing *went* do so in the context of the other vocabulary items that are also stored in the same connections. There is no guarantee that these connections will produce *went* in the context of a different vocabulary. As the child acquires additional vocabulary items, most of which are regular, the context radically changes. Connections that were, so to speak, perfectly adequate for creating *went* in the old context now have to work in a context where very strong connections are trying to create forms ending in *-ed*; the old connections are not up to the new task. Only through extensive experience trying to produce *went* in the new context of many regular verbs can the old connections be modified to work in the new context. In particular, strong new connections must be added that, when the input pattern encodes *go*, cancel the *-ed* in the output; these were not needed before.

These observations about context-dependence can also be framed in terms of inference. If we choose to regard the child as using knowledge to infer the correct answer *went*, then we can say that after the child has added more knowledge (about new verbs), the ability to make the (correct) inference is lost. In this sense the child's inference process is non-monotonic – perhaps this is why we find the phenomenon surprising. As will be discussed in section 8, non-monotonocity is a fundamental property of sub-symbolic inference.

To summarize:

(18) (a) Knowledge in sub-symbolic systems can take two forms, both resident in the connections.
    (b) The knowledge used by the conscious rule interpreter lies in connections that reinstantiate patterns encoding rules; task constraints are coded in context-independent rules and satisfied serially.
    (c) The knowledge used in intuitive processing lies in connections that constitute highly context-dependent encodings of task constraints that can be satisfied with massive parallelism.
    (d) Learning such encodings requires much experience.

7 Sub-symbolic Definition of Cognitive Systems and Some Foundational Issues

In order for the sub-conceptual level to be rightly viewed as a level for practicing cognitive science, it is necessary that the principles formulated at this level truly be principles of cognition. Since sub-symbolic principles are neither conceptual-level nor neural-level principles, it is not immediately apparent what kind of cognitive principles they might be. The structure of sub-symbolic models is that of a dynamical system; in what sense do these models embody principles of cognition rather than principles of physics?

What distinguishes those dynamical systems that are cognitive from those that are not? At this point the types of dynamical systems being studied in Connectionist cognitive science lack anything that could justly be called an intentional psychology. In this section I wish to show that it is none the less possible to distinguish the sort of dynamical systems that have so far been the object of study in connectionist cognitive science from the dynamical systems that have traditionally been the subject matter of physics, and that the questions being studied are indeed questions of cognition.

A crucial property of cognitive systems broadly construed is that over a wide variety of environments they can maintain, at an adequately constant level, the degree to which a significant number of *goal conditions* are met. Here I intend the teleological, rather than the intentional, sense of 'goal'. A river, for example, is a complex dynamical system that responds sensitively to its environment – but about the only condition that it can satisfy over a large range of environments is going downhill. A cockroach manages, over an annoyingly extensive range of environments, to maintain its nutritive intake, its reproductive demands, its oxygen intake, even its probability of getting smashed, all within a relatively narrow band. The repertoire of conditions that people can keep satisfied, and the range of environments under which this relative constancy can be maintained, provides a measure worthy of the human cognitive capacity.

(19)   *Cognitive system*: A necessary condition for a dynamical system to be *cognitive* is that, under a wide variety of environmental conditions, it maintains a large number of goal conditions. The greater the repertoire of goals and variety of tolerable environmental conditions, the greater the cognitive capacity of the system.

The issue of complexity is crucial here. A river (or a thermostat) only fails to be a cognitive dynamical system because it cannot satisfy a *large* range of goals under a *wide* range of conditions.[10] Complexity is largely what distinguishes the dynamical systems studied in the sub-symbolic paradigm from those traditionally studied in physics. Connectionist dynamical systems have great complexity: the information content in their weights is very high. Studying the extent to which a connectionist dynamical system can achieve complex goals in complex environments requires grappling with complexity in dynamical systems in a way that is traditionally avoided in physics. In cognitive modeling, many of the basic questions concern the detailed dynamics of a distinct pattern of activation in a system with a particular initial state and a particular set of interaction strengths that are highly non-homogeneous. This is like asking a physicist: 'Suppose we have a gas with 10,000 particles with the following 10,000 different masses and the following 500,000 different forces between them. Suppose we start them at rest in the following 10,000 positions. What are the trajectories of the following 20 particles?' This is indeed a question about a dynamical system, and is, in a sense, a question of physics. It is this kind of question, however, that is avoided at all costs in physics. The physicist we consulted is likely to compute the mean collision times for the particles assuming equal masses, random starting positions, and uniformly random interactions, and say 'if that isn't good enough, then take your question to a computer.'[11]

None the less, physics has valuable concepts and techniques to contribute to the study of connectionist dynamical systems. Insights from physics have already proved important in various ways in the sub-symbolic paradigm (Sejnowski, 1976; Hinton and Sejnowski, 1983a; Smolensky, 1983).

Various sub-symbolic models have addressed various goals and environments. A very general goal that is of particular importance is:

(20)   *The prediction goal*: given some partial information about the environmental state, correctly infer missing information.

What is maintained here is the degree of match between predicted values and the actual values for the unknowns. Maintenance of this match over the wide range of conditions found in a complex environment is a difficult task. Special cases of this task include predicting the depth of an object from retinal images, the future location of a moving object, the change in certain aspects of an electric circuit given the changes in other aspects, or the propositions implied by a text. The prediction goal is obviously an important one, because it can serve so many other goals: accurate prediction of the effects of actions allows the selection of those leading to desired effects.

A closely related goal is:

(21)   *The prediction-from-examples goal*: given more and more examples of states from an environment, achieve the prediction goal with increasing accuracy in that environment.

For the prediction goal we ask: what inference procedures and knowledge about an environment must a dynamical system possess to be able to predict that environment? For the prediction-from-examples goal we go further and ask: what learning procedures must a dynamical system possess to be able to acquire the necessary knowledge about an environment from examples?

The goals of prediction and prediction-from-examples are the subject of many principles of the sub-symbolic paradigm. These are indeed cognitive principles. They will be taken up in the next section; first, however, I would like to consider some implications of this characterization of a cognitive system for certain foundational issues: semantics, rationality, and the constituent structure of mental states. It would be absurd to suggest that the following few paragraphs constitute definitive treatments of these issues; the intent is rather to indicate specific points where sub-symbolic research touches on these issues and to sow seeds for further analysis.

7.1   Semantics and rationality in the sub-symbolic paradigm

The sub-symbolic characterization of a cognitive system (19) intrinsically binds cognitive systems both to states of the environment and to goal conditions. It therefore has implications for the question: how do states of a sub-symbolic system get their meanings and truth conditions? A starting point for an answer is suggested in the following hypothesis:

(22)   *Sub-symbolic semantics*: a cognitive system adopts various internal states in various environmental conditions. To the extent that the cognitive system meets its goal conditions in various environmental conditions, its internal states are *veridical representations* of the corresponding environmental states, with respect to the given goal conditions.

For the prediction goal, for example, a state of the sub-symbolic system is a veridical representation of the current environmental state to the extent that it leads to correct predictions.

According to hypothesis (22), it is not possible to localize a failure of veridical representation. Any particular state is part of a large causal system of states, and failures of the system to meet goal conditions cannot in general be localized to any particular state or state component.[12] In sub-symbolic systems, this *assignment of blame problem* (Minsky, 1963) is a difficult one, and it makes programming sub-symbolic models by hand very tricky. Solving the assignment of blame problem is one of the central accomplishments of the automatic network programming procedures: the learning procedures of the sub-symbolic paradigm.

The characterization (19) of cognitive systems relates to rationality as well. How can one build a rational machine? How can internal processes (e.g. inference) be guaranteed to preserve veridical semantic relationships (e.g. be truth preserving)? These questions now become: how can the connection strengths be set so that the sub-symbolic system will meet its goal conditions? Again, this is a question answered by the scientific discoveries of the sub-symbolic paradigm: particular procedures for programming machines to meet certain goals, especially learning procedures to meet adaptation goals such as prediction-from-examples.

Let me compare this sub-symbolic approach to veridicality with a symbolic approach to truth preservation offered by Fodor (1975, 1987). In the context of model-theoretic semantics for a set of symbolic formulae, proof theory provides a set of symbol manipulations (rules of inference) guaranteed to preserve truth conditions. Thus if an agent possesses knowledge in the symbolic form $p \rightarrow q$ and additional knowledge p, then by syntactic operations the agent can produce q; proof theory guarantees that the truth conditions of the agent's knowledge (or beliefs) has not changed.

There are fairly direct sub-symbolic counterparts to this proof-theoretic account. The role of logical inference is played by statistical inference. By explicitly formalizing tasks like prediction as statistical inference tasks, it is possible to prove for appropriate systems that sub-symbolic computation is valid in a sense directly comparable to symbolic proof. Further discussion of this point, which will appear in section 9.1, must await further examination of the computational framework of the sub-symbolic paradigm, which is the subject of section 8.

Note that the proof-theoretic account explains the tautological inference of q from p and $p \rightarrow q$, but it leaves to an independent module an account of how the agent acquired the knowledge $p \rightarrow q$ that licenses the inference from p to q. In the sub-symbolic account, the veridicality problem is tied inextricably to the environment in which the agent is trying to satisfy the goal conditions – sub-symbolic semantics is intrinsically situated. The sub-symbolic analysis of veridicality involves the following basic questions: how can a cognitive system be put in a novel environment and learn to create veridical internal representations that allow valid inferences about that environment so that goal conditions can be satisfied? How can it pick up information from its environment? These are exactly the questions addressed by sub-symbolic learning procedures.

Note that in the sub-symbolic case, the internal processing mechanisms (which can appropriately be called inference procedures) do not, of course, directly depend causally on the environmental state that may be internally represented or on the veridicality of that representation. In that sense, they are just as formal as syntactic symbol manipulations. The fact that a sub-symbolic system can generate veridical representations of the environment (e.g. make valid predictions) is a result of extracting information from the environment and internally coding it in its weights through a learning procedure.

7.2   Constituent structure of mental states

Fodor and Pylyshyn have argued (e.g. Fodor, 1975; Pylyshyn, 1984) that mental states must have constituent structure, and they have used this argument agaisnt the Connectionist approach (See chapter 3). Their argument applies, however, only to ultra-local connectionist models (Ballard and Hayes, 1984); it is quite inapplicable to the distributed connectionist systems considered here. A mental state in a sub-symbolic system is a pattern of activity with a constituent structure that can be analyzed at both the conceptual and the sub-conceptual levels. In this section I offer a few general observations on this issue; the connectionist representation of complex structures is an active area of research (Touretzky, 1986; Smolensky, 1987), and many difficult problems remain to be solved (for futher discussion, see Smolensky, 1988).

At the conceptual level, a connectionist mental state contains constituent sub-patterns that have conceptual interpretations. Pylyshyn, in a debate over the connectionist approach at the 1984 meeting of the Cognitive Science Society, suggested how to extract these conceptual constituents with the following example. The Connectionist representation of *coffee* is the representation of *cup with coffee* minus the representation of *cup without coffee*. To carry out this suggestion, imagine a crude but adequate kind of distributed semantic representation, in which the interpretation of *cup with coffee* involves the activity of network units representing features like brown liquid with flat top surface, brown liquid with curved sides and bottom surface, brown liquid contacting porcelain, hot liquid, upright container with a handle, burnt odor, and so forth. We should really use sub-conceptual features, but even these features are sufficiently low-level to make the point. Following Pylyshyn, we take this representation of the interpretation of *Cup with coffee* and subtract from it the representation of the interpretation of *Cup without coffee*, leaving the representation of *coffee*. What remains, in fact, is a pattern of activity with active features such as brown liquid with flat top surface, brown liquid with curved sides and bottom surface, brown liquid contacting porcelain, hot liquid, and burnt odor. This represents *coffee*, in some sense – but *coffee in the context of cup*.

In using Pylyshyn's procedure for determining the Connectionist representation of *coffee*, there is nothing sacred about starting with *cup with coffee*: why not start with *can with coffee, tree with coffee, or man with coffee*, and subtract the corresponding representation of X *without coffee?* Thinking back to the distributed featural representation, it is clear that each of these procedures produces quite a different result for 'the' Connectionist representation of *coffee*. The pattern representing *coffee* in the context of *cup* is quite different from the pattern representing *coffee* in the context of *can, tree or man*.

The pattern representing *cup with coffee* can be decomposed into conceptual-level constituents, one for *coffee* and another for *cup*. This decomposition differs in two significant ways from the decomposition of the symbolic expression *cup with coffee*, into the three constituents, *coffee*, *cup* and *with*. First, the decomposition is quite approximate. The pattern of features representing *Cup with coffee* may well, as in the imagined case above, possess a sub-pattern that can be identified with *coffee*, as well as a sub-pattern that can be identified with *cup*; but these sub-patterns will in general not be defined precisely and there will typically remain features that can be identified only with the interaction of the two (as in brown liquid contacting porcelain). Secondly, whatever the sub-pattern identified with *coffee*, unlike the symbol *coffee*, it is a context-dependent constituent, one whose internal structure is heavily influenced by the structure of which it is a part.

These constituent sub-patterns representing *coffee* in varying contexts are activity vectors that are not identical, but possess a rich structure of commonalities and differences (a family resemblance, one might say). The commonalities are directly responsible for the common processing implications of the interpretations of these various phrases, so the approximate equivalence of the *coffee* vectors across contexts plays a functional role in sub-symbolic processing that is quite close to the role played by the exact equivalence of the *coffee* tokens across different contexts in a symbolic processing system.

The conceptual-level constituents of mental states are activity vectors, which themselves have constituent structure at the sub-conceptual level: the individual units' activities. To summarize the relationship between these notions of constituent structure in the symbolic and sub-symbolic paradigms, let's call each *coffee* vector the (Connectionist) symbol for coffee in the given context. Then we can say that the context alters the internal structure of the symbol; the activities of the sub-conceptual units that comprise the symbol – its sub-symbols – change across contexts. In the symbolic paradigm, a symbol is effectively contextualized by surrounding it with other symbols in some larger structure. In other words:

(23)   *Symbols and context dependence:* in the symbolic paradigm, the context of a symbol is manifest around it and consists of other symbols; in the sub-symbolic paradigm, the context of a symbol is manifest inside it and consists of subsymbols.

(Compare Hofstadter, 1979, 1985a, b)

8   Computation at the Sub-conceptual Level

Hypothesis (8a) offers a brief characterization of the connectionist architecture assumed at the sub-conceptual level by the sub-symbolic paradigm. It is time to bring out the computational principles implicit in that hypothesis.

8.1   Continuity

According to (8a), a connectionist dynamical system has a continuous space of states and changes state continuously in time. I take time in this section to motivate at some length this assumption of continuity, because it plays a central role in the characterization of sub-symbolic computation and because readers familiar with the literature on connectionist models will no doubt require that I reconcile the continuity assumption with some salient candidate counter-examples.

Within the symbolic paradigm, the simplest, most straightforward formalizations of a number of cognitive processes have quite discrete characters:

(24)   (a)   Discrete memory locations, in which items are stored without mutual interaction.
   (b)   Discrete memory storage and retrieval operations, in which an entire item is stored or retrieved in a single, atomic (primitive) operation.
   (c)   Discrete learning operations, in which new rules become available for use in an all-or-none fashion.
   (d)   Discrete inference operations, in which conclusions become available for use in an all-or-none fashion.
   (e)   Discrete categories, to which items either belong or do not belong.

(f) Discrete production rules, with conditions that are either satisfied or not satisfied, and actions that either execute or do not execute.

These discrete features come 'for free' in the symbolic paradigm: of course, any one of them can be softened but only by explicitly building in machinery to do so.

Obviously (24) is a pretty crude characterization of cognitive behavior. Cognition seems to be a richly interwoven fabric of graded, continuous processes and discrete, all-or-none processes. One way to model this interplay is to posit separate discrete and continuous processors in interaction. Some theoretical problems with this move were mentioned in section 6, where a unified formalism was advocated. It is difficult to introduce a hard separation between the soft and the hard components of processing. An alternative is to adopt a fundamentally symbolic approach, but to soften various forms of discreteness by hand. For example, the degree of match to conditions of production rules can be given numerical values, productions can be given strengths, interactions between separately stored memory items can be put in by hand, and so on (Anderson, 1983).

The sub-symbolic paradigm offers another alternative. All the discrete features of (24) are neatly swept aside in one stroke by adopting a continuous framework that applies at the sub-conceptual level. Then, when the continuous system is analyzed at the higher, conceptual level, various aspects of discreteness emerge naturally and inevitably, without explicit machinery having been devised to create this discreteness. These aspects of 'hardness' are intrinsically embedded in a fundamentally 'soft' system. The dilemma of accounting for both the hard and soft aspects of cognition is solved by using the passage from a lower level of analysis to a higher level to introduce natural changes in the character of the system: the emergent properties can have a different nature from the fundamental properties. This is the story to be fleshed out in the remainder of the chapter. It rests on the fundamental continuity of sub-symbolic computation, which is further motivated in the remainder of this section (for further discussion see Smolensky, 1987b).

It may appear that the continuous nature of sub-symbolic systems is contradicted by the fact that it is easy to find in the connectionist literature models that are quite within the spirit of the sub-symbolic paradigm, but which have neither continuous state spaces nor continuous dynamics. For example, models having units with binary values that jump discretely on the ticks of a discrete clock (the Boltzmann machine: Hinton and Sejnowski 1983a; Ackley et al., 1985; harmony theory: Smolensky, 1983, 1986a). I will now argue that these models should be viewed as discrete simulations of an underlying continuous model, considering first discretization of time and then discretization of the units' values.

Dynamical systems evolving in continuous time are almost always simulated on digital computers by discretizing time. Since sub-symbolic models have almost always been simulated on digital computers, it is no surprise that they too have been simulated by discretizing time. The equations defining the dynamics of the models can be understood more easily by most cognitive scientists if the differential equations of the underlying continuous dynamical system are avoided in favor of the discrete-time approximations that actually get simulated.

When sub-symbolic models use binary-valued units, these values are best viewed not as symbols like T and NIL that are used for conditional branching tests, but as numbers (not numerals!) like 1 and 0 that are used for numerical operations (e.g. multiplication by weights, summation, exponentiation). These models are formulated in such a way that they are perfectly well defined for continuous values of the units. Discrete numerical unit values are no more than a simplification that is sometimes convenient.[13]

As historical evidence that underlying sub-symbolic models are continuous systems, it is interesting to note that when the theoretical conditions that license the discrete approximation have changed, the models have reverted to continuous values. In the harmony/energy optima model, when the jumpy stochastic search was replaced by a smooth deterministic one (Rumelhart et al. 1986c), the units were changed to continuous ones.[14]

A second, quite dramatic, piece of historical evidence is a case where switching from discrete to continuous units made possible a revolution in sub-symbolic learning theory. In their classic book, *Perceptrons*, Minsky and Papert (1969) exploited primarily discrete mathematical methods that were compatible with the choice of binary units. They were incapable of analyzing any but the simplest learning networks. By changing the discrete threshold function of perceptrons to a smooth, differentiable curve, and thereby defining continuous-valued units, Rumelhart et al. (1986a) were able to apply continuous analytic methods to more complex learning networks. The result was a major advance in the power of sub-symbolic learning.

A third historical example of the power of a continuous conception of sub-symbolic computation relates to the connectionist generation of sequences. Traditionally, this task has been viewed as making a connectionist system jump discretely between states to generate an arbitrary discrete sequence of actions A_1, A_2 $\cdots$. This view of the task reduces the connectionist system to a finite state machine that can offer little new to the analysis of sequential behavior. Jordan (1986) shows how a sub-symbolic approach can give 'for free' co-articulation effects where the manner in which actions are executed is influenced by future actions. Such effects are just what should come automatically from implementing serial behavior in a fundamentally parallel machine. Jordan's trick is to view the connectionist system as evolving continuously in time, with the task being the generation of a continuous trajectory through state space, a trajectory that meets as boundary conditions certain constraints, for example, that at the discrete times 1, 2, $\cdots$ the system state must be in regions corresponding to the actions A_1, A_2, $\cdots$.

The final point is a foundational one. The theory of discrete computation is quite well understood. If there is any new theory of computation implicit in the sub-symbolic approach, it is likely to be a result of a fundamentally different, continuous formulation of computation. It therefore seems fruitful, in order to maximize the opportunity for the sub-symbolic paradigm to contribute new computational insights, to hypothesize that sub-symbolic computation is fundamentally continuous.

It must be emphasized that the discrete/continuous distinction cannot be understood completely by looking at simulations. Discrete and continuous machines can of course simulate each other. The claim here is that the most analytically powerful descriptions of sub-symbolic models are continuous ones, whereas those of symbolic models are not continuous.

This has profound significance because it means that many of the concepts used to understand cognition in the sub-symbolic paradigm come from the category of continuous mathematics, while those used in the symbolic paradigm come nearly exclusively from discrete mathematics. Concepts from physics, from the theory of dynamical systems, are at least as likely to be important as concepts from the theory of digital computation. And analog computers, both electronic and optical, provide natural implementation media for sub-symbolic systems (Anderson, 1986; Cohen, 1986).

8.2   Sub-symbolic computation

An important illustration of the continuous/discrete mathematics contrast that distinguishes sub-symbolic from symbolic computation is found in inference. A natural way to look at the knowledge stored in connections is to view each connection as a *soft constraint*. A positive (excitatory) connection from unit *a* to unit *b* represents a soft constraint to the effect that if *a* is active, then *b* should be too. A negative (inhibitory) connection represents the opposite constraint. The numerical magnitude of a connection represents the strength of the constraint.

Formalizing knowledge in soft constraints rather than hard rules has important consequences. Hard constraints have consequences singly; they are rules that can be applied separately and sequentially – the operation of each proceeding independently of whatever other rules may exist. But soft constraints have no implications singly; any one can be overridden by the others. It is only the entire set of soft constraints that has any implications. Inference must be a cooperative process, like the parallel relaxation processes typically found in sub-symbolic systems. Furthermore, adding additional soft constraints can repeal conclusions that were formerly valid: sub-symbolic inference is fundamentally non-monotonic.

One way of formalizing soft-constraint satisfaction is in terms of statistical inference. In certain sub-symbolic systems, the soft constraints can be identified as statistical parameters, and the activation-passing procedures can be identified as statistical-inference procedures (Hinton and Sejnowski, 1983b; Geman and Geman, 1984; Pearl, 1985; Shastri, 1985; Smolensky, 1986a). This identification is usually rather complex and subtle: unlike in classical 'spreading activation' models and in many local connectionist models, the strength of the connection between two units is *not* determined solely by the correlation between their activity (or their 'degree of association'). To implement sub-symbolic statistical inference, the correct connection strength between two units will typically depend on all the other connection strengths. The sub-symbolic learning procedures that sort out this interdependence through simple, strictly local, computations and ultimately assign the correct strength to each connection are performing no trivial task.

To sum up:

(25) (a) Knowledge in sub-symbolic computation is formalized as a large set of soft constraints.
(b) Inference with soft constraints is fundamentally a parallel process.
(c) Inference with soft constraints is fundamentally non-monotonic.
(d) Certain sub-symbolic systems can be identified as using statistical inference.

9   Conceptual-level Descriptions of Intuition

The previous section concerned computation in sub-symbolic systems analyzed at the sub-conceptual level, the level of units and connections. In this final section I consider analyses of sub-symbolic computation at the higher, conceptual level. Section 6 discussed sub-symbolic modeling of conscious rule interpretation; here I consider sub-symbolic models of intuitive processes. I will elaborate the point foreshadowed in section 5: conceptual-level descriptions of aspects of sub-symbolic models of intuitive processing roughly approximate symbolic accounts. The picture that emerges is of a symbiosis between the symbolic and sub-symbolic paradigms: the symbolic paradigm offers concepts for better understanding sub-symbolic models, and those concepts are in turn illuminated with a fresh light by the sub-symbolic paradigm.

9.1   The best fit principle

The notion that each connection represents a soft constraint can be formulated at a higher level:

(26)   *The best fit principle*: Given an input, a sub-symbolic system outputs a set of inferences that, as a whole, gives a best fit to the input, in a statistical sense defined by the statistical knowledge stored in the system's connections.

In this vague form, this principle can be regarded as a desideratum of sub-symbolic systems. Giving the principle, formal embodiment in a class of connectionist dynamical systems was the goal of harmony theory (Smolensky, 1983, 1984a, b; 1986a, c; Riley and Smolensky, 1984).

   To render the best fit principle precise, it is necessary to provide precise definitions of 'inferences', 'best fit' and 'statistical knowledge stored in the system's connections'. This is done in harmony theory, where the central object is the harmony function H which measures, for any possible set of inferences, the goodness of fit to the input with respect to the soft constraints stored in the connection strengths. The set of inferences with the largest value of H, that is, highest harmony, is the best set of inferences, with respect to a well-defined statistical problem.

   Harmony theory offers three things. It gives a mathematically precise characterization of the prediction-from-examples goal as a statistical inference problem. It tells how the prediction goal can be achieved using a network with a certain set of connections. Moreover, it gives a procedure by which the network can learn the correct connections with experience, thereby satisfying the prediction-from-examples goal.

The units in harmony networks are stochastic: the differential equations defining the system are stochastic. There is a system parameter called the *computational temperature* that governs the degree of randomness in the units' behavior, it goes to zero as the computation proceeds. (The process is *simulated annealing*, like in the Boltzmann machine: Ackley et al., 1985; Hinton and Sejnowski, 1983a, b, 1986. See Rumelhart et al. 1986b, p. 148, and Smolensky, 1986a, for the relations between harmony theory and the Boltzmann machine.)

9.2   Productions, sequential processing and logical inference

A simple harmony model of expert intuition in qualitative physics was described by Riley and Smolensky (1984) and Smolensky (1986a, c). The model answers questions such as 'What happens to the voltages in this circuit if I increase this resistor?' (The questions refer to a particular simple circuit; the model's expertise is built in and not the result of learning.) This connectionist problem-solving system illustrates several points about the relations between sub-conceptual- and conceptual-level descriptions of sub-symbolic computation.

Very briefly, the model looks like this. The state of the circuit is represented as a vector of activity over a set of network units we can call *circuit state feature units* – 'feature units' for short. A sub-part of this activity pattern represents whether the circuit's *current* has gone up, down or stayed the same; other sub-parts indicate what has happened to the *voltage drops*, and so on. Some of these sub-patterns are fixed by the givens in the problem, and the remainder comprise the answer to be computed by the network. There is a second set of network units, called *knowledge atoms*, each of which corresponds to a sub-pattern of activity over feature units. The sub-patterns of features encoded by knowledge atoms are those that can appear in representations of possible states of the circuit: they are sub-patterns that are allowed by the laws of circuit physics. The system's knowledge of Ohm's Law, for example, is distributed over the many knowledge atoms whose sub-patterns encode the legal feature combinations for current, voltage and resistance. The connections in the network determine which feature sub-pattern corresponds to a given knowledge atom. The sub-pattern corresponding to knowledge atom α includes a positive (negative) value for a particular feature f if there is a positive (negative) connection between unit α and unit f; the sub-pattern for α does not include f at all if there is no connection between α and f. All connections are two-way: activity can propagate from feature units to knowledge atoms and vice versa. The soft constraints encoded by these connections, then, say that 'if sub-pattern α is present, then feature f should be positive (negative), and vice versa.'

In the course of computing an answer to a question, the units in the network change their values hundreds of times. Each time a unit recomputes its value, we have a *micro-decision*. As the network converges to a solution, it is possible to identify *macro-decisions*, each of which amounts to a commitment of part of the network to a portion of the solution. Each macro-decision is the result of many individual micro-decisions. These macro-decisions are approximately like the firing of production rules. In fact, these productions fire in essentially the same order as in a symbolic forward-chaining inference system.[15] One can measure the total amount of order in the system and see that there is a qualitative change in the system when the first micro-decisions are made – the system changes from a disordered phase to an ordered one.

It is a corollary of the way this network embodies the problem domain constraints, and the general theorems of harmony theory, that the system, when given a well-posed problem and unlimited relaxation time, will always give the correct answer. So under that idealization, the *competence* of the system is described by *hard* constraints: Ohm's Law, Kirchoff's Law, the laws of simple circuits. It's as though the model had those laws written down inside it. However, as in all sub-symbolic systems, the *performance* of the system is achieved by satisfying a large set of *soft* constraints. What this means is that if we depart from the ideal conditions under which hard constraints seem to be obeyed, the illusion that the system has hard constraints inside is quickly dispelled. The system can violate Ohm's Law if it has to, but if it needn't violate the law, it won't. Outside the idealized domain of well-posed problems and unlimited processing time, the system gives sensible performance. It isn't brittle the way that symbolic inference systems are. If the system is given an ill-posed problem, it satisfies as many constraints as possible. If it is given inconsistent information, it doesn't fall flat and deduce just anything at all. If it is given insufficient information, it doesn't sit there and deduce nothing at all. Given limited processing time, the performance degrades gracefully as well. All these features emerge 'for free', as automatic consequences of performing inference in a sub-symbolic system; no extra machinery is added on to handle the deviations from ideal circumstances.

Returning to a physics-level analogy introduced in section 5, we have a 'quantum' system that appears to be 'Newtonian' under the proper conditions. A system that has, at the micro-level, soft constraints satisfied in parallel, has at the macro-level, under the right circumstances, to have hard constraints, satisfied serially. But it doesn't *really*, and if you go outside the Newtonian domain, you see that it's really been a quantum system all along.

This model exemplifies the competence/performance distinction as it appears in the sub-symbolic paradigm. We have an inference system (albeit a very limited one) whose performance is completely characterizable at the sub-conceptual level in terms of standard sub-symbolic computation: massively parallel satisfaction of multiple soft constraints. The system is fundamentally soft. Just the same, the behavior of the system can be analyzed at a higher level, and, under appropriate situations (well-posed problems), and under suitable processing idealizations (unlimited computation time), the competence of the system can be described in utterly different computational terms: the hard rules of the circuit domain. The competence theory is extremely important, but the performance theory uses radically different computational mechanisms.

The relation of the competence theory and the performance theory for this model can be viewed as follows. The behavior of the system is determined by its harmony function, which determines a surface or 'landscape' of harmony values over the space of network states. In this landscape there are peaks where the harmony achieves its maximal value: these global maxima correspond to network states representing circuit conditions that satisfy all the laws of physics. The competence theory nicely describes the structure of this discrete constellation of global harmony maxima. But these maxima are a tiny sub-set of an extended harmony landscape in which they are embedded, and the network's performance is a stochastic search over the harmony landscape for these peaks. The givens of a problem restrict the search to the portion of the space consistent with those givens. If the problem is well posed, exactly one of the global harmony peaks will be accessible to the system. Given unlimited search time, the system will provably end up at this peak: this is the limit in which the performance theory is governed by the competence theory. As the search time is reduced, the probability of the system's not ending up at the correct harmony peak increases. If insufficient information is given in the problem, multiple global harmony peaks will be accessible, and the system will converge to one of those peaks. If inconsistent information is given in the problem, none of the global harmony peaks will be accessible. But within the space of states accessible to the network there will be highest peaks of harmony – these peaks are not as high as the inaccessible global maxima; they correspond to network states representing circuit states that satisfy as many as possible of the circuit laws. As the network computes, it will converge toward these best-available peaks.

Sub-symbolic computation is the evolution of a dynamical system. The input to the computation is a set of constraints on which states are accessible to the system (or, possibly, the state of the system at time zero). The dynamical system evolves in time under its defining differential equations; typically, it asymptotically approaches some equilibrium state – the output. The function relating the system's input to its output is its competence theory. This function is extremely important to characterize. But it is quite different from the performance theory of the system, which is the differential equation governing the system's moment-to-moment evolution. Relating the performance and competence of cognitive systems coincides with one of the principal tasks of dynamical systems theory: relating a system's local description (differential equations) to its global (asymptotic) behavior.

9.3   Conceptual-level spreading activation

In section 7.2 it was pointed out that states of a sub-symbolic model can be approximately analyzed as superpositions of vectors with individual conceptual-level semantics. It is possible to approximately analyze connectionist dynamical systems at the conceptual level, using the mathematics of the superposition operation. If the connectionist system is purely linear (so that the activity of each unit is precisely a weighted sum of the activities of the units giving it input), it can easily be proved that the higher-level description obeys formal laws of just the same sort as the lower level: the computations at the sub-conceptual and conceptual levels are isomorphic. Linear connectionist systems are of limited computational power, however; most interesting connectionist systems are non-linear. Nevertheless, most of these are in fact *quasi-linear*: a unit's value is computed by taking the weighted sum of its inputs and passing this through a non-linear function like a threshold or sigmoid. In quasi-linear systems, each unit combines its inputs linearly even though the effects of this combination on the unit's activity is non-linear. Furthermore, the problem-specific knowledge in such systems is in the combination weights, that is, the linear part of the dynamical equations; and in learning systems, it is generally only these linear weights that adapt. For these reasons, even though the higher level is not isomorphic to the lower level in non-linear systems, there are senses in which the higher level approximately obeys formal laws similar to the lower level (For details, see Smolensky, 1986b).

The conclusion here is a rather different one from the preceding section, where we saw how there are senses in which higher-level characterizations of certain sub-symbolic systems approximate productions, serial processing and logical inference. Now what we see is that there are also senses in which the laws describing cognition at the conceptual level are activation-passing laws like those at the sub-conceptual level but operating between units with individual conceptual semantics. Such semantic-level descriptions of mental processing (which include *local* connectionist models; see note 3) have been of considerable value in cognitive science. We can now see how these 'spreading activation' accounts of mental processing can fit into the sub-symbolic paradigm.

9.4   Schemata

The final conceptual-level notion I will consider is that of the *schema* (e.g. Rumelhart, 1980). This concept goes back at least to Kant (1787/ 1963) as a description of mental concepts and mental categories. Schemata appear in many AI systems in the forms of frames, scripts or similar structures: they are prepackaged bundles of information that support inference in prototypical situations (see also Arbib, 1987).

Briefly, I will summarize work on schemata in connectionist systems reported in Rumelhart et al. (1986c) (see also Feldman, 1981; Smolensky, 1986a, c). This work addressed the case of schemata for rooms. Subjects were asked to described some imagined rooms using a set of 40 features like has-ceiling, has-window, contains-toilet, and so on. Statistics were computed on these data and were used to construct a network containing one node for each feature as well as connections computed from the statistical data.

The resulting network can perform inference of the same general kind as that carried out by symbolic systems with schemata for various types of rooms. The network is told that some room contains a ceiling and an oven; the question is, what else is likely to be in the room? The system settles down into a final state, and among the inferences contained in that final state are: the room contains a coffee cup but no fireplace, a coffee pot but no computer.

The inference process in this system is simply one of greedily maximizing harmony. (Cf. the multiple book review of Sperber and Wilson's *Relevance* in *Behavioral and Brain Sciences* 10(4).) To describe the inference of this system on a higher level, we can examine the global states of the system in terms of their harmony values. How internally consistent are the various states in the space? It's a 40-dimensional state space, but various 2-dimensional sub-spaces can be selected, and the harmony values there can be graphically displayed. The harmony landscape has various peaks; looking at the features of the state corresponding to one of the peaks, we find that it corresponds to a prototypical bathroom; others correspond to a prototypical office, and so on for all the kinds of rooms subjects were asked to describe. There are no *units* in this system for bathrooms or offices – there are just lower-level descriptors. The prototypical bathroom is a pattern of activation, and the system's recognition of its prototypicality is reflected in the harmony peak for that pattern. It is a consistent, 'harmonious' combination of features: better than neighboring points, such as one representing a bathroom without a bathtub, which has distinctly lower harmony.

During inference, this system climbs directly uphill on the harmony landscape. When the system state is in the vicinity of the harmony peak representing the prototypical bathroom, the inferences it makes are governed by the shape of the harmony landscape there. This shape is like a schema that governs inferences about bathrooms. (In fact, harmony theory was created to give a connectionist formalization of the notion of schema; see Smolensky, 1984b, 1986a, c.) Looking closely at the harmony landscape, we can see that the terrain around the 'bathroom' peak has many of the properties of a bathroom schema: variables and constants, default values, schemata embedded inside schemata, and even cross-variable dependencies, which are rather difficult to incorporate into symbolic formalizations of schemata. The system behaves as though it had schemata for bathrooms, offices and so forth, even though they are not really there at the fundamental level: these schemata are strictly properties of a higher-level description. They are informal, approximate descriptions – one might even say they are merely metaphorical descriptions – of an inference process too subtle to admit such high-level descriptions with great precision. Even though these schemata may not be the sort of object on which to base a formal model, none the less they are useful descriptions that help us understand a rather complex inference system.

9.5 Summary

In this section the symbolic structures in the intuitive processor have been viewed as entities in high-level descriptions of cognitive dynamical systems. From this perspective, these structures assume rather different forms from those arising in the symbolic paradigm. To sum up:

(27) (a) Macro-inference is not a process of firing a symbolic production but rather of qualitative state change in a dynamical system, such as a phase transition.

(b) Schemata are not large symbolic data structures but rather the potentially intricate shapes of harmony maxima.

(c) Categories (it turns out) are attractors in connectionist dynamical systems: states that 'suck in' to a common place many nearby states, like peaks of harmony functions.

(d) Categorization is not the execution of a symbolic algorithm but rather the continuous evolution of the dynamical system – the evolution that drives states into the attractors that maximize harmony.

(e) Learning is not the construction and editing of formulae, but rather the gradual adjustment of connection strengths with experience, with the effect of slowly shifting harmony landscapes, adapting old and creating new concepts, categories and schemata.

The heterogeneous assortment of high-level mental structures that have been embraced in this section suggests that the conceptual level lacks formal unity. This is precisely what one expects of approximate higher-level descriptions, which, capturing different aspects of global properties, can have quite different characters. According to the sub-symbolic paradigm, the unity underlying cognition is to be found not at the conceptual level, but rather at the sub-conceptual level, where relatively few principles in a single formal framework lead to a rich variety of global behaviors.

10   Conclusion

In this chapter I have not argued for the validity of a Connectionist approach to cognitive modeling, but rather for a particular view of the role a connectionist approach might play in cognitive science. An important question remains: should the goal of connectionist research be to replace other methodologies in cognitive science? Here it is important to avoid the confusion discussed in section 2.1. There I argued that for the purpose of science, it is sound to formalize knowledge in linguistically expressed laws and rules, but it does not follow therefore that knowledge in an individual's mind is best formalized by such rules. It is equally true that even if the knowledge in a native speaker's mind is well formalized by a huge mass of connection strengths, it does not follow that the science of language should be such a set of numbers. On the contrary, the argument of section 2.1 implies that the science of language should be a set of linguistically expressed laws, to the maximal extent possible.

The view that the goal of connectionist research should be to replace other methodologies may represent a naive form of eliminative reductionism. Successful lower-level theories generally serve not to replace higher-level ones, but to enrich them, to explain their successes and failures, to fill in where the higher-level theories are inadequate, and to unify disparate higher-level accounts. The goal of sub-symbolic research should not be to replace symbolic cognitive science, but rather to explain the strengths and weaknesses of existing symbolic theory, to explain how symbolic computation can emerge out of non-symbolic computation, to enrich conceptual-level research with new computational concepts and techniques that reflect an understanding of how conceptual-level theoretical constructs emerge from sub-conceptual computation, to provide a uniform sub-conceptual theory from which the multiplicity of conceptual theories can all be seen to emerge, to develop new empirical methodologies that reveal sub-conceptual regularities of cognitive behavior that are invisible at the conceptual level, and to provide new subconceptual-level cognitive principles that explain these regularities.

The rich behavior displayed by cognitive systems has the paradoxical character of appearing on the one hand tightly governed by complex systems of hard rules, and on the other to be awash with variance, deviation, exception and a degree of flexibility and fluidity that has quite eluded our attempts at simulation. *Homo sapiens* is the rational animal, with a mental life ruled by the hard laws of logic, but real human behaviour is riddled with strong non-rational tendencies that display a systematicity of their own. Human language is an intricate crystal defined by tight sets of intertwining constraints, but real linguistic behaviour is remarkably robust under deviations from those constraints. This ancient paradox has produced a deep chasm in both the philosophy and the science of mind: on one side, those placing the essence of intelligent behavior in the hardness of mental competence; on the other, those placing it in the subtle softness of human performance.

The sub-symbolic paradigm suggests a solution to this paradox. It provides a formal framework for studying how a cognitive system can possess knowledge which is fundamentally *soft*, but at the same time, under ideal circumstances, admit good higher-level descriptions that are undeniably *hard*. The passage from the lower, sub-conceptual level of analysis to the higher, conceptual level naturally and inevitably introduces changes in the character of the sub-symbolic system: the computation that emerges at the higher level incorporates elements with a nature profoundly different from that of the fundamental computational processes.

To turn this story into a scientific reality, a multitude of serious conceptual and technical obstacles must be overcome. The story does, however, seem to merit serious consideration. It is to be hoped that the story's appeal will prove sufficient to sustain the intense effort that will be required to tackle the obstacles.

Acknowledgments

I am indebted to Dave Rumelhart for several years of provocative conversations on many of these issues; his contributions permeate the ideas formulated here. Sincere thanks to Jerry Fodor and Zenon Pylyshyn for most instructive conversations. Comments on earlier drafts from Geoff Hinton, Mark Fanty and Dan Lloyd were very helpful, as were pointers from Kathleen Akins. Extended comments on the manuscript by Georges Rey were extremely helpful. I am particularly grateful for a number of insights that Rob Cummins and Denise Dellarosa have generously contributed to this paper.

This research has been supported by NSF grant IST-8609599 and by the Department of Computer Science and Institute of Cognitive Science at the University of Colorado at Boulder.

Notes

1   In this chapter, when *interpretation* is used to refer to a process, the sense intended is that of computer science: the process of taking a linguistic description of a procedure and executing that procedure.

2   Consider, for example, the connectionist symposium at the University of Geneva held 9 September 1986. The advertised program featured Feldman, Minsky, Rumelhart, Sejnowski and Waltz. Of these five researchers, three were major contributors to the symbolic paradigm for many years (Minsky, 1975; Rumelhart, 1975; 1980; Waltz, 1978).

3   This is an issue that divides connectionist approaches. 'Local connectionist models' (e.g., McClelland and Rumelhart, 1981; Rumelhart and McClelland, 1982; Dell, 1985; Feldman; 1985; Waltz and Pollack, 1985) accept (9), and often deviate significantly from (8a). This approach has been championed by the Rochester connectionists (Feldman et al., 1985). Like the symbolic paradigm, this school favors simple semantics and more complex operations. The processors in their networks are usually more powerful than those allowed by (8); they are often like digital computers running a few lines of simple code. ('If there is a 1 on this input line then do X else do Y', where X and Y are quite different simple procedures; e.g. Shastri, 1985.) This style of connectionism, quite different from the sub-

symbolic style, has much in common with techniques if traditional computer science for 'parallelizing' serial algorithms by decomposing them into routines that can run in parallel, often with certain synchronization points built in. The grain size of the Rochester parallelism, although large compared to the sub-symbolic paradigm, is small compared to standard parallel programming: the processors are allowed only a few internal states and can transmit only a few different values (Feldman and Ballard, 1982).

4   As indicated in the introduction, a sizeable sample of research that by and large falls under the sub-symbolic paradigm can be found in the two volumes of *Parallel Distributed Processing: Explorations in the Microstructure of Cognition* (Rumelhart *et al.*, 1986B, McClelland *et al.*, 1986). While this work has since come to be labeled 'Connectionist', the term 'PDP' was deliberately chosen to distinguish it from the localist approach which had previously adopted the name 'Connectionist' (Feldman and Ballard, 1982).

5   The phrase is Roger Schank's, in reference to 'parallel processing' (Waldrop, 1984). Whether he was referring to connectionist systems I do not know; in any event, I don't mean to imply that the grounds for his comment are addressed here.

6   In this section the disclaimer in the introduction is particularly relevant: The arguments I offer are not intended to represent a consensus among connectionists.

7   For example, two recently discovered learning rules that allow the training of hidden units, the Boltzmann machine learning procedure (Hinton and Sejnowski, 1983a) and the back-propagation procedure (Rumelhart et al., 1986), both involve introducing computational machinery that is motivated purely mathematically; the neural counterparts of which are so far unknown (unit-by-unit connection strength symmetry, alternating Hebbian and anti-Hebbian learning, simulated annealing, and backwards error propagation along connections of identical strength to forward activation propagation).

8   A notable exception is Touretzky and Hinton (1985).

9   Furthermore, when a network makes a mistake, it can be told the correct answer, but it cannot be told the precise rule it violated. Thus it must assign blame for its error in an undirected way. It is quite plausible that the large amount of training currently required by sub-symbolic systems could be significantly reduced if blame could be focused by citing violated rules.

10   There is a trade-off between the number of goal conditions one chooses to attribute to a system, and the corresponding range of tolerable environmental conditions. Considering a large variety of environmental conditions for a river, there is only the 'flow downhill' goal; by appropriately narrowing the class of conditions, one can increase the corresponding goal repertoire. A river can meet the goal of carrying messages from A to B, if A and B are appropriately restricted. But a homing pigeon can meet this goal over a much greater variety of situations.

11   Consider a model that physicists like, to apply to 'neural nets' – the *spin glass* (Toulouse et al. 1986). Spin glasses seem relevant because they are

dynamical systems in which the interactions of the variables ('spins') are spatially in-homogeneous. But a spin glass is a system in which the interactions between spins are random variables that all obey the same probability distribution p: The system has *homogeneous in-homogeneity*. The analysis of spin glasses relates the properties of p to the bulk properties of the medium as a whole; the analysis of a single spin subject to a particular set of in-homogeneous interactions is regarded as quite meaningless, and techniques for such analysis are not generally developed.

12   This problem is closely related to the localization of a failure of veridicality in a scientific theory. Pursuing the remarks of section 2.1, scientific theories can be viewed as cognitive systems, indeed ones having the prediction goal. Veridicality is a property of a scientific theory as a whole, gauged ultimately by the success or failure of the theory to meet the prediction goal. The veridicality of abstract representations in a theory derives solely from their causal role in the accurate predictions of observable representations.

13   For example, in both harmony theory and the Boltzmann machine, discrete units have typically been used because (a) discrete units simplify both analysis and simulation; (b) for the quadratic harmony or energy functions that are being optimized, it can be proved that no optima are lost by simplifying to binary values; (c) these models' stochastic search has a 'jumpy' quality to it anyway. These, at least, are the computational reasons for discrete units; in the case of the Boltzmann machine, the discrete nature of action potentials is also cited as a motivation for discrete units (Hinton et al., 1984).

14   Alternatively, if the original harmony/Boltzmann approach is extended to include non-quadratic harmony/energy functions, non-binary optima appear so again one switches to continuous units (Derthick, in progress; Smolensky, in progress).

15   Note that these (procedural) 'productions' that occur in intuitive processing are very different from the (declarative) production rules of section 6 that occur in conscious rule application.

References

Ackley, D.H., Hinton, G.E. and Sejnowski, T.J. (1985) A learning algorithm for Boltzmann machines. *Cognitive Science* 9, 147–69.

Anderson, D.Z. (1986) Coherent optical eigenstate memory. *Optics Letters* 11, 56–8.

Anderson, J.R. (1981) *Cognitive Skills and their Acquisition*. Hillsdale, NJ, Erlbaum.

Anderson, J.R. (1983) *The Architecture of Cognition*. Cambridge, Mass., Harvard University Press.

Anderson, J.R. (1987) Methodologies for studying human knowledge. *Behavioral and Brain Sciences* 10 (3), 467–77.

Arbib, M. (1987) Levels of modeling of mechanisms of visually guided behavior. *Behavioral and Brain Sciences* 10 (3), 407–36.

Ballard, D.H. (1986) Cortical connections and parallel processing: structure and function. *Behavioral and Brain Sciences* 9, 67–120.

Ballard, D.H. and Hayes, P.J. (1984) Parallel logical inference. *Proceedings of the Sixth Conference of the Cognitive Science Society*, Rochester, New York. Hillsdale, NJ, Erlbaum.

Cognitive Science (1985) Special issue on connectionist models and their applications 9 (1).

Cohen, M.S. (1986) Design of a new medium for volume holographic information processing. *Applied Optics* 14, 2288–94.

Crick, F. and Asanuma, C. (1986) Certain aspects of the anatomy and physiology of the cerebral cortex. In J.L. McClelland, D.E. Rumelhart and the PDP Research Group (eds), *Parallel Distributed Processing: Explorations in the Microstructure of Cognition*. Vol. 2: *Psychological and Biological Models*. Cambridge, Mass., MIT Press/Bradford Books.

Dell, G.S. (1985) Positive feedback in hierarchical connectionist models: applications to language production. *Cognitive Science* 9, 3–23.

Feldman, J.A. (1981) A connectionist model of visual memory. In G.E. Hinton and J.A. Anderson (eds), *Parallel Models of Associative Memory*. Hillsdale, NJ, Erlbaum.

Feldman, J.A. (1985) Four frames suffice: a provisional model of vision and space. *Behavioral and Brain Sciences* 8, 265–89.

Feldman, J.A. (1986) Neural representation of conceptual knowledge. Technical Report 189, Department of Computer Science, University of Rochester.

Feldman, J.A. and Ballard, D.H. (1982) Connectionist models and their properties. *Cognitive Science* 6, 205–54.

Feldman, J.A., Ballard, D.H., Brown, C.M. and Dell, G.S. (1985) Rochester connectionist papers: 1979–1985. Technical Report 172, Department of Computer Science, University of Rochester.

Fodor, J.A. (1975) *The Language of Thought*. Cambridge, Mass., Harvard University Press.

Fodor, J.A. (1987) Why there still has to be a language of thought. In *Psychosemantics*. Cambridge, Mass., MIT Press/Bradford Books.

Geman, S. and Geman, D. (1984) Stochastic relaxation. Gibbs distributions, and the Bayesian restoration of images. *IEEE Transactions on Pattern Analysis and Machine Intelligence* 6, 721–41.

Haugeland, J. (1978) The nature and plausibility of cognitivism. *Behavioral and Brain Sciences* 1, 215–26.

Hebb, D.O. (1949) *The Organization of Behavior*. New York, Wiley.

Hinton, G.E. and Anderson, J.A. (eds) (1981) *Parallel Models of Associative Memory*. Hillsdale, NJ, Erlbaum.

Hinton, G.E., McClelland, J.L. and Rumelhart, D.E. (1986) Distributed representations. In D.E. Rumelhart, J.L. McClelland and the PDP Research Group (eds), *Parallel Distributed Processing: Explorations in the*

Microstructure of Cognition. Vol. 1: *Foundations.* Cambridge, Mass., MIT Press/Bradford Books.

Hinton, G.E. and Sejnowski, T.J. (1983a) Analyzing cooperative computation. *Proceedings of the Fifth Annual Conference of the Cognitive Science Society.*

Hinton, G.E. and Sejnowski, T.J. (1983b) Optimal perceptual inference. *Proceedings of the IEEE Conference on Computer Vision and Pattern Recognition.*

Hinton, G.E. and Sejnowski, T.J. (1986) Learning and relearning in Boltzmann machines. In D.E. Rumelhart, J.L. McClelland and the PDP Research Group (eds), *Parallel Distributed Processing: Explorations in the Microstructure of Cognition.* Vol. 1: *Foundations.* Cambridge, Mass., MIT Press/Bradford Books.

Hinton, G.E., Sejnowski, T.J. and Ackley, D.H. (1984) Boltzmann machines: constraint satisfaction networks that learn. Technical Report CMU-CS-84-119. Computer Science Department, Carnegie-Mellon University.

Hofstadter, D.R. (1979) *Gödel, Escher, Bach: an Eternal Golden Braid.* New York, Basic Books.

Hofstadter, D.R. (1985a) Variations on a theme as the crux of creativity. In *Metamagical Themas.* New York, Basic Books.

Hofstadter, D.R. (1985b) Waking up from the Boolean dream, or, subcognition as computation. In *Metamagical Themas.* New York, Basic Books.

Hopcroft, J.E. and Ullman, J.D. (1979) *Introduction to Automata Theory, Languages, and Computation.* London, Addison-Wesley.

Jordan, M.I. (1986) Attractor dynamics and parallelism in a connectionist sequential machine. *Proceedings of the Eighth Meeting of the Cognitive Science Society.*

Kant, I. (1787/1963) *Critique of Pure Reason,* 2nd edn. Trans. N. Kemp Smith. London, Macmillan.

Larkin, J.H., McDermott, J., Simon, D.P. and Simon, H.A. (1980) Models of competence in solving physics problems. *Cognitive Science* 4, 317–45.

Lashley, K. (1950) In search of the engram. In *Psychological Mechanisms in Animal Behavior,* Symposia of the Society for Experimental Biology, no. 4. London, Academic Press.

Lewis, C.H. (1978) Production system models of practice effects. Unpublished PhD thesis, University of Michigan.

McClelland, J.L. and Rumelhart, D.E. (1981) An interactive activation model on context effects in letter perception: Part 1. An account of the basic findings. *Psychological Review* 88, 375–407.

McClelland, J.L., Rumelhart, D.E. and the PDP Research Group (eds) (1986) *Parallel Distributed Processing: Explorations in the Microstructure of Cognition.* Vol. 2: *Psychological and Biological Models.* Cambridge, Mass., MIT Press/Bradford Books.

Minsky, M. (1963) Steps towards artificial intelligence. In E.A. Feigenbaum and J. Feldman (eds), *Computers and Thought.* New York, McGraw-Hill.

Minsky, M. (1975) A framework for representing knowledge. In P.H. Winston (ed.), *The Psychology of Computer Vision.* New York, McGraw-Hill.

Minsky, M. and Papert, S. (1969) *Perceptrons*. Cambridge, Mass., MIT Press.

Newell, A. (1980) Physical symbol systems. *Cognitive Science* 4, 135–83.

Newell, A. and Simon, H.A. (1976) Computer science as empirical inquiry: symbols and search. *Communications of the Association for Computing Machinery* 19, 113–26.

Pearl, J. (1985) Bayesian networks: a model of self-activated memory for evidential reasoning. *Proceedings of the Seventh Conference of the Cognitive Science Society*.

Pylyshyn, Z.W. (1984) *Computation and Cognition: Toward a Foundation for Cognitive Science*. Cambridge, Mass., MIT Press/Bradford Books.

Riley, M.S. and Smolensky, P. (1984) A parallel model of (sequential) problem solving. *Proceedings of the Sixth Annual Conference of the Cognitive Science Society*. Hillsdale, NJ, Erlbaum.

Rumelhart, D.E. (1975) Notes on a schema for stories. In D.G. Bobrow and A. Collins (eds), *Representation and Understanding*. New York, Academic Press.

Rumelhart, D.E. (1980) Schemata: the building blocks of cognition. In R. Spiro, B. Bruce and W. Brewer (eds), *Theoretical Issues in Reading Comprehension*. Hillsdale, NJ, Erlbaum.

Rumelhart, D.E. and McClelland, J.L. (1982) An interactive activation model of context effects in letter perception: Part 2. The contextual enhancement effect and some tests and extensions of the model. *Psychological Review* 89, 60–94.

Rumelhart, D.E. and McClelland, J.L. (1986) On learning the past tenses of English verbs. In J.L. McClelland, D.E. Rumelhart and the PDP Research Group (eds), *Parallel Distributed Processing: Explorations in the Microstructure of Cognition*. Vol. 2: *Psychological and Biological Models*. Cambridge, Mass., MIT Press/Bradford Books.

Rumelhart, D.E., Hinton, G.E. and Williams, R.J (1986a) Learning and internal representations by error propagation. In D.E. Rumelhart, J.L. McClelland and the PDP Research Group (eds), *Parallel Distributed Processing: Explorations in the Microstructure of Cognition*. Vol. 1: *Foundations*. Cambridge, Mass., MIT Press/Bradford Books.

Rumelhart, D.E., McClelland, J.L. and the PDP Research Group (eds) (1986b) *Parallel Distributed Processing: Explorations in the Microstructure of Cognition*. Vol. 1: *Foundations*. Cambridge, Mass., MIT Press/Bradford Books.

Rumelhart, D.E., Smolensky, P., McClelland, J.L. and Hinton, G.E. (1986c) Schemata and sequential thought processes in parallel distributed models. In J.L. McClelland, D.E. Rumelhart and the PDP Research Group (eds), *Parallel Distributed Processing: Explorations in the Microstructure of Cognition*. Vol. 2: *Psychological and Biological Models*. Cambridge, Mass., MIT Press/Bradford Books.

Sejnowski, T.J. (1976) On the stochastic dynamics of neuronal interactions. *Biological Cybernetics* 22, 203–11.

Sejnowski, T.J. and Rosenberg, C.R. (1986) NETtalk: a parallel network that learns to read aloud. Technical Report JHU/EECS-86/01. Department of Electrical Engineering and Computer Science, The Johns Hopkins University.

Shastri, L. (1985) Evidential reasoning in semantic networks: a formal theory and its parallel implementation. Technical Report TR 166, Department of Computer Science, University of Rochester.

Shepard, R.N. (1962) The analysis of proximities: multidimensional scaling with an unknown distance function. I and II. *Psychometrika* 27, 125–40, 219–46.

Smolensky, P. (1983) Schema selection and stochastic inference in modular environments. *Proceedings of the National Conference on Artificial Intelligence.*

Smolensky, P. (1984a) Harmony theory: thermal parallel models in a computational context. In P. Smolensky and M.S. Riley (eds), *Harmony Theory: Problem Solving, Parallel Cognitive Models, and Thermal Physics.* Technical Report 8404, Institute for Cognitive Science, University of California at San Diego.

Smolensky, P. (1984b) The mathematical role of self-consistency in parallel computation. *Proceedings of the Sixth Annual Conference of the Cognitive Science Society.* Hillsdale, NJ, Erlbaum.

Smolensky, P. (1986a) Information processing in dynamical systems: foundations of harmony theory. In D.E. Rumelhart, J.L. McClelland and the PDP Research Group (eds), *Parallel Distributed Processing: Explorations in the Microstructure of Cognition.* Vol. 1: *Foundations.* Cambridge, Mass., MIT Press/Bradford Books.

Smolensky, P. (1986b) Neural and conceptual interpretations of parallel distributed processing models. In J.L. McClelland, D.E. Rumelhart and the PDP Research Group (eds), *Parallel Distributed Processing: Explorations in the Microstructure of Cognition.* Vol. 2: *Psychological and Biological Models.* Cambridge, Mass., MIT Press/Bradford Books.

Smolensky, P. (1986c) Formal modeling of subsymbolic processes: an introduction to harmony theory. In N.E. Sharkey (ed.), *Directions in the Science of Cognition.* Ellis Horwood.

Smolensky, P. (1987a) On variable binding and the representation of symbolic structures in connectionist systems. Technical Report CU-CS-355-87, Department of Computer Science, University of Colorado at Boulder.

Smolensky, P. (1987b) The constituent structure of connectionist mental states: a reply to Fodor and Pylyshyn. *Southern Journal of Philosophy* 26 (suppl.), 137–63.

Toulouse, G., Dehaene, S. and Changeux, J-P. (1986) A spin glass model of learning by selection. Technical Report, Unité de Neurobiologie Moléculaire, Institut Pasteur, Paris.

Touretzky, D.S. (1986) BoltzCONS: reconciling connectionism with the recursive nature of stacks and trees. *Proceedings of the Eighth Conference of the Cognitive Society.* Hillsdale, NJ, Erlbaum.

Touretzky, D.S. and Hinton, G.E. (1985) Symbols among the neurons: details of a connectionist inference architecture. In A. Joshi (ed.), *Proceedings of the International Joint Conference on Artificial Intelligence*, pp. 238–43. California, Morgan Kaufmann.

Turing, A. (1936) On computable numbers, with an application to Entscheidungs problem. *Proceedings of the London Mathematical Society* (ser. 2) 42, 230–65; 43, 544–6.

Waldrop, M.M. (1984) Artificial intelligence in parallel. *Science* 225, 608–10.

Waltz, D.L. (1978) An English language question answering system for a large related database. *Communications of the Association for Computing Machinery* 21, 526–39.

Waltz, D.L. and Pollack, J.B. (1985) Massively parallel parsing: a strongly interactive model of natural language interpretation. *Cognitive Science* 9, 51–74.

3

Connectionism and Cognitive Architecture: A Critical Analysis

Jerry A. Fodor and Zenon W. Pylyshyn

1 Introduction

Connectionist or PDP models are catching on. There are conferences and new books nearly every day, and the popular science press hails this new wave of theorizing as a breakthrough in understanding the mind (a typical example is the article in the May issue of *Science 86*, called 'How we think: a new theory'). There are also, inevitably, descriptions of the emergence of connectionism as a Kuhnian 'paradigm shift' (see Schneider, 1987, for an example of this and for further evidence of the tendency to view connectionism as the 'new wave' of cognitive science.)

The fan club includes the most unlikely collection of people. Connectionism gives solace both to philosophers who think that relying on the pseudo-scientific intentional or semantic notions of folk psychology (like goals and beliefs) mislead psychologists into taking the computational approach (e.g. P.M. Churchland, 1981; P.S. Churchland, 1986; Dennett, 1986); and to those with nearly the opposite perspective, who think that computational psychology is bankrupt because it doesn't address issues of intentionality or meaning (e.g. Dreyfus and Dreyfus, 1988). On the computer science side, connectionism appeals to theorists who think that serial machines are too weak and must be replaced by radically new parallel machines (Fahlman and Hinton, 1987), while on the biological side it appeals to those who believe that cognition can only be understood if we study it as neuroscience (e.g. Arbib, 1975; Sejnowski, 1981). It is also attractive to psychologists who think that much of the mind (including the part involved in using imagery) is not discrete (e.g. Kosslyn and Hatfield, 1984), or who think that cognitive science has not paid enough attention to stochastic mechanisms or to 'holistic' mechanisms (e.g. Lakoff, 1986), and so on and on. It also appeals to many young cognitive scientists who view the approach as not only anti-establishment (and therefore desirable) but also rigorous and mathematical (see, however, note 2 below). Almost everyone who is discontented with contemporary cognitive psychology and current 'information-processing' models of the mind has rushed to embrace 'the connectionist alternative'.

When taken as a way of modeling *cognitive architecture*, connectionism really does represent an approach that is quite different from that of the classical cognitive science that it seeks to replace. Classical models of the mind were derived from the structure of Turing and von Neumann machines. They are not, of course, committed to the details of these machines as exemplified in Turing's original formulation or in typical commercial computers; only to the basic idea that the kind of computing that is relevant to understanding cognition involves operations on symbols (see Fodor, 1976, 1987; Newell, 1980, 1982; Pylyshyn, 1980, 1984a, b). In contrast, connectionists propose to design systems that can exhibit intelligent behavior without storing, retrieving or otherwise operating on structured symbolic expressions. The style of processing carried out in such models is thus strikingly unlike what goes on when conventional machines are computing some function.

Connectionist systems are networks consisting of very large numbers of simple but highly interconnected 'units'. Certain assumptions are generally made both about the units and the connections: each unit is assumed to receive real-valued activity (either excitatory or inhibitory or both) along its input lines. Typically the units do little more than sum this activity and change their state as a function (usually a threshold function) of this sum. Each connection is allowed to modulate the activity it transmits as a function of an intrinsic (but modifiable) property called its 'weight'. Hence the activity on an input line is typically some non-linear function of the state of activity of its sources. The behavior of the network as a whole is a function of the initial state of activation of the units and of the weights on its connections, which serve as its only form of memory.

Numerous elaborations of this basic connectionist architecture are possible. For example, connectionist models often have stochastic mechanisms for determining the level of activity or the state of a unit. Moreover, units may be connected to outside environments. In this case the units are sometimes assumed to respond to a narrow range of combinations of parameter values and are said to have a certain 'receptive field' in parameter-space. These are called 'value units' (Ballard, 1986). In some versions of connectionist architecture, environmental properties are encoded by the pattern of states of entire populations of units. Such 'coarse coding' techniques are among the ways of achieving what connectionists call 'distributed representation'.[1] The term 'connectionist model' (like 'Turing machine' or 'van Neumann machine') is thus applied to a family of mechanisms that differ in detail but share a galaxy of architectural commitments. We shall return to the characterization of these commitments below.

Connectionist networks have been analyzed extensively, in some cases using advanced mathematical techniques.[2] They have also been simulated on computers and shown to exhibit interesting aggregate properties. For example, they can be 'wired' to recognize patterns, to exhibit rule-like behavioral regularities and to realize virtually any mapping from patterns of (input) parameters to patterns of (output) parameters, though in most cases multi-parameter, multi-valued mappings require very large numbers of units. Of even greater interest is the fact that such networks can be made to learn; this is achieved by modifying the weights on the connections as a function of certain kinds of feedback (the exact way in which this is done constitutes a preoccupation of connectionist research and has lead to the development of such important techniques as 'back propagation').

In short, the study of connectionist machines has led to a number of striking and unanticipated findings; it's surprising how much computing can be done with a uniform network of simple interconnected elements. Moreover, these models have an appearance of neural plausibility that classical architectures are sometimes said to lack. Perhaps, then, a new cognitive science based on connectionist networks should replace the old cognitive science based on classical computers. Surely this is a proposal that ought to be taken seriously: if it is warranted, it implies a major redirection of research.

Unfortunately, however, discussions of the relative merits of the two architectures have thus far been marked by a variety of confusions and irrelevances. It's our view that when you clear away these misconceptions what's left is a real disagreement about the nature of mental processes and mental representations. But it seems to us that it is a matter that was substantially put to rest about 30 years ago; and the arguments that then appeared to militate decisively in favor of the Classical view appear to us to do so still.

In the present chapter we will proceed as follows. First, we discuss some methodological questions about levels of explanation that have become enmeshed in the substantive controversy over connectionism. Secondly, we try to say what it is that makes Connectionist and Classical theories of mental structure incompatible. Thirdly, we review and extend some of the traditional arguments for the classical architecture. Though these arguments have been somewhat recast, very little that we'll have to say here is entirely new. But we hope to make it clear how various aspects of the Classical doctrine cohere, and why rejecting the Classical picture of reasoning leads connectionists to say the very implausible things they do about logic and semantics. In section 4, we return to the question of what makes the connectionist approach appear attractive to so many people. In doing so we'll consider some arguments that have been offered in favor of connectionist networks as general models of cognitive processing.

1.1 Levels of explanation

There are two major traditions in modern theorizing about the mind, one that we'll call 'representationalist' and one that we'll call 'eliminativist'. Representationalists hold that postulating representational (or 'intentional' or 'semantic') states is essential to a theory of cognition; according to representationalists, there are states of the mind which function to encode states of the world. Eliminativists, by contrast, think that psychological theories can dispense with such semantic notions as representation. According to eliminativists, the appropriate vocabulary for psychological theorizing is neurological or, perhaps behavioral, or perhaps syntactic; in any event, not a vocabulary that characterizes mental states in terms of what they represent. (For a neurological version of eliminativism, see P.S. Churchland, 1986; for a behavioral version, see Watson, 1930; for a syntactic version, see Stich, 1983.)

Connectionists are on the representationalist side of this issue. As Rumelhart and McClelland (1986b, p. 121) say, PDPs 'are explicitly concerned with the problem of internal representation'. Correspondingly, the specification of what the states of a network *represent* is an essential part of a connectionist model. Consider, for example, the well-known connectionist account of the bi-stability of the Necker cube (Feldman and Ballard, 1982): 'Simple units representing the visual features of the two alternatives are arranged in competing coalitions, with inhibitory . . . links between rival features and positive links within each coalition. . . . The result is a network that has two dominant stable states' (see figure 3.1). Notice that, in this as in all other such connectionist models, the commitment to mental representation is explicit: the label of a node is taken to express the representational content of the state that the device is in when the node is excited, and there are nodes corresponding to monadic and to relational properties of the reversible cube when it is seen in one way or the other.

There are, to be sure, times when connectionists appear to vacillate between representationalism and the claim that the 'cognitive level' is

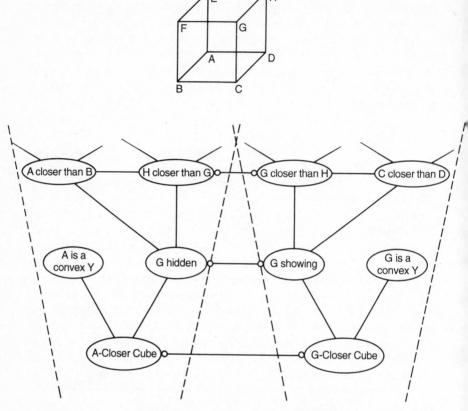

Figure 3.1 A connectionist network model illustrating the two stable representations of the Necker cube. (Reproduced with permission from Feldman and Ballard, 1982, p. 221.)

dispensable in favor of a more precise and biologically motivated level of theory. In particular, there is a lot of talk in the connectionist literature about processes that are 'sub-symbolic' – and therefore presumably *not* representational. But this is misleading: connectionist modeling is consistently representationalist in practice, and representationalism is generally endorsed by the very theorists who also like the idea of cognition 'emerging from the sub-symbolic'. Thus, Rumelhart and McClelland (1986b, p. 121) insist that PDP models are 'strongly committed to the study of representation and process'. Similarly, though Smolensky (chapter 2) takes connectionism to articulate regularities at the 'sub-symbolic level' of analysis, it turns out that sub-symbolic states do have a semantics, though it's not the semantics of representations at the 'conceptual level'. According to Smolensky (chapter 2, p. 34), the semantical distinction between symbolic and sub-symbolic theories is just that 'entities that are typically represented in the symbolic paradigm by [single] symbols are typically represented in the sub-symbolic paradigm by a large number of sub-symbols'.[3] Both the conceptual and the sub-symbolic levels thus postulate representational states, but sub-symbolic theories slice them thinner.

We are stressing the representationalist character of connectionist theorizing because much connectionist methodological writing has been preoccupied with the question 'What level of explanation is appropriate for theories of cognitive architecture? (see, for example, the exchange between Broadbent, 1985, and Rumelhart and McClelland, 1985). And, as we're about to see, what one says about the levels question depends a lot on what stand one takes about whether there are representational states.

It seems certain that the world has causal structure at very many different levels of analysis, with the individuals recognized at the lowest levels being, in general, very small and the individuals recognized at the highest levels being, in general, very large. Thus there is a scientific story to be told about quarks; and a scientific story to be told about atoms; and a scientific story to be told about molecules . . . ditto rocks and stones and rivers . . . ditto galaxies. And the story that scientists tell about the causal structure that the world has at any one of these levels may be quite different from the story that they tell about its causal structure at the next level up or down. The methodological implication for psychology is this: if you want to have an argument about *cognitive* architecture, you have to specify the level of analysis that's supposed to be at issue.

If you're *not* a representationalist, this is quite tricky since it is then not obvious what makes a phenomenon cognitive. But specifying the level of analysis relevant for theories of cognitive architecture is no problem for either classicists or connectionists. Since classicists and connectionists are both representationalists, for them any level at which states of the system are taken to encode properties of the world counts as a *cognitive* level; and no other levels do. (Representations of 'the world' include, of course, representations of symbols; for example, the concept WORD is a construct at the cognitive level because it represents something, namely words.) Correspondingly, it's the architecture of representational states and processes that discussions of *cognitive architecture* are about. Put differently, the architecture of the cognitive system consists of the set of basic operations, resources, functions, principles etc. (generally the sorts of properties that would be described in a 'user's manual' for that architecture if it were available on a computer), whose domain and range are the *representational states* of the organism.[4]

It follows, that, if you want to make good the Connectionist theory *as a theory of cognitive architecture*, you have to show that the processes which operate on *the representational states* of an organism are those which are specified by a connectionist architecture. It is, for example, *no use at all*, from the cognitive psychologist's point of view, to show that the *non*-representational (e.g. neurological, or molecular, or quantum mechanical) states of an organism constitute a connectionist network, because that would *leave open* the question of whether the mind is a such a network *at the psychological level*. It is, in particular, perfectly possible that non-representational neurological states are interconnected in the ways described by connectionist models *but that the representational states themselves are not*. This is because, just as it is possible to implement a *connectionist* cognitive architecture in a network of causally interacting non-representational elements, so too it is perfectly possibly to implement a *classical* cognitive architecture in such a network.[5] In fact, the question of whether connectionist networks should be treated as models at some level of implementation is moot, and will be discussed at some length in section 4.

It is important to be clear about this matter of levels on pain of simply trivializing the issues about cognitive architecture. Consider, for example, the following remark of Rumelhart's:

> It has seemed to me for some years now that there must be a unified account in which the so-called rule-governed and [the] exceptional cases were dealt with by a unified underlying process – a process which produces rule-like and rule-exception behaviour through the application of a single process . . . [In this process] . . . both the rule-like and non-rule-like behaviour is a product of the interaction of a very large number of 'sub-symbolic' processes. (Rumelhart, 1984, p. 60)

It's clear from the context that Rumelhart takes this idea to be very tendentious; one of the connectionist claims that Classical theories are required to deny.

But in fact it's not. For, *of course* there are 'sub-symbolic' interactions that implement both rule-like and rule-violating behaviour; for example, quantum mechanical processes do. *That's* not what Classical theorists deny; indeed, it's not denied by anybody who is even vaguely a materialist. Nor does a Classical theorist deny that rule-following and rule-violating behaviors are both implemented by the very same neurological machinery. For a Classical theorist, neurons implement *all* cognitive process in precisely the same way: viz., by supporting the basic operations that are required for symbol-processing.

What *would* be an interesting and tendentious claim is that there's no distinction between rule-following and rule-violating mentation *at the cognitive or representational or symbolic level*; specifically, that it is not the case that the etiology of rule-following behavior is mediated by the representation of explicit rules.[6] We will consider this idea in section 4, where we will argue that it too is *not* what divides classical from connectionist architecture; classical models *permit* a principled distinction between the etiologies of mental processes that are explicitly rule-governed and mental processes that aren't; but they don't demand one.

In short, the issue between classical and connectionist architecture is not about the explicitness of rules; as we'll presently see, classical architecture is not, *per se*, committed to the idea that explicit rules mediate the etiology of behavior. And it is not about the reality of representational states; classicists and connectionists are all representational realists. And it is not about non-representational architecture; a connectionist neural network can perfectly well implement a classical architecture at the cognitive level.

So, then, what *is* the disagreement between classical and connectionist architecture about?

2   The Nature of the Dispute

Classicists and connectionists all assign semantic content to *something*. Roughly, connectionists assign semantic content to 'nodes' (that is, to units or aggregates of units; see note 1) – i.e. to the sorts of things that are typically labeled in connectionist diagrams; whereas classicists assign semantic content to *expressions* – i.e., to the sorts of things that get written on the tapes of Turing machines and stored at addresses in von Neumann machines.[7] But Classical theories disagree with Connectionist theories about what primitive relations hold among these content-bearing entities. Connectionist theories acknowledge *only causal connectedness* as a primitive relation among nodes; when you know how activation and inhibition flow among them, you know everything there is to know about how the nodes in a network are related. By contrast, Classical theories acknowledge not only causal relations among the semantically evaluable objects that they posit, but also a range of structural relations, of which constituency is paradigmatic.

This difference has far-reaching consequences for the ways that the two kinds of theories treat a variety of cognitive phenomena, some of which we will presently examine at length. But, underlying the disagreements about details are two architectural differences between the theories:

(1) *Combinatorial syntax and semantics for mental representations.* Classical theories – but not Connectionist theories – postulate a 'language of thought' (see, for example, Fodor, 1976); they take mental representations to have *a combinatorial syntax and semantics*, in which (a) there is a distinction between structurally atomic and structurally molecular representations; (b) structurally molecular representations have syntactic constituents that are themselves either structurally molecular or structurally atomic; and (c) the semantic content of a (molecular) representation is a function of the semantic contents of its syntactic parts, together with its constituent structure. For purposes of convenience, we'll sometime abbreviate (a)-(c) by speaking of Classical theories as committed to 'complex' mental representations or to 'symbol structures'.[8]

(2) *Structure sensitivity of processes.* In classical models, the principles by which mental states are transformed, or by which an input selects the corresponding output, are defined over structural properties of mental representations. Because Classical mental *representations* have combinatorial structure, it is possible for Classical mental *operations* to apply to them by reference to their form. The result is that a paradigmatic Classical mental process operates upon any mental representation that satisfies a given structural description, and transforms it into a mental representation that satisfies another structural description. (So, for example, in a model of inference one might recognize an operation that applies to any representation of the form $P \, \& \, Q$ and transforms it into a representation of the form P.) Notice that since formal properties can be defined at a variety of levels of abstraction, such an operation can apply equally to representations that differ widely in their structural complexity. The operation that applies to representations of the form $P \, \& \, Q$ to produce P is satisfied by, for example, an expression like '(AvBvC) & (DvEvF)', from which it derives the expression '(AvBvC)'.

We take (1) and (2) as the claims that define classical models, and we take these claims quite literally; they constrain the physical realizations of symbol structures. In particular, the symbol structures in a classical model are assumed to correspond to real physical structures in the brain and the *combinatorial structure* of a representation is supposed to have a counterpart in structural relations among physical properties of the brain. For example, the relation 'part of', which holds between a relatively simple symbol and a more complex one, is assumed to correspond to some physical relation among brain states.[9] This is why Newell (1980) speaks of computational systems such as brains and classical computers as '*physical* symbols systems'.

This bears emphasis because the Classical theory is committed not only to there being a system of physically instantiated symbols, but also to the claim that the physical properties onto which the structure of the symbols is mapped *are the very properties that cause the system to behave as it does.* In other words, the physical counterparts of the symbols, and their structural properties, *cause* the system's behavior. A system which has symbolic expressions, but whose operation does not depend upon the structure of these expressions, does not qualify as a classical machine since it fails to satisfy condition (2). In this respect, a classical model is very different from one in which behavior is caused by mechanisms, such as energy minimization, that are not responsive to the physical encoding of the structure of representations.

From now on, when we speak of 'classical' models, we will have in mind *any* model that has complex mental representations, as characterized in (1) and structure-sensitive mental processes, as characterized in (2). Our account of classical architecture is therefore neutral with respect to such issues as whether or not there is a separate executive. For example, classical machines can have an 'object-oriented' architecture, like that of the computer language *Smalltalk*, or a 'message passing' architecture, like that of Hewett's (1977) *Actors*, so long as the objects or the messages have a combinatorial structure which is causally implicated in the processing. Classical architecture is also neutral on the question of whether the operations on the symbols are constrained to occur one at a time or whether many operations can occur at the same time.

Here, then, is the plan for what follows. In the rest of this section, we will sketch the connectionist proposal for a computational architecture that does away with complex mental representations and structure-sensitive operations. (Although our purpose here is merely expository, it turns out that describing exactly what connectionists are committed to requires substantial reconstruction of their remarks and practices. Since there is a great variety of points of view within the connectionist community, we are prepared to find that some connectionists in good standing may not fully endorse the program when it is laid out in what we take to be its bare essentials.) Following this general expository (or reconstructive) discussion, section 3 provides a series of arguments favoring the Classical story. Then the remainder of the chapter considers some of the reasons why connectionism appears attractive to many people and offers further general comments on the relation between the classical and the connectionist enterprise.

2.1   Complex mental representations

To begin with, consider a case of the most trivial sort: two machines, one classical in spirit and one connectionist.[10] Here is how the connectionist machine might reason. There is a network of labelled nodes as in figure 3.2. Paths between the nodes indicate the routes along which activation can spread (that is, they indicate the consequences that exciting one of the nodes has for determining the level of excitation of others). Drawing an inference from A & B to A thus corresponds to an excitation of node 2 being caused by an excitation of node 1 (alternatively, if the system is in a state in which node 1 is excited, it eventually settles into a state in which node 2 is excited; see note 7).

Now consider a classical machine. This machine has a tape on which it writes expressions. Among the expressions that can appear on this tape are: 'A', 'B', 'A&B', 'C', 'D', 'C&D', 'A&C&D' ... etc. The machine's causal constitution is as follows: whenever a token of the form P&Q appears on the tape, the machine writes a token of the form P. An inference from A&B to A thus corresponds to a tokening of type 'A&B' on the tape causing a tokening of type 'A'.

So then, what does the architectural difference between the machines consist in? In the classical machine, the objects to which the content A&B is ascribed (viz. tokens of the expression 'A&B') literally contain, as proper parts, objects to which the content A is ascribed (viz., tokens of the expression 'A'.) Moreover, the semantics (e.g. the satisfaction conditions) of the expression 'A&B' is determined in a uniform way by the semantics of its constituents.[11] By contrast, in the connectionist machine none of this is true; the object to which the content A&B is ascribed (viz. node 1) is causally connected to the object to which the content A is ascribed (viz. node 2); but there is no structural (e.g. no part/whole) relation that holds between them. In short, it is character-

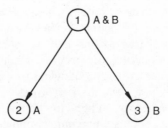

Figure 3.2   A possible connectionist network for drawing inferences from A&B to A or to B.

istic of classical systems, but not of connectionist systems, to exploit arrays of symbols some of which are atomic (e.g. expressions like 'A') but indefinitely many of which have other symbols as syntactic and semantic parts (e.g. expressions like 'A&B').

It is easy to overlook this difference between Classical and connectionist architectures when reading the connectionist polemical literature or examining a connectionist model. There are at least four ways in which one might be lead to do so:

1 By failing to understand the difference between what arrays of symbols do in classical machines and what node labels do in connectionist machines.
2 By confusing the question of whether the nodes in connectionist networks have *constituent* structure with the question of whether they are *neurologically distributed*.
3 By failing to distinguish between a representation having semantic and syntactic constituents and a concept being encoded in terms of microfeatures.
4 By assuming that since representations of connectionist networks have a graph structure, it follows that the nodes in the networks have a corresponding constituent structure.

We shall now need rather a long digression to clear up these misunderstandings.

2.1.1 The role of labels in Connectionist theories   In the course of setting out a connectionist model, intentional content will be assigned to machine states, and the expressions of some language or other will, of course, be used to express this assignment; for example, nodes may be labeled to indicate their representational content. Such labels often have a combinatorial syntax and semantics; in this respect, they can look a lot like Classical mental representations. The point to emphasize, however, is that it doesn't follow (and it isn't true) that the nodes to which these labels are assigned have a combinatorial syntax and semantics. 'A&B', for example, can be tokened on the tape of the classical machine *and can also appear as a label in a connectionist machine* as it does in figure 3.2 above. And, of course, the expression 'A&B' is syntactically and semantically complex: it has a token of 'A' as one of its syntactic constituents, and the semantics of the expression 'A&B' is a function of the semantics of the expression 'A'. But it isn't part of the intended reading of the figure that node 1 itself has constituents; the node – unlike its label – has no semantically interpreted parts.

It is, in short, important to understand the difference between connectionist labels and the symbols over which Classical computations are defined. The difference is this: strictly speaking, the labels play *no role at all* in determining the operation of a connectionist machine; in particular, the operation of the machine is unaffected by the syntactic and semantic relations that hold among the expressions that are used as labels. To put this another way, the node labels in a connectionist machine are not part of the causal structure of the machine. Thus, the machine depicted in figure 3.2 will continue to make the same state transitions regardless of what labels we assign to the nodes. Whereas, by contrast, the state transitions of classical machines are causally determined *by the structure – including the constituent structure – of the symbol arrays that the machines transform:* change the symbols and the system behaves quite differently. (In fact, since the behavior of a classical machine is sensitive to the syntax of the representations it computes on, even interchanging *synonymous* – semantically equivalent – representations affects the course of computation.) So, although the connectionist's labels and the classicist's data structures both constitute languages, only the latter language constitutes a medium of computation.[12]

2.1.2   Connectionist networks and graph structures   The *second* reason that the lack of syntactic and semantic structure in Connectionist representations has largely been ignored may be that connectionist networks look like general graphs; and it is, of course, perfectly possible to use graphs to describe the internal structure of a complex symbol. That's precisely what linguists do when they use 'trees' to exhibit the constituent structure of sentences. Correspondingly, one could imagine a graph notation that expresses the internal structure of mental representations by using arcs and labelled nodes. So, for example, you might express the syntax of the mental representation that corresponds to the thought that John loves the girl like this:

John → loves → the girl

Under the intended interpretation, this would be the structural description of a mental representation whose content is that John loves the girl, and whose constituents are: a mental representation that refers to *John*, a mental representation that refers to *the girl*, and a mental representation that expresses the two-place relation represented by '→ loves →'.

But although graphs can sustain an interpretation as specifying the logical syntax of a complex mental representation, this interpretation is inappropriate for graphs of connectionist networks. Connectionist graphs are not structural descriptions of mental representations; they're specifications of causal relations. All that a connectionist can mean by a graph of the form X → Y is: *states of node X causally affect states of node Y.* In particular, the graph can't mean *X is a constituent of Y* or *X is grammatically related to Y* etc. since these sorts of relations are, in general, not defined for the kinds of mental representations that connectionists recognize.

Another way to put this is that the links in connectionist diagrams are not generalized pointers that can be made to take on different functional significance *by an independent interpreter*, but are confined to meaning something like 'sends activation to'. The intended interpretation of the links as causal connections is intrinsic to the theory. If you ignore this point, you are likely to take connectionism to offer a much richer notion of mental representation than it actually does.

2.1.3   Distributed representations   The *third* mistake that can lead to a failure to notice that the mental representations in connectionist models lack combinatorial syntactic and semantic structure is the fact that many connectionists view representations as being *neurologically distributed*; and, presumably, whatever is distributed must have parts. It doesn't follow, however, that whatever is distributed must have *constituents*; being neurologically distributed is very different from having semantic or syntactic constituent structure.

You have constituent structure when (and only when) the parts of semantically evaluable entities are themselves semantically evaluable. Constituency relations thus hold among objects all of which are at the representational level; they are, in that sense, *within* level relations.[13] By contrast, neural distributedness – the sort of relation that is assumed to hold between 'nodes' and the 'units' by which they are realized – is a *between* level relation: the nodes, but not the units, count as representations. To claim that a node is neurally distributed is presumably to claim that its states of activation correspond to patterns of neural activity – to aggregates of neural 'units' – rather than to activations of single neurons. The important point is that nodes that are distributed in this sense can perfectly well be syntactically and semantically atomic: complex spatially distributed implementation in no way implies constituent structure.

There is, however, a different sense in which the representational states in a network might be distributed, and this sort of distribution also raises questions relevant to the constituency issue.

2.1.4   Representations as 'distributed' over micro-features   Many connectionists hold that the mental representations that correspond to common-sense concepts (CHAIR, JOHN, CUP etc.) are 'distributed' over galaxies of lower-level units which themselves have representational content. To use common connectionist terminology (see Smolensky, chapter 2), the higher or 'conceptual-level' units correspond to vectors in a 'sub-conceptual' space of micro-features. The model here is something like the relation between a defined expression and its defining feature analysis: thus, the concept BACHELOR might be thought to correspond to a vector in a space of features that includes ADULT, HUMAN, MALE and MARRIED; i.e. as an assignment of the value + to the first two features and − to the last. Notice that distribution over micro-features (unlike distribution over neural units) is a relation among representations, hence a relation at the cognitive level.

Since micro-features are frequently assumed to be derived automatically (i.e. via learning procedures) from the statistical properties of samples of stimuli, we can think of them as expressing the sorts of properties that are revealed by multivariate analysis of sets of stimuli (e.g. by multi-dimensional scaling of similarity judgments). In particular, they need not correspond to English words; they can be finer-grained than, or otherwise atypical of, the terms for which a non-specialist needs to have a word. Other than that, however, they are perfectly ordinary semantic features, much like those that lexicographers have traditionally used to represent the meanings of words.

On the most frequent Connectionist accounts, theories articulated in terms of micro-feature vectors are supposed to show how concepts are *actually* encoded, hence the feature vectors are intended to *replace* 'less precise' specifications of macro-level concepts. For example, where a Classical theorist might recognize a psychological state of entertaining the concept CUP, a connectionist may acknowledge only a *roughly analogous* state of tokening the corresponding feature vector. (One reason that the analogy is only rough is that which feature vector 'corresponds' to a given concept may be viewed as heavily context dependent.) The generalizations that 'concept-level' theories frame are thus taken to be only approximately true, the exact truth being stateable only in the vocabulary of the micro-features. Smolensky, for example (p. 42), is explicit in endorsing this picture: 'Complete, formal and precise descriptions of the intuitive processor are generally tractable not at the conceptual level, but only at the sub-conceptual level.'[14] This treatment of the relation between common-sense concepts and micro-features is exactly analogous to the standard connectionist treatment of rules; in both cases, macro-level theory is said to provide a vocabulary adequate for formulating generalizations that roughly approximate the facts about behavioral regularities. But the constructs of the macro-theory do *not* correspond to the causal mechanisms that generate these regularities. If you want a theory of these mechanisms, you need to replace talk about rules and concepts with talk about nodes, connections, micro-features, vectors and the like.[15]

Now, it is among the major misfortunes of the connectionist literature that the issue about whether common-sense concepts should be represented by sets of micro-features has gotten thoroughly mixed up with the issue about combinatorial structure in mental representations. The crux of the mix-up is the fact that sets of micro-features can overlap, so that, for example, if a micro-feature corresponding to '+ has-a-handle' is part of the array of nodes over which the common-sense concept CUP is distributed, then you might think of the theory as representing '+ has-a-handle' as a *constituent* of the concept CUP; from which you might conclude that connectionists have a notion of constituency after all, contrary to the claim that connectionism is not a language-of-thought architecture (see chapter 2).

A moment's consideration will make it clear, however, that even on the assumption that concepts are distributed over microfeatures, '+ has-a-handle' is not a constituent of CUP in anything like the sense that 'Mary' (the word) is a constituent of (the sentence) 'John loves Mary'. In the former case, 'constituency' is being (mis)used to refer to a semantic relation between predicates; roughly, the idea is that macro-level predicates like CUP are defined by sets of micro-features like 'has-a-handle', so that it's some sort of semantic truth that CUP applies to a subset of what 'has-a-handle' applies to. Notice that while the extensions of these predicates are in a set/subset relation, the predicates themselves are not in any sort of part-to-whole relation. The expression 'has-a-handle' isn't *part of* the expression CUP any more than the English phrase 'is an unmarried man' is part of the English phrase 'is a bachelor'.

Real constituency does have to do with parts and wholes; the symbol 'Mary' is literally a part of the symbol 'John loves Mary'. It is because their symbols enter into real-constituency relations that natural languages have both atomic symbols and complex ones. By contrast, the definition relation can hold in a language where *all* the symbols are syntactically atomic; e.g. a language which contains both 'cup' and 'has-a-handle' as atomic predicates. This point is worth stressing. The question of whether a representational system has real-constituency is independent of the question of micro-feature analysis; it arises both for systems in which you have CUP as semantically primitive, and for systems in which the semantic primitives are things like '+ has-a-handle', and CUP and the like are defined in terms of these primitives. It really is very important not to confuse the semantic distinction between primitive expressions and defined expressions with the syntactic distinction between atomic symbols and complex symbols.

So far as we know, there are no worked out attempts in the connectionist literature to deal with the syntactic and semantical issues raised by relations of real-constituency. There is, however, a proposal that comes up from time to time: viz. that what are traditionally treated as complex symbols should actually be viewed as just sets of units, with the role relations that traditionally get coded by constituent structure represented by units belonging to these sets. So, for example, the mental representation corresponding to the belief that John loves Mary might be the feature vector {+*John-subject;* +*loves;* +*Mary-object*}. Here 'John-subject' 'Mary-object' and the like are the labels of units; that is, they are atomic (i.e. micro-) features, whose status is analogous to 'has-a-handle'. In particular, they have no internal syntactic analysis, and there is no structural relation (except the orthographic one) between the feature 'Mary-object' that occurs in the set {John-subject; loves; Mary-object} and the feature 'Mary-subject' that occurs in the set {Mary-subject; loves; John-object}. (See, for example, the discussion in Hinton, 1987 of 'role-specific descriptors that represent the conjunction of an identity and a role [by the use of which] we can implement part-whole hierarchies using set intersection as the composition rule.' See also, McClelland et al., 1986b, p. 82–5, where what appears to be the same treatment is proposed in somewhat different terms.)

Since, as we remarked, these sorts of ideas aren't elaborated in the connectionist literature, detailed discussion is probably not warranted here. But it's worth a word to make clear what sort of trouble you would get into if you were to take them seriously.

As we understand it, the proposal really has two parts: on the one hand, it's suggested that although Connectionist representations cannot exhibit real-constituency, nevertheless the Classical distinction between complex symbols and their constituents can be replaced by the distinction between feature sets and their subsets; and, on the other hand, it's suggested that role relations can be captured by features. We'll consider these ideas in turn.

(1)   Instead of having complex symbols like 'John loves Mary' in the representational system, you have feature sets like {+*John-subject;* +*loves;* +*Mary-object*}. Since this set has {+*John-subject*}, {+*loves;* +*Mary-object*} and so forth as subsets, it may be supposed that the force of the constituency relation has been captured by employing the subset relation.

However, it's clear that this idea won't work since not all subsets of features correspond to genuine constituents. For example, among the subsets of {+*John-subject;* +*loves;* +*Mary-object*} are the sets {+*John-subject;* +*Mary-object*}) and the set {+*John-subject;* + *loves*} which do not, of course, correspond to constituents of the complex symbol 'John loves Mary'.

(2)   Instead of defining roles in terms of relations among constituents, as one does in classical architecture, introduce them as micro-features.

Consider a system in which the mental representation that is entertained when one believes that John loves Mary is the feature set {+*John-subject;* +*loves;* +*Mary-object*}. What representation corresponds to the belief that John loves Mary and Bill hates Sally? Suppose, pursuant to the present proposal, that it's the set {+*John-subject;* +*loves;* +*Mary-object;* +*Bill-subject;* +*hates;* +*Sally-object*}. We now have the problem of distinguishing that belief from the belief that John loves Sally and Bill hates Mary; and from the belief that John hates Mary and Bill loves Sally; and from the belief that John hates Mary and Sally and Bill loves Mary; etc., since these other beliefs will all correspond to precisely the same set of features. The problem is, of course, that nothing in the representation of Mary as +*Mary-object* specifies whether it's the loving or the hating that she is the object of; similarly, *mutatis mutandis*, for the representation of John as +*John-subject*.

What has gone wrong isn't disastrous (yet). All that's required is to enrich the system of representations by recognizing features that correspond not to (for example) just being a subject, but rather to being the subject of a loving of Mary (the property that John has when John loves Mary) and being the subject of a hating of Sally (the property that Bill has when Bill hates Sally). So, the representation of John that's entertained when one believes that John loves Mary and Bill hates Sally might be something like +*John-subject-hates-Mary-object*.

The disadvantage of this proposal is that it requires rather a lot of micro-features.[16] How many? Well, a number of the order of magnitude of the *sentences* of a natural language (whereas one might have hoped to get by with a vocabulary of basic expressions that is not vastly larger than the *lexicon* of a natural language; after all, natural languages do). We leave it to the reader to estimate the number of micro-features you would need, assuming that there is a distinct belief corresponding to every grammatical sentence of English of up to, say, fifteen words of length, and assuming that there is an average of, say, five roles associated with each belief. (Hint: George Miller once estimated that the number of well-formed 20-word sentences of English is of the order of magnitude of the number of seconds in the history of the universe.)

The alternative to this grotesque explosion of atomic symbols would be to have *a combinatorial syntax and semantics for the features*. But, of course, this is just to give up the game since the syntactic and semantic relations that hold among the parts of the complex feature +((*John subject) loves (Mary object)*) are the very same ones that Classically hold among the constituents of the complex symbol 'John loves Mary'; these include the role relations which connectionists had proposed to reconstruct using just sets of atomic features. It is, of course, no accident that the connectionist proposal for dealing with role relations runs into these sorts of problems. Subject, object and the rest are Classically defined *with respect to the geometry of constituent structure trees*. And connectionist representations don't have constituents.

The idea that we should capture role relations by allowing features like *John-subject* thus turns out to be bankrupt; and there doesn't seem to be any other way to get the force of structured symbols in a connectionist architecture. Or, if there is, nobody has given any indication of how to do it. This becomes clear once the crucial issue about structure in mental representations is disentangled from the relatively secondary (and orthogonal) issue about whether the representation of common sense concepts is 'distributed' (i.e. from questions like whether it's CUP or 'has-a-handle' or both that are semantically primitive in the language of thought).

It's worth adding that these problems about expressing the role relations are actually just a symptom of a more pervasive difficulty: a consequence of restricting the vehicles of mental representation to sets of atomic symbols is a notation that fails quite generally to express the way that concepts group into propositions. To see this, let's continue to suppose that we have a network in which the nodes represent concepts rather than propositions (so that what corresponds to the thought that John loves Mary is a distribution of activation over the set of nodes. {JOHN; LOVES; MARY} rather than the activation of a single node labelled JOHN LOVES MARY). Notice that it cannot plausibly be assumed that all the nodes that happen to be active at a given time will correspond to concepts that are constituents of the *same* proposition; least of all if the architecture is 'massively parallel' so that many things are allowed to go on – many concepts are allowed to be entertained – simultaneously in a given mind. Imagine, then, the following situation: at time t, a man is looking at the sky (so the nodes corresponding to SKY and BLUE are active) and thinking that John loves Fido (so the nodes corresponding to JOHN, LOVES and FIDO are active), and the node FIDO is connected to the node DOG (which is in turn connected to the node ANIMAL) in such fashion that DOG and ANIMAL are active too. We can, if you like, throw it in that the man has got an itch, so ITCH is also on.

According to the current theory of mental representation, this man's mind at t is specified by the vector {+JOHN, +LOVES, +FIDO, +DOG, +SKY, +BLUE, +ITCH, +ANIMAL}. And the question is: *which sub-vectors of this vector correspond to thoughts that the man is thinking?* Specifically, what is it about the man's representational state that determines that the simultaneous activation of the nodes, {JOHN, LOVES, FIDO} constitutes his thinking that John loves Fido, but the simultaneous activation of FIDO, ANIMAL and BLUE does *not* constitute his thinking that Fido is a blue animal? It seems that we made it too easy for ourselves when we identified the thought that John loves Mary with the vector {+JOHN, +LOVES, +MARY}; at best that works only on the assumption that JOHN, LOVES and MARY are the only nodes active when someone has that thought. And that's an assumption to which no theory of mental representation is entitled.

It's important to see that this problem arises precisely because the theory is trying to use sets of atomic representations to do a job that you really need complex representations for. Thus, the question we're wanting to answer is: given the total set of nodes active at a time, what distinguishes the sub-vectors that correspond to propositions from the sub-vectors that don't? This question has a straightforward answer if, contrary to the present proposal, complex representations are assumed: when representations express concepts that belong to the same proposition, they are not merely simultaneously active, but also *in construction with each other.* By contrast, representations that express concepts that don't belong to the same proposition may be simultaneously active; but, they are *ipso facto not* in construction with each other.

In short, you need two degrees of freedom to specify the thoughts that an intentional system is entertaining at a time: one parameter (active *v.* inactive) picks out the nodes that express concepts that the system has in mind; the other (in construction *v.* not) determines how the concepts that the system has in mind are distributed in the propositions that it entertains. For symbols to be 'in construction' in this sense is just for them to be constituents of a complex symbol. Representations that are in construction form parts of a geometrical whole, *where the geometrical relations are themselves semantically significant.* Thus the representation that corresponds to the thought that John loves Fido is not a *set* of concepts but something like a *tree* of concepts, and it's the geometrical relations in this tree that mark (for example) the difference between the thought that John loves Fido and the thought that Fido loves John.

We've occasionally heard it suggested that you could solve the present problem consonant with the restriction against complex representations if you allow networks like this:

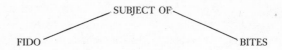

The intended interpretation is that the thought that Fido bites corresponds to the simultaneous activation of these nodes; that is, to the vector {+ FIDO, + SUBJECT OF, + BITES} – with similar though longer vectors for more complex role relations.

But, on second thought, this proposal merely begs the question that it set out to solve. For, if there's a problem about what justifies assigning the proposition *John loves Fido* as the content of the set {JOHN, LOVES, FIDO}, there is surely the same problem about what justifies assigning the proposition *Fido is the subject of bites* to the set {FIDO, SUBJECT OF, BITES}. If this is not immediately clear, consider the case where the simultaneously active nodes are {FIDO, SUBJECT OF, BITES, JOHN}. Is the propositional content that Fido bites or that John does?[17]

Strikingly enough, the point that we've been making in the past several paragraphs is very close to one that Kant made against the associationists of his day. In 'Transcendental Deduction (B)' of The First Critique, Kant remarks that:

> if I investigate . . . the relation of the given modes of knowledge in any judgement, and distinguish it, as belonging to the understanding, from the relation according to laws of the reproductive imagination [e.g. according to the principles of association], which has only subjective validity, I find that a judgement is nothing but the manner in which given modes of knowledge are brought to the objective unity of apperception. This is what is intended by the copula 'is'. It is employed to distinguish the objective unity of given representations from the subjective . . . Only in this way does there arise from the relation a *judgement*, that is a relation which is *objectively valid*, and so can be adequately distinguished from a relation of the same representations that would have only subjective validity – as when they are connected according to laws of association. In the latter case, all that I could say would be 'If I support a body, I feel an impression of weight'; I could not say, 'It, the body, is heavy.' Thus to say 'The body is heavy' is not merely to state that the two representations have always been conjoined in my perception . . . what we are asserting is that they are combined *in the object* . . . Kant, 1929, p. 159; emphasis in original)

A modern paraphrase might be: a theory of mental representation must distinguish the case when two concepts (e.g. THIS BODY, HEAVY) are merely *simultaneously entertained* from the case where, to put it roughly, the property that one of the concepts expresses is predicated of the thing that the other concept denotes (as in the thought: THIS BODY IS HEAVY). The relevant distinction is that while both concepts are 'active' in both cases, in the latter case but *not* in the former the active concepts are in construction. Kant thinks that 'this is what is intended by the copula "is".' But, of course, there are other notational devices that can serve to specify that concepts are in construction; notably the bracketing structure of constituency trees.

There are, to reiterate, two questions that you need to answer to specify the content of a mental state: 'Which concepts are "active"' and 'Which of the active concepts are in construction with which others?' Identifying mental states with sets of active nodes provides resources to answer the first of these questions but not the second. That's why the version of network theory that acknowledges sets of atomic representations but no complex representations fails, in indefinitely many cases, to distinguish mental states that are in fact distinct.

But we are *not* claiming that you can't reconcile a connectionist architecture with an adequate theory of mental representation (specifically with a combinatorial syntax and semantics for mental representations). On the contrary, of course you can: all that's required is that you use your network to implement a Turing machine, and specify a combinatorial structure for its computational language. What it appears that you can't do, however, is have both a combinatorial representational system and a connectionist architecture *at the cognitive level*.

So much, then, for our long digression. We have now reviewed one of the major respects in which Connectionist and Classical theories differ; viz. their accounts of mental *representations*. We turn to the second major difference, which concerns their accounts of mental *processes*.

2.2   Structure-sensitive operations

Classicists and connectionists both offer accounts of mental processes, but their theories differ sharply. In particular, the Classical theory relies heavily on the notion of the logico-syntactic form of mental representations to define the ranges and domains of mental operations. This notion is, however, unavailable to orthodox connectionists since it presupposes that there are non-atomic mental representations.

The Classical treatment of mental processes rests on two ideas, each of which corresponds to an aspect of the Classical theory of computation. Together they explain why the Classical view postulates at least three distinct levels of organization in computational systems: not just a physical level and a semantic (or 'knowledge') level, but a syntactic level as well.

The first idea is that it is possible to construct languages in which certain features of the syntactic structures of formulas correspond systematically to certain of their semantic features. Intuitively, the idea is that in such languages the syntax of a formula encodes its meaning; most especially, those aspects of its meaning that determine its role in inference. All the artificial languages that are used for logic have this property and English has it more or less. Classicists believe that it is a crucial property of the Language of Thought.

A simple example of how a language can use syntactic structure to encode inferential roles and relations among meanings may help to illustrate this point. Thus, consider the relation between the following two sentences:

(1)   John went to the store and Mary went to the store.
(2)   Mary went to the store.

On the one hand, from the semantic point of view, (1) entails (2) (so, of course, inferences from (1) to (2) are truth-preserving). On the other hand, from the syntactic point of view, (2) is a constituent of (1). These two facts can be brought into phase by exploiting the principle that sentences with the *syntactic* structure '(S1 and S2)$_s$' entail their sentential constituents. Notice that this principle connects the syntax of these sentences with their inferential roles. Notice too that the trick relies on facts about the grammar of English; it wouldn't work in a language where the formula that expresses the conjunctive content *John went to the store and Mary went to the store* is *syntactically* atomic.[18]

Here is another example. We can reconstruct such truth-preserving inferences as *if Rover bites then something bites* on the assumption that (a) the sentence 'Rover bites' is of the syntactic type Fa, (b) the sentence 'something bites' is of the syntactic type $\exists x$ (Fx) and (c) every formula of the first type entails a corresponding formula of the second type (where the notion 'corresponding formula' is cashed syntactically; roughly the two formulas must differ only in that the one has an existentially bound variable at the syntactic position that is occupied by a constant in the other). Once again, the point to notice is the blending of syntactical and semantical notions: the rule of existential generalization applies to formulas in virtue of their syntactic form. But the salient property that's preserved under applications of the rule is semantical: what's claimed for the transformation that the rule performs is that it is *truth-preserving*.[19]

There are, as it turns out, examples that are quite a lot more complicated than these. The whole of the branch of logic known as proof theory is devoted to exploring them.[20] It would not be unreasonable to describe Classical cognitive science as an extended attempt to apply the methods of proof theory to the modeling of thought (and, similarly, of whatever other mental processes are plausibly viewed as involving inferences; pre-eminently learning and perception). Classical theory construction rests on the hope that syntactic analogues can be constructed for non-demonstrative inferences (or informal, common-sense reasoning) in something like the way that proof theory has provided syntactic analogues for validity.

The second main idea underlying the Classical treatment of mental processes is that it is possible to devise machines whose function is the transformation of symbols, and whose operations are sensitive to the syntactical structure of the symbols that they operate upon. This is the Classical conception of a computer: it's what the various architectures that derive from Turing and von Neumann machines all have in common.

Perhaps it's obvious how the two 'main ideas' fit together. If, in principle, syntactic relations can be made to parallel semantic relations, and if, in principle, you can have a mechanism whose operations on formulas are sensitive to their syntax, then it may be possible to construct a *syntactically* driven machine whose state transitions satisfy *semantical* criteria of coherence. Such a machine would be just what's required for a mechanical model of the semantical coherence of thought; correspondingly, the idea that the brain *is* such a machine is the foundational hypothesis of Classical cognitive science.

So much for the Classical story about mental processes. The Connectionist story must, of course, be quite different: since connectionists eschew postulating mental representations with combinatorial syntactic/semantic structure, they are precluded from postulating mental processes that operate on mental representations in a way that is sensitive to their structure. The sorts of operations that connectionist models do have are of two sorts, depending on whether the process under examination is learning or reasoning.

2.2.1 Learning If a connectionist model is intended to learn, there will be processes that determine the weights of the connections among its units as a function of the character of its training. Typically in a connectionist machine (such as a 'Boltzman machine') the weights among connections are adjusted until the system's behavior comes to model the statistical properties of its inputs. In the limit, the stochastic relations among machine states recapitulates the stochastic relations among the environmental events that they represent.

This should bring to mind the old associationist principle that the strength of association between 'ideas' is a function of the frequency with which they are paired 'in experience' and the learning theoretic principle that the strength of a stimulus–response connection is a function of the frequency with which the response is rewarded in the presence of the stimulus. But though connectionists, like other associationists, are committed to learning processes that model statistical properties of inputs and outputs, the simple mechanisms based on co-occurrence statistics that were the hallmarks of old-fashioned associationism have been augmented in connectionist models by a number of technical devices. (Hence the 'new' in 'new connectionism'.) For example, some of the earlier limitations of associative mechanisms are overcome by allowing the network to contain 'hidden' units (or aggregates) that are not directly connected to the environment and whose purpose is, in effect, to detect statistical patterns in the activity of the 'visible' units including, perhaps, patterns that are more abstract or more 'global' than the ones that could be detected by old-fashioned perceptrons.[21]

In short, sophisticated versions of the associative principles for weight-setting are on offer in the connectionist literature. The point of present concern, however, is what all versions of these principles have in common with one another and with older kinds of associationism: viz. these processes are all *frequency*-sensitive. To return to the example discussed above: if a connectionist learning machine converges on a state where it is prepared to infer A from A&B (i.e. to a state in which when the 'A&B' node is excited it tends to settle into a state in which the 'A' node is excited) the convergence will typically be caused by statistical properties of the machine's training experience: e.g. by correlation between firing of the 'A&B' node and firing of the 'A' node, or by correlations of the firing of both with some feedback signal. Like traditional associationism, connectionism treats learning as basically a sort of statistical modeling.

2.2.2 Reasoning Association operates to alter the structure of a network *diachronically* as a function of its training. Connectionist models also contain a variety of types of 'relaxation' processes which determine the *synchronic* behavior of a network; specifically, they determine what output the device provides for a given pattern of inputs. In this respect, one can think of a connectionist model as a species of analog machine constructed to realize a certain function. The inputs to the function are (a) a specification of the connectedness of the machine (of which nodes are connected to which); (b) a specification of the weights along the connections; (c) a specification of the values of a variety of idiosyncratic parameters of the nodes (e.g. intrinsic thresholds; time since last firing etc.); (d) a specification of a pattern of excitation over the input nodes. The output of the function is a specification of a pattern of excitation over the output nodes; intuitively, the machine chooses the output pattern that is most highly associated to its input.

Much of the mathematical sophistication of connectionist theorizing has been devoted to devising analog solutions to this problem of finding a 'most highly associated' output corresponding to an arbitrary input; but, once again, the details needn't concern us. What is important, for our purposes, is another property that Connectionist theories share with other forms of associationism. In traditional associationism, the probability that one idea will elicit another is sensitive to the strength of the association between them (including 'mediating' associations, if any). And the strength of this association is in turn sensitive to the extent to which the ideas have previously been correlated. Associative strength was not, however, presumed to be sensitive to features of the content or the structure of representations *per se*. Similarly, in connectionist models, the selection of an output corresponding to a given input is a function of properties of the paths that connect them (including the weights, the states of intermediate units etc.). And the weights, in turn, are a function of the statistical properties of events in the environment (or of relations between patterns of events in the environment and implicit 'predictions' made by the network etc.). But the syntactic/semantic structure of the representation of an input is *not* presumed to be a factor in determining the selection of a corresponding output since, as we have seen, syntactic/semantic structure is not defined for the sorts of representations that connectionist models acknowledge.

To summarize: Classical and Connectionist theories disagree about the nature of mental representation; for the former, but not for the latter, mental representations characteristically exhibit a combinatorial constituent structure and a combinatorial semantics. Classical and Connectionist theories also disagree about the nature of mental processes; for the former, but not for the latter, mental processes are characteristically sensitive to the combinatorial structure of the representations on which they operate.

We take it that these two issues define the present dispute about the nature of cognitive architecture. We now propose to argue that the connectionists are on the wrong side of both.

3   The Need for Symbol Systems: Productivity, Systematicity, Compositionality and Inferential Coherence

Classical psychological theories appeal to the constituent structure of mental representations to explain three closely related features of cognition: its productivity, its compositionality and its inferential coherence. The traditional argument has been that these features of cognition are, on the one hand, pervasive and, on the other hand, explicable only on the assumption that mental representations have internal structure. This argument – familiar in more or less explicit versions for the last 30 years or so – is still intact, so far as we can tell. It appears to offer something close to a demonstration that an empirically adequate cognitive theory must recognize not just causal relations among representational states but also relations of syntactic and semantic constituency; hence that the mind cannot be, in its general structure, a connectionist network.

3.1   Productivity of thought

There is a classical productivity argument for the existence of combinatorial structure in any rich representational system (including natural languages and the language of thought). The representational capacities of such a system are, by assumption, unbounded under appropriate idealization; in particular, there are indefinitely many propositions which the system can encode.[22] However, this unbounded expressive power must presumably be achieved by finite means. The way to do this is to treat the system of representations as consisting of expressions belonging to a generated set. More precisely, the correspondence between a representation and the proposition it expresses is, in arbitrarily many cases, built up recursively out of correspondences between parts of the expression and parts of the proposition. But, of course, this strategy can operate only when an unbounded number of the expressions are non-atomic. So linguistic (and mental) representations must constitute *symbol systems* (in the sense of note 8). So the mind cannot be a PDP.

Very often, when people reject this sort of reasoning, it is because they doubt that human cognitive capacities are correctly viewed as productive. In the long run there can be no *a priori* arguments for (or against) idealizing to productive capacities; whether you accept the idealization depends on whether you believe that the inference from finite performance to finite capacity is justified, or whether you think that finite performance is typically a result of the interaction of an unbounded competence with resource constraints. Classicists have traditionally offered a mixture of methodological and empirical considerations in favor of the latter view.

From a methodological perspective, the least that can be said for assuming productivity is that it precludes solutions that rest on inappropriate tricks (such as storing all the pairs that define a function);

tricks that would be unreasonable in practical terms even for solving finite tasks that place sufficiently large demands on memory. The idealization to unbounded productive capacity forces the theorist to separate the finite specification of a method for solving a computational problem from such factors as the resources that the system (or person) brings to bear on the problem at any given moment.

The empirical arguments for productivity have been made most frequently in connection with linguistic competence. They are familiar from the work of Chomsky (1968) who has claimed (convincingly, in our view) that the knowledge underlying linguistic competence is generative, i.e. that it allows us *in principle* to generate (/understand) an unbounded number of sentences. It goes without saying that no one does, or could, *in fact* utter or understand tokens of more than a finite number of sentence types; this is a trivial consequence of the fact that nobody can utter or understand more than a finite number of sentence tokens. But there are a number of considerations which suggest that, despite *de facto* constraints on performance, one's knowledge of one's language supports an unbounded productive capacity in much the same way that one's knowledge of addition supports an unbounded number of sums. Among these considerations are, for example, the fact that a speaker/hearer's performance can often be improved by relaxing time constraints, increasing motivation or supplying pencil and paper. It seems very natural to treat such manipulations as affecting the transient state of the speaker's memory and attention rather than what he/she knows about – or how he/she represents – his/her language. But this treatment is available only on the assumption that the character of the subject's performance is determined by interactions between the available knowledge base and the available computational resources.

Classical theories are able to accommodate these sorts of considerations because they assume architectures in which there is a functional distinction between memory and program. In a system such as a Turing machine, where the length of the tape is not fixed in advance, changes in the amount of available memory *can be affected without changing the computational structure of the machine*, viz. by making more tape available. By contrast, in a finite state automaton or a connectionist machine, adding to the memory (e.g. by adding units to a network) alters the connectivity relations among nodes and thus does affect the machine's computational structure. Connectionist cognitive architectures cannot, by their very nature, support an expandable memory, so they cannot support productive cognitive capacities. The long and short is that if productivity arguments are sound, then they show that the architecture of the mind can't be connectionist. Connectionists have, by and large, acknowledged this; so they are forced to reject productivity arguments.

The test of a good scientific idealization is simply and solely whether it produces successful science in the long term. It seems to us that the productivity idealization has more than earned its keep, especially in linguistics and in theories of reasoning. Connectionists, however, have not been persuaded. For example, Rumelhart and McClelland (1986b, p. 119) say that they:

> do not agree that [productive] capabilities are of the essence of human computation. As anyone who has ever attempted to process sentences like 'The man the boy the girl hit kissed moved' can attest, our ability to process even moderate degrees of center-embedded structure is grossly impaired relative to an ATN [Augmented Transition Network] parser. . . . What is needed, then, is not a mechanism for flawless and effortless processing of embedded constructions . . . The challenge is to explain how those processes that others have chosen to explain in terms of recursive mechanisms can be better explained by the kinds of processes natural for PDP networks.

These remarks suggest that Rumelhart and McClelland think that the fact that center-embedding sentences are hard is somehow an *embarrassment* for theories that view linguistic capacities as productive. But of course it's not since, according to such theories, performance is an effect of interactions between a productive competence and restricted resources. There are, in fact, quite plausible Classical accounts of why center-embeddings ought to impose especially heavy demands on resources, and there is a reasonable amount of experimental support for these models (see, for example, Wanner and Maratsos, 1978).

In any event, it should be obvious that the difficulty of parsing center-embeddings can't be a consequence of their recursiveness *per se* since there are many recursive structures that are strikingly easy to understand. Consider: This is the dog that chased the cat that ate the rat that lived in the house that Jack built.' The classicist's case for productive capacities in parsing rests on the transparency of sentences like these.[23] In short, the fact that center-embedded sentences are hard perhaps shows that there are some recursive structures that we can't parse. But what Rumelhart and McClelland need if they are to deny the productivity of linguistic capacities is the much stronger claim that there are no recursive structures that we can parse; and this stronger claim would appear to be simply false.

Rumelhart and McClelland's discussion of recursion (1986b, pp. 119–20) nevertheless repays close attention. They are apparently prepared to concede that PDPs can model recursive capacities only indirectly, viz. by implementing classical architectures like ATNs; so that *if* human cognition exhibited recursive capacities, that would suffice to show that minds have classical rather than connectionist architecture at the psychological level. 'We have not dwelt on PDP implementations of Turing machines and recursive processing engines *because we do not agree with those who would argue that such capacities are of the essence of human computation*' (p. 119, our emphasis). Their argument that recursive capacities *aren't* 'of the essence of human computation' is, however, just the unconvincing stuff about center-embedding quoted above.

So the Rumelhart and McClelland view is apparently that if you take it to be independently obvious that some cognitive capacities are productive, then you should take the existence of such capacities to argue for classical cognitive architecture and hence for treating connectionism as at best an implementation theory. We think that this is quite a plausible understanding of the bearing that the issues about productivity and recursion have on the issues about cognitive architecture; in section 4 we will return to the suggestion that connectionist models can plausibly be construed as models of the implementation of a classical architecture.

In the meantime, however, we propose to view the status of productivity arguments for classical architectures as moot; we're about to present a different sort of argument for the claim that mental representations need an articulated internal structure. It is closely related to the productivity argument, but it doesn't require the idealization to unbounded competence. Its assumptions should thus be acceptable even to theorists who – like connectionists – hold that the finitistic character of cognitive capacities is intrinsic to their architecture.

3.2 Systematicity of cognitive representation

The form of the argument is this: whether or not cognitive capacities are really *productive*, it seems indubitable that they are what we shall call 'systematic'. And we'll see that the systematicity of cognition provides as good a reason for postulating combinatorial structure in mental representation as the productivity of cognition does: you get, in effect, the same conclusion, but from a weaker premise.

The easiest way to understand what the systematicity of cognitive capacities amounts to is to focus on the systematicity of language comprehension and production. In fact, the systematicity argument for combinatorial structure in *thought* exactly recapitulates the traditional structuralist argument for constituent structure in sentences. But we pause to remark upon a point that we'll re-emphasize later; linguistic capacity is a paradigm of systematic cognition, but it's widly unlikely that it's the only example. On the contrary, there's every reason to believe that systematicity is a thoroughly pervasive feature of human and infra-human mentation.

What we mean when we say that linguistic capacities are *systematic* is that the ability to produce/understand some sentences is *intrinsically* connected to the ability to produce/understand certain others. You can see the force of this if you compare learning languages the way we really do learn them with learning a language by memorizing an enormous phrase book. The point isn't that phrase books are finite and can therefore exhaustively specify only *non*-productive languages; that's true, but we've agreed not to rely on productivity arguments for our present purposes. Our point is rather that you can learn *any part of a phrase book without learning the rest*. Hence, on the phrase book model, it would be perfectly possible to learn that uttering the form of words 'Granny's cat is on Uncle Arthur's mat' is the way to say (in English) that Granny's cat is on Uncle Arthur's mat, and yet have no idea at all how to say that it's raining (or, for that matter, how to say that Uncle Arthur's cat is on Granny's mat). Perhaps it's self-evident that the phrase book story must be wrong about language acquisition because a speaker's knowledge of his native language is never like that. You don't, for example, find native speakers who know how to say in English that John loves the girl but don't know how to say in English that the girl loves John.

Notice, in passing, that systematicity is a property of the mastery of the syntax of a language, not of its lexicon. The phrase book model really does fit what it's like to learn the *vocabulary* of English since when you learn English vocabulary you acquire a lot of basically *independent* capacities. So you might perfectly well learn that using the expression 'cat' is the way to refer to cats and yet have no idea that using the expression 'deciduous conifer' is the way to refer to deciduous conifers. Systematicity, like productivity, is the sort of property of cognitive capacities that you're likely to miss if you concentrate on the psychology of learning and searching lists.

There is, as we remarked, a straightforward (and quite traditional) argument from the systematicity of language capacity to the conclusion that sentences must have syntactic and semantic structure. If you assume that sentences are constructed out of words and phrases, and that many different sequences of words can be phrases of the same type, the very fact that one formula is a sentence of the language will often imply that other formulas must be too: in effect, systematicity follows from the postulation of constituent structure.

Suppose, for example, that it's a fact about English that formulas with the constituent analysis 'NP Vt NP' are well formed; and suppose that 'John' and 'the girl' are NPs and 'loves' is a Vt. It follows from these assumptions that 'John loves the girl,' 'John loves John,' 'the girl loves the girl,' and 'the girl loves John' must all be sentences. It follows too that anybody who has mastered the grammar of English must have linguistic capacities that are systematic in respect of these sentences; he/she *can't but* assume that all of them are sentences if he/she assumes that any of them are. Compare the situation on the view that the sentences of English are all atomic. There is then no structural analogy between 'John loves the girl' and 'the girl loves John' and hence no reason why understanding one sentence should imply understanding the other; no more than understanding 'rabbit' implies understanding 'tree'.[24]

On the view that the sentences are atomic, the systematicity of linguistic capacities is a mystery; on the view that they have constituent structure, the systematicity of linguistic capacities is what you would predict. So we should prefer the latter view to the former.

Notice that you can make this argument for constituent structure in sentences without idealizing to astronomical computational capacities. There are productivity arguments for constituent structure, but they're concerned with our ability – in principle – to understand sentences that are arbitrarily long. Systematicity, by contrast, appeals to premises that are much nearer home; such considerations as the ones mentioned above, that no speaker understands the form of words 'John loves the girl' except as he/she also understands the form of words 'the girl loves John'. The assumption that linguistic capacities are productive 'in principle' is one that a connectionist might refuse to grant. But that they are systematic *in fact* no one can plausibly deny.

We can now, finally, come to the point: the argument from the systematicity of linguistic capacities to constituent structure in sentences is quite clear. *But thought is systematic too*, so there is a precisely parallel argument from the systematicity of thought to syntactic and semantic structure in mental representations.

What does it mean to say that thought is systematic? Well, just as you don't find people who can understand the sentence 'John loves the girl' but not the sentence 'the girl loves John', so too you don't find people who can *think the thought* that John loves the girl but can't think the thought that the girl loves John. Indeed, in the case of verbal organisms the systematicity of thought *follows from* the systematicity of language if you assume – as most psychologists do – that understanding a sentence involves entertaining the thought that it expresses; on that assumption, nobody *could* understand both the sentences about John and the girl unless he/she were able to think both the thoughts about John and the girl.

But now if the ability to think that John loves the girl is intrinsically connected to the ability to think that the girl loves John, that fact will somehow have to be explained. For a representationalist (which, as we have seen, connectionists are), the explanation is obvious: entertaining thoughts requires being in representational states (i.e. it requires tokening mental representations). And, just as the systematicity of language shows that there must be structural relations between the sentence 'John loves the girl' and the sentence 'the girl loves John,' so the systematicity of thought shows that there must be structural relations between the mental representation that corresponds to the thought that John loves the girl and the mental representation that corresponds to the thought that the girl loves John;[25] namely, the two mental representations, like the two sentences, *must be made of the same parts*. But if this explanation is right (and there don't seem to be any others on offer), then mental representations have internal structure and there is a language of thought. So the architecture of the mind is not a connectionist network.[26]

To summarize the discussion so far: productivity arguments infer the internal structure of mental representations from the presumed fact that nobody has a *finite* intellectual competence. By contrast, systematicity arguments infer the internal structure of mental representations from the patent fact that nobody has a *punctate* intellectual competence. Just as you don't find linguistic capacities that consist of the ability to understand 67 unrelated sentences, so too you don't find cognitive capacities that consist of the ability to think 74 unrelated thoughts. Our claim is that this isn't, in either case, an accident: a linguistic theory that allowed for the possibility of punctate languages would have gone not just wrong, but *very profoundly* wrong. And similarly for a cognitive theory that allowed for the possibility of punctate minds.

But perhaps not being punctate is a property only of the minds of language users; perhaps the representational capacities of infra-verbal organisms do have just the kind of gaps that connectionist models permit? A connectionist might then claim that he/she can do everything 'up to language' on the assumption that mental representations lack combinatorial syntactic and semantic structure. Everything up to language may not be everything, but it's a lot. (On the other hand, a lot may be a lot, but it isn't everything. Infra-verbal cognitive architecture mustn't be so represented as to make the eventual acquisition of language in phylogeny and in ontogeny require a miracle.)

It is not, however, plausible that only the minds of verbal organisms are systematic. Think what it would mean for this to be the case. It would have to be quite usual to find, for example, animals capable of representing the state of affairs *aRb*, but incapable of representing the state of affairs *bRa*. Such an animal would be, as it were, *aRb* sighted but *bRa* blind since, presumably, the representational capacities of its mind affect not just what an organism can think, but also what it can perceive. In consequence, such animals would be able to learn to respond selectively to *aRb* situations but quite *un*able to learn to respond selectively to *bRa* situations. (So that, though you could teach the creature to choose the picture with the square larger than the triangle, you couldn't for the life of you teach it to choose the picture with the triangle larger than the square.)

It is, to be sure, an empirical question whether the cognitive capacities of infra-verbal organisms are often structured that way, but we're prepared to bet that they are not. Ethological cases are the exceptions that prove the rule. There *are* examples where salient environmental configurations act as '*gestalten*'; and in such cases it's reasonable to doubt that the mental representation of the stimulus is complex. But the point is precisely that these cases are *exceptional*; they're exactly the ones where you expect that there will be some special story to tell about the ecological significance of the stimulus: that it's the shape of a predator, or the song of a conspecific etc. Conversely, when there is no such story to tell, you expect structurally similar stimuli to elicit correspondingly similar cognitive capacities. That, surely, is the least that a respectable principle of stimulus generalization has got to require.

That infra-verbal cognition is pretty generally systematic seems, in short, to be about as secure as any empirical premise in this area can be. And, as we've just seen, it's a premise from which the inadequacy of connectionist models as cognitive theories follows quite straight-forwardly; as straightforwardly, in any event, as it would from the assumption that such capacities are generally productive.

3.3 Compositionality of representations

Compositionality is closely related to systematicity; perhaps they're best viewed as aspects of a single phenomenon. We will therefore follow much the same course here as in the preceding discussion: first, we introduce the concept by recalling the standard arguments for the compositionality of natural languages. We then suggest that parallel arguments secure the compositionality of mental representations. Since compositionality requires combinatorial syntactic and semantic structure, the compositionality of thought is evidence that the mind is not a connectionist network.

We said that the systematicity of linguistic competence consists in the fact that 'the ability to produce/understand some of the sentences is intrinsically connected to the ability to produce/understand certain of the others.' We now add that which sentences are systematically related is not arbitrary from a semantic point of view. For example, being able to understand 'John loves the girl' goes along with being able to understand 'the girl loves John', and there are correspondingly close semantic relations between these sentences: in order for the first to be true, John must bear to the girl the very same relation that the truth of the second requires the girl to bear to John. By contrast, there is no intrinsic connection between understanding either of the John/girl sentences and understanding semantically unrelated formulas like 'quarks are made of gluons' or 'the cat is on the mat' or '2 + 2 = 4'; it looks as though semantical relatedness and systematicity keep quite close company.

You might suppose that this co-variance is covered by the same explanation that accounts for systematicity *per se*; roughly, that sentences that are systematically related are composed from the same syntactic constituents. But, in fact, you need a further assumption, which we'll call the 'principle of compositionality': in so far as a language is systematic, a lexical item must make approximately the same semantic contribution to each expression in which it occurs. It is, for example, only in so far as 'the', 'girl', 'loves' and 'John' make the same semantic contribution to 'John loves the girl' that they make to 'the girl loves John' that understanding the one sentence implies understanding the other. Similarity of constituent structure accounts for the semantic relatedness between systematically related sentences only to the extent that the semantical properties of the shared constituents are context-independent.

Here idioms prove the rule: being able to understand 'the', 'man', 'kicked' and 'bucket' isn't much help with understanding 'the man kicked the bucket', since 'kicked' and 'bucket' don't bear their standard meanings in this context. And, just as you'd expect, 'the man kicked the bucket' is *not* systematic even with respect to syntactically closely related sentences like 'the man kicked over the bucket' (for that matter, it's not systematic with respect to the 'the man kicked the bucket' read literally).

It's uncertain exactly how compositional natural languages actually are (just as it's uncertain exactly how systematic they are). We suspect that the amount of context-induced variation of lexical meaning is often

overestimated because other sorts of context sensitivity are miscon-
strued as violations of compositionality. For example, the difference
between 'feed the chicken' and 'chicken to eat' must involve an *animal/
food* ambiguity in 'chicken' rather than a violation of compositionality
since if the context 'feed the . . .' could *induce* (rather than select) the
meaning *animal*, you would expect 'feed the veal', 'feed the pork' and
the like.[27] Similarly, the difference between 'good book', 'good rest' and
'good fight' is probably not meaning shift but syncategorematicity.
'Good *NP*' means something like *NP that answers to the relevant interest
in NPs:* a good book is one that answers to our interest in books (viz. it's
good to read); a good rest is one that answers to our interest in rests
(viz. it leaves one refreshed); a good fight is one that answers to our
interest in fights (viz. it's fun to watch or to be in, or it clears the air);
and so on. It's because the meaning of 'good' is syncategorematic and
has a variable in it for relevant interests, that you can know that a good
flurg is a flurg that answers to the relevant interest in flurgs without
knowing what flurgs are or what the relevant interest in flurgs is (see
Ziff, 1960).

In any event, the main argument stands: systematicity depends on
compositionality, so to the extent that a natural language is systematic it
must be compositional too. This illustrates another respect in which
systematicity arguments can do the work for which productivity
arguments have previously been employed. The traditional argument for
compositionality is that it is required to explain how a finitely
representable language can contain infinitely many non-synonymous
expressions.

Considerations about systematicity offer one argument for compositionality; considerations about entailment offer another. Consider
predicates like '. . . is a brown cow'. This expression bears a
straightforward semantical relation to the predicates '. . . is a cow' and
'. . . is brown'; viz. that the first predicate is true of a thing if and only if
both of the others are. That is, '. . . is a brown cow' severally entails '. . .
is brown' and '. . . is a cow' and is entailed by their conjunction.
Moreover – and this is important – this semantical pattern is not
peculiar to the cases cited. On the contrary, it holds for a very large
range of predicates (see '. . . is a red square', '. . . is a funny old German
soldier', '. . . is a child prodigy' and so forth).

How are we to account for these sorts of regularities? The answer
seems clear enough; '. . . is a brown cow' entails '. . . is brown' because
(a) the second expression is a constituent of the first; (b) the syntactical
form '(adjective noun)$_N$' has (in many cases) the semantic force of a
conjunction; and (c) 'brown' retains its semantical value under
simplification of conjunction. Notice that you need (c) to rule out the

possibility that 'brown' means *brown* when it modifies a noun but (as it might be) *dead* when it's a predicate adjective; in which case '. . . is a brown cow' wouldn't entail '. . . is brown' after all. Notice too that (c) is just an application of the principle of composition.

So, here's the argument so far: you need to assume some degree of compositionality of English sentences to account for the fact that systematically related sentences are always semantically related; and to account for certain regular parallelisms between the syntactical structure of sentences and their entailments. So, beyond any serious doubt, the sentences of English must be compositional to some serious extent. But the principle of compositionality governs the semantic relations between words *and the expressions of which they are constituents*. So compositionality implies that (some) expressions *have* constituents. So compositionality argues for (specifically, presupposes) syntactic/semantic structure in sentences.

Now what about the compositionality of mental representations? There is, as you'd expect, a bridging argument based on the usual psycho-linguistic premise that one uses language to express ones thoughts. Sentences are used to express thoughts; so if the ability to use some sentences is connected with the ability to use certain other, semantically related, sentences, then the ability to think some thoughts must be correspondingly connected with the ability to think certain other, semantically related, thoughts. But you can only think the thoughts that your mental representations can express. So, if the ability to think certain thoughts is interconnected, then the corresponding representational capacities must be interconnected too; specifically, the ability to be in some representational states must imply the ability to be in certain other, semantically related representational states.

But then the question arise: *how could* the mind be so arranged that the ability to be in one representational state is connected with the ability to be in others that are semantically nearby? What account of mental representation would have this consequence? The answer is just what you'd expect from the discussion of the linguistic material. Mental representations must have internal structure, just the way that sentences do. In particular, it must be that the mental representation that corresponds to the thought that John loves the girl contains, as its parts, the same constituents as the mental representation that corresponds to the thought that the girl loves John. That would explain why these thoughts are *systematically* related; *and, to the extent that the semantic value of these parts is context-independent, that would explain why these systematically related thoughts are also semantically related.* So, by this chain of argument, evidence for the compositionality of sentences is evidence for the compositionality of the representational states of speaker/hearers.

Finally, what about the compositionality of infra-verbal thought? The argument isn't much different from the one that we've just run through. We assume that animal thought is largely systematic: the organism that can perceive (hence learn) that *aRb* can generally perceive (/learn) that *bRa*. But, systematically related thoughts (just like systematically related sentences) are generally semantically related too. It's no surprise that being able to learn that the triangle is above the square implies being able to learn that the square is above the triangle; whereas it would be *very* surprising if being able to learn the square/triangle facts implied being able to learn that quarks are made of gluons or that Washington was the first President of America.

So, then, what explains the correlation between systematic relations and semantic relations in infraverbal thought? Clearly, connectionist models don't address this question; the fact that a network contains a node labelled X has, so far as the constraints imposed by connectionist architecture are concerned, *no implications at all* for the labels of the other nodes in the network; in particular, it doesn't imply that there will be nodes that represent thoughts that are semantically close to X. This is just the semantical side of the fact that network architectures permit arbitrarily punctate mental lives.

But if, on the other hand, we make the usual Classicist assumptions (viz. that systematically related thoughts share constituents and that the semantic values of these shared constituents are context-independent) the correlation between systematicity and semantic relatedness follows immediately. For a classicist, this correlation is an 'architectural' property of minds; it couldn't but hold if mental representations have the general properties that classical models suppose them to.

What have connectionists to say about these matters? There is some textual evidence that they are tempted to deny the facts of compositionality wholesale. For example, Smolensky (chapter 2) claims that:

Surely . . . we would get quite a different representation of 'coffee' if we examined the difference between 'can with coffee' and 'can without coffee' or 'tree with coffee' and 'tree without coffee'; or 'man with coffee' and 'man without coffee' . . . context insensitivity is not something we expect to be reflected in connectionist representations. . . .

It's certainly true that compositionality is not generally a feature of connectionist representations. Connectionists can't acknowledge the facts of compositionality because they are committed to mental representations that don't have combinatorial structure. But to give up on compositionality is to take 'kick the bucket' as a model for the relation between syntax and semantics; and the consequence is, as we've

seen, that you make the systematicity of language (and of thought) a
mystery. On the other hand, to say that 'kick the bucket' is aberrant, and
that the right model for the syntax/semantics relation is (e.g.) 'brown
cow', is to start down a trail which leads, pretty inevitably, to
acknowledging combinatorial structure in mental representation, hence
to the rejection of connectionist networks as cognitive models.

We don't think there's any way out of the need to acknowledge the
compositionality of natural languages and of mental representations.
However, it's been suggested (see Smolensky, chapter 2) that while the
principle of compositionality is false (because content isn't context
invariant) there is nevertheless a 'family resemblance' between the
various meanings that a symbol has in the various contexts in which it
occurs. Since such proposals generally aren't elaborated, it's unclear
how they're supposed to handle the salient facts about systematicity and
inference. But surely there are going to be serious problems. Consider,
for example, such inferences as

(i)   Turtles are slower than rabbits.
(ii) Rabbits are slower than Ferraris.
. . . .
(iii) Turtles are slower than Ferraris.

The soundness of this inference appears to depend upon (a) the fact
that the same relation (viz. *slower than*) holds between turtles and rabbits
on the one hand, and rabbits and Ferraris on the other; and (b) the fact
that that relation is transitive. If, however, it's assumed (contrary to the
principle of compositionality) that 'slower than' means something
different in premises (i) and (ii) (and presumably in (iii) as well) – so
that, strictly speaking, the relation that holds between turtles and rabbits
is *not* the same one that holds between rabbits and Ferraris – then it's
hard to see why the inference should be valid.

Talk about the relations being 'similar' only papers over the difficulty
since the problem is then to provide a notion of similarity that will
guaranty that if (i) and (ii) are true, so too is (iii). And, so far at least, no
such notion of similarity has been forthcoming. Notice that it won't do
to require just that the relations all be similar in respect of their
transitivity, i.e. that they all be transitive. On that account, the argument
from 'turtles are slower than rabbits' and 'rabbits are furrier than
Ferraris' to 'turtles are slower than Ferraris' would be valid since
'furrier than' is transitive too.

Until these sorts of issues are attended to, the proposal to replace the
compositional principle of context invariance with a notion of 'approxi-

mate equivalence ... across contexts' (Smolensky, chapter 2, p. 67) doesn't seem to be much more than hand waving.

3.4 The systematicity of inference

In section 2 we saw that, according to Classical theories, the syntax of mental representations mediates between their semantic properties and their causal role in mental processes. Take a simple case: it's a 'logical' principle that conjunctions entail their constituents (so the argument from $P\&Q$ to P and to Q is valid). Correspondingly, it's a psychological law that thoughts that $P\&Q$ tend to cause thoughts that P and thoughts that Q, all else being equal. Classical theory exploits the constituent structure of mental representations to account for both these facts, the first by assuming that the combinatorial semantics of mental representations is sensitive to their syntax and the second by assuming that mental processes apply to mental representations in virtue of their constituent structure.

A consequence of these assumptions is that Classical theories are committed to the following striking prediction: inferences that are of similar logical type ought, pretty generally,[28] to elicit correspondingly similar cognitive capacities. You shouldn't, for example, find a kind of mental life in which you get inferences from $P\&Q\&R$ to P but you don't get inferences from $P\&Q$ to P. This is because, according to the Classical account, this logically homogeneous class of inferences is carried out by a correspondingly homogeneous class of psychological mechanisms. The premises of both inferences are expressed by mental representations that satisfy the same syntactic analysis (viz. $S_1\&S_2\&S_3\&$ ... S_n); and the process of drawing the inference corresponds, in both cases, to the same formal operation of detaching the constituent that expresses the conclusion.

The idea that organisms should exhibit similar cognitive capacities in respect of logically similar inferences is so natural that it may seem unavoidable. But, on the contrary: there's nothing in principle to preclude a kind of cognitive model in which inferences that are quite similar from the logician's point of view are nevertheless computed by quite different mechanisms; or in which some inferences of a given logical type are computed and other inferences of the same logical type are not. Consider, in particular, the Connectionist account. A connectionist can certainly model a mental life in which, if you can reason from $P\&Q\&R$ to P, then you can also reason from $P\&Q$ to P. For example, the network in figure 3.3 would do.

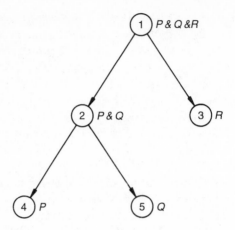

Figure 3.3   A possible connectionist network which draws inferences from
P&Q&R to *P* and also draws inferences from *P&Q* to *P*.

But notice that a *connectionist can equally model a mental life in which
you get one of these inferences and not the other*. In the present case, since
there is no structural relation between the *P&Q&R* node and the *P&Q*
node (remember, all nodes are atomic; don't be misled by the node
labels), there's no reason why a mind that contains the first should also
contain the second, or vice versa. Analogously, there's no reason why
you shouldn't get minds that simplify the premises *John loves Mary and
Bill hates Mary* but no others; or minds that simplify premises with 1, 3
or 5 conjuncts, but don't simplify premises with 2, 4 or 6 conjuncts; or,
for that matter, minds that simplify only premises that were acquired on
Tuesdays ... etc.

In fact, the connectionist architecture is *utterly indifferent* as among
these possibilities. That's because it recognizes no notion of syntax
according to which thoughts that are alike in inferential role (e.g.
thoughts that are all subject to simplification of conjunction) are
expressed by mental representations of correspondingly similar syntactic
form (e.g. by mental representations that are all syntactically conjunctive). So, the connectionist architecture tolerates gaps in cognitive
capacities; it has no mechanism to enforce the requirement that logically
homogeneous inferences should be executed by correspondingly homogeneous computational processes.

But, we claim, you don't find cognitive capacities that have these sorts
of gaps. You don't, for example, get minds that are prepared to infer
John went to the store from *John and Mary and Susan and Sally went to the
store* and from *John and Mary went to the store* but not from *John and*

Mary and Susan went to the store. Given a notion of logical syntax – the very notion that the Classical theory of mentation requires to get its account of mental processes off the ground – it is a *truism* that you don't get such minds. Lacking a notion of logical syntax, it is a *mystery* that you don't.

3.5   Summary

It is perhaps obvious by now that all the arguments that we've been reviewing – the argument from systematicity, the argument from compositionality, and the argument from inferential coherence – are really much the same. If you hold the kind of theory that acknowledges structured representations, it must perforce acknowledge representations with *similar* or *identical* structures. In the linguistic cases, constituent analysis implies a taxonomy of sentences by their syntactic form, and in the inferential cases, it implies a taxonomy of arguments by their logical form. So, if your theory also acknowledges mental processes that are structure sensitive, then it will predict that similarly structured representations will generally play similar roles in thought. A theory that says that the sentence 'John loves the girl' is made out of the same parts as the sentence 'the girl loves John', and made by applications of the same rules of composition, will have to go out of its way to explain a linguistic competence which embraces one sentence but not the other. And, similarly, if a theory says that the mental representation that corresponds to the thought that *P&Q&R* has the same (conjunctive) syntax as the mental representation that corresponds to the thought that *P&Q* and that mental processes of drawing inferences subsume mental representations in virtue of their syntax, it will have to go out of its way to explain inferential capacities which embrace the one thought but not the other. Such a competence would be, at best, an embarrassment for the theory, and at worst a refutation.

By contrast, since the connectionist architecture recognizes no combinatorial structure in mental representations, gaps in cognitive competence should proliferate arbitrarily. It's not just that you'd expect to get them from time to time; it's that, on the 'no-structure' story, *gaps are the unmarked case.* It's the *systematic* competence that the theory is required to treat as an embarrassment. But, as a matter of fact, inferential competences are *blatantly* systematic. So there must be something deeply wrong with connectionist architecture.

What's deeply wrong with connectionist architecture is this: because it acknowledges neither syntactic nor semantic structure in mental representations, it perforce treats them not as a generated set but as a list. But lists, *qua* lists, have no structure; any collection of items is a possible list. And, correspondingly, on Connectionist principles, any collection of (causally connected) representational states is a possible mind. So, as far as connectionist architecture is concerned, there is nothing to prevent minds that are arbitrarily unsystematic. But that result is *preposterous*. Cognitive capacities come in structurally related clusters; their systematicity is pervasive. All the evidence suggests that *punctate minds can't happen*. This argument seemed conclusive against the connectionism of Hebb, Osgood and Hull 20 or 30 years ago. So far as we can tell, nothing of any importance has happened to change the situation in the meantime.[29]

A final comment to round off this part of the discussion. It's possible to imagine a connectionist being prepared to admit that while systematicity doesn't *follow from* – and hence is not explained by – connectionist architecture, it is none the less *compatible* with that architecture. It is, after all, perfectly possible to follow a policy of building networks that have *aRb* nodes only if they have *bRa* nodes . . . etc. There is therefore nothing to stop a connectionist from stipulating – as an independent postulate of his/her theory of mind – that all biologically instantiated networks are, *de facto*, systematic.

But this misses a crucial point: it's not enough just to stipulate systematicity; one is also required to specify a mechanism that is able to enforce the stipulation. To put it another way, it's not enough for a connectionist to agree that all minds are systematic; he/she must also explain *how nature contrives to produce only systematic minds*. Presumably there would have to be some sort of mechanism, over and above the ones that connectionism *per se* posits, the functioning of which insures the systematicity of biologically instantiated networks; a mechanism such that, in virtue of its operation, every network that has an *aRb* node also has a *bRa* node . . . and so forth. There are, however, no proposals for such a mechanism. Or, rather, there is just one: the only mechanism that is known to be able to produce pervasive systematicity is classical architecture. And, as we have seen, classical architecture is not compatible with connectionism since it requires internally structured representations.

4   The Lure of Connectionism

The current popularity of the connectionist approach among psychologists and philosophers is puzzling in view of the sorts of problems raised above; problems which were largely responsible for the development of a syntax-based (proof theoretic) notion of computation and a Turing-style, symbol-processing notion of cognitive architecture in the first place. There are, however, a number of apparently plausible arguments, repeatedly encountered in the literature, that stress certain limitations of conventional computers as models of brains. These may be seen as favoring the connectionist alternative. We will sketch a number of these before discussing the general problems which they appear to raise.

Rapidity of cognitive processes in relation to neural speeds: the 'hundred step' constraint It has been observed (e.g. Feldman and Ballard, 1982) that the time required to execute computer instructions is in the order of nanoseconds, whereas neurons take tens of milliseconds to fire. Consequently, in the time it takes people to carry out many of the tasks at which they are fluent (like recognizing a word or a picture, either of which may require considerably less than a second) a *serial* neurally instantiated program would only be able to carry out about 100 instructions. Yet such tasks might typically require many thousands – or even millions – of instructions in present-day computers (if they can be done at all). Thus, it is argued, the brain must operate quite differently from computers. In fact, the argument goes, the brain must be organized in a highly parallel manner ('massively parallel' is the preferred term of art).

Difficulty of achieving large-capacity pattern recognition and content-based retrieval in conventional architectures Closely related to the issues about time constraints is the fact that humans can store and make use of an enormous amount of information, apparently without effort (Fahlman and Hinton, 1987). One particularly dramatic skill that people exhibit is the ability to recognize patterns from among tens or even hundreds of thousands of alternatives (e.g. word or face recognition). In fact, there is reason to believe that many expert skills may be based on large, fast recognition memories (see Simon and Chase, 1973). If one had to search through one's memory serially, the way conventional computers do, the complexity would overwhelm any machine. Thus, the knowledge that people have must be stored and retrieved differently from the way conventional computers do it.

Conventional computer models are committed to a different etiology for 'rule-governed' behavior and 'exceptional' behavior Classical psychological theories, which are based on conventional computer ideas, typically distinguish between mechanisms that cause regular and divergent behavior by postulating systems of explicit unconscious rules to explain the former, and then attributing departures from these rules to secondary (performance) factors. Since the divergent behaviors occur very frequently, a better strategy would be to try to account for both types of behavior in terms of the same mechanism.

Lack of progress in dealing with processes that are non-verbal or intuitive   Most of our fluent cognitive skills do not consist in accessing verbal knowledge or carrying out deliberate conscious reasoning (Fahlman and Hinton, 1987; Smolensky, Chapter 2). We appear to know many things that we would have great difficulty in describing verbally, including how to ride a bicycle, what our close friends look like, and how to recall the name of the President etc. Such knowledge, it is argued, must not be stored in linguistic form, but in some other 'implicit' form. The fact that conventional computers typically operate in a 'linguistic mode', inasmuch as they process information by operating on syntactically structured expressions, may explain why there has been relatively little success in modeling implicit knowledge.

Acute sensitivity of conventional architectures to damage and noise   Unlike digital circuits, brain circuits must tolerate noise arising from spontaneous neural activity. Moreover, they must tolerate a moderate degree of damage without failing completely. With a few notable exceptions, if a part of the brain is damaged, the degradation in performance is usually not catastrophic but varies more or less gradually with the extent of the damage. This is especially true of memory. Damage to the temporal cortex (usually thought to house memory traces) does not result in selective loss of particular facts and memories. This and similar facts about brain-damaged patients suggests that human memory representations, and perhaps many other cognitive skills as well, are *distributed* spatially, rather than being neurally localized. This appears to contrast with conventional computers, where hierarchical-style control keeps the crucial decisions highly localized and where memory storage consists of an array of location-addressable registers.

Storage in conventional architectures is passive   Conventional computers have a passive memory store which is accessed in what has been called a 'fetch and execute cycle'. This appears to be quite unlike human memory. For example, according to Kosslyn and Hatfield (1984, pp. 1022, 1029):

> In computers the memory is static: once an entry is put in a given location, it just sits there until it is operated upon by the CPU ... But consider a very simple experiment: Imagine a letter *A* over and over again

... then switch to the letter *B*. In a model employing a von Neumann architecture the 'fatigue' that inhibited imaging the *A* would be due to some quirk in the way the CPU executes a given instruction ... Such fatigue should generalize to all objects imaged because the routine responsible for imaging was less effective. But experiments have demonstrated that this is not true: specific objects become more difficult to image, not all objects. This finding is more easily explained by an analogy to the way invisible ink fades of its own accord ... with invisible ink, the representation itself is doing something – there is no separate processor working over it. ...

Conventional rule-based systems depict cognition as 'all-or-none' But cognitive skills appear to be characterized by various kinds of continuities. For example:

1　*Continuous variation in degree of applicability of different principles*, or in the degree of relevance of different constraints, 'rules' or procedures. There are frequent cases (especially in perception and memory retrieval), in which it appears that a variety of different constraints is brought to bear on a problem simultaneously and the outcome is a combined effect of all the different factors (see for example, the informal discussion by McClelland et al., 1986b, pp. 3–9). That's why 'constraint propagation' techniques are receiving a great deal of attention in artificial intelligence (see Mackworth, 1987).

2　*Non-determinism of human behavior*: cognitive processes are never rigidly determined or precisely replicable. Rather, they appear to have a significant random or stochastic component. Perhaps that's because there is randomness at a microscopic level, caused by irrelevant biochemical or electrical activity or perhaps even by quantum mechanical events. To model this activity by rigid deterministic rules can only lead to poor predictions because it ignores the fundamentally stochastic nature of the underlying mechanisms. Moreover, deterministic, all-or-none models will be unable to account for the gradual aspect of learning and skill acqusition.

3　*Failure to display graceful degradation*: when humans are unable to do a task perfectly, they none the less do something reasonable. If the particular task does not fit exactly into some known pattern, or if it is only partly understood, a person will not give up or produce nonsensical behavior. By contrast, if a Classical rule-based computer program fails to recognize the task, or fails to match a pattern to its stored representations or rules, it usually will be unable to do anything at all. This suggests that in order to display graceful degradation, we must be able to represent prototypes, match patterns, recognize problems etc. in various *degrees*.

4 *Conventional models are dictated by current technical features of computers and take little or no account of the facts of neuroscience.* Classical symbol-processing systems provide no indication of how the kinds of processes that they postulate could be realized by a brain. The fact that this gap between high-level systems and brain architecture is so large might be an indication that these models are on the wrong track.

Whereas the architecture of the mind has evolved under the pressures of natural selection, some of the Classical assumptions about the mind may derive from features that computers have only because they are explicitly designed for the convenience of programmers. Perhaps this includes even the assumption that the description of mental processes at the cognitive level can be divorced from the description of their physical realization. At a minimum, by building our models to take account of what is known about neural structures we may reduce the risk of being misled by metaphors based on contemporary computer architectures.

5   Replies: Why the Usual Reasons Given for Preferring a Connectionist Architecture are Invalid

It seems to us that, as arguments against classical cognitive architecture, all these points suffer from one or other of the following two defects.

1 The objections depend on properties that are not in fact intrinsic to classical architectures, since there can be perfectly natural classical models that don't exhibit the objectionable features. (We believe this to be true, for example, of the arguments that Classical rules are explicit and Classical operations are 'all or none'.)

2 The objections are true to classical architectures in so far as they are implemented on current computers, but need not be true of such architectures when differently (e.g. neurally) implemented. They are, in other words, directed at the implementation level rather than the cognitive level, as these were distinguished in our earlier discussion. (We believe that this is true, for example, of the arguments about speed, resistance to damage and noise, and the passivity of memory.)

In the remainder of this section we will expand on these two points and relate them to some of the arguments presented above. Following this analysis, we will present what we believe may be the most tenable view of connectionism; namely, that it is a theory of how (classical) cognitive systems might be implemented, either in real brains or in some 'abstract neurology'.

5.1   Parallel computation and the issue of speed

Consider the argument that cognitive processes must involve large-scale parallel computation. In the form that it takes in typical connectionist discussions, this issue is irrelevant to the adequacy of classical *cognitive* architecture. The 'hundred step' constraint, for example, is clearly directed at the implementation level. All it rules out is the (absurd) hypothesis that cognitive architectures are implemented in the brain in the same way as they are implemented on electronic computers.

If you ever have doubts about whether a proposal pertains to the implementation level or the symbolic level, a useful heuristic is to ask yourself whether what is being claimed is true of a conventional computer – such as the DEC VAX – at *its* implementation level. Thus although most algorithms that run on the VAX are serial,[30] at the implementation level such computers are 'massively parallel'; they quite literally involve simultaneous electrical activity throughout almost the entire device. For example, every memory access cycle involves pulsing every bit in a significant fraction of the system's memory registers – since memory access is essentially a destructive read and rewrite process, the system clock regularly pulses and activates most of the central processing unit, and so on.

The moral is that the absolute speed of a process is a property *par excellence* of its implementation. (By contrast, the *relative* speed with which a system responds to different inputs is often diagnostic of distinct processes; but this has always been a prime empirical basis for deciding among alternative algorithms in information-processing psychology.) Thus, the fact that individual neurons require tens of milliseconds to fire can have no bearing on the predicted speed at which an algorithm will run *unless there is at least a partial, independently motivated, theory of how the operations of the functional architecture are implemented in neurons*. Since, in the case of the brain, it is not even certain that the firing[31] of neurons is invariably the relevant implementation property (at least for higher-level cognitive processes like learning and memory) the hundred step 'constraint' excludes nothing.

Finally, absolute constraints on the number of serial steps that a mental process can require, or on the time that can be required to execute them, provide weak arguments against classical architecture because classical architecture in no way excludes parallel execution of multiple symbolic processes. Indeed, it seems extremely likely that many Classical symbolic processes are going on in parallel in cognition, and that these processes interact with one another (e.g. they may be involved in some sort of symbolic constraint propagation). Operating on symbols can even involve 'massively parallel' organizations; that might indeed imply new architectures, but they are all *classical* in our sense, since they all share the Classical conception of computation as symbol-processing. (For examples of serious and interesting proposals on organizing classical processors into large parallel networks, see Hewett's, 1977, *Actor* system, Hillis', 1985, 'Connection Machine', as well as any of a number of recent commercial multi-processor machines.) The point here is that an argument for a network of parallel computers is not in and of itself either an argument against a classical architecture or an argument for a connectionist architecture.

5.2   Resistance to noise and physical damage (and the argument for distributed representation)

Some of the other advantages claimed for connectionist architectures over classical ones are just as clearly aimed at the implementation level. For example, the 'resistance to physical damage' criterion is so obviously a matter of implementation that it should hardly arise in discussions of cognitive-level theories.

It is true that a certain kind of damage resistance appears to be incompatible with localization, and it is also true that representations in PDPs are distributed over groups of units (at least when 'coarse coding' is used). But distribution over units achieves damage resistance only if it entails that representations are also *neurally* distributed.[32] However, neural distribution of representations is just as compatible with classical architectures as it is with connectionist networks. In the classical case all you need are memory registers that distribute their contents over physical space. You can get that with fancy storage systems like optical ones, or chemical ones, or even with registers made of connectionist nets. Come to think of it, we already had it in the old style 'ferrite core' memories!

The physical requirements of a Classical symbol-processing system are easily misunderstood. (Confounding of physical and functional properties is widespread in psychological theorizing in general; for a discussion of this confusion in relation to metrical properties in models of mental imagery, see Pylyshyn, 1981.) For example, conventional architecture requires that there be distinct symbolic expressions for each state of affairs that it can represent. Since such expressions often have a structure consisting of concatenated parts, the adjacency relation must be instantiated by *some* physical relation when the architecture is implemented (see the discussion in note 9). However, since the relation to be physically realized is *functional* adjacency, there is no necessity that physical instantiations of adjacent symbols be *spatially* adjacent. Similarly, although complex expressions are made out of atomic elements, and the distinction between atomic and complex symbols must somehow be physically instantiated, there is no necessity that a token of an atomic symbol be assigned a smaller region in space than a token of a complex symbol; even a token of a complex symbol of which it is a constituent. In Classical architectures, as in Connectionist networks, functional elements can be physically distributed or localized to any extent whatever. In a VAX (to use our heuristic again) pairs of symbols may certainly be functionally adjacent, but the symbol tokens are none the less spatially spread through many locations in physical memory.

In short, the fact that a property (like the position of a symbol within an expression) is functionally local has no implications one way or the other for damage-resistance or noise tolerance unless the functional-neighborhood metric corresponds to some appropriate *physical* dimension. When that is the case, we may be able to predict adverse consequences that varying the physical property has on objects localized in functional space (e.g. varying the voltage or line frequency might damage the left part of an expression). But, of course, the situation is exactly the same for connectionist systems: even when they are resistant to spatially local damage, they may not be resistant to damage that is local along some other physical dimensions. Since spatially local damage is particularly frequent in real world traumas, this may have important practical consequences. But so long as our knowledge of how cognitive processes might be mapped onto brain tissue remains very nearly non-existent, its message for cognitive science remains moot.

5.3   'Soft' constraints, continuous magnitudes, stochastic mechanisms and active symbols

The notion that 'soft' constraints which can vary continuously (as degree of activation does) are incompatible with Classical rule-based symbolic systems is another example of the failure to keep the psychological (or symbol-processing) and the implementation levels separate. One can have a Classical rule system in which the decision concerning which rule will fire resides in the functional architecture and depends on continuously varying magnitudes. Indeed, this is typically how it is done in practical 'expert systems' which, for example, use a Bayesian mechanism in their production-system rule interpreter. The soft or stochastic nature of rule-based processes arises from the interaction of deterministic rules with real-valued properties of the implementation, or with noisy inputs or noisy information transmission.

It should also be noted that rule applications need not issue in 'all-or-none' behaviors since several rules may be activated at once and can have interactive effects on the outcome. Or, alternatively, each of the activated rules can generate independent parallel effects, which might get sorted out later – depending say, on which of the parallel streams reaches a goal first. An important, though sometimes neglected, point about such aggregate properties of overt behavior as continuity, 'fuzziness', randomness etc. is that they need not arise from underlying mechanisms that are themselves fuzzy, continuous or random. It is not only possible in principle, but often quite reasonable in practice, to assume that apparently variable or non-deterministic behavior arises from the interaction of multiple deterministic sources.

A similar point can be made about the issue of 'graceful degradation', classical architecture does not require that when the conditions for applying the available rules aren't precisely met, the process should simply fail to do anything at all. As noted above, rules could be activated in some measure depending upon how close their conditions are to holding. Exactly what happens in these cases may depend on how the rule system is implemented. On the other hand, it could be that the failure to display 'graceful degradation' really is an intrinsic limit of the current class of models or even of current approaches to designing intelligent systems. It seems clear that the psychological models now available are inadequate over a broad spectrum of measures, so their problems with graceful degradation may be a special case of their general unintelligence: they may simply not be smart enough to know what to do when a limited stock of methods fails to apply. But this needn't be a principled limitation of classical architectures. There is, to our knowledge, no reason to believe that something like Newell's (1969) 'hierarchy of weak methods' or Laird et al. (1986) 'universal subgoaling', is in principle incapable of dealing with the problem of graceful degradation. (Nor, to our knowledge, has any argument yet been offered that connectionist architectures are in principle capable of dealing with it. In fact, current connectionist models are every bit as graceless in their modes of failure as ones based on classical architectures. For example, contrary to some claims, models such as that of McClelland

and Kawamoto, 1986, fail quite unnaturally when given incomplete information.)

In short, the Classical theorist can view stochastic properties of behavior as emerging from interactions between the model and the intrinsic properties of the physical medium in which it is realized. It is essential to remember that, from the Classical point of view, overt behaviour is *par excellence* an interaction effect, and symbol manipulations are supposed to be only one of the interacting causes.

These same considerations apply to Kosslyn and Hatfield's (1984) remarks (quoted earlier) about the commitment of Classical models to 'passive' versus 'active' representations. It is true, as Kosslyn and Hatfield say, that the representations that von Neumann machines manipulate 'don't *do* anything until a CPU operates upon them (they don't decay, for example). But, even on the absurd assumption that the mind has *exactly* the architecture of some contemporary (von Neumann) computer, it is obvious that its behavior, and hence the behavior of an organism, is determined not just by the logical machine that the mind instantiates, but also by the protoplasmic machine in which the logic is realized. Instantiated representations *are* therefore bound to be active, even according to classical models; the question is whether the kind of activity they exhibit should be accounted for by the cognitive model or by the theory of its implementation. This question is empirical and must not be begged on behalf of the Connectionist view. (As it is, for example, in such passages as:

> The brain itself does not manipulate symbols; the brain is the medium in which the symbols are floating and in which they trigger each other. There is no central manipulator, no central program. There is simply a vast collection of 'teams' – patterns of neural firings that, like teams of ants, trigger other patterns of neutral firings . . . . We feel those symbols churning within ourselves in somewhat the same way we feel our stomach churning. (Hofstadter, 1983, p. 279)

This appears to be a serious case of *Formicidae in machina*: ants in the stomach of the ghost in the machine.)

5.4 Explicitness of rules

According to McClelland et al. (1986a, p. 6),

> connectionist models are leading to a reconceptualization of key psychological issues, such as the nature of the representation of

knowledge . . . One traditional approach to such issues treats knowledge as a body of rules that are consulted by processing mechanisms in the course of processing; in connectionist models, such knowledge is represented, often in widely distributed form, in the connections among the processing units.

As we remarked in the introduction, we think that the claim that most psychological processes are rule implicit, and the corresponding claim that divergent and compliant behaviors result from the same cognitive mechanisms, are both interesting and tendentious. We regard these matters as entirely empirical and, in many cases, open. In any case, however, one should not confuse the rule-implicit/rule-explicit distinction with the distinction between classical and connectionist architecture.[33]

This confusion is just ubiquitous in the connectionist literature: it is universally assumed by connectionists that classical models are committed to claiming that regular behaviors must arise from explicitly encoded rules. But this is simply untrue. Not only is there no reason why classical models are required to be rule explicit but – as a matter of fact – arguments over which, if any, rules are explicitly mentally represented have raged for decades *within* the classicist camp. (See, for examples, the discussion of the explicitness of grammatical rules in Stabler, 1985, and replies; for a philosophical discussion, see Cummins, 1983.) The one thing that classical theorists do agree about is that it *can't* be that *all* behavioral regularities are determined by explicit rules; at least some of the causal determinants of compliant behavior *must* be *im*plicit. (The arguments for this parallel Lewis Carroll's observations in 'What the Tortoise Said to Achilles'; see Carroll, 1956.) All other questions of the explicitness of rules are viewed by classicists as moot; and every shade of opinion on the issue can be found in the classicist camp.

The basic point is this: not all the functions of a classical computer can be encoded in the form of an explicit program; some of them must be wired in. In fact, the entire program can be hard-wired in cases where it does not need to modify or otherwise examine itself. In such cases, classical machines can be *rule implicit* with respect to their programs, and the mechanism of their state transitions is entirely sub-computational (i.e. sub-symbolic).

What *does* need to be explicit in a classical machine is not its program but the symbols that it writes on its tapes (or stores in its registers). These, however, correspond not to the machine's rules of state transition but to its data structures. Data structures are *the objects that the machine transforms, not the rules of transformation*. In the case of programs that parse natural language, for example, classical architecture requires the explicit representation of the structural descriptions of sentences, but is entirely neutral on the explicitness of grammars, contrary to what many connectionists believe.

One of the important inventions in the history of computers – the stored-program computer – makes it *possible* for programs to take on the role of data structures. But nothing in the architecture *requires* that they always do so. Similarly, Turing demonstrated that there exists an abstract machine (the so-called universal Turing machine) which can simulate the behavior of any target (Turing) machine. A universal machine is 'rule explicit' about the machine it is simulating (in the sense that it has an explicit representation of that machine which is sufficient to specify its behavior uniquely). Yet the target machine can perfectly well be 'rule implicit' with respect to the rules that govern *its* behavior.

So, then, you can't attack Classical theories of cognitive architecture by showing that a cognitive process is rule implicit; classical architecture *permits* rule-explicit processes but does *not* require them. However, you *can* attack connectionist architectures by showing that a cognitive process is rule *explicit* since, by definition, connectionist architecture precludes the sorts of logico-syntactic capacities that are required to encode rules and the sorts of executive mechanisms that are required to apply them.[34]

If, therefore, there should prove to be persuasive arguments for rule-explicit cognitive processes, that would be very embarrassing for connectionists. A natural place to look for such arguments would be in the theory of the acquisition of cognitive competences. For example, much traditional work in linguistics (see Prince and Pinker, 1988), and all recent work in mathematical learning theory (see Osherson et al., 1984), assumes that the characteristic output of a cognitive acquisition device is a recursive rule system (a grammar, in the linguistic case). Suppose such theories prove to be well founded; then that would be incompatible with the assumption that the cognitive architecture of the capacities acquired is connectionist.

5.5   On 'brain style' modeling

The relation of connectionist models to neuroscience is open to many interpretations. On the one hand, people like Ballard (1986) and Sejnowski (1981) are explicitly attempting to build models based on properties of neurons and neural organizations, even though the neuronal units in question are idealized (some would say more than a little idealized: see, for example the commentaries following Ballard, 1986). On the other hand, Smolensky (chapter 2) views connectionist units as mathematical objects which can be given an interpretation in either neural or psychological terms. Most connectionists find themselves somewhere in between, frequently referring to their approach as 'brain-style' theorizing.[35]

Understanding both psychological principles *and* the way that they are neurophysiologically implemented is much better (and, indeed, more empirically secure) than only understanding one or the other. That is not at issue. The question is whether there is anything to be gained by designing 'brain style' models that are uncommitted about how the models map onto brains.

Presumably the point of 'brain style' modeling is that theories of cognitive processing should be influenced by the facts of biology (especially neuroscience). The biological facts that influence connectionist models appear to include the following: neuronal connections are important to the patterns of brain activity; the memory 'engram' does not appear to be spatially local; to a first approximation, neurons appear to be threshold elements which sum the activity arriving at their dendrites; many of the neurons in the cortex have multi-dimensional 'receptive fields' that are sensitive to a narrow range of values of a number of parameters; the tendency for activity at a synapse to cause a neuron to 'fire' is modulated by the frequency and recency of past firings.

Let us suppose that these and similar claims are both true and relevant to the way the brain functions – an assumption that is by no means unproblematic. The question we might then ask is: what follows from such facts that is relevant to inferring the nature of the cognitive architecture? The unavoidable answer appears to be, very little. That's not an *a priori* claim. The degree of relationship between facts at different levels of organization of a system is an empirical matter. However, there is reason to be skeptical about whether the sorts of properties listed above are reflected in any more-or-less direct way in the structure of the system that carries out reasoning.

Consider, for example, one of the most salient properties of neural systems: they are networks which transmit activation culminating in state changes of some quasi-threshold elements. Surely it is not warranted to conclude that reasoning consists of the spread of excitation among representations, or even among semantic components of representations. After all, a VAX is also correctly characterized as consisting of a network over which excitation is transmitted culminating in state changes of quasi-threshold elements. Yet at the level at which it processes representations, a VAX is *literally* organized as a von Neumann architecture.

The point is that the structure of 'higher levels' of a system are rarely isomorphic, or even similar, to the structure of 'lower levels' of a system.

No one expects the theory of protons to look very much like the theory of rocks and rivers, even though, to be sure, it is protons and the like that rocks and rivers are 'implemented in'. Lucretius got into trouble precisely by assuming that there must be a simple correspondence between the structure of macro-level and micro-level theories. He thought, for example, that hooks and eyes hold the atoms together. He was wrong, as it turns out.

There are, no doubt, cases where special empirical considerations suggest detailed structure/function correspondences or other analogies between different levels of a system's organization. For example, the input to the most peripheral stages of vision and motor control *must* be specified in terms of anatomically projected patterns (of light, in one case, and of muscular activity in the other); and independence of structure and function is perhaps less likely in a system whose input or output must be specified somatotopically. Thus, at these stages it is reasonable to expect an anatomically distributed structure to be reflected by a distributed functional architecture. When, however, the cognitive process under investigation is as abstract as reasoning, there is simply no reason to expect isomorphisms between structure and function; as, indeed, the computer case proves.

Perhaps this is all too obvious to be worth saying. Yet it seems that the commitment to 'brain style' modeling leads to many of the characteristic connectionist claims about psychology, and that it does so via the implicit – and unwarranted – assumption that there ought to be similarity of structure among the different levels of organization of a computational system. This is distressing since much of the psychology that this search for structural analogies has produced is strikingly recidivist. Thus the idea that the brain is a neural network motivates the revival of a largely discredited associationist psychology. Similarly, the idea that brain activity is anatomically distributed leads to functionally distributed representations for concepts which in turn leads to the postulation of micro-features; yet the inadequacies of feature-based theories of concepts are well known and, to our knowledge, micro-feature theory has done nothing to address them (see Bolinger, 1965; J.D. Fodor, 1977). Or again, the idea that the strength of a connection between neurons is affected by the frequency of their co-activation gets projected onto the cognitive level. The consequence is a resurgence of statistical models of learning that had been widely acknowledged (both in psychology and in AI) to be extremely limited in their applicability (e.g. Chomsky, 1957; Minsky and Papert, 1972).

So although, *in principle*, knowledge of how the brain works could direct cognitive modeling in a beneficial manner, *in fact* a research strategy has to be judged by its fruits. The main fruit of 'brain style-modeling' has been to revive psychological theories whose limitations had previously been pretty widely appreciated. It has done so largely because assumptions about the structure of the brain have been adopted in an all-too-direct manner as hypotheses about cognitive architecture; it's an instructive paradox that the current attempt to be thoroughly modern and 'take the brain seriously' should lead to a psychology not readily distinguishable from the worst of Hume and Berkeley. The moral seems to be that one should be deeply suspicious of the heroic sort of brain modeling that purports to address the problems of cognition. We sympathize with the craving for biologically respectable theories that many psychologists seem to feel. But, given a choice, truth is more important than respectability.

5.6   Concluding comments: connectionism as a theory of implementation

A recurring theme in the previous discussion is that many of the arguments for connectionism are best construed as claiming that cognitive architecture is *implemented* in a certain kind of network (of abstract 'units'). Understood this way, these arguments are neutral on the question of what the cognitive architecture is.[36] In these concluding remarks, we will briefly consider connectionism from this point of view.

Almost every student who enters a course on computational or information-processing models of cognition must be disabused of a very general misunderstanding concerning the role of the physical computer in such models. Students are almost always skeptical about 'the computer as a model of cognition' on such grounds as 'computers don't forget or make mistakes', 'computers function by exhaustive search', 'computers are too logical and unmotivated', 'computers can't learn by themselves; they can only do what they're told', or 'computers are too fast (or too slow)', or 'computers never get tired or bored' and so on. If we add to this list such relatively more sophisticated complaints as that 'computers don't exhibit graceful degradation' or 'computers are too sensitive to physical damage' this list will begin to look much like the arguments put forward by connectionists.

The answer to all these complaints has always been that the *implementation*, and all properties associated with the particular realization of the algorithm that the theorist happens to use in a particular case, is irrelevant to the psychological theory; only the algorithm and the representations on which it operates are intended as a psychological hypothesis. Students are taught the notion of a 'virtual machine' and shown that *some* virtual machines *can* learn, forget, get bored, make mistakes and whatever else one likes, providing one has a theory of the origins of each of the empirical phenomena in question.

Given this principled distinction between a model and its implementation, a theorist who is impressed by the virtues of connectionism has the option of proposing PDPs as theories of implementation. But then, far from providing a revolutionary new basis for cognitive science, these models are in principle neutral about the nature of cognitive processes. In fact, they might be viewed as advancing the goals of Classical information-processing psychology by attempting to explain how the brain (or perhaps some idealized brain-like network) might realize the types of processes that conventional cognitive science has hypothesized.

Connectionists do sometimes explicitly take their models to be theories of implementation. Ballard (1986) even refers to connectionism as 'the implementational approach'. Touretzky (1986) clearly views his BoltzCONS model this way; he uses connectionist techniques to implement conventional symbol-processing mechanisms such as push-down stacks and other LISP facilities.[37]

Rumelhart and McClelland (1986b, p. 117), who are convinced that connectionism signals a radical departure from the conventional symbol-processing approach, none the less refer to 'PDP implementations' of various mechanisms such as attention. Later in the same essay, they make their position explicit: unlike 'reductionists', they believe 'that new and useful concepts emerge at different levels of organization' (1986b, p. 128). Although they then defend the claim that one should understand the higher levels 'through the study of the interactions among lower level units', the basic idea that there *are* autonomous levels seems implicit everywhere in the essay.

But once one admits that there really are cognitive-level principles distinct from the (putative) architectural principles that connectionism articulates, there seems to be little left to argue about. Clearly it is pointless to ask whether one should or shouldn't do cognitive science by studying 'the interaction of lower levels' as opposed to studying processes at the cognitive level since we surely have to do *both*. Some scientists study geological principles, others study 'the interaction of lower level units' like molecules. But since the fact that there are genuine, autonomously stateable principles of geology is never in dispute, people who build molecular level models do not claim to have invented a 'new theory of geology' that will dispense with all that old fashioned 'folk geological' talk about rocks, rivers and mountains!

We have, in short, no objection at all to networks as potential implementation models, nor do we suppose that any of the arguments we've given are incompatible with this proposal. The trouble is, however, that if connectionists do want their models to be construed this way, then they will have to radically alter their practice. For, it seems utterly clear that most of the connectionist models that have actually been proposed must be construed as theories of cognition, not as theories of implementation. This follows from the fact that it is intrinsic to these theories to ascribe representational content to the units (and/or aggregates) that they postulate. And, as we remarked at the beginning, a theory of the relations among representational states is *ipso facto* a theory at the level of cognition, not at the level of implementation. It has been the burden of our argument that when construed as a cognitive theory, rather than as an implementation theory, connectionism appears to have fatal limitations. The problem with connectionist models is that all the reasons for thinking that they might be true are reasons for thinking that they couldn't be *psychology*.

6   Conclusions

What, in light of all of this, are the options for the further development of connectionist theories? As far as we can see, there are four routes that they could follow. First, they could hold out for unstructured mental representations as against the Classical view that mental representations have a combinational syntax and semantics. Productivity and systematicity arguments make this option appear not attractive.

Secondly, they could abandon network architecture to the extent of opting for structured mental *representations* but continue to insist upon an associationistic account of the nature of mental *processes*. This is, in effect, a retreat to Hume's picture of the mind (see note 29), and it has a problem that we don't believe can be solved. Although mental representations are, on the present assumption, structured objects, *association is not a structure sensitive relation*. The problem is thus how to reconstruct the semantical coherence of thought without postulating psychological processes that are sensitive to the structure of mental representations. (Equivalently, in more modern terms, it's how to get the causal relations among mental representations to mirror their semantical relations without assuming a proof-theoretic treatment of inference and – more generally – a treatment of semantic coherence that is syntactically expressed, in the spirit of proof-theory.) This is the problem on which traditional associationism foundered, and the prospects for solving it now strike us as not appreciably better than they were a couple of hundred years ago. To put it a little differently: if you need structure in mental representations anyway to account for the productivity and systematicity of minds, why not postulate mental processes that are structure sensitive to account for the coherence of mental processes? Why not be a Classicist, in short? In any event, notice that the present option gives the Classical picture a lot of what it wants: viz. the identification of semantic states with relations to structured arrays of symbols and the identification of mental processes with transformations of such arrays. Notice too that, as things now stand, this proposal is Utopian since there are no serious proposals for incorporating syntactic structure in connectionist architectures.

Thirdly, there is the route that treats connectionism as an implementation theory. We have no principled objection to this view (though there are, as connectionists are discovering, technical reasons why networks are often an awkward way to implement classical machines). This option would entail rewriting quite a lot of the polemical material in the connectionist literature, as well as redescribing what the networks are doing as operating on symbol structures, rather than spreading activation among semantically interpreted nodes. Moreover, this revision of policy is sure to lose the movement a lot of fans. As we have pointed out, many people have been attracted to the connectionist approach because of its promise to (a) do away with the symbol level of analysis, and (b) elevate neuroscience to the position of providing evidence that bears directly on issues of cognition. If connectionism is considered simply as a theory of how cognition is neurally implemented, it may constrain cognitive models no more than theories in biophysics, biochemistry or, for that matter, quantum mechanics do. All of these theories are also concerned with processes that *implement* cognition, and all of them are likely to postulate structures that are quite different from cognitive architecture. The point is that 'implements' is transitive, and it goes all the way down.

Fourthly, connectionists could give up on the idea that networks offer (to quote Rumelhart and McClelland, 1986b, p. 110) 'a reasonable basis for modeling cognitive processes in general'. It could still be held that networks sustain *some* cognitive processes. A good bet might be that they sustain such processes as can be analyzed as the drawing of statistical inferences; as far as we can tell, what network models really are is just analog machines for computing such inferences. Since we doubt that much of cognitive processing does consist of analyzing statistical relations, this would be quite a modest estimate of the prospects for network theory compared to what the connectionists themselves have been offering.

This is, for example, one way of understanding what's going on in the argument between Rumelhart and McClelland (1986a) and Prince and

Pinker (1988), though neither paper puts it in quite these terms. In effect, Rumelhart and McClelland postulate a mechanism which, given a corpus of pairings that a 'teacher' provides as data, computes the statistical correlation between the phonological form of the ending of a verb and the phonological form of its past tense inflection. (The magnitude of the correlations so computed is analogically represented by the weights that the network exhibits at asymptote.) Given the problem of inflecting a new verb stem ending in a specified phonological sequence, the machine chooses the form of the past tense that was most highly correlated with that sequence in the training set. By contrast, Prince and Pinker (1988) argue (in effect) that more must be going on in learning past tense morphology than merely estimating correlations since the statistical hypothesis provides neither a close fit to the ontogenetic data nor a plausible account of the adult competence on which the ontogenetic processes converge. It seems to us that Pinker and Prince have, by quite a lot, the best of this argument.

There is an alternative to the empiricist idea that all learning consists of a kind of statistical inference, realized by adjusting parameters; it's the rationalist idea that some learning is a kind of theory construction, effected by framing hypotheses and evaluating them against evidence. We seem to remember having been through this argument before. We find ourselves with a gnawing sense of *déjà vu*.

Acknowledgments

We wish to thank the Alfred P. Sloan Foundation for their generous support of this research. The preparation of this chapter was also aided by a Killam Research Fellowship and a Senior Fellowship from the Canadian Institute for Advanced Research to ZWP. We also gratefully acknowledge comments and criticisms of earlier drafts by: Professors Noam Chomsky, William Demopoulos, Lila Gleitman, Russ Greiner, Norbert Hornstein, Keith Humphrey, Sandy Pentland, Steven Pinker, David Rosenthal and Edward Stabler.

Notes

1   The difference between connectionist networks in which the state of a single unit encodes properties of the world (i.e. the so-called 'localist' networks) and ones in which the pattern of states of an entire population of units does the encoding (the so-called 'distributed' representation networks) is considered to be important by many people working on connectionists models. Although connectionists debate the relative merits of localist (or 'compact') versus distributed representations (e.g. Feldman,

1986), the distinction will usually be of little consequence for our purposes, for reasons that we give later. For simplicity, when we wish to refer indifferently to either single unit codes or aggregate distributed codes, we shall refer to the 'nodes' in a network. When the distinction is relevant to our discussion, however, we shall explicitly mark the difference by referring either to units or to aggregate of units.

2 One of the attractions of connectionism for many people is that it does employ some heavy mathematical machinery, as can be seen from a glance at many of the chapters of the two-volume collection by Rumelhart, McClelland and the PDP Research Group (1986). But in contrast to many other mathematically sophisticated areas of cognitive science, such as automata theory or parts of Artificial Intelligence (particularly the study of search or of reasoning and knowledge representation), the mathematics has not been used to map out the limits of what the proposed class of mechanisms can do. Like a great deal of Artificial Intelligence research, the connectionist approach remains almost entirely experimental; mechanisms that look interesting are proposed and explored by implementing them on computers and subjecting them to empirical trials to see what they will do. As a consequence, although there is a great deal of mathematical work within the tradition, one has very little idea what various connectionist networks and mechanisms are good for in general.

3 Smolensky seems to think that the idea of postulating a level of representations with a semantics of sub-conceptual features is unique to network theories. This is an extraordinary view considering the extent to which *Classical* theorists have been concerned with feature analyses in every area of psychology from phonetics to visual perception to lexicography. In fact, the question whether there are 'sub-conceptual' features is *neutral* with respect to the question whether cognitive architecture is classical or connectionist.

4 Sometimes, however, even representationalists fail to appreciate that it is *representation* that distinguishes cognitive from non-cognitive levels. Thus, for example, although Smolensky (chapter 2) is clearly a representationalist, his official answer to the question 'What distinguishes those dynamical systems that are cognitive from those that are not?' makes the mistake of appealing to complexity rather than intentionality: 'A river . . . fails to be a cognitive dynamical system only because it cannot satisfy a *large* range of goals under a *large* range of conditions.' But, of course, that depends on how you individuate goals and conditions; the river that wants to get to the sea wants first to get half-way to the sea, and then to get half-way more, . . ., and so on; quite a lot of goals all told. The real point, of course, is that states that represent goals play a role in the etiology of the behaviors of people but not in the etiology of the 'behavior' of rivers.

5 That classical architectures can be implemented in networks is not disputed by connectionists; see for example Rumelhart and McClelland (1986b, p. 118): 'one can make an arbitrary computational machine out of linear threshold units, including, for example, a machine that can carry out

all the operations necessary for implementing a Turing machine; the one limitation is that real biological systems cannot be Turing machines because they have finite hardware.'

6   There is a different idea, frequently encountered in the connectionist literature, that this one is easily confused with: viz., that the distinction between regularities and exceptions is merely stochastic (what makes 'went' an irregular past tense is just that the *more frequent* construction is the one exhibited by 'walked'). It seems obvious that if this claim is correct it can be readily assimilated to Classical architecture (see section 4).

7   This way of putting it will do for present purposes. But a subtler reading of connectionist theories might take it to be total machine *states* that have content, e.g. the state of *having such and such a node excited*. Postulating connections among labeled nodes would then be equivalent to postulating causal relations among the corresponding content-bearing machine states: to say that the excitation of the node labelled 'dog' is caused by the excitation of nodes labelled [d], [o], [g] is to say that the machine's representing its input as consisting of the phonetic sequence [dog] causes it to represent its input as consisting of the word 'dog'. And so forth. Most of the time the distinction between these two ways of talking does not matter for our purposes, so we shall adopt one or the other as convenient.

8   Sometimes the difference between simply postulating representational states and postulating representations with a combinatorial syntax and semantics is marked by distinguishing theories that postulate *symbols* from theories that postulate *symbol systems*. The latter theories, but not the former, are committed to a 'language of thought'. For this usage, see Kosslyn and Hatfield (1984) who take the refusal to postulate symbol systems to be the characteristic respect in which connectionist architectures differ from classical architectures. We agree with this diagnosis.

9   Perhaps the notion that relations among physical properties of the brain instantiate (or encode) the *combinatorial structure* of an expression bears some elaboration. One way to understand what is involved is to consider the conditions that must hold on a mapping (which we refer to as the 'physical instantiation mapping') from expressions to brain states if the causal relations among brain states are to depend on the combinatorial structure of the encoded expressions. In defining this mapping it is not enough merely to specify a physical encoding for each symbol; in order for the *structures* of expressions to have causal roles, structural relations must be encoded by physical properties of brain states (or by sets of functionally equivalent physical properties of brain states).

Because, in general, classical models assume that the expressions that get physically instantiated in brains have a generative syntax, the definition of an appropriate physical instantiation mapping has to be built up in terms of (a) the definition of a primitive mapping from atomic symbols to relatively elementary physical states, and (b) a specification of how the structure of complex expressions maps onto the structure of relatively complex or composite physical states. Such a structure-preserving mapping is typically given recursively, making use of the combinatorial syntax by which complex expressions are built up out of simpler ones. For example, the physical instantiation mapping F for complex expressions would be defined by recursion, given the definition of F for *atomic* symbols and given the *structure* of the complex expression, the latter being specified in terms of the 'structure building' rules which constitute the generative syntax for complex expressions. Take, for example, the expression '(A&B)&C'. A suitable definition for a mapping in this case might contain the statement that for any expressions P and Q, $F[P\&Q] = B(F[P].F[Q])$, where the function B specifies the physical relation that holds between physical states $F[P]$ and $F[Q]$. Here the property B serves to physically encode (or 'instantiate') the relation that holds between the expressions P and Q, on the one hand, and the expression $P\&Q$ on the other.

In using this rule for the example above P and Q would have the values 'A&B' and 'C' respectively, so that the mapping rule would have to be applied twice to pick the relevant physical structures. In defining the mapping recursively in this way we ensure that the relation between the expressions 'A' and 'B', and the composite expression 'A&B', is encoded in terms of a physical relation between constituent states that is identical (or functionally equivalent) to the physical relation used to encode the relation between expressions 'A&B' and 'C', and their composite expression '(A&B)&C'. This type of mapping is well known because of its use in Tarski's definition of an interpretation of a language in a model. The idea of a mapping from symbolic expressions to a structure of physical states is discussed in Pylyshyn (1984a, pp. 54–69), where it is referred to as an 'instantiation function' and in Stabler (1985), where it is called a 'realization mapping'.

10   This illustration has not any particular connectionist model in mind, though the caricature presented is, in fact, a simplified version of the Ballard (1987) connectionist theorem proving system (which actually uses a more restricted proof procedure based on the *unification* of Horn clauses). To simplify the exposition, we assume a 'localist' approach, in which each semantically interpreted node corresponds to a single connectionist unit: but nothing relevant to this discussion is changed if these nodes actually consist of patterns over a cluster of units.

11   This makes the 'compositionality' of data structures a defining property of classical architecture. But, of course, it leaves open the question of the degree to which *natural* languages (like English) are also compositional.

12   Labels aren't part of the *causal structure* of a connectionist machine, but they may play an essential role in its *causal history* in so far as designers wire their machines to respect the semantical relations that the labels express. For example, in Ballard's (1987) connectionist model of theorem proving, there is a mechanical procedure for wiring a network which will carry out proofs by unification. This procedure is a function from a set of node labels to a wired-up machine. There is thus an interesting and revealing respect in which node labels are relevant to the operations that

get performed when the function is executed. But, of course, the machine on which the labels have the effect is not the machine whose states they are labels of; and the effect of the labels occurs at the time that the theorem-proving machine is constructed, not at the time its reasoning process is carried out. *This* sort of case of labels 'having effects' is thus quite different from the way that symbol tokens (e.g. tokened data structures) can affect the causal processes of a classical machine.

13   Any relation specified as holding among representational states is, by definition, within the 'cognitive level'. It goes without saying that relations that are 'within-level' by this criterion can count as 'between-level' when we use criteria of finer grain. There is, for example, nothing to prevent hierarchies of levels of representational states.

14   Smolensky (chapter 2, p. 45) remarks that 'Unlike symbolic tokens, these vectors lie in a topological space in which some are close together and others are far apart.' However, this seems to radically conflate claims about the connectionist model and claims about its implementation (a conflation that is not unusual in the connectionist literature as we'll see in section 4). If the space at issue is *physical*, then Smolensky is committed to extremely strong claims about adjacency relations in the brain; claims which there is, in fact, no reason at all to believe. But if, as seems more plausible, the space at issue is *semantical* then what Smolensky says isn't true. Practically any cognitive theory will imply distance measures between mental representations. In Classical theories, for example, the distance between two representations is plausibly related to the number of computational steps it takes to derive one representation from the other. In Connectionist theories, it is plausibly related to the number of intervening nodes (or to the degree of overlap between vectors, depending on the version of connectionism one has in mind). The interesting claim is not that an architecture offers *a* distance measure but that it offers the *right* distance measure – one that is empirically certifiable.

15   The primary use that connectionists make of micro-features is in their accounts of generalization and abstraction (see, for example, Hinton, et al. 1986). Roughly, you get generalization by using overlap of micro-features to define a similarity space, and you get abstraction by making the vectors that correspond to *types* be sub-vectors of the ones that correspond to their *tokens*. Similar proposals have quite a long history in traditional empiricist analysis; and have been roundly criticized over the centuries. (For a discussion of abstractionism, see Geach, 1957; that similarity is a primitive relation – hence not reducible to partial identity of feature sets – was, of course, a main tenet of Gestalt psychology, as well as more recent approaches based on 'prototypes'). The treatment of micro-features in the connectionist literature would appear to be very close to early proposals by Katz and Fodor (1963) and Katz and Postal (1964), where both the idea of a feature analysis of concepts and the idea that relations of semantical containment among concepts should be identified with set-theoretic relations among feature arrays are explicitly endorsed.

16   Another disadvantage is that, strictly speaking, it doesn't work; although it allows us to distinguish the belief that John loves Mary and Bill hates Sally from the belief that John loves Sally and Bill hates Mary, we don't yet have a way to distinguish believing that (John loves Mary because Bill hates Sally) from believing that (Bill hates Sally because John loves Mary). Presumably nobody would want to have micro-features corresponding to these.

17   It's especially important at this point not to make the mistake of confusing diagrams of connectionist networks with constituent structure diagrams (see section 2.1.2 above). Connecting SUBJECT OF with FIDO and BITES does not mean that when all three are active FIDO is the subject of BITES. A network diagram is not a specification of the internal structure of a complex mental representation. Rather, it's a specification of a pattern of causal dependencies among the states of activation of nodes. Connectivity in a network determines which sets of simultaneously active nodes are possible; but it has no *semantical* significance.

The difference between the paths between nodes that network diagrams exhibit and the paths between nodes that constituent structure diagrams exhibit is precisely that the latter but not the former specify parameters of mental representations. (In particular, they specify part/whole relations among the constituents of complex symbols.) Whereas network theories define semantic interpretations over sets of (causally interconnected) representations of concepts, theories that acknowledge complex symbols define semantic interpretations over sets of representations of concepts *together with specifications of the constituency relations that hold among these representations.*

18   And it doesn't work uniformly for English conjunction. Compare: *John and Mary are friends* → **John are friends*; or *The flag is red, white and blue* → *The flag is blue.* Such cases show either that English is not the language of thought, or that, if it is, the relation between syntax and semantics is a good deal subtler for the language of thought than it is for the standard logical languages.

19   It needn't, however, be strict truth-preservation that makes the syntactic approach relevant to cognition. Other semantic properties might be preserved under syntactic transformation in the course of mental processing, e.g. warrant, plausibility, heuristic value, or simply *semantic non-arbitrariness*. The point of Classical modeling isn't to characterize human thought as supremely logical; rather, it's to show how a family of types of semantically coherent (or knowledge-dependent) reasoning are mechanically possible. Valid inference is the paradigm only in that it is the best understood member of this family; the one for which syntactical analogues for semantical relations have been most systematically elaborated.

20   It is not uncommon for connectionists to make disparaging remarks about the relevance of logic to psychology, even thought they accept the idea that inference is involved in reasoning. Sometimes the suggestion seems to be

that it's all right if connectionism can't reconstruct the theory of inference that formal deductive logic provides since it has something even better on offer. For example, in their report to the US National Science Foundation, McClelland et al. (1986a) state that 'connectionist models realize an evidential logic *in contrast to* the symbolic logic of conventional computing' (p. 6; our emphasis) and that 'evidential logics are becoming increasingly important in cognitive science and have a natural map to connectionist modeling' (p. 7). It is, however, hard to understand the implied contrast since, on the one hand, evidential logic must surely be a fairly conservative extension of 'the symbolic logic of conventional computing' (i.e. most of the theorems of the latter have to come out true in the former) and, on the other, there is not the slightest reason to doubt that an evidential logic would 'run' on a Classical machine. Prima facie, the problem about evidential logic isn't that we've got one that we don't know how to implement; it's that we haven't got one.

21   Compare the 'little s's' and 'little r's' of neo-Hullean 'mediational' Asociationists like Charles Osgood.

22   This way of putting the productivity argument is most closely identified with Chomsky (1965, 1968). However, one does not have to rest the argument upon a basic assumption of infinite generative capacity. Infinite generative capacity can be viewed, instead, as a consequence or a corollary of theories formulated so as to capture the greatest number of generalizations with the fewest independent principles. This more neutral approach is, in fact, very much in the spirit of what we shall propose below. We are putting it in the present form for expository and historical reasons.

23   McClelland and Kawamoto (1986) discuss this sort of recursion briefly. Their suggestion seems to be that parsing such sentences doesn't really require recovering their recursive structure: 'the job of the parser [with respect to right-recursive sentences] is to spit out phrases in a way that captures their *local* context. Such a representation may prove sufficient to allow us to reconstruct the correct bindings of noun phrases to verbs and prepositional phrases to *nearby* nouns and verbs' (p. 324; emphasis ours). It is, however, by no means the case that all of the semantically relevant grammatical relations in readily intelligible embedded sentences are local in surface structure. Consider: '*Where* did the man who owns the cat that chased the rat that frightened the girl say that he was going to move to (X)?' or '*What* did the girl that the children loved to listen to promise your friends that she would read (X) to them?' Notice that, in such examples, a binding element (italicized) can be arbitrarily displaced from the position whose interpretation it controls (marked 'X') without making the sentence particularly difficult to understand. Notice too that the 'semantics' doesn't determine the binding relations in either example.

24   See Pinker (1984, ch. 4) for evidence that children never go through a stage in which they distinguish between the internal structures of NPs depending on whether they are in subject or object position; i.e. the

dialects that children speak are always systematic with respect to the syntactic structures that can appear in these positions.

25   It may be worth emphasizing that the structural complexity of a mental representation is not the same thing as, and does *not* follow from, the structural complexity of its propositional content (i.e. of what we're calling 'the thought that one has'). Thus, connectionists and classicists can agree to agree that *the thought that P&Q* is complex (and has the thought that *P* among its parts), while agreeing to disagree about whether mental representations have internal syntactic structure.

26   These considerations throw further light on a proposal we discussed in section 2. Suppose that the mental representation corresponding to the thought that John loves the girl is the feature vector {+*John-subject*; +*loves*; +*the-girl-object*} where '*John-subject*' and '*the-girl-object*' are atomic features; as such, they bear no more structural relation to '*John-object*' and '*the-girl-subject*' than they do to one another or to, say, '*has-a-handle*'. Since this theory recognizes no structural relation between '*John-subject*' and '*John-object*', it offers no reason why a representational system that provides the means to express one of these concepts should also provide the means to express the other. This treatment of role relations thus makes a mystery of the (presumed) fact that anybody who can entertain the thought that John loves the girl can also entertain the thought that the girl loves John (and, *mutatis mutandis*, that any natural language that can express the proposition that John loves the girl can also express the proposition that the girl loves John). This consequence of the proposal that role relations be handled by 'role specific descriptors that represent the conjunction of an identity and a role' (Hinton, 1987) offers a particularly clear example of how failure to postulate internal structure in representations leads to failure to capture the systematicity of representational systems.

27   We are indebted to Steve Pinker for this point.

28   The hedge is meant to exclude cases where inferences of the same logical type nevertheless differ in complexity in virtue of, for example, the length of their premises. The inference from (AvBvCvDvE) and (−B&−C&−D&−E) to A is of the same logical type as the inference from AvB and −B to A. But it wouldn't be very surprising, or very interesting, if there were minds that could handle the second inference but not the first.

29   *Historical footnote.* Connectionists are associationists, but not every associationist holds that mental representations must be unstructured. Hume didn't, for example. Hume thought that mental representations are rather like pictures, and pictures typically have a compositional semantics: the parts of a picture of a horse are generally pictures of horse parts. On the other hand, allowing a compositional semantics for mental representations doesn't do associationist much good so long as he/she is true to this spirit of his/her associationism. The virtue of having mental representations with structure is that it allows for structure-sensitive operations to be defined

over them; specifically, it allows for the sort of operations that eventuate in productivity and systematicity. Association is not, however, such an operation; all *it* can do is build an internal model of redundancies in experience by altering the probabilities of transitions among mental states. So far as the problems of productivity and systematicity are concerned, an associationist who acknowledges structured representations is in the position of having the can but not the opener. Hume, in fact, cheated: he allowed himself not just association but also 'imagination', which he takes to be an 'active' faculty that can produce new concepts out of old parts by a process of analysis and recombination. (The idea of a unicorn is pieced together out of the idea of a horse and the idea of a horn, for example.) *Qua* associationist Hume had, of course, no right to active mental faculties. But allowing imagination in gave Hume precisely what modern connectionists don't have: an answer to the question how mental processes can be productive. The moral is that if you've got structured representations, the temptation to postulate structure-sensitive operations and an executive to apply them is practically irresistible.

30 Even in the case of a conventional computer, whether it should be viewed as executing a serial or a parallel algorithm depends on what 'virtual machine' is being considered in the case in question. After all, a VAX *can* be used to simulate (i.e. to implement) a virtual machine with a parallel architecture. In that case the relevant algorithm would be a parallel one.

31 There are, in fact, a number of different mechanisms of neural interaction (e.g. the 'local interactions' described by Rakie, 1975). Moreover, a large number of chemical processes takes place at the dendrites, covering a wide range of time-scales, so even if dendritic transmission were the only relevant mechanism, we still wouldn't know what time-scale to use as our estimate of neural action in general (see, for example, Black, 1986).

32 Unless the 'units' in a connectionist network really are assumed to have different spatially focused loci in the brain, talk about distributed representation is likely to be extremely misleading. In particular, if units are merely *functionally* individuated, any amount of distribution of functional entities is compatible with any amount of spatial compactness of their neural representations. But it is not clear that units do, in fact, correspond to any anatomically identifiable locations in the brain. In the light of the way connectionist mechanisms are designed, it may be appropriate to view units and links as functional/mathematical entities (what psychologists would call 'hypothetical constructs') whose neurological interpretation remains entirely open. (This is, in fact, the view that some connectionists take; see Smolensky, Chapter 2). The point is that distribution over mathematical constructs does not buy you damage resistance; only *neural* distribution does!

33 An especially flagrant example of how issues about architecture get confused with issues about the explicitness of rules in the connectionist literature occurs in *Parallel Distributed Processing*, ch. 4, where Rumelhart and McClelland (1986b) argue that PDP models provide 'a rather

plausible account of how we can come to have innate "knowledge". To the extent that stored knowledge is assumed to be in the form of explicit, inaccessible rules . . . it is hard to see how it could "get into the head" of the newborn. It seems to us implausible that the newborn possesses elaborate symbol systems and the systems for interpreting them required to put these explicit, inaccessible rules to use in guiding behavior. On our account, we do not need to attribute such complex machinery. If the innate knowledge is simply the prewired connections, it is encoded from the start in just the right way to be of use by the processing mechanisms' (p. 42). Apriorizing about what it does and doesn't seem likely that newborns possess strikes us as a bad way to do developmental cognitive psychology. But Rumelhart and McClelland's argument is doubly beside the point since a classicist who shares their prejudices can perfectly well avail him or herself of the same solution that they endorse. Classical architecture does *not* require 'complex machinery' for 'interpreting' explicit rules since classical machines do not *require* explicit rules at all. Classical architecture is therefore *neutral* on the empiricism/nativism issue (and so is connectionism, as Rumelhart and McClelland elsewhere correctly remark).

34 Of course, it *is* possible to simulate a 'rule-explicit process' in a connectionist network by first implementing a classical architecture in the network. The slippage between networks as architectures and as implementations is ubiquitous in connectionist writings, as we remarked above.

35 The PDP Research Group views its goal as being 'to replace the "computer metaphor" as a model of the mind with the "brain metaphor"' (Rumelhart and McClelland, 1986b, ch. 6, p. 75). But the issue is not at all which metaphor we should adopt; metaphors (whether 'computer' or 'brain') tend to be a license to take one's claims as something less than serious hypotheses. As Pylyshyn (1984a) points out, the claim that the mind has the architecture of a classical computer is not a metaphor but a literal empirical hypothesis.

36 Rumelhart and McClelland (1986b) maintain that PDP models are more than *just* theories of implementation because (a) they add to our understanding of the problem (p. 116), and (b) studying PDPs can lead to the postulation of different macro-level processes (p. 126). Both these points deal with the heuristic value of 'brain style' theorizing. Hence, though correct in principle, they are irrelevant to the crucial question of whether connectionism is best understood as an attempt to model neural implementation, or whether it really does promise a '*new*' theory of the mind' incompatible with Classical information-processing approaches. It is an empirical question whether the heuristic value of this approach will turn out to be positive or negative. We have already commented on our view of the recent history of this attempt.

37 Even in this case, where the model is specifically designed to implement LISP-like features, some of the rhetoric fails to keep the implementation-algorithm levels distinct. This leads to talk about 'emergent properties' and to the claim that even when they implement LISP-like mechanisms,

connectionist systems 'can compute things in ways in which Turing machines and von Neumann computers can't' (Touretzky, 1986). Such a claim suggests that Touretzky distinguishes different 'ways of computing' not in terms of different algorithms, but in terms of different ways of implementing the same algorithm. While nobody has proprietary rights to terms like 'ways of computing', this is a misleading way of putting it; it means that a DEC machine has a 'different way of computing' from an IBM machine even when executing the identical program.

References

Arbib, M. (1975) Artificial intelligence and brain theory: unities and diversities. *Biomedical Engineering* 3, 238–74.

Ballard, D.H. (1986) Cortical connections and parallel processing: structure and function. *Behavioral and Brain Sciences* 9, 67–120.

Ballard, D.H. (1987) Parallel logical inference and energy minimization. Technical report 142, Computer Science Department, University of Rochester.

Black, I.B. (1986) Molecular memory mechanisms. In G. Lynch (ed.), *Synapses, Circuits, and the Beginnings of Memory*. Cambridge, Mass., MIT Press/ Bradford Books.

Bolinger, D. (1965) The atomization of meaning. *Language* 41, 555–73.

Broadbent, D. (1985) A question of levels: comments on McClelland and Rumelhart. *Journal of Experimental Psychology; General* 114, 189–92.

Carroll, L. (1956) What the tortoise said to Achilles and other riddles. In J.R. Newman (ed.), *The World of Mathematics*, Vol. 4. New York, Simon and Schuster.

Chomsky, N. (1957) *Syntactic Structures*. The Hague, Mouton.

Chomsky, N. (1965) *Aspects of the Theory of Syntax*. Cambridge, Mass., MIT Press.

Chomsky, N. (1968) *Language and Mind*. New York, Harcourt, Brace and World.

Churchland, P.M. (1981) Eliminative materialism and the propositional attitudes. *Journal of Philosophy*, 78, 67–90.

Churchland, P.S. (1986) *Neurophilosophy*. Cambridge, Mass., MIT Press.

Cummins, R. (1983) *The Nature of Psychological Explanation*. Cambridge, Mass., MIT Press.

Dennett, D. (1986) The logical geography of computational approaches: a view from the east pole. In M. Brand and R.M. Harnish (eds). *The Representation of Knowledge*. Tucson, Arizona, University of Arizona Press.

Dreyfus, H. and Dreyfus, S. (1988) Making a mind vs modelling the brain: AI back at a branch point. *Daedalus* 117(1), 15–43.

Fahlman, S.E. and Hinton, G.E. (1987) Connectionist architectures for artificial intelligence. *Computer* 20, 100–109.

Feldman, J.A. (1986) Neural representation of conceptual knowledge. Technical Report 189. Department of Computer Science, University of Rochester.

Feldman, J.A. and Ballard, D.H. (1982) Connectionist models and their properties. *Cognitive Science* 6, 205–54.

Fodor, J.A. (1976) *The Language of Thought*. Brighton, Harvester Press (Harvard University Press paperback).

Fodor, J.A. (1987) *Psychosemantics*. Cambridge, Mass., MIT Press.

Fodor, J.D. (1977) *Semantics: Theories of Meaning in Generative Grammar*. New York, Thomas Y. Crowell.

Frohn, H., Geiger, H. and Singer, W. (1987) A self-organizing neural network sharing features of the mammalian visual system. *Biological Cybernetics* 55, 333–43.

Geach, P. (1957) *Mental Acts*. London, Routledge and Kegan Paul.

Hewett, C. (1977) Viewing control structures as patterns of passing messages. *The Artificial Intelligence Journal* 8, 232–364.

Hillis, D (1985) *The Connection Machine*. Cambridge, Mass., MIT Press.

Hinton, G.E. (1987) Representing part-whole hiearchies in connectionist networks. Unpublished manuscript.

Hinton, G.E., McClelland, J.L. and Rumelhart, D.E. (1986) Distributed representations. In D.E. Rumelhart, J.L. McClelland and the PDP Research Group (eds), *Parallel Distributed Processing: Explorations in the Microstructure of Cognition. Vol. 1: Foundations*. Cambridge, Mass., MIT Press/Bradford Books.

Hofstadter, D.R. (1983) Artificial intelligence: sub-cognition as computation. In F. Machlup and U. Mansfield (eds), *The Study of Information: Interdisciplinary Messages*. New York, Wiley.

Kant, I. (1929) *The Critique of Pure Reason*. New York, St Martins Press.

Katz, J.J. (1972) *Semantic Theory*. New York, Harper & Row.

Katz, J.J. and Fodor, J.A. (1963) The structure of a semantic theory. *Language* 39, 170–210.

Katz, J.J. and Postal, P. (1964) *An Integrated Theory of Linguistic Descriptions*. Cambridge, Mass., MIT Press.

Kosslyn, S.M. and Hatfield, G. (1984) Representation without symbol systems. *Social Research* 51, 1019–54.

Laird, J., Rosenbloom, P. and Newell, A. (1986) *Universal Subgoaling and Chunking: The Automatic Generation and Learning of Goal Hierarchies*. Boston, Mass., Kluwer.

Lakoff, G. (1986) Connectionism and cognitive linguistics. Seminar delivered at Princeton University, 8 December 1986.

McClelland, J.L. and Kawamoto, A.H. (1986). Mechanisms of sentence processing: assigning roles to constituents. In J.L. McClelland, D.E. Rumelhart and the PDP Research Group (eds), *Parallel Distributed Processing. Vol. 2: Psychological and Biological Models*. Cambridge, Mass., MIT Press/Bradford Books.

McClelland, J.L., Feldman, J., Adelson, B., Bower, G. and McDermott, D. (1986a). Connectionist models and cognitive science: goals, directions and implications. Report to the National Science Foundation, June, 1986.

McClelland, J.L., Rumelhart, D.E. and Hinton, G.E. (1986b) The appeal of parallel distributed processing. In D.E. Rumelhart, J.L. McClelland and the PDP Research Group (eds), *Parallel Distributed Processing*. Vol. 1: *Foundations*. Cambridge, Mass., MIT Press/Bradford Books.

Mackworth, A. (1987) Constraint propagation. In S.C. Shapiro (ed.), *The Encyclopedia of Artificial Intelligence*, Vol. 1. New York, Wiley.

Minsky, M. and Papert, F. (1972) Artificial intelligence progress report. AI Memo 252, Massachusetts Institute of Technology.

Newell, A. (1969) Heuristic programming: ill-structured problems. In J. Aronofsky (ed.), *Progress in Operations Research*, vol. III. New York, Wiley.

Newell, A. (1980) Physical symbol systems. *Cognitive Science* 4, 135–83.

Newell, A. (1982) The knowledge level. *Artificial Intelligence* 18, 87–127.

Osherson, D., Stov, M. and Weinstein, S. (1984) Learning theory and natural language, *Cognition* 17, 1–28.

Pinker, S. (1984) *Language Learnability and Language Development*. Cambridge, Mass., Harvard University Press.

Prince, A. and Pinker, S. (1988) On language and connectionism: analysis of a parallel distributed processing model of language acquisition. *Cognition* 28, 73–193.

Pylyshyn, Z.W. (1980) Cognition and computation: issues in the foundations of cognitive science. *Behavioral and Brain Sciences* 31, 154–69.

Pylyshyn, Z.W. (1981) The imagery debate: analogue media versus tacit knowledge. *Psychological Review* 88, 16–45.

Pylyshyn, Z.W. (1984a) *Computation and Cognition: Toward a Foundation for Cognitive Science*. Cambridge. Mass., MIT Press/Bradford Books.

Pylyshyn, Z.W. (1984b) Why computation requires symbols. *Proceedings of the Sixth Annual Conference of the Cognitive Science Society*, Boulder, Colorado, August, 1984. Hillsdale, NJ, Erlbaum.

Rakic, P. (1975) Local circuit neurons. *Neurosciences Research Program Bulletin* 13, 299–313.

Rumelhart, D.E. (1984) The emergence of cognitive phenomena from sub-symbolic processes. In *Proceedings of the Sixth Annual Conference of the Cognitive Science Society*, Boulder, Colorado, August, 1984. Hillsdale, NJ, Erlbaum.

Rumelhart, D.E. and McClelland, J.L. (1985) Level's indeed! A response to Broadbent. *Journal of Experimental Psychology: General* 114, 193–7.

Rumelhart, D.E. and McClelland, J.L. (1986a) On learning the past tenses of English verbs. In J.L. McClelland, D.E. Rumelhart and the PDP Research Group (eds), *Parallel Distributed Processing: Explorations in the Microstructure of Cognition*. Vol. 2: *Psychological and Biological Models*. Cambridge, Mass., MIT Press/Bradford Books.

Rumelhart, D.E. and McClelland, J.L. (1986b) PDP models and general issues in cognitive science. In D.L. Rumelhart, J.L. McClelland and the PDP

Research Group (eds), *Parallel Distributed Processing: Explorations in the Microstructure of Cognition*. Vol. 1: *Foundations*. Cambridge, Mass., MIT Press/Bradford Books.

Schneider, W. (1987) Connectionism: is it a paradigm shift for psychology? *Behavior Research Methods, Instruments and Computers* 19, 73–83.

Sejnowski, T.J. (1981) Skeleton filters in the brain. In G.E. Hinton and A.J. Anderson (eds). *Parallel Models of Associative Memory*, Hillsdale, NJ, Erlbaum.

Simon, H.A. and Chase, W.G. (1973) Skill in chess. *American Scientist* 621, 394–403.

Stabler, E. (1985) How are grammars represented? *Behavioral and Brain Sciences* 36, 391–420.

Stich, S. (1983) *From Folk Psychology to Cognitive Science*. Cambridge, Mass., MIT Press.

Touretzky, D.S. (1986) BoltzCONS: reconciling connectionism with the recursive nature of stacks and trees. *Proceedings of the Eighth Annual Conference of the Cognitive Science Society*, Amherst, Mass., August, 1986. Hillsdale, NJ, Erlbaum.

Wanner, E. and Maratsos, M. (1978) An ATN approach to comprehension. In M. Halle, J. Bresnan and G.A. Miller (eds), *Linguistic Theory and Psychological Reality*. Cambridge, Mass., MIT Press.

Watson, J. (1930) *Behaviorism*. Chicago, University of Chicago Press.

Woods, W.A. (1975) What's in a link? In D. Bobrow, and A. Collins (eds), *Representation and Understanding*, New York, Academic Press.

Ziff, P. (1960) *Semantic Analysis*. Ithaca, NY, Cornell University Press.

4

Connectionism, Constituency and the Language of Thought

Paul Smolensky

I'm the only President you've got.

(Lyndon Johnson)[1]

In chapter 3, Fodor and Pylyshyn argue that connectionism cannot offer a cognitive architecture that is both viable and different from the Classical language of thought architecture: if it differs from the Classical architecture it is because it reinstantiates simple associationism, and is therefore not a viable candidate; if it is viable, it is because it implements the Classical view and therefore does not offer a new cognitive architecture – just a new implementation of the old one. It is my purpose here to expose the false dichotomy in this argument, to show that the space of connectionist cognitive architectures is much richer than this simple dichotomy presumes, and that in this space is a large region of architectures that are implementations neither of a Classical architecture nor of a simple associationist architecture; these architectures provide structured mental representations and structure-sensitive processes in a truly non-Classical way.

In section 1, I make a number of general remarks about connectionism, Fodor and Pylyshyn's argumentation, and the abuse of the term 'implementation'. In section 2, I focus on the crux of their argument, which turns on the compositional structure of mental states. I develop in some detail the argument that, unlike simple associationist models, connectionist models using *distributed representations* can embody compositionality at the same time as providing a new cognitive architecture that is not an implementation of a Classical language of thought. In section 3, I bring the more technical discussion of section 2 back in contact with the more general issues raised in section 1. I argue that the debate surrounding compositionality illustrates the general point that by finding new formal instantiations of basic computational notions in the category of continuous mathematics, connectionism can open up genuinely new and powerful accounts of computation and cognition that go well beyond the limited progress that can be afforded by the kind of implementationalist strategy that Fodor and Pylyshyn advocate.

1   General Remarks

1.1   The true commitment of connectionism: PTC version

In this chapter I adopt a view of connectionism that was presented and discussed at some length in chapter 2 and in Smolensky 1988, a view I call PTC (for the Proper Treatment of Connectionism). Oversimplifying a bit, according to PTC, the true commitment of connectionism is to a very general formalism for describing mental representations and mental processes. The Classical view is, of course, committed to the hypothesis that mental representations are elements of a *symbol system*, and that mental processes consist of symbol-manipulation operations. PTC is committed to the hypothesis that mental representations are *vectors* partially specifying the state of a dynamical system (the activities of units in a connectionist network), and that mental processes are specified by the differential equations governing the evolution of that dynamical system.

The main point is this: under the influence of the Classical view, computation and cognition have been studied almost exclusively under the umbrella of discrete mathematics; the connectionist approach, on the other hand, brings the study of computation and cognition squarely into contact with the other half of mathematics: continuous mathematics. The true commitment, according to PTC, is to uncovering the insights into the nature of computation and cognition that this other half of mathematics can provide us.

On the PTC account, simple associationism is a particularly impoverished and impotent corner of the connectionist universe. It may well be that the attraction a number of people feel to connectionism is an attraction to neo-associationism; but it is none the less a serious mistake to presume connectionism to be committed to simple associationist principles. To equate connectionism with simple associationism is no more appropriate than equating. Classical symbolic theory with Aristotelean logic. (The temptation Fodor may provide his readers notwithstanding, I don't recommend the second identification any more than the first.)

In fact, the comparison with Aristotle is not wholly inappropriate. Our current understanding of the power of connectionist computation might well be compared with Aristotle's understanding of symbolic computation; before connectionists can take really serious shots at cognitive modeling, we probably have at least as far to go in developing connectionist computation as symbolic computation had to go between Aristotle and Turing. In giving up symbolic computation to undertake connectionist modeling, we connectionists have taken out an enormous loan, on which we are still paying nearly all interest: solving the basic problems we have created for ourselves rather than solving the problems of cognition. In my view, the loan is worth taking out for the goal of understanding how symbolic computation, or approximations to it, can emerge from numerical computation in a class of dynamical systems sharing the most general characteristics of neural computation.

Because cognitive modeling demands so much further progress in the development of connectionist computational techniques, I will argue here not for the superiority (nor even the plausibility) of a connectionist approach to cognitive modeling. Rather, I will argue that connectionism should be given a chance to progress unhampered by the misconception, fueled in significant part by Fodor and Pylyshyn (chapter 3; henceforth, F&P), that there is little point in pursuing the connectionist approach since it is doomed at the outset on fundamental grounds.

Given this characterization of the commitments of the Classical and connectionist approaches, to claim, as F&P explicitly do, that any cognitive architecture that incorporates structured mental representations and processes sensitive to that structure is a classical architecture, is to bloat the notion of 'classical architecture' well beyond reasonable bounds.

1.2   Implementation v. refinement

The bottom line of F&P can be paraphrased as follows. '*Standard* connectionism is just simple associationism wrapped in new jargon, and as such, is fatally flawed. Connectionists should pursue instead a *nonstandard* connectionism, embracing the principles of compositionality and structure-sensitive processing: they should accept the Classical view and should design their nets to be implementations of classical architectures.' Behind this moral is the assumption that connectionist models with compositionally structured representations must necessarily be implementations of a classical architecture; it will be my major purpose to show that this is false. The connectionist systems I will advocate hypothesize models that are not an *implementation* but rather a *refinement* of the Classical symbolic approach; these connectionist models hypothesize a truly different cognitive architecture, to which the classical architecture is a scientifically important approximation. The reader may suspect that I will be splitting hairs and that the difference between 'implementation' and 'refinement' will be of no philosophical significance. But in fact the new cognitive architecture I will hypothesize lacks the most crucial property of Fodor and Pylyshyn's classical architecture: mental representations and mental processes are *not* supported by the same formal entities – there are no 'symbols' that can do both jobs.[2] The new cognitive architecture is fundamentally two-level: formal, algorithmic specification of processing mechanisms, on the one hand, and semantic interpretation, on the other, must be done at two different levels of description.

There is a sense of 'implementation' that cognitive science has inherited from computer science, and I propose that we use it. If there is an account of a computational system at one level and an account at a lower level, then the lower one is an *implementation* of the higher one if and only if the higher description is a complete, precise, algorithmic account of the behavior of that system. It is *not* sufficient that the higher-level account provide some sort of rough summary of the interactions at the lower level. It is *not* sufficient that the lower-level account involve some of the same basic ideas of how the problem is to be solved (for example, a decomposition of the problem into sub-problems). Such weak usages of 'implementation' abound in the literature, particularly in the numerous attempts to dismiss connectionism as 'mere implementation'. But in its correct usage, *implementation* requires that the higher-level account provide an exact, precise, algorithmic account of the system's behavior.

It's important to see that, unless this definition of implementation is adopted, it is impossible to legitimately argue to F&P's ultimate conclusion: as long as connectionists are doing implementation, they're not going to provide a new cognitive architecture. If it is shown only that connectionism 'implements' the classical architecture under a looser definition of the term, then the conclusion that follows is that the Classical account provides a rough, higher-level approximation to the connectionist account, or involves some of the same basic ideas about how information is represented and processed. This is a *much weaker* conclusion than what F&P are after. They want the conclusion that only true implementation will license: since the Classical account provides a complete, precise, algorithmic account of the cognitive system, there is nothing to be gained by going to the lower-level account, as long as the phenomena of interest can be seen at the higher level; and, of course, it is exactly those phenomena that the classicist will count as 'truly cognitive'. To account for intrinsically lower-level phenomena – in which category the classicist will certainly include neural phenomena and may also include certain perceptual/motor phenomena – the classicist will acknowledge the need to condescend to a lower-level account; but within the domain of 'pure cognition', classicists won't need to get their hands so dirty. These are the sorts of conclusions that classicists have pushed for decades on the basis of analogies to higher- and lower-level computer languages. But, of course, these languages, *by design*, satisfy the *correct* definition of implementation; none of these conclusions follows from weaker definitions, and none follows from the connectionist position I defend here. Far from the conclusion that '*nothing* can be gained from going to the lower-level account', there is *plenty* to be gained: completeness, precision, and algorithmic accounts of processing, none of which is in general available at the higher level, according to PTC.

To see how the distributed connectionist architecture differs fundamentally from the classical one – fails to provide an 'implementation' using the correct definition of the term – I will now sketch how the connectionist architecture is intrinsically split over two levels of description. We'll consider the purest case: distributed connectionist models having the following two properties:

(1) (a) Interpretation can be assigned to large-scale activity patterns but not to individual units.
     (b) The dynamics governing the interaction of individual units is sufficiently complex that the algorithm defining the interactions of individual units cannot be translated into a tractably specified algorithm for the interaction of whole patterns.[3]

As a result of these two properties, we can see that there are two levels of analysis with very different characteristics. At the lower level, where the state variables are the activities of individual units, the processing is described by a complete, precise and formal algorithm, but semantic interpretation cannot be done. At the higher level, where the system's state is described in terms of the presence of certain large-scale patterns, semantic interpretation can be done, but now complete, precise algorithms for the processing cannot be stated. As I have characterized this in Chapter 2, the *syntax* or processing algorithm strictly resides at the lower level, while the *semantics* strictly resides at the upper level. Since both the syntax and the semantics are essential to the cognitive architecture, we have an intrinsically split-level cognitive architecture here: there is no account of the architecture in which the same elements carry both the syntax and the semantics. Thus we have a fundamentally new candidate for the cognitive architecture which is simply *not* an implementation of the classical one.

Note that the conclusions of this section depend crucially on the assumption (1a) that connectionist representations are *distributed* (when viewed at the level of individual units, the level at which processing algorithms can be identified (1b)). Thus, while F&P attempt to give the impression that the issue of local *v.* distributed representations is a little technical squabble between connectionists of no philosophical consequence, I believe this to be a profound mistake. Distributed representations, when combined with (1b), entail that in the connectionist cognitive architecture, mental representations bear a fundamentally different relation to mental processes than' is true in the Classical account. I will return to this crucial point in section 3.

2   Compositionality and Distributed Connectionist Representations

I shall not seek, and I will not accept, the nomination of my party for another term as your President.

(Lyndon Johnson)

In this section I consider the crux of F&P's argument, and argue that distributed connectionist architectures, without implementing the classical architecture, can none the less provide structured mental representations and mental processes sensitive to that structure.

2.1   The ultra-local case

Here is a quick summary of what I take to be the central argument of F&P.

(2)   (a) Thoughts have composite structure.

By this they mean things like: the thought that *John loves the girl* is not atomic; it's a composite mental state built out of thoughts about *John*, *loves* and *the girl*.

(2)   (b) Mental processes are sensitive to this composite structure.

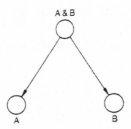

Figure 4.1 Fodor and Pylyshyn's network.

For example, from any thought of the form p & q – regardless of what p and q are – we can deduce p.

F&P elevate (2) to the status of defining the Classical view of cognition, and claim that this is what is being challenged by connectionism. I am arguing that this is wrong, but for now we continue with F&P's argument.

Having identified claims (2) as definitive of the Classical view, F&P go on to argue that there are compelling arguments for these claims.[4] According to these arguments, mental states have the properties of productivity, systematicity, compositionality and inferential coherence. Without going into all these arguments, let me simply state that for present purposes I'm willing to accept that they are convincing enough to justify the conclusion that (2) must be taken quite seriously.

Now for F&P's analysis of connectionism. They assert that in (standard) connectionism, all representations are atomic; mental states have no composite structure, violating (2a). Furthermore, they assert, (standard) connectionist processing is association which is sensitive only to *statistics*, not to *structure* – in violation of (2b). Therefore, they conclude, (standard) connectionism is maximally non-Classical: it violates both the defining principles. Therefore connectionism is defeated by the compelling arguments in favor of the Classical view.

What makes F&P say that connectionist representations are atomic? Their figure 3.2 (in chapter 3 (p. 100) says it all – it is rendered here as figure 4.1. This network is supposed to illustrate the standard connectionist account of the inference from A & B to A and to B. It is true that Ballard and Hayes wrote a paper (Ballard and Hayes, 1984; also Ballard, 1986) about using connectionist networks to do automated resolution theorem proving in which networks like this appear. However, it is a serious mistake to view this as the paradigmatic connectionist account for anything like human inferences of this sort. The kind of *ultra-local* connectionist representation, in which entire propositions are represented by individual nodes, is far from typical of connectionist models, and certainly not to be taken as *definitive* of the connectionist approach.[5]

A central claim in my response to F&P is that any critique of the connectionist approach must consider the consequences of using distributed representations, in which the representations of high-level conceptual entities such as propositions are distributed over many nodes, and the same nodes simultaneously participate in the representation of many entities. Their response, in section 2.1.3 (p. 103), is as follows. The distributed/local representation issue concerns (they assume) whether each of the nodes in figure 4.1 refers to something complicated and lower level (the distributed case) or not (the local case). But, they claim, this issue is irrelevant, because it pertains to a *between-level* issue, and the compositionality of mental states is a *within level* issue.

My response is that they are correct that compositionality is a within-level issue, and correct that the distributed/local distinction is a between-level issue. Their argument presumes that because of this difference, one issue cannot influence the other. But that is a fallacy. It assumes that the between-level relation in distributed representations cannot have any consequences on the *within-level* structure of the relationships between the representations of *A & B* and the representation of *A*. And that's simply false. There are profound implications of distributed representations for compositionality; these are the subject of all of section 2 of this chapter. In particular, it will turn out that figure 4.1 is exactly as relevant to a distributed connectionist account of inference as it is to a symbolic account. In the ultra-local case, figure 4.1 is relevant and their critique stands; in the distributed case, figure 4.1 is a bogus characterization of the connectionist account and their critique completely misses its target. It will further turn out that a valid analysis of the actual distributed case, based on suggestions of Pylyshyn himself, leads to quite the opposite conclusion: connectionist models using distributed representations describe mental states with a relevant kind of (within-level) constituent structure. The rather weak sense of constituent structure in generic distributed representations, identified in section 2.2, will be made much stronger in explicitly designed distributed representations, discussed in section 2.3, in which constituents can fill varying structural roles.

2.2 The distributed (weakly compositional) case

For now, the goal is to show that generic connectionist models using distributed representations ascribe to mental states the kind of compositional structure demanded by (2a), contrary to F&P's conclusion based on the ultra-local network of figure 4.1.

2.2.1 The coffee story   My argument consists primarily in carrying out an analysis that was suggested by Zenon Pylyshyn himself at the 1984 Cognitive Science Meeting in Boulder.[6] We'll take a *distributed* representation of *cup with coffee* and subtract from it a distributed representation of *cup without coffee* and call what's left, following Pylyshyn, 'the connectionist representation of *coffee*'.

To generate these distributed representations I will use a set of 'micro-features' (Hinton et al., 1986) that are not very micro – but that's always what happens in examples that are cooked up to be intuitively understandable in a non-technical exposition. These micro-features are shown in figure 4.2.

Figure 4.2 shows a distributed representation of *cup with coffee*: a pattern of activity in which those units that are active (black) are those that correspond to micro-features present in the description of a cup containing coffee. Obviously, this is a crude, nearly sensory-level representation, but, again, that helps make the example more intuitive – it's not essential.

Given the representation of *cup with coffee* displayed in figure 4.2, Pylyshyn suggests we subtract the representation of *cup without coffee*. The representation of *cup without coffee* is shown in figure 4.3, and figure 4.4 shows the result of subtracting it from the representation of *cup with coffee*.

So what does this procedure produce as 'the connectionist representation of *coffee*'? Reading off from figure 4.4, we have a burnt

Units	Micro-features
●	upright container
●	hot liquid
○	glass contacting wood
●	porcelain curved surface
●	burnt odour
●	brown liquid contacting porcelain
○	oblong silver object
●	finger -sized handle
●	brown liquid with curved sides and bottom

Figure 4.2   Representation of cup with coffee.

Units	Micro-features
●	upright container
○	hot liquid
○	glass contacting wood
◕	porcelain curved surface
○	burnt odour
○	brown liquid contacting porcelain
○	oblong silver object
◕	finger-sized handle
○	brown liquid with curved sides and bottom

Figure 4.3   Representation of cup without coffee.

Units	Micro-features
○	upright container
◕	hot liquid
○	glass contacting wood
○	porcelain curved surface
◕	burnt odour
●	brown liquid contacting porcelain
○	oblong silver object
○	finger-sized handle
●	brown liquid with curved sides and bottom

Figure 4.4   'Representation of coffee'.

odor and hot brown liquid with curved sides and bottom surfaces contacting porcelain. This is indeed a representation of *coffee*, but in a very particular context: the context provided by *cup*.

What does this mean for Pylyshyn's conclusion that 'the connectionist representation of *cup with coffee* is just the representation of *cup without coffee* combined with the representation of *coffee*'? What is involved in combining the representations of figures 4.3 and 4.4 back together to form that of figure 4.2? We assemble the representation of *cup with coffee* from a representation of a *cup*, and a representation of *coffee*, but it's a rather strange combination. There's also the representation of the *interaction* of the cup with coffee – like *brown liquid contacting porcelain*. Thus the composite representation is built from coffee *extracted* from the situation *cup with coffee*, together with *cup* extracted from the situation *cup with coffee*, together with their interaction.

So the compositional structure is there, but it's there in an *approximate* sense. It's *not* equivalent to taking a context-independent representation of *coffee* and a context-independent representation of *cup* – and certainly not equivalent to taking a context-independent representation of the relationship *in* or *with* – and sticking them all together in a symbolic structure, concatenating them together to form the kind of syntactic compositional structures like WITH (CUP, COFFEE) that F&P want connectionist nets to implement.

To draw this point out further, let's reconsider the representation of *coffee* once the cup has been subtracted off. This, suggests Pylyshyn, is the connectionist representation of *coffee*. But as we have already observed, this is really a representation of *coffee* in the particular context of being inside a cup. According to Pylyshyn's formula, to get the connectionist representation of *coffee* it should have been in principle possible to take the connectionist representation of *can with coffee* and subtract from it the connectionist representation of *can without coffee*. What would happen if we actually did this? We would get a representation of ground, brown, burnt-smelling granules stacked in a cylindrical shape, together with granules contacting tin. This is the connectionist representation of *coffee* we get by starting with *can with coffee* instead of *cup with coffee*. Or we could start with the representation of *tree with coffee* and subtract off *tree without coffee*. We would get a connectionist representation for *coffee* which would be a representation of brown beans in a funny shape hanging suspended in mid-air. Or again we could start with *man with coffee* and get still another connectionist representation of *coffee*: one quite similar to the entire representation of *cup with coffee* from which we extracted our first representation of *coffee*.

The point is that the representation of *coffee* that we get out of the construction starting with *cup with coffee* leads to a different representation of *coffee* than we get out of other constructions that have equivalent *a priori* status. That means that if you want to talk about the connectionist representation of *coffee* in this distributed scheme, you have to talk about a *family of distributed activity patterns*. What knits together all these particular representations of *coffee* is nothing other than a type of family resemblance.

2.2.2 Morals of the coffee story   The first moral I want to draw out of this *coffee* story is this: unlike the ultra-local case of figure 4.1, with distributed representations, complex representations *are* composed of representations of constituents. The constituency relation here is a *within-level* relation, as F&P require: the pattern or *vector* representing *cup with coffee* is composed of a *vector* that can be identified as a distributed representation of *cup without coffee* together with a *vector* that can be identified as a particular distributed representation of *coffee*. In characterizing the constituent vectors of the vector representing the composite, we are *not* concerned with the fact that the vector representing *cup with coffee* is a vector comprised of the activity of individual micro-feature units. The *between-level* relation between the vector and its individual numerical elements is *not* the constituency relation, and so section 2.1.4 (pp. 103–11) of F&P is irrelevant – it addresses a mistake that is not being made.

The second moral is that the constituency relation among distributed representations is one that is important for the analysis of connectionist models, and for explaining their behavior, but it is *not* a part of the information-processing mechanism within the connectionist model. In order to process the vector representing *cup with coffee*, the network does not have to decompose it into constituents. For processing, it is the *between-level* relation, not the within-level relation, that matters. The processing of the vector representing *cup with coffee* is determined by the individual numerical activities that make up the vector: it is over these lower-level activities that the processes are defined. Thus the fact that there is considerable arbitrariness in the way the constituents of *cup with coffee* are defined introduces no ambiguities in the way the network processes that representation – the ambiguities exist only for us who analyze the model and try to explain its behavior. Any particular definition of constituency that gives us explanatory leverage is a valid definition of constituency; lack of uniqueness is not a problem.

This leads directly to the third moral: the decomposition of composite states into their constituents is not precise and uniquely defined. The notion of constituency is important but attempts to formalize it are likely to crucially involve *approximation*. As discussed at some length in chapter 2, this is the typical case: notions from symbolic computation provide important tools for constructing higher-level accounts of the behavior of connectionist models using distributed representation – but these notions provide approximate, not precise, accounts.

Which leads to the fourth moral: while connectionist networks using distributed representations *do* describe mental states with the type of constituency required by (2a), they do *not* provide an implementation – correctly defined – of a symbolic language of thought. The context-dependency of the constituents, the interactions that must be accommodated when they are combined, the inability to uniquely and precisely identify constituents, the imperative to take seriously the notion that the representation of *coffee* is a collection of vectors knit together by family resemblance – all these entail that the relation between connectionist constituency and syntactic-symbolic constituency is *not* one of implementation. In particular, it would be absurd to claim that even if the connectionist story is correct then that would have no implications for the cognitive architecture, that it would merely fill in lower-level details without important implications for the higher-level account.

These conclusions all address compositional representation (2a) without explicitly addressing structure-sensitive processing (2b). Addressing structure sensitivity to the depth necessary to grapple with real cognitive modeling is far beyond the scope of this chapter; to a considerable extent, it is beyond the scope of current connectionism. However, let me simply state the fundamental hypothesis of PTC that weaves the statistical sensitivity characteristic of connectionist processing together with the notion of structure sensitivity: *the mind is a statistics-sensitive engine operating on structure-sensitive (numerical) representations.* The previous arguments have shown that distributed representations do possess constituency relations, and that, properly analyzed, these representations can be seen to encode structure. Extending this to grapple with the complexity of the kinds of rich structures implicated in complex cognitive processes is the topic of the next section. Here it suffices to observe that once we have complex structured information represented in distributed numerical patterns, statistics-sensitive processes can proceed to analyze the statistical regularities in a fully structure-sensitive way. Whether such processes can provide structure sensitivity that is adequate to cope with the demands of linguistic and inferential processing is sure to be unknown for some time yet.

The conclusion, then, is that distributed models *can* satisfy (2). Whether (2) can be satisfied to the depth required by the full demands of cognitive modeling is of course an open empirical question – just as it is for the symbolic approach to satisfying (2). At the same time, distributed connectionist models do *not* amount to an implementation of the symbolic instantiations of (2) that F&P are committed to.

Before summing up, I'd like to return to figure 4.1. In what sense can figure 4.1 be said to describe the relation between the distributed representation of *A&B* and the distributed representations of *A* and *B*? It was the intent of the *coffee* story to show that the distributed representations of the constituents are, in an approximate but explanation-relevant sense, part of the representation of the composite. Thus, in the distributed case, the relation between the node of figure 4.1 labeled *A&B* and the others is one kind of whole/part relation. An inference mechanism that takes as input the vector representing *A&B*

and produces as output the vector representing A is a mechanism that extracts a part from a whole. And in this sense it is no different from a symbolic inference mechanism that takes the syntactic structure **A & B** and extracts from it the syntactic constituent **A**. The connectionist mechanisms for doing this are, of course, quite different from the symbolic mechanisms, and the approximate nature of the whole/part relation gives the connectionist computation different overall characteristics: we don't have simply a new implementation of the old computation.

It is clear that, just as figure 4.1 offers a crude summary of the symbolic process of passing from **A & B** to **A**, a summary that uses the labels to encode hidden internal structures within the nodes, *exactly the same is true of the distributed connectionist case.* In the distributed connectionist case – *just as in the symbolic case* – the links in figure 4.1 are crude summaries of complex processes and not simple-minded causal channels that pass activity from the top node to the lower nodes. Such a simple causal story applies only to the ultra-local connectionist case, which is the only legitimate target of F&P's attack.

Let me be clear: there is no serious distributed connectionist model, as far as I know, of the kind of formal inference F&P have in mind here. Many proponents of connectionism would be content to claim that formal inference is a specially trained, poorly practiced skill that is far from central to cognition, and that therefore we can afford to put off worrying about providing a connectionist model of it for a long time. I prefer to say that, at root, the F&P argument concerns an important and central issue: the constituent structure of mental states; formal inference is just one setting in which to see the importance of that constituent structure. So the preceding discussion of the constituent structure of distributed representations does address the heart of their critique, even if a well-developed connectionist account of formal inference remains unavailable.

2.3 The distributed (strongly compositional) case

But, one might well argue, the sense in which the vector encoding the distributed representation of *cup with coffee* has constituent vectors representing *cup* and *coffee* is too weak to serve all the uses of constituent structure – in particular, too weak to support formal inference – because the vector representing *cup* cannot fill multiple structural roles. A true constituent can move around and fill any of a number of different roles in different structures. Can *this* be done with vectors encoding distributed representations, and be done in a way that doesn't amount to simply implementing symbolic syntactic constituency? The purpose of this section is to describe research showing that the answer is affirmative.

A large class of connectionist representations, which I call *tensor product representations*, is defined and analyzed in Smolensky (1987a), and applied in Dolan and Smolensky (1988). We generate various members of this class by variously specifying several parameters in a highly general method for creating connectionist representations of structured information. The resulting parametric variation in the representations is very broad, encompassing very simple representations such as the case of figure I, as well as representations that are close to true implementations of a syntactic language of thought. This class of representations covers the spectrum from fully distributed representations to ultra-local ones, and includes representations with a full sense of constituency, where role-independent constituents are assigned to roles in a structure and the representation of the structure is built up systematically from the representation of the constituents.

The problem that motivates this work is mapping complex structure such as parse trees into vectors of activity in connectionist networks, in such a way that the constituent structure is available for connectionist processing. A general formal framework for stating this problem is to assume that there is a set of discrete structures S (like parse trees) and a vector space V – a space of activity states of a connectionist network. A connectionist representation is a mapping from S to V; the theorist's job is to identify such mappings having various desirable properties. Tensor product representations can provide many of these properties.

A particular tensor product representation is constructed in two steps.

(3) (a) Specify a decompositional process whereby the discrete structures are explicitly broken down as a set of constituents, each filling a particular role in the structure as a whole. This step has nothing to do with connectionism *per se*; it just amounts to being specific about the kind of constituent structure we want to represent.

   (b) Specify two connectionist representations: one for the structural roles and another for their fillers (the constituents). Thus, for every filler, we assign a vector in the state space of some network for representing fillers; similarly, we assign to every role a vector in the state space of some network for representing roles.

These two steps indicate the 'parameters' in the general tensor product representational scheme that must be specified to individuate a particular representation. Once these parameters are specified, two very simple operations from the theory of vector spaces are used to generate the representation of a particular discrete structure. The representation of the whole is built from the representation of its constituent parts by the operation of *superposition* which is simply *vector addition*: the vector representing the whole is the sum of the vectors representing the parts. Step (3a) above specifies exactly what constituents are involved in this process. The vector representing a given constituent is actually a role-sensitive representation: a representation of that constituent *in the role it plays in the whole*. This vector is built by taking a particular vector product of the vector that represents the constituent independent of any role, and the vector representing the role in the structure that is filled by the constituent. Step (3b) specifies a set of vectors that represent individual structural roles and another set of vectors that represent individual fillers for those roles (constituents) independently of any role. The product operation here is a vector operation called the *tensor product* that takes two vectors and produces a new vector; if the two vectors consist of n and m activity values, then their tensor product is a vector of nm activity values, each one being a different product (using ordinary numerical multiplication) of two activity values, one from each of the original vectors.[7]

The tensor product provides a general solution to a problem that has been nagging the distributed connectionist representational world for a long time, the so-called *variable binding problem*. How can we take an activity pattern representing a variable and another pattern representing a value and generate a connectionist representation of their binding that has the right computational properties? The simplicity of the tensor product makes it possible to show it does in fact satisfy the computational demands of (distributed) connectionist variable binding. The tensor product technique is a generalization, of specific tricks (especially, *conjunctive coding*: Hinton et al., 1986; McClelland and Kawamoto, 1986; Smolensky, forthcoming) that have been used to solve this problem in particular instances in the past.

The tensor product representation of constituent structure considerably strengthens the notion of constituency brought out in the previous section through the *coffee* story. There we saw that the whole/part relation between *cup with coffee* and *coffee* is mirrored in a whole/part relation between their respective representations: the latter relation was not the whole/part relation between molecular symbolic structures and their atomic constituents, as in a symbolic language of thought, but rather the relation between a sum vector $\mathbf{w}$ and the component vectors that add up to it: $\mathbf{w} = \mathbf{c}_1 + \mathbf{c}_2 + \ldots$ The same is true here generally with respect to tensor product representations, but now in addition we can identify the representations of each constituent as a role-*dependent* representation built in a systematic way (through tensor product variable binding) from a role-*independent* representation of the filler and a filler-independent representation of its role.

Among the computational properties required of the variable binding mechanism is the possibility of *unbinding*: from the role-dependent representation of some constituent we must be able to extract the role-independent representation of that constituent. Similarly, given the vector representing a symbolic structure as a whole, it should be possible to extract the role-independent representation of the filler of any given role in the structure. Under a wide variety of conditions this is possible with the tensor product representation, although when so many roles are simultaneously filled that the capacity of the representing network is exceeded, corruptions, confusions and errors can be introduced during unbinding. The conditions under which error-free unbinding can be performed, and characterization of the errors occurring when these conditions are violated, can be computed (Smolensky, 1987a). Thus, for example, if we have a tensor product representation for $P\&Q$, and we wish to extract the first element P as part of a deductive process, then as long as the representing network is not trivially small, we can easily do so without error, using very simple (linear) connectionist processes.

So, returning to F&P's critique, let's see what the tensor product representational scheme can do for us in terms of the simple inference problems they talk about.

Using the tensor product technique, it is possible to define a family of representations of tree structures. We can consider a simple tree for $P\&Q$ consisting of $\&$ at the top, P as its left child, and Q as its right child; and we can view the roles as positions in the tree, the simplest kind of role decomposition. The tensor product representation of that tree structure is a vector $F(P\&Q)$ which is related to the vectors representing the constituents, $F(P)$ and $F(Q)$, by a function $\mathbf{B}_\&$ that is particular to constructing conjunctions:

$$F(P\&Q) = \mathbf{B}_\& \ [F(P), F(Q)]$$

The function $B_\&$ is defined by

$$\mathbf{B}_\&(\mathbf{u}, \mathbf{v}) = \mathbf{c}_\& + \tau_0\mathbf{u} + \tau_1\mathbf{v}$$

where $\mathbf{c}_\&$ is a constant vector and τ_0 and τ_1, are linear operators (the most natural vector operators) that vary depending on how the parameters individuating the tensor product representation are chosen.

I have descended to this level of detail and used this notation because in note 9 of F&P (chapter 2, p. 152) exactly this property is chosen to define F as a 'physical instantiation mapping of combinatorial structure'. In this sense the tensor product representation meets F&P's formal requirements for a representation of combinatorial structure.

But have we merely provided an implementation then of a symbolic language of thought? In general, the answer is 'no'. Depending on how we have chosen to set the parameters in specifying the tensor product representation (which determines the properties of τ_o and τ_l), we can fail to have any of the following properties holding (Smolensky, 1987a):

(4) (a) *Uniqueness with respect to roles or fillers.* If we're not careful, even though the above equation is satisfied, we can end up with *P&Q* having the same representation as *Q&P*, or other more subtle ambiguities about what fills various roles in the structure.

(b) *Unbounded depth.* We may avoid the first problem (4a) for sufficiently small structures, but when representing sufficiently large or deep structures, these problems may appear. Unless the vector space in which we do our representation is infinite-dimensional (corresponding to a network with infinitely many units), we cannot solve (4a) for unbounded depth. (Of course, the same is true of Turing/von Neumann machines if they are only allowed bounded resources; but whereas the capacity limit in the symbolic case is a hard one, the tensor product representation allows for graceful degradation as resources are saturated.)

(c) *Non-confusability in memory.* Even when problem (4a) is avoided, when we have representations with uniquely determined filler/role bindings, it can easily happen that we cannot simultaneously store many such structures in a connectionist memory without getting intrusions of undesired memories during the retrieval of a given memory.

(d) *Processing independence.* This is in a sense a generalization of the preceding point, concerning processing constraints that may arise even when problem (4a) is avoided. In simple associative processing, for example, we may find that we can associate two vectors representing symbolic structures with what we like, but then find ourselves unable to associate the representation of a third structure with what we like, because its associate is constrained by the other two.

With all these properties potentially failing to hold, it doesn't sound to me like we're dealing with an implementation of a symbolic language of thought. But at this point somebody's going to want to say, 'Well, you've just got a *lousy* implementation of a symbolic language of thought.' But it's not that simple. We may have lost some (superficially desirable, at least) features of a symbolic language of thought, but we've gained some (superficially desirable, at least) features of connectionist processing in return.

(5) (a) *Massive parallelism.* Since we have a vector that represents an entire tree at once, we can feed it into the usual connectionist massively parallel processes. Unlike traditional AI programs, we don't have to spend all our time painfully traversing step-by-step long descending chains into the bowels of complex symbolic data structures: it's all there at once, all accessible in parallel.[8]

   (b) *Content-addressable memory.* This is the usual distributed connectionist story, but now it applies to *structural information.*

   (c) *Statistical inference.* F&P are among the first to attack connectionism for basing its processing mechanisms on statistical inference. One more reason for them to deny that the connectionist framework I am discussing truly constitutes an implementation of their preferred architecture. Yet their arguments *against* statistical processing are much less compelling than their arguments *for* structure-sensitive processing. We are now in a position to go after *both*, in a unified framework, dissolving a long-standing tension arising from a failure to see how to formally unify structure-sensitive and statistical processing. Rather than having to model the mind as *either* a structure cruncher *or* a number cruncher, we can now see it as a number cruncher in which the numbers crunched are in fact representing complex structures.[9]

   (d) *Statistical learning.* Since structure can now be brought fully into the world of connectionist learning research, we can move from declarations of dogma to actual empirical results about what structurally rich representations and processes can and cannot be acquired from experience through statistically based learning. We can now foresee a time when it will be too late to put your money down on the fate of the 'poverty of the stimulus' dogma.

The point is that the parametric variation in tensor product representations covers a rich territory, and an important item on the connectionist cognitive modeling agenda is to determine whether in that territory there is a set of representations that has the right mixture of the power of (5) and the limitations of (4) to capture real human behavior. This large space of tensor product representations extends from simple ultra-local representations of the sort F&P correctly dismiss towards – I hesitate to say all the way up to, but quite close to – a true implementation of a symbolic language of thought. If you want such an implementation, you have to go to a limit that includes the following characteristics:

(6) (a) *Orthogonality*. The angle between the vectors representing different roles needs to go to 90 degrees, and similarly for vectors representing the fillers, to eliminate non-uniqueness and minimize interference in memory.

   (b) *Infinite-dimensional representations*. Otherwise, we can't represent unboundedly deep structures without confusion.

   (c) *Simple operations*. If we happen to want an implementation of sequential algorithms, then in processing these representations we insist that the vector equivalent of the primitive symbolic operations (like LISP's car, cdr and cons) are all that can be done in one time step: we don't avail ourselves of the massively parallel operations that otherwise would be available to us.

I have talked so far mostly about representations and little about processing. If we are interested, as F&P are, in inferences such as that from *P & Q* to *P*, it turns out that with tensor product representations, this operation can be achieved by a simple linear transformation upon these representational vectors, the kind of transformation most natural in this category of representations.[10] Not only can this structure-sensitive process be achieved by connectionist mechanisms on connectionist representations, but it can be achieved through the simplest of all connectionist operations: linear mapping. All in an architecture that differs fundamentally from the classical one; we have not implemented a symbolic language of thought.

3   Connectionism, Implementationalism and Limitivism

I am not a crook.

(Richard Nixon)

Let me now bring the arguments of section 2 to bear on the general issues raised in section 1.

3.1   The methodological implications of implementationalism and limitivism

It seems to me most likely that symbolic descriptions *will* provide scientifically important *approximate* higher-level accounts of how the ultimate connectionist cognitive models compute – but that these distributed connectionist models will not implement a symbolic language of thought, under the relevant (and correct) definition of the word. The approximations involved demand a willingness to accept context-sensitive symbols and interactional components present in compositional structures, and the other funny business that came out in the *coffee* example. If we're willing to live with all those degrees of approximation, then we can usefully view these symbolic-level descriptions as approximate higher-level accounts of the processing in a connectionist network.

An important overall conclusion in the constituency issue, then, is that the Classical and connectionist approaches differ *not* in whether they accept principles (2), *but in how they formally instantiate them.* To really confront the Classical/connectionist dispute, one has to be willing to descend to the level of the particular formal instantiations they give to the non-formal principles (2). To fail to descend to this level of detail is to miss much of the issue. In the Classical approach, principles (2) are formalized using syntactic structures for mental representations and symbol manipulation for mental processes. In the distributed connectionist approach, principles (2) are formalized using vectorial representations for mental representations, and the corresponding notion of compositionality, together with numerical mental processes that derive their structure sensitivity from the differential way that they treat the parts of vectors corresponding to different structural roles.

In terms of research methodology, this means that the agenda for connectionism should not be to develop a connectionist implementation of the symbolic language of thought, but rather to develop formal analysis of vectorial representations of complex structures and operations on those structures that are sufficiently structure sensitive to do the required work. This is exactly the kind of research that, for example, tensor product representations are being used to support.

Thus the PTC position is that distributed representations provide a description of mental states with semantically interpretable constituents, but that there is no complete, precise formal account of the construction of composites or of mental processes in general that can be stated solely in terms of context-independent semantically interpretable constitu-

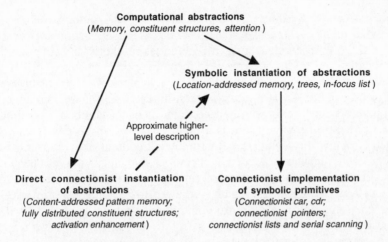

Figure 4.5   PTC *v.* implementationalism. (Reprinted with permission of *Behavioral and Brain Sciences.*)

ents. On this account, there *is* a language of thought – but only approximately; the language of thought by itself does not provide a basis for an exact formal account of mental structure or processes – it cannot by itself support a precise formal account of the cognitive architecture.

Constituency is one illustration of a central component of the general PTC approach to connectionism: the relation hypothesized between connectionist models based on continuous mathematics and classical models based on discrete, symbolic computation. That relationship might be called the *cognitive correspondence principle*: when powerful connectionist computational systems are appropriately analyzed at higher levels, elements of symbolic computation appear as emergent properties.

Figures 4.5 schematically illustrates the cognitive correspondence principle. At the top are non-formal notions: the central hypotheses that the principles of cognition consist in principles of memory, of inference, of compositionality and constituent structure, etc. In the F&P argument, the relevant non-formal principles are their compositionality principles (2).

The non-formal principles at the top of figure 4.5 have certain formalizations in the discrete mathematical category, which are shown one level down on the right branch. For example, memory is formalized as standard location-addressed memory or some appropriately more sophisticated related notion. Inference gets formalized in the discrete category as logical inference, a particular form of symbol manipulation. And so on.

The PTC research agenda consists in taking these kinds of cognitive principles and finding new ways to instantiate them in formal principles based on the continuous mathematics of dynamical systems; these are shown in figure 4.5 at the lowest level on the left branch. The concept of memory retrieval is reformalized in terms of the continuous evolution of a dynamical system towards a point attractor whose position in the state space is the memory; we naturally get content-addressed memory instead of location-addressed memory. (Memory storage becomes modification of the dynamics of the system so that its attractors are located where the memories are supposed to be; thus the principles of memory storage are even more unlike their symbolic counterparts than those of memory retrieval.) When reformalizing inference principles, the continuous formalism leads naturally to principles of statistical inference rather than logical inference. And so on.

The cognitive correspondence principle states that the general relationship between the connectionist formal principles and the symbolic formal principles – given that they are both instantiations of common non-formal notions, and to the extent that ultimately they are both scientifically valid descriptions of the same cognitive system – is that if we take a higher-level analysis of what's going on in the connectionist systems we find that it matches, to some kind of approximation, what's going on in the symbolic formalism. This relation is indicated in figure 4.5 by the dotted arrow.

This is to be contrasted with an implementational view of connectionism such as that which F&P advocate. As portrayed in figure 4.5, the implementational methodology is to proceed from the top to the bottom not directly, via the left branch, but indirectly, via the right branch: connectionists should take the symbolic instantiations of the non-formal principles and should find ways of implementing *them* in connectionist networks.

The PTC methodology is to be contrasted not just with the implementational approach, but also with the eliminativist one. In terms of these methodological considerations, eliminativism has a strong and a weak form. The weak form advocates taking the left branch of figure 4.5 but ignoring altogether the symbolic formalizations, on the belief that the symbolic notions will confuse rather than enlighten us in our attempts to understand connectionist computation. The strong eliminativist position states that even viewing the non-formal principles at the top of figure 4.5 as a starting point for thinking about cognition is a mistake – that it is better, for example, to pursue a blind bottom-up strategy in which we take low-level connectionist principles from neuroscience and see where they lead us, without being prejudiced by archaic pre-scientifc notions such as those at the top of figure 4.5.

In rejecting both the implementationalist and eliminativist positions, PTC views connectionist accounts in significant part as reducing and explaining symbolic accounts. Connectionist accounts serve to refine symbolic accounts, to reduce the degree of approximation required, to enrich the computational notions from the symbolic and discrete world, to fill them out with notions of continuous computation. Primarily that's done by descending to a lower level of analysis, by exposing the hidden micro-structure in these kinds of large-scale, discrete symbolic operations.

I have dubbed the PTC position *limitivism* because it views connectionism as delimiting the domain D of validity of symbolic accounts, and explaining the validity of the symbolic approximation through passage to the 'Classical limit', a general theoretical limit incorporating, e.g. the specifics described in (6), in which connectionist accounts admit, more and more exactly, higher-level symbolic accounts – at least in the limited domain *D*. This limitivist position on the relation between connectionism and symbolic theory is obviously modeled after a relation frequently observed in the refinement of physical theories, e.g. the relation between quantum and Newtonian mechanics.

The cognitive correspondence principle is so named because I believe that it has a role to play in the developing micro-theory of cognition that's analogous to the role that the quantum correspondence principle played in the development of micro-theory in physics. This case from physics instantiates the structure of figure 4.5 quite directly. There are certain fundamental physical principles that arch over both the classical and quantum formalisms: the notions of space and time and associated invariance principles, the principles of energy and momentum conservation, force laws, and so on. These principles at the top of figure 4.5 are instantiated in particular ways in the Classical formalism, corresponding to the point one level down on the right branch. To go to a lower level of physical analysis requires the development of a new formalism. In this quantum formalism the fundamental principles are reinstantiated: they occupy the bottom of the left branch. The Classical formalism can be looked at as a higher-level description of the same principles operating at the lower quantum level: the dotted line of figure 4.5. Of course, quantum mechanics does not *implement* classical mechanics: the accounts are intimately related, but classical mechanics provides an approximate, not an exact, higher-level account.[11] In a fundamental sense, the quantum and classical theories are quite incompatible: according to the ontology of quantum mechanics, the ontology of classical mechanics is quite impossible to realize in this world. But there is no denying that the classical ontology and the accompanying principles are theoretically essential, for at least two reasons: (a) to provide explanations (literally, perhaps, approximate ones) of an enormous range of classical phenomena for which direct explanation from quantum principles is hopelessly infeasible; and (b) historically, to provide the guidance necessary to discover the quantum principles in the first place. To try to develop lower-level principles without looking at the higher-level principles for guidance, given the insights we have gained from those principles, would seem – to put it mildly – inadvisable. It is basically this pragmatic consideration that motivates the cognitive correspondence principle and the PTC position it leads to.

3.2   Constituency via vector decomposition, explanatory relevance and causal efficacy

As a final topic I would like to show how the previous methodological considerations relate specifically to the technical heart of this chapter. I want to show that, if we take the general position advocated above that the research agenda of distributed connectionism is to find formal means within the continuous mathematics of dynamical systems for naturally and powerfully embodying central non-formal principles of computation and cognition, then the connectionist analysis of constituent structure I have described here is, if not inevitable, then at least perfectly natural. I take up this topic because it has been suggested that in my analysis, perhaps in order to cook up a refutation of F&P, I have seriously contorted the notion of constituency; that superposition of vectors, and tensor product binding, are just not appropriate means of instantiating constituency.

At the same time, I will consider the central question: 'Is the sense in which vector decomposition constitutes a constituency relation adequate to make constituency *explanatorily relevant* to or *causally efficacious* in the account of the systematicity of thought, the basic problem motivating F&P's critique?'

Let me begin with a few words about the idea of decomposing a vector into a sum or superposition of component vectors: $w = c_1 + c_2 + \ldots$. This technique is very commonly used to explain the behavior of dynamical systems; it works best for simple linear systems, where the equations governing the interaction between state variables are linear (such as the very simplest connectionist models). In that case – and the technique gets more complicated from there – the story is as follows.

We want to know, if we start the system off in some initial state described by the vector w, what will the system's subsequent behavior be? (In the connectionist case, w characterizes the input, and we want to know what states the system will then go through; especially, what the later state that determines the output will be.) First we ask, how can the vector w be decomposed: $w = c_1 + c_2 + \ldots$, so that the component vectors c_i are along certain special directions, determined by the linear interaction equations of the system; these directions e_i are called the 'normal modes' of the system, and each $c_i = c_i e_i$, where the coefficient c_i, tells how strongly represented in this particular input w the ith normal mode is. Once we have decomposed the vector into components in the directions of the normal modes, we can write down in a closed form expression the state of the system at any later time: it is just the superposition of the states arising from each of the normal modes independently, and those normal modes are defined exactly so that it is possible to write down how they evolve in time.[12] Thus, knowing the interaction equations of the system, we can compute the normal modes and how they evolve in time, and then we can explain how *any* state evolves in time, simply by decomposing that state into components in the directions of the normal modes. To see an example of this technique applied to actual connectionist networks, see the general analysis of Smolensky (1986) and the specific analysis in Anderson and Mozer (1981) of the categorization performed in J.A. Anderson's 'Brain-State-in-a-Box' model. (Both these analyses deal with what I call *quasi-linear* networks, a class covering many actual connectionist systems, in which the heart of the computation is linear, but a certain degree of non-linearity is also important.)

Thus, to explain the behavior of the system, we usually choose to decompose the state vector into components in the directions of the normal modes, which are conveniently related to the particular dynamics of this system. If there is change in how the system interacts with itself (as in connectionist networks that learn), over time we'll change the way we choose to break up the state in order to explain the behavior. There's no unique way to decompose a vector. That is to say, there are lots of ways that this input vector could be viewed as composed of constituents, but normal mode decomposition happens to enable a good explanation for behavior over time. In general, there may well be other compositions that are explanatorily relevant.

So, far from being an unnatural way to break up the part of a connectionist state vector that represents an input, decomposing the vector into components is exactly what we'd expect to need to do to explain the processing of that input.[13] If the connections that mediate processing of the vectors representing composite structures have the effect of sensible processing of the vector in terms of the task demands, it is very likely that in order to *understand and explain* the regularities in the network's behavior we will need to break the vector for the structure into the vectors for the constituents, and relate the processing of the whole to the processing of the parts. That this decomposition, and not arbitrary decompositions into meaningless component vectors, is useful for explaining the processing is a consequence of the connections that embody the process. Those particular components are useful for those particular connections. In general, what distinguishes one decomposition of a state vector that is useful for predicting behavior from other decompositions that are not is that the useful decomposition bears some special relation to the dynamics of the system. It may well turn out that to explain various aspects of the system's behavior (for example, various cognitive processes acting on a given input), we will want to exploit various decompositions.

Are the vector constituents in physical and connectionist systems causally efficacious? It would appear not, since the real mechanism driving the behavior of the system operates oblivious to our descriptive predilection to vector decomposition. It is the numerical values comprising the vector (in the connectionist case, the individual activity values) that really drive the machine.

As Fodor and Pylyshyn will, I believe, agree, caution in treating 'causal efficacy' is required even for the Classical case. When we write a LISP program, are the symbolic structures we think in terms of causally efficacious in the operation of the computer that runs the program? There is a sense in which they are: even though we normally think of the 'real' causes as physical and far below the symbolic level, there is none the less a complete and precise algorithmic (temporal) story to tell about the states of the machine described at the level of symbols. Traditional computers (the hardware and especially the software) are designed to make that true, and it is the main source of their power.

The hypothesis I have attributed to distributed connectionism is that there is no comparable story at the symbolic level in the human cognitive architecture: no algorithm in terms of semantically interpretable elements that gives a precise formal algorithmic account of the system's behavior over time. That is a difference with the Classical view that I have made much of. It may be that a good way to characterize the difference is in terms of whether the constituents in mental structures are causally efficacious in mental processing.

Such causal efficacy was not my goal in developing the tensor product representation; rather, the goal was and is the design of connectionist systems that display the kinds of complex systematic behavior seen, for example, in language processing – and the mathematical explanation of that systematicity. As the examples from physics show, it is not only wrong to claim that to explain systematicity by reference to constituent structures requires that those constituents be causally efficacious: it is also wrong (but more honest) to claim (as Fodor often does) that such an explanatory strategy, while not provably unique, constitutes 'the only game in town'. There is an alternative explanatory strategy that has been practiced very effectively in physics for centuries, and that strategy can be applied in cognitive science as well. There are now at least two games in town, and rather than pretending otherwise, we should get on with the business of playing those games for all we can. Odds are, given how hard cognitive science is, we'll need to be playing other games before too long.

The Classical strategy for explaining the systematicity of thought is to hypothesize that there is a precise formal account of the cognitive architecture in which the constituents of mental representations have causally efficacious roles in the mental processes acting on them. The PTC view denies that such an account of the cognitive architecture exists,[14] and hypothesizes instead that, like the constituents of structures in quantum mechanics, the systematic effects observed in the processing of mental representations arise because the evolution of vectors can be (at least partially and approximately) explained in terms of the evolution of their components, even though the precise dynamical equations apply at the lower level of the individual numbers comprising the vectors and cannot be pulled up to provide a precise temporal account of the processing at the level of entire constituents, i.e. even though the constituents are not causally efficacious.[15]

4   Summary

Therefore, I shall resign the presidency effective at noon tomorrow.
(Richard Nixon)

Shifting attention away from the refutation of F&P's argument, let me summarize what I take to be the positive contributions of this chapter.

(7)   (a)   As F&P plead, it *is* crucial for connectionism to separate itself from simplistic associationist psychology, and to accept the importance of a number of computational principles fundamental to traditional cognitive science, such as those relating to structure that F&P emphasize, which go beyond the computational repertoire of simple traditional connectionist networks.

(b) The computational repertoire of connectionism should be extended by finding ways of directly, naturally and powerfully realizing these computational principles within the continuous mathematics of dynamical systems.

(c) Just as a set of symbolic structures offers a domain for modeling structured mental representation and processing, so do sets of vectors, once the appropriate notions (such as variable binding via tensor products) are recognized in the new mathematical category. Thus distributed connectionist representations provide a computational arena for structure processing.

(d) The resulting connectionist model of mental processing is characterized by context-sensitive constituents, approximately (but not exactly) compositional semantics, massively parallel structure-sensitive processing, statistical inference and statistical learning with structured representations.

(e) This connectionist cognitive architecture is intrinsically two-level: semantic interpretation is carried out at the level of patterns of activity while the complete, precise and formal account of mental processing must be carried out at the level of individual activity values and connections. Mental processes reside at a lower level of analysis than mental representations.

(f) Thus, not only is the connectionist cognitive architecture fundamentally different from the classical one, so is the basic strategy for explaining the systematicity of thought. The systematic behavior of the cognitive system is to be explained by appealing to the systematic constituent structure of the representational vectors, and the connectivity patterns that give rise to and manipulate these vectors: but the mechanism responsible for that behavior does not (unlike in the Classical account) operate through laws or rules that are expressible formally at the level of the constituents.

The wind is changing

(Mary Poppins)

Only connect

(E.M. Forster)[16]

Acknowledgments

I have benefited greatly from conversations with Jerry Fodor and Zenon Pylyshyn, extending from February 1986, when Fodor presented an early version of the argument ('Against connectionism') at the Workshop on the Foundations of AI in Las Cruces, New Mexico, through a (surprisingly enjoyable) public debate held at MIT in March 1988. The concerns that drove my research to tensor product representations were kindled through that interaction. I have learned a tremendous amount from Georges Rey, thanks to his wonderful insight, open-mindedness and patience; I would also like to thank him for his most helpful suggestions for this chapter. Thanks, too, to Terry Horgan for very helpful discussions, as well as to the other participants of the Spindel Conference on Connectionism and the Philosophy of Mind (which resulted in the collection of papers in which Smolensky, 1987b, appears). I thank Horgan, John Tienson, and the *Southern Journal of Philosophy* for permission to include a portion of Smolensky (1987b) here. Rob Cummins and Georg Schwarz have helped me enormously in sorting out a number of the issues discussed here, and I refer the reader to their papers for a number of important insights that have not been given their due here. Kevin Markey gets the credit for the crucial Presidential quotes. Finally I would like to thank Geoff Hinton, Jay McClelland, Dave Rumelhart, David Touretzky, and more recently, Alan Prince, for many helpful discussions on issues relating to connectionism and structure processing.

This work has been supported by NSF grants IRI-8609599 and ECE-8617947, by a grant from the Sloan Foundation's computational neuroscience program, and by the Optical Connectionist Machine Program of the NSF Engineering Research Center for Optoelectronic Computing Systems at the University of Colorado at Boulder.

Notes

1   Quoted in Fodor, 1975, p. 27.
2   This point is brought out nicely in Cummins and Schwarz (1987), Schwarz (1987) and Cummins (1989).
3   The complexity criterion here is very low: the interactions should be more complex than purely linear. A lengthy and, I hope, accessible discussion may be found in Smolensky (1986).
4   They admit up front that these arguments are a re-run updated for the 1980s, a colorized version of a film that was shown in black and white some time ago – where the colour comes mainly from replacing everywhere the word 'behaviorism' by 'connectionism'.
5   The conception of connectionist representation and processing embodied in figure 4.1. is at the center of this entire argument, so it is important to properly locate this network and the Ballard and Hayes paper in the connectionist landscape; for those not well familiar with the territory, this may be facilitated by a sociogeographical digression. Hayes is a leading figure in the logic-based approach to symbolic AI, and (to my knowledge) this collaborative exercise is his only foray onto connectionist turf. Ballard is a leading connectionist of the 'Rochester school', which tends to favour local representations over distributed ones, and which as a result

represents a radically different set of foundational commitments (see Feldman and Ballard, 1982) from those of the 'San Diego' or 'PDP' school, as articulated for example in the PDP books (McClelland et al., 1986; Rumelhart et al., 1986); my version of the PDP framework is articulated as PTC in chapter 2 and in Smolensky (1988), which explicitly address the contrast with Feldman and Ballard (1982). (Incidentally, the name 'PDP' was coined to differentiate the approach from the 'connectionist' approach already defined by Feldman and Ballard, 1982; the referent of 'connectionist' subsequently expanded to engulf the PDP approach (e.g. *Cognitive Science*, 1985). This left what I have referred to as the 'Rochester' approach without a distinctive name; the term 'structured connectionist networks' is now sometimes used, but it is potentially quite misleading.) As already evidenced in section 1, it turns out that on foundational issues generally, the local v distributed issues forces the two schools of connectionism to take quite different positions; a response to F&P from the Feldman and Ballard (1982) perspective would have to differ completely from the one I offer here. While F&P argue that distributed representations make no difference, I now proceed to identify a crucial fallacy in that argument, which this chapter as a whole shows to be quite inadequate.

6   A sort of debate about connectionism was held between Geoffrey Hinton and David Rumelhart on the one hand, and Zenon Pylyshyn and Kurt VanLehn on the other. While pursuing the nature of connectionist representations, Pylyshyn asked Rumelhart: 'Look, can you guys represent a cup of coffee in these networks?' Rumelhart's reply was 'Sure' so Pylyshyn continued: 'And can you represent a cup without coffee in it?' Waiting for the trap to close, Rumelhart said 'Yes', at which point Pylyshyn pounced: 'Ah-hah, well, the difference between the two is just the representation of *coffee* – you've just built a representation of *cup with coffee* by combining a representation of *cup* with a representation of *coffee*.'

7   As suggested to me by Georges Rey, the tensor product representation scheme can be understood by analogy to Gödel number encodings. In the Gödel encoding, the representation of a string ab . . . x . . . is the number $v = p_1{}^a p_2{}^b \ldots p_i{}^x \ldots$ where x is the ith symbol in the string. Each of the symbols in the alphabet, a, b, . . ., x, . . . is assigned a unique whole number code, a, b, . . ., x, . . . To each possible position i in the string corresponds a certain prime number p_i. Given v, it is possible to recover the string it represents, provided we know both the set of primes used to code positions, $\{p_i\}$, and the encoding of the alphabet; this is because v has a unique decomposition into powers of primes. In the tensor product scheme, this string would be represented by a vector $\mathbf{v} = \mathbf{p}_1 \otimes \mathbf{a} + \mathbf{p}_2 \otimes \mathbf{b} + \ldots + \mathbf{p}_i \otimes \mathbf{x} + \ldots$ Instead of numbers, each symbol is now encoded by a vector of activity values (x is represented by $\mathbf{x}$ etc.); instead of primes, each position i is represented by an activity vector $\mathbf{p}_i$. In going from the Gödel scheme to the tensor product representation, numbers become vectors, the exponentiation used to bind symbols to their positions

becomes the tensor product, and the multiplication used to combine the symbol/position bindings becomes vector addition. From v we can exactly recover the string if the vectors $\{p_i\}$ are all linearly independent: if none can be expressed as a weighted sum of the others. This is the property that guarantees we can undo the vector addition operation, just as using primes ensures in the Gödel scheme that we can undo the multiplication operation (none of the p_i can be expressed as a product of the others). Gödel numbering can be done recursively, so that the exponents representing consecutive objects (e.g. lines in a proof) can themselves be the Gödel numbers of strings; likewise, tensor product representations can be built recursively, so that the vector representing a filler (or role) can itself be the tensor product representation of a structure. This is possible because the tensor product takes two vectors and creates a new vector which can then be used in a subsequent tensor product. (This is the reason that tensor algebra is natural here; in matrix algebra, which is to some degree a subset of tensor algebra, the outer product of two vectors, which is the same set of numbers as the tensor product of those vectors, is treated as a new type of object: a matrix – this blocks recursion.)

8   It's all well and good to say, as F&P do, that the Classical view has no commitment to serial processing. 'We like parallel computation too.' Fine, give me a massively parallel symbolic model that processes tree structures and I'll be happy to compare it to this. But I don't see it out there. See Dolan and Smolensky (1988) for an actual distributed connectionist model, TPPS, that uses the tensor product to represent a symbolic structure and operate on it with massive parallelism. The system is an exercise in applying the tensor product representation to put on a somewhat more general and simple mathematical footing Touretzky and Hinton's (1985) Boltzmann machine implementation of a distributed connectionist production system, DCPS. Each production in TPPS does pattern matching against the whole symbolic structure in working memory in parallel, and does all parts of its action in parallel. Since it is an implementation of a traditional production system, however, productions are fired one at a time, although conflict resolution is done in parallel.

9   Like connectionist networks, traditional computers were originally viewed exclusively as number processors. Newell and Simon are credited with teaching us that traditional computers could also be used as powerful structure processors. I am essentially trying to make the same point about connectionist networks.

10   This is true provided the parameter values defining the representation satisfy the very weak constraint that the simplest possible confusions are avoided (such as confusing $P \,\&\, Q$ with $Q \,\&\, P$ or with $P \text{ or } Q$).

11   Many cases analogous to 'implementation' *are* found in physics: Newton's laws provide an 'implementation' of Kepler's laws; Maxwell's theory 'implements' Coulomb's law; the quantum principles of the hydrogen atom 'implement' Balmer's formula.

12　For example, in a dynamical system that oscillates, the evolution of the normal modes in time is given by: $e_n(t) = e^{i\omega_n t}e_n$. Each particular normal mode e_n consists of an oscillation with a particular frequency ω_n.

13　How reasonable is it to view this decomposition process as a formalization of the notion of decomposing a 'structure' into its 'constituents'? (I am indebted to Tim van Gelder, personal communication, for very useful discussion of this issue; see also van Gelder, 1989.) I take it that it is a reasonable use of the term 'constituent' to say that 'electrons are constituents of atom.' In modern physics, what is the relation between the representation of the electron and the representation of the atom?

　　The state of the atom, like the states of all systems in quantum theory, is represented by a vector in an abstract vector space. Each electron has an internal state (its 'spin'); it also has a role it plays in the atom as a whole: it occupies some 'orbital', essentially a cloud of probability for finding it at particular places in the atom. The internal state of an electron is represented by a 'spin vector'; the orbital or role of the electron (part) in the atom (whole) is represented by another vector, which describes the probability cloud. The vector representing the electron as situated in the atom is the tensor product of the vector representing the internal state of the electron and the vector representing its orbital. The atom as a whole is represented by a vector that is the sum or superposition of vectors, each of which represents a particular electron situated in its orbital. (There are also contributions of the same sort from nucleons.)

　　Thus the vector representing the whole is the sum of tensor products of pairs of vectors; in each pair, one vector represents the part independent of its role in the whole, and the other represent the role in the whole independent of the part that fills the role. This is exactly the way I have used tensor products to construct distributed connectionist representations for wholes from distributed connectionist representations of their parts (and from distributed representations of the roles of parts in the whole) – and this is exactly where the idea came from.

　　So someone who claims that the tensor product representational scheme distorts the notion of constituency has some explaining to do.

　　So does someone who claims that the sense in which the whole has parts is not explanatorily relevant. We explain the properties of atoms by invoking properties of their electronic configuration all the time. Quantum theory aside, physical systems whose states are described by vectors have for centuries had their behavior explained by viewing the state vector as a superposition of component vectors, and explaining the evolution of the total state in terms of the evolution of its component vectors – as I have indicated in the preceding discussion of normal modes.

　　Are the constituents of mental representations as I have characterized them in distributed connectionist systems causally efficacious in mental processing?

　　The term 'causally efficacious' must be used with some caution. The equations that drive the atom do not work by first figuring out what the component particles are, and then working on each of them separately. The equations take the elements comprising the vector for the whole atom and change them in time. We can *analyze* the system by breaking up the vector for the whole into the vectors for the parts, and in general that's a good way to do the analysis; but nature doesn't do that in updating the state of the system from one moment to the next. So, in this case, are the constituents causally efficacious or not? The same question arises in the connectionist case.

14 Except for that limited part of the architecture I have called the 'conscious rule interpreter'; see chapter 2.
15 I use this characterization rather tentatively because I am not yet convinced that the notion of causal efficacy it presupposes is less problematic than what it is being invoked to elucidate.
16 Quoted in Fodor, 1975, p. vi.

References

Anderson, J.A. and Mozer, M.C. (1981) Categorization and selective neurons. In G.E. Hinton and J.A. Anderson (eds), *Parallel Models of Associative Memory*. Hillsdale, NJ, Erlbaum.

Ballard, D. (1986) Parallel logical inference and energy minimization, Technical report 142, Computer Science Department, University of Rochester.

Ballard, D. and Hayes, P.J. (1984) Parallel logical inference. *Proceedings of the Sixth Annual Conference of the Cognitive Science Society*, Rochester, New York. Hillsdale, NJ, Erlbaum.

Cognitive Science (1985) Special issue on connectionist models and their applications 9 (1).

Cummins, R. (1989) *Meaning and Mental Representation*. Cambridge, Mass. MIT Press/Bradford Books.

Cummins, R. and Schwarz, G. (1987) Radical connectionism. *Southern Journal of Philosophy* 26 (suppl.), 43–61.

Dolan, C. and Smolensky, P. (1988) Implementing a connectionist production system using tensor products. In Morgan Kaufmann. D. Touretzky, G.E. Hinton and T.J. Sejnowski (eds), *Proceedings of the Connectionist Models Summer School, 1988*.

Feldman, J.A. and Ballard, D.H. (1982) Connectionist models and their properties. *Cognitive Science* 6, 205–54.

Fodor, J.A. (1975) *The Language of Thought*. New York, Thomas Y, Crowell. (Harvard University Press paperback.)

Gelder, T. van (1989) Compositionality: variation on a classical theme. Unpublished manuscript.

Hinton, G.E., McClelland, J.L. and Rumelhart, D.E. (1986) Distributed representations. In D.E. Rumelhart, J.L. McClelland and the PDP Research Group (eds), *Parallel Distributed Processing: Explorations in the*

Microstructure of Cognition. Vol. 1: *Foundations*. Cambridge, Mass., MIT Press/Bradford Books.

McClelland, J.L. and Kawamoto, A.H. (1986) Mechanisms of sentence processing: assigning roles to constituents of sentences. In J.L. McClelland, D.E. Rumelhart and the PDP Research Group (eds), *Parallel Distributed Processing: Explorations in the Microstructure of Cognition*. Vol. 2: *Psychological and Biological Models*. Cambridge, Mass., MIT Press/Bradford Books.

McClelland, J.L., Rumelhart, D.E. and the PDP Research Group (eds) (1986) *Parallel Distributed Processing: Explorations in the Microstructure of Cognition*. Vol. 2: *Psychological and Biological Models*. Cambridge, Mass., MIT Press/Bradford Books.

Newell, A. and Simon, H. (1981) Computer science as an empirical inquiry. In J. Haugeland (ed.), *Mind Design*. Cambridge, Mass., MIT Press/Bradford Books.

Rumelhart, D.E., McClelland, J.L. and the PDP Research Group (eds) (1986) *Parallel Distributed Processing: Explorations in the Microstructure of Cognition*. Vol. 1: *Foundations*. Cambridge, Mass., MIT Press/Bradford Books.

Schwarz, G. (1987) Explaining cognition as computation. Unpublished Master's thesis, University of Colorado at Boulder.

Smolensky, P. (1986) Neural and conceptual interpretations of parallel distributed processing models. In J.L. McClelland, D.E. Rumelhart and the PDP Research Group (eds), *Parallel Distributed Processing: Explorations in the Microstructure of Cognition*. Vol. 2: *Psychological and Biological Models*. Cambridge, Mass., MIT Press/Bradford Books.

Smolensky, P. (1987a) On variable binding and the representation of symbolic structures in connectionist systems. Technical Report CU-CS-355-87, Department of Computer Science, University of Colorado at Boulder.

Smolensky, P. (1987b) The constituent structure of connectionist mental states: a reply to Fodor and Pylyshyn. *Southern Journal of Philosophy* 26 (suppl.), 137–63.

Smolensky, P. (1988) Putting together connectionism – again. *Behavioral and Brain Sciences* 11, 59–74.

Smolensky, P. (forthcoming) *Lectures on Connectionist Cognitive Modeling*. Hillsdale, NJ, Erlbaum.

Touretzky, D.S. and Hinton, G.E. (1985) Symbols among the neurons: details of a connectionist inference architecture. In A. Joshi (ed.), *Proceedings of the International Joint Conference on Artificial Intelligence*, pp. 238–43. California, Morgan Kaufmann.

5

Connectionism and the Problem of Systematicity: Why Smolensky's Solution Doesn't Work

Jerry A. Fodor and Brian P. McLaughlin

Introduction

Paul Smolensky (1987, chapter 4) has responded to a challenge Jerry Fodor and Zenon Pylyshyn (chapter 3) posed for connectionist theories of cognition: to explain the existence of systematic relations among cognitive capacities without assuming that cognitive processes are causally sensitive to the constituent structure of mental representations. This challenge implies a dilemma: if connectionism can't account for systematicity, it thereby fails to provide an adequate basis for a theory of cognition; but if its account of systematicity requires mental processes that are sensitive to the constituent structure of mental representations, then the theory of cognition it offers will be, at best, an implementation architecture for a 'classical' (language of thought) model. Smolensky thinks connectionists can steer between the horns of this dilemma if they avail themselves of certain kinds of distributed mental representation. In what follows, we will examine this proposal.

Our discussion has three parts. In section 1, we briefly outline the phenomenon of systematicity and its Classical explanation. As we will see, Smolensky actually offers two alternatives to this Classical treatment, corresponding to two ways in which complex mental representations can be distributed; the first kind of distribution yields complex mental representations with 'weak compositional structure', the second yields mental representations with 'strong compositional structure'. We will consider these two notions of distribution in turn: in section 2, we argue that Smolensky's proposal that complex mental representations have weak compositional structure should be rejected both as inadequate to explain systematicity and on internal grounds; in section 3, we argue that postulating mental representations with strong compositional structure also fails to provide for an explanation of systematicity. The upshot will be that Smolensky avoids only one horn of the dilemma that Fodor and Pylyshyn proposed. We shall see that his architecture is genuinely non-classical since the representations he postulates are not 'distributed over' constituents in the sense that Classical representations are; and we shall see that for that very reason Smolensky's architecture leaves systematicity unexplained.

1   The Systematicity Problem and its Classical Solution

The systematicity problem is that cognitive capacities come in clumps. For example, it appears that there are families of semantically related mental states such that, as a matter of psychological law, an organism is able to be in one of the states belonging to the family only if it is able to be in many of the others. Thus, you don't find organisms that can learn to prefer the green triangle to the red square but can't learn to prefer the red triangle to the green square. You don't find organisms that can think the thought that the girl loves John but can't think the thought that John loves the girl. You don't find organisms that can infer P from $P\&Q\&R$ but can't infer P from $P\&Q$ And so on over a very wide range of cases. For the purposes of this paper, we assume without argument:

(a) that cognitive capacities are generally systematic in this sense, both in humans and in many infra-human organisms;
(b) that it is nomologically necessary (hence counterfactual supporting) that this is so;
(c) that there must therefore be some psychological mechanism in virtue of the functioning of which cognitive capacities are systematic;
(d) and that an adequate theory of cognitive architecture should exhibit this mechanism.

Any of (a)-(d) may be viewed as tendentious; but, so far as we can tell, all four are accepted by Smolensky. So we will take them to be common ground in what follows.[1]

The Classical account of the mechanism of systematicity depends crucially on the idea that mental representation is language-like. In particular, mental representations have a combinatorial syntax and semantics. We turn to a brief discussion of the Classical picture of the syntax and semantics of mental representations; this provides the basis for understanding the Classical treatment of systematicity.

Classical syntax and Classical constituents

The Classical view holds that the syntax of mental representations is like the syntax of natural language sentences in the following respect: both include complex symbols (bracketing trees) which are constructed out of what we will call *Classical constituents*. Thus, for example, the English sentence 'John loves the girl' is a complex symbol whose decomposition into Classical constituents is exhibited by some such bracketing tree as:

Sentence

Subject   Predicate

Object

John   loves   the girl

Correspondingly, it is assumed that the mental representation that is entertained when one thinks the thought that John loves the girl is a complex symbol of which the Classical constituents include representations of John, the girl, and loving.

It will become clear in section 3 that it is a major issue whether the sort of complex mental representations that are postulated in Smolensky's theory have constituent structure. We do not wish to see this issue degenerate into a terminological wrangle. We therefore stipulate that, for a pair of expression types E1, E2, the first is a *Classical* constituent of the second *only if* the first is tokened whenever the second is tokened. For example, the English word 'John' is a Classical constituent of the English sentence 'John loves the girl' and every tokening of the latter implies a tokening of the former (specifically, every token of the latter *contains* a token of the former; you can't say 'John loves the girl' without saying 'John').[2] Likewise, it is assumed that a mentalese symbol which names John is a Classical constituent of the mentalese symbol that means that John loves the girl. So again tokenings of the one symbol require tokenings of the other.

It is precisely because Classical constituents have this property that they are always accessible to operations that are defined over the complex symbols that contain them; in particular, it is precisely because Classical mental representations have Classical constituents that they provide domains for structure-sensitive mental processes. We shall see presently that what Smolensky offers as the 'constituents' of connectionist mental representations are non-Classical in this respect, and that that is why his theory provides no account of systematicity.

Classical semantics

It is part of the Classical picture, both for mental representation and for representation in natural languages, that generally when a complex formula (e.g. a sentence) S expresses the proposition P, S's constituents express (or refer to) the elements of P.[3] For example, the proposition that John loves the girl contains as its elements the individuals John and the girl, and the two-place relation 'loving'. Correspondingly, the formula 'John loves the girl', which English uses to express this proposition, contains as constituents the expressions 'John', 'loves' and 'the girl'. The sentence 'John left and the girl wept', whose constituents include the formulas 'John left' and 'the girl wept', expresses the proposition that John left and the girl wept, whose elements include the proposition that John left and the proposition that the girl wept. And so on.

These assumptions about the syntax and semantics of mental representations are summarized by condition (C):

(C): If a proposition P can be expressed in a system of mental representation M, then M contains some complex mental representation (a 'mental sentence') S, such that S expresses P and the (Classical) constituents of S express (or refer to) the elements of P.

Systematicity

The Classical explanation of systematicity assumes that (C) holds by nomological necessity; it expresses a *psychological law* that subsumes all systematic minds. It should be fairly clear why systematicity is readily explicable on the assumptions, first, that mental representations satisfy (C), and, secondly, that mental processes have access to the constituent structure of mental representations. Thus, for example, since (C) implies that anyone who can represent a proposition can, *ipso facto*, represent its elements, it implies, in particular, that anyone who can represent the proposition that John loves the girl can, *ipso facto*, represent John, the girl and the two-place relation *loving*. Notice, however, that the proposition that *the girl loves John* is *also* constituted by these same individuals/relations. So, then, assuming that the processes that integrate the mental representations that express propositions have access to their constituents, it follows that anyone who can represent John's loving the girl can also represent the girl's loving John. Similarly, suppose that the constituents of the mental representation that gets tokened when one thinks that $P\&Q\&R$ and the constituents of the mental representation that gets tokened when one thinks that $P\&Q$ both include the mental representation that gets tokened when one thinks that P. And suppose that the mental processes that mediate the drawing of inferences have access to the constituent structure of mental representations. Then it should be no surprise that anyone who can infer P from $P\&Q\&R$ can likewise infer P from $P\&Q$.

To summarize: the Classical solution to the systematicity problem entails that (a) systems of mental representation satisfy (C) (*a fortiori*, complex mental representations have Classical constituents); and (b) mental processes are sensitive to the constituent structure of mental representations. We can now say quite succinctly what our claim against Smolensky will be: on the one hand, the cognitive architecture he endorses does not provide for mental representations with Classical constituents; on the other Hall, he provides no suggestion as to how Mental processes could be structure sensitive unless mental representations have Classical constituents; and, on the third hand (as it were) he provides no suggestion as to how minds could be systematic if mental processes aren't structure sensitive. So his reply to Fodor and Pylyshyn fails.

Most of the rest of the chapter will be devoted to making this analysis stick.

2   Weak Compositionality

Smolensky's views about 'weak' compositional structure are largely inexplicit and must be extrapolated from his 'coffee story', which he tells in both of the papers under discussion (and also in chapter 2). We turn now to considering this story.

Smolensky begins by asking how we are to understand the relation between the mental representation COFFEE and the mental representation

CUP WITH COFFEE.[4] His answer to this question has four aspects that are of present interest:

1   COFFEE and CUP WITH COFFEE are activity vectors (according to Smolensky's weak compositional account, this is true of the mental representations corresponding to all common-sense concepts; whether it also holds for (for example) technical concepts won't matter for what follows). A vector is, of course, a magnitude with a certain direction. A pattern of activity over a group of 'units' is a state consisting of the members of the group each having an activation value of 1 or 0.[5] Activity vectors are representations of such patterns of activity.

2   CUP WITH COFFEE representations contain COFFEE representations as (non-Classical)[6] constituents in the following sense: they contain them as *component* vectors. By stipulation, a, is a component vector of b, if there is a vector x such that $a + x = b$ (where '+' is the operation of vector addition). More generally, according to Smolensky, the relation between vectors and their non-Classical constituents is that the former are derivable from the latter by operations of vector analysis.

3   COFFEE representations and CUP WITH COFFEE representations are activity vectors over units which represent micro-features (units like BROWN, LIQUID, MADE OF PORCELAIN etc.).

4   COFFEE (and, presumably, any other representation vector) is *context dependent*. In particular, the activity vector that is the COFFEE representation in CUP WITH COFFEE *is distinct from* the activity vector that is the COFFEE representation in, as it might be, GLASS WITH COFFEE or CAN WITH COFFEE. Presumably this means that the vector in question, with no context specified, does not give necessary conditions for being *coffee*. (We shall see later that Smolensky apparently holds that it doesn't specify sufficient conditions for being *coffee* either.)

Claims (1) and (2) introduce the ideas that mental representations are activity vectors and that they have (non-Classical) constituents. These ideas are neutral with respect to the distinction between strong and weak compositionality so we propose to postpone discussing them until section 3. Claim (3), is, in our view, a red herring. The idea that there are micro-features is orthogonal both to the question of systematicity and to the issues about compositionality. We therefore propose to discuss it only very briefly. It is claim (4) that distinguishes the strong from the weak notion of compositional structure: a representation has weak compositional structure iff it contains context-dependent constituents. We propose to take up the question of context dependent-representation here.

We commence by reciting the coffee story (in a slightly condensed form).

Since, following Smolensky, we are assuming heuristically that units have bivalent activity levels, vectors can be represented by ordered sets of zeros (indicating that a unit is 'off') and ones (indicating that a unit is 'on'). Thus, Smolensky says, the CUP WITH COFFEE representation might be the following activity vector over micro-features:

1-UPRIGHT CONTAINER
1-HOT LIQUID
0-GLASS CONTACTING WOOD[7]
1-PORCELAIN CURVED SURFACE
1-BURNT ODOR
1-BROWN LIQUID CONTACTING PORCELAIN
1-PORCELAIN CURVED SURFACE
0-OBLONG SILVER OBJECT
1-FINGER-SIZED HANDLE
1-BROWN LIQUID WITH CURVED SIDES AND BOTTOM[8]
(taken from the draft copy of chapter 4)

This vector, according to Smolensky, contains a COFFEE representation as a constituent. This constituent can, he claims, be derived from CUP WITH COFFEE by subtracting CUP WITHOUT COFFEE from CUP WITH COFFEE. The vector that is the remainder of this subtraction will be COFFEE.

The reader will object that this treatment presupposes that CUP WITHOUT COFFEE is a constituent of CUP WITH COFFEE. Quite so. Smolensky is explicit in claiming that 'the pattern or *vector* representing *cup with coffee* is composed of a *vector* that can be identified as a distributed representation of *cup without coffee* together with a *vector* that can be identified as a particular distributed representation of *coffee*' (chapter 4, p. 175).

One is inclined to think that this must surely be wrong. If you combine a representation with the content *cup without coffee* with a representation with the content *coffee*, you get not a representation with the content *cup with coffee* but rather a representation with the self-contradictory content *cup without coffee with coffee*. Smolensky's subtraction procedure appears to confuse the representation of *cup without coffee* (viz. CUP WITHOUT COFFEE) with the representation of *cup* without the representation of *coffee* (viz. CUP). CUP WITHOUT COFFEE expresses the content *cup without coffee*; CUP combines consistently with COFFEE. But nothing does both.

On the other hand, it must be remembered that Smolensky's mental representations are advertised as context dependent, hence non-compositional. Indeed, we are given *no clue at all* about what sorts of relations between the semantic properties of complex symbols and the semantic properties of their constituents his theory acknowledges. Perhaps in a semantics where constituents don't contribute their contents to the symbols they belong to, it's all right after all if CUP WITH COFFEE has CUP WITHOUT COFFEE (or, for that matter, PRIME NUMBER, or GRANDMOTHER, or FLYING SAUCER or THE LAST OF THE MOHICANS) among its constituents.

In any event, to complete the story, Smolensky gives the following features for CUP WITHOUT COFFEE:

1-UPRIGHT CONTAINER
0-HOT LIQUID
0-GLASS CONTACTING WOOD
1-PORCELAIN CURVED SURFACE
0-BURNT ODOR
0-BROWN LIQUID CONTACTING PORCELAIN
1-PORCELAIN CURVED SURFACE
0-OBLONG SILVER OBJECT
1-FINGER-SIZED HANDLE
0-BROWN LIQUID WITH CURVED SIDES AND BOTTOM etc.
(taken from the draft copy of chapter 4)

Subtracting this vector from CUP WITH COFFEE, we get the following COFFEE representation:

0-UPRIGHT CONTAINER
1-HOT LIQUID
0-GLASS CONTACTING WOOD
0-PORCELAIN CURVED SURFACE
1-BURNT ODOR
1-BROWN LIQUID CONTACTING PORCELAIN
0-PORCELAIN CURVED SURFACE
0-OBLONG SILVER OBJECT
0-FINGER-SIZED HANDLE
1-BROWN LIQUID WITH CURVED SIDES AND BOTTOM
(taken from the draft copy of chapter 4)

That, then, is Smolensky's 'coffee story'.

Comments

Micro-features It's common ground in this discussion that the explanation of systematicity must somehow appeal to relations between complex mental representations and their constituents (on Smolensky's view, to combinatorial relations among vectors). The issue about whether there are micro-features is entirely orthogonal; it concerns only the question *which properties the activation states of individual units express.* (To put it in more Classical terms, it concerns the question which symbols constitute the *primitive vocabulary* of the system of mental representations.) If there are micro-features, then the activation states of individual units are constrained to express only (as it might be) 'sensory' properties (Smolensky, 1987, p. 146). If there aren't, then activation states of individual units can express not only such properties as *being brown* and *being hot*, but also such properties as *being coffee*. It should be evident upon even casual reflection that, whichever way this issue is settled, the constituency question – viz. the question how the representation COFFEE relates to the representation CUP WITH COFFEE – remains wide open. We therefore propose to drop the discussion of micro-features in what follows.

Context-dependent representation As far as we can tell, Smolensky holds that the representation of *coffee* that he derives by subtraction from CUP WITH COFFEE is context dependent in the sense that it need bear no more than a 'family resemblance' to the vector that represents *coffee* in CAN WITH COFFEE, GLASS WITH COFFEE etc. There is thus no single vector that counts as *the* COFFEE representation, hence no single vector that is a component of all the representations which, in a classical system, would have COFFEE as a Classical constituent.

Smolensky himself apparently agrees that this is the wrong sort of constituency to account for systematicity and related phenomena. As he remarks, 'a true constituent can move around and fill any of a number of different roles in different structures' (chapter 4, p. 177) and the connection between constituency and systematicity would appear to turn on this. For example, the solution to the systematicity problem mooted in section 1 depends exactly on the assumption that tokens of the representation type JOHN express the same content in the context LOVES THE GIRL that they do in the context THE GIRL LOVES; (viz. that they pick out *John*, who is an element both of the proposition *John loves the girl* and of the proposition *the girl loves John*.) It thus appears, prima facie, that the explanation of systematicity requires context-independent constituents.

How, then, does Smolensky suppose that the assumption that mental representations have weak compositional structure, that is, that mental representation is context dependent, bears on the explanation of systematicity? He simply doesn't say. And we don't have a clue. In fact, having introduced the notion of weak compositional structure, Smolensky to all intents and purposes drops it in favour of the notion of strong compositional structure, and the discussion of systematicity is carried out entirely in terms of the latter. What, then, he takes the relation between weak and strong compositional structure to be – and, for that matter, which kind of structure he actually thinks that mental representations haves[9] – is thoroughly unclear.

In fact, quite independent of its bearing on systematicity, the notion of weak compositional structure as Smolensky presents it is of very dubious coherence. We close this section with a remark or two about this point.

It looks as though Smolensky holds that the COFFEE vector that you get by subtraction from CUP WITH COFFEE is not a COFFEE representation when it stands alone. 'This representation is indeed a representation of coffee, but [only?] in a very particular context: the context provided by *cup* [i.e. CUP]' (Smolensky, 1987, p. 147). If this is the view, it has bizarre consequences. Take a liquid that has the properties specified by the micro-features that comprise COFFEE in isolation, but that isn't coffee. Pour it into a cup, *et voila!* it *becomes* coffee by semantical magic.

Smolensky explicitly doesn't think that the vector COFFEE that you get from CUP WITH COFFEE gives necessary conditions for being coffee, since you'd get a different COFFEE vector by subtraction from, say, GLASS WITH COFFEE. And the passage just quoted suggests that he thinks it doesn't give sufficient conditions either. But, then, if the micro-features associated with COFFEE are neither necessary nor sufficient for being *coffee*[10] the question arises what, according to this story, *does* makes a vector a COFFEE representation; when does a vector have the content *coffee*?

As far as we can tell, Smolensky holds that what makes the COFFEE component of CUP WITH COFFEE a representation with the content *coffee* is that it is distributed over units representing certain micro-features *and* that it figures as a component vector of a vector which is a CUP WITH COFFEE representation. As remarked above, we are given no details at all about this reverse compositionality according to which the embedding vector determines the contents of its constituents; how it is supposed to work isn't even discussed in Smolensky's papers. But, in any event, a regress threatens since the question now arises: if being a component of a CUP OF COFFEE representation is required to make a vector a *coffee* representation, what is required to make a vector a *cup of coffee* representation? Well, presumably CUP OF COFFEE represents *cup of coffee* because it involves the micro-features it does *and* because it is a component of still another vector; perhaps one that is a THERE IS A CUP OF COFFEE ON THE TABLE representation. Does this go on forever? If it doesn't, then presumably there are some vectors which aren't constituents of any others. But now, what determines *their* contents? Not the contents of their constituents because, by assumption, Smolensky's semantics isn't compositional (CUP WITHOUT COFFEE is a constituent of CUP WITH COFFEE etc.). And not the vectors that they are constituents of, because, by assumption, there aren't any of those.

We think it is unclear whether Smolensky has a coherent story about how a system of representations could have weak compositional structure.

What, in the light of all this, leads Smolensky to embrace his account of weak compositionality? Here's one suggestion: perhaps Smolensky confuses being a representation of a cup with coffee with being a CUP WITH COFFEE representation. Espying some cup with coffee on a particular occasion, in a particular context, one might come to be in a mental state that represents it as having roughly the micro-features that Smolensky lists. That mental state would then be a representation of a cup with coffee in this sense: there is a cup of coffee that it's a mental representation of. But it wouldn't, of course, follow, that it's a CUP WITH COFFEE representation; and the mental representation of that cup with coffee might be quite different from the mental representation of the cup with coffee that you espied on some other occasion or in some other context. So *which mental representation a cup of coffee gets is context dependent*, just as Smolensky says. But that doesn't give Smolensky what he needs to make mental representations themselves context dependent. In particular, from the fact that cups with coffee get different representations in different contexts, it patently doesn't follow that the mental symbol that represents something as *being* a cup of coffee in one context might represent something as being something else (a giraffe say, or *The Last of the Mohicans*) in some other context. We doubt that anything will give Smolensky that, since we know of no reason to suppose that it is true.

In short, it is natural to confuse the true but uninteresting thought that how you mentally represent some coffee depends on the context, with the much more tendentious thought that the mental representation COFFEE is context dependent. Assuming that he is a victim of this confusion makes sense of many of the puzzling things that Smolensky says in the coffee story. Notice, for example, that all the micro-features in his examples express more or less perceptual properties (cf. Smolensky's own remark that his micro-features yield a 'nearly sensory level representation'). Notice, too, the peculiarity that the micro-feature 'porcelain curved surface' occurs *twice* in the vector for CUP WITH COFFEE, COFFEE, CUP WITHOUT COFFEE and the like. Presumably, what Smolensky has in mind is that, when you look at a cup, you get to see two curved surfaces, one going off to the left and the other going off to the right.

Though we suspect this really is what's going on, we won't pursue this interpretation further since, if it's correct, then the coffee story is completely irrelevant to the question of what kind of constituency relation a COFFEE representation bears to a CUP WITH COFFEE; and that, remember, is the question that bears on the issues about systematicity.

3   Strong Compositional Structure

So much, then, for 'weak' compositional structure. Let us turn to Smolensky's account of 'strong' compositional structure. Smolensky says that:

> A true constituent can move around and fill any of a number of different roles in different structures. Can *this* be done with vectors encoding distributed representations, and be done in a way that doesn't amount to simply implementing symbolic syntactic constituency? The purpose of this section is to describe research showing that the answer is affirmative. (Chapter 4, pp. 177–8)

The idea that mental representations are activity vectors over units, and the idea that some mental representations have other mental representations as components, is common to the treatment of both weak and strong compositional structure. However, Smolensky's discussion of the latter differs in several respects from his discussion of the former. First, units are explicitly supposed to have continuous activation levels between 0 and 1; secondly, he does not invoke the idea of micro-features when discussing strong compositional structure; thirdly, he introduces a new vector operation (multiplication) to the two previously mentioned (addition and subtraction); fourthly, and most important, strong compositional structure does not invoke – indeed, would appear to be incompatible with – the notion that mental representations are context dependent. So strong compositional structure does not exhibit the incoherences of Smolensky's theory of context-dependent representation.

We will proceed as follows. First we briefly present the notion of strong compositional structure. Then we shall turn to criticism.

Smolensky explains the notion of strong compositional structure, in part, by appeal to the ideas of a tensor product representation and a superposition representation. To illustrate these ideas, consider how a connectionist machine might represent four-letter English words. Words can be decomposed into roles (viz. ordinal positions that letters can occupy) and things that can fill these roles (viz. letters). Correspondingly, the machine might contain activity vectors over units which represent the relevant roles (i.e. over the *role units*) and activity vectors over units which represent the fillers (i.e. over the *filler units*). Finally, it might contain activity vectors over units which represent *filled roles* (i.e. letters in letter positions); these are the *binding units*. The key idea is that the activity vectors over the binding units might be tensor products of activity vectors over the role units and the filler units. The representation of a word would then be a superposition vector over the binding units; that is, a vector that is arrived at by superimposing the tensor product vectors.

The two operations used here to derive complex vectors from component vectors are vector multiplication in the case of tensor product vectors and vector addition in the case of superposition vectors. These are iterative operations in the sense that activity vectors that result from the multiplication of role vectors and filler vectors might themselves represent the fillers of roles in more complex structures. Thus, a tensor product which represents the word 'John' as *'J' in first position, 'o' in second position . . . etc.* might itself be bound to the representation of a syntactical function to indicate, for example, that 'John' has the role subject-of in 'John loves the girl'. Such tensor product representations could themselves be superimposed over yet another group of binding units to yield a superposition vector which represents the bracketing tree (John) (loves (the girl)).

It is, in fact, unclear whether this sort of apparatus is adequate to represent all the semantically relevant syntactic relations that Classical theories express by using bracketing trees with Classical constituents. (There are, for example, problems about long-distance binding relations, as between quantifiers and bound variables.) But we do not wish to press this point. For present polemical purposes, we propose simply to assume that each Classical bracketing tree can be coded into a complex vector in such fashion that the constituents of the tree correspond in some regular way to components of the vector.

But this is not, of course, to grant that either tensor product or superposition vectors *have* Classical constituent structure. In particular, from the assumptions that bracketing trees have Classical constituents and that bracketing trees can be coded by activity vectors, it does *not* follow that activity vectors have Classical constituents. On the contrary, a point about which Smolensky is himself explicit is vital in this regard: the components of a complex vector need not even correspond to patterns of activity over units actually in the machine. As Smolensky puts it, the activity states of the filler and role units can be 'imaginary' even though the ultimate activity vectors – the ones which do not themselves serve as filler or role components of more complex structures – must be actual activity patterns over units in the machine. Consider again our machine for representing four-letter words. The superposition pattern that represents, say, the word 'John' will be an activity vector actually realized in the machine. However, the activity vector representing 'J' will be merely imaginary, as will the activity vector representing *the first letter position*. Similarly for the tensor product activity vector representing *'J' in the first letter position*. The only pattern of activity that will be *actually tokened* in the machine is the superposition vector representing 'John'.

These considerations are of central importance for the following reason. Smolensky's main strategy is, in effect, to invite us to consider the components of tensor product and superposition vectors to be analogous to the Classical constituents of a complex symbol; hence to view them as providing a means by which connectionist architectures can capture the causal and semantic consequences of Classical constituency in mental representations. However, the components of tensor product and superposition vectors differ from Classical constituents in the following way: when a complex Classical symbol is tokened, its constituents are tokened. When a tensor product vector or superposition vector is tokened, its components are not (except *per accidens*). The implication of this difference, from the point of view of the theory of mental processes, is that whereas the Classical constituents of a complex symbol are, *ipso facto*, available to contribute to the causal consequences of its tokenings – in particular, they are available to provide domains for mental processes – the components of tensor product and superposition vectors can have no causal status as such. What is merely imaginary can't make things happen, to put this point in a nutshell.

We will return presently to what all this implies for the treatment of the systematicity problem. There is, however, a preliminary issue that needs to be discussed.

We have seen that the components of tensor product/superposition vectors, unlike Classical constituents, are not, in general, tokened whenever the activity vector of which they are the components is tokened. It is worth emphasizing, in addition, the familiar point that there is, in general, no *unique* decomposition of a tensor product or superposition vector into components. Indeed, given that units are assumed to have continuous levels of activation, there will be *infinitely* many decompositions of a given activity vector. One might wonder, therefore, what sense there is in talk of *the* decomposition of a mental representation into significant constituents given the notion of constituency that Smolensky's theory provides.[11]

Smolensky replies to this point as follows. Cognitive systems will be dynamical systems; there will be dynamic equations over the activation values of individual units, and these will determine certain regularities over activity vectors. Given the dynamical equations of the system, certain decompositions can be especially useful for 'explaining and understanding' its behavior. In this sense, the dynamics of a system may determine 'normal modes' of decomposition into components. So, for example, though a given superposition vector can, in principle, be taken to be the sum of many different sets of vectors, yet it may turn out that we get a small group of sets – even a unique set – when we decompose in the direction of normal modes; and likewise for decomposing tensor product vectors. The long and short is that *it could, in principle, turn out* that, given the (thus far undefined) normal modes of a dynamical cognitive system, complex superposition vectors will have it in common with Classical complex symbols that they have a unique decomposition into semantically significant parts. Of course, it also could turn out that they don't, and no ground for optimism on this point has thus far been supplied.

Having noted this problem, however, we propose simply to ignore it. So here is where we now stand: by assumption (though quite possibly contrary to fact), tensor product vectors and superposition vectors can code constituent structure in a way that makes them adequate vehicles for the expression of propositional content; and, by assumption (though again quite possibly contrary to fact), the superposition vectors that cognitive theories acknowledge have a unique decomposition into semantically interpretable tensor product vectors which, in turn, have a unique decomposition into semantically interpretable filler vectors and role vectors; so it's determinate which proposition a given complex activity vector represents.

Now, assuming all this, what about the systematicity problem?

The first point to make is this: if tensor product/superposition vector representation solves the systematicity problem, the solution must be quite different from the Classical proposal sketched in section 1. True tensor product vectors and superposition vectors 'have constituents' in some suitably extended sense: tensor product vectors have semantically evaluable components, and superposition vectors are decomposable into semantically evaluable tensor product vectors. But the Classical solution to the systematicity problem assumes that *the constituents of mental representations have causal roles*; that they provide domains for mental processes. The Classical constituents of a complex symbol thus contribute to determining the causal consequences of the tokening of that symbol, and it seems clear that the 'extended' constituents of a tensor product/superposition representation can't do that. On the contrary, the components of a complex vector are typically not even tokened when the complex vector itself is tokened; they are simply constituents into which the complex vector *could be* resolved consonant with decomposition in the direction of normal modes. But, to put it crudely, the fact that six *could be* represented as '3 × 2' cannot, in and of itself, affect the causal processes in a computer (or a brain) in which six *is* represented as '6'. Merely counterfactual representations have no causal consequences; only actually tokened representations do.

Smolensky is, of course, sensitive to the question of whether activity vectors really do have constituent structure. He defends at length the claim that he has not contorted the notion of constituency in claiming that they do. Part of this defense adverts to the role that tensor products and superpositions play in physical theory:

> The state of the atom, like the states of all systems in quantum theory, is represented by a vector in an abstract vector space. Each electron has an internal state (its 'spin'); it also has a role it plays in the atom as a whole: it occupies some 'orbital', essentially a cloud of probability for finding it at particular places in the atom. The internal state of an electron is represented by a 'spin vector'; the orbital or role of the electron (part) in the atom (whole) is represented by another vector, which describes the probability cloud. The vector representing the electron as situated in the atom is the tensor product of the vector representing the internal state of the electron and the vector representing its orbital. The atom as a whole is represented by a vector that is the sum or superposition of vectors, each of which represents a particular electron in its orbital. (chapter 4, p. 196)

'So', Smolensky adds, 'someone who claims that the tensor product representational scheme distorts the notion of constituency has some explaining to do' (p. 196).

The physics lesson is greatly appreciated; but it is important to be clear on just what it is supposed to show. It's not, at least for present purposes, in doubt that tensor products *can represent* constituent structure. The relevant question is whether tensor product representations *have* constituent structure; or, since we have agreed that they may be said to have constituent structure 'in an extended sense', it's whether they have the kind of constituent structure to which causal processes can be sensitive, hence the kind of constituent structure to which an explanation of systematicity might appeal.[12] But we have already seen the answer to *this* question: the constituents of complex activity vectors typically aren't 'there', so if the causal consequences of tokening a complex vector are sensitive to its constituent structure, that's a miracle.

We conclude that assuming that mental representations are activation vectors does not allow Smolensky to endorse the Classical solution of the systematicity problem. And, indeed, we think Smolensky would grant this since he admits up front that mental processes will not be causally sensitive to the strong compositional structure of mental representations. That is, he acknowledges that the constituents of complex mental representations play no causal role in determining what happens when the representations get tokened. 'Causal efficacy was not my goal in developing the tensor product representation' (Chapter 4, p. 190). What are causally efficacious according to connectionists are the activation values of individual units; the dynamical equations that govern the evolution of the system will be defined over these. It would thus appear that Smolensky must have some *non*-Classical solution to the systematicity problem up his sleeve; some solution that does *not* depend on assuming mental processes that are causally sensitive to constituent structure. So then, after all this, what *is* Smolensky's solution to the systematicity problem? Remarkably enough, *Smolensky doesn't say*. All he does say is that he

> hypothesizes . . . that . . . the systematic effects observed in the processing of mental representations arise because the evolution of vectors can be (at least partially and approximately) explained in terms of the evolution of their components, even though the precise dynamical equations apply [only] at the lower level of the individual numbers comprising the vectors and cannot be pulled up to provide a precise temporal account of the processing at the level of entire constituents, i.e. even though the constituents, are not causally efficacious. (Chapter 4, p. 191).

It is left unclear how the constituents ('components') of complex vectors are to explain their evolution (even partially and approximately) when they are, by assumption, at best causally inert and, at worst, merely imaginary. In any event, what Smolensky clearly does think is causally responsible for the 'evolution of vectors' (and hence for the systematicity of cognition) are unspecified processes that affect the states of activation of the individual units (the neuron analogs) out of which the vectors are composed. So, then, as far as we can tell, the proposed connectionist explanation of systematicity (and related features of cognition) comes down to this: Smolensky 'hypothesizes' that systematicity is somehow a consequence of underlying neural pro-cesses.[13] Needless to say, if that *is* Smolensky's theory, it is, on the one hand, certainly true, and, on the other hand, not intimately dependent upon his long story about fillers, binders, tensor products, superposition vectors and the rest.

By way of rounding out the argument, we want to reply to a question raised by an anonymous. *Cognition* reviewer, who asks: 'couldn't Smolensky easily build in mechanisms to accomplish the matrix algebra operations that would make the necessary vector explicit (or better yet, from his point of view ... mechanisms that are sensitive to the imaginary components without literally making them explicit in some string of units)?'[14] But this misses the point of the problem that systematicity poses for connectionists, which is not to show that systematic cognitive capacities are *possible* given the assumptions of a connectionist architecture, but to explain how systematicity could be *necessary* – how it could be a *law* that cognitive capacities are systematic – given those assumptions.[15]

No doubt it is possible for Smolensky to wire a network so that it supports a vector that represents *aRb* if and only if it supports a vector that represents *bRa*; and perhaps it is possible for him to do that without making the imaginary units explicit[16] (though there is, so far, no proposal about how to ensure this for *arbitrary a, R* and *b*). The trouble is that, although the architecture permits this, it equally permits Smolensky to wire a network so that it supports a vector that represents *aRb* if and only if it supports a vector that represents *zSq*; or, for that matter, if and only if it supports a vector that represents *The Last of the Mohicans*. The architecture would appear to be absolutely indifferent as among these options.

Whereas, as we keep saying, in the Classical architecture, if you meet the conditions for being able to represent *aRb*, YOU CANNOT BUT MEET THE CONDITIONS FOR BEING ABLE TO REPRESENT *bRa*; the architecture won't let you do so because (a) the representation of *a, R* and *b* are constituents of the representation of *aRb*, and (b) you have to token the constituents of the representations that you token, so Classical constituents can't be just imaginary. So then: it is *built into* the Classical picture that you can't think *aRb* unless you are able to think *bRa*, but the connectionist picture is *neutral* on whether you can think *aRb* even if you can't think *bRa*. But it is a law of nature that you can't think *aRb* if you can't think *bRa*. So the Classical picture explains systematicity and the connectionist picture doesn't. So the Classical picture wins.

Conclusion

At one point in his discussion, Smolensky makes some remarks that we find quite revealing: he says that, even in cases that are paradigms of classical architectures (LISP machine and the like), 'we normally think of the "real" causes as physical and far below the symbolic level ...' Hence, even in Classical machines, the sense in which operations at the symbol level are real causes is just that 'there is ... a complete and precise algorithmic (temporal) story to tell about the states of the machine described' at that level (Chapter 4, p. 190). Smolensky, of course, denies that there is a 'comparable story at the symbolic level in the human cognitive architecture ... [T]hat is a difference with the Classical view that I have made much of. *It may be that a good way to characterize the difference is in terms of whether the constituents in mental structures are causally efficacious in mental processing*' (p. 190; our emphasis).

We say that this is revealing because it suggests a diagnosis: it would seem that Smolensky has succumbed to a sort of generalized epiphenomenalism. The idea is that even Classical constituents participate in causal processes solely by virtue of their physical micro-structure, so even on the Classical story it's what happens at the neural level that *really* counts. Though the evolution of vectors can perhaps be explained in a predictively adequate sort of way by appeal to macro-processes like operations on constituents, still if you want to know what's *really* going on – if you want the *causal* explanation – you need to go down to the 'precise dynamical equations' that apply to activation states of units. That intentional generalizations can only approximate these precise dynamical equations is among Smolensky's recurrent themes. By conflating the issue about 'precision' with the issue about causal efficacy, Smolensky makes it seem that to the extent that macro-level generalizations are imprecise, to that extent macro-level processes are epiphenomenal.

It would need a philosophy lesson to say all of what's wrong with this. Suffice it for present purposes that the argument iterates in a way that Smolensky ought to find embarrassing. No doubt, we do get greater precision when we go from generalizations about operations on constituents to generalizations about operations on units. But if that shows that symbol-level processes aren't really causal, then it must be that unit-level processes aren't really causal either. After all, we get *still more* precision when we go down from unit-sensitive operations to molecule-sensitive operations, and more precision yet when we go down from molecule-sensitive operations to quark-sensitive operations. The moral is not, however, that the causal laws of psychology should be stated in terms of the behavior of quarks. Rather, the moral is that whether you have a level of causal explanation is a question, not just of how much precision you are able to achieve, but also of *what generalizations you are able to express*. The price you pay for doing psychology at the level of units is that you lose causal generalizations that symbol-level theories are able to state. Smolensky's problems with capturing the generalizations about systematicity provide a graphic illustration of these truths.

It turns out, at any event, that there is a crucial caveat to Smolensky's repeated claim that connectionist mechanisms can reconstruct everything that's interesting about the notion of constituency. Strictly speaking, he claims only to reconstruct whatever is interesting about constituents *except their causes and effects*. The explanation of systematicity turns on the causal role of the constituents of mental representations and is therefore among the casualties. Hilary Putnam, back in the days when he was still a metaphysical realist, used to tell a joke about a physicist who actually managed to build a perpetual motion machine; all except for a part that goes back and forth, back and forth, back and forth, forever. Smolensky's explanation of systematicity has very much the character of this machine.

We conclude that Fodor and Pylyshyn's challenge to connectionists has yet to be met. We still don't have *even a suggestion* of how to account for systematicity within the assumptions of connectionist cognitive architecture.

Notes

1   Since the two are often confused, we wish to emphasize that taking *systematicity* for granted leaves the question of *compositionality* wide open. The systematicity of cognition consists of, for example, the fact that organisms that can think aRb can think bRa and vice versa. *Compositionality* proposes a certain explanation of systematicity: viz. that the content of thoughts is determined, in a uniform way, by the content of the context-independent concepts that are their constituents; and that the thought that bRa is constituted of the same concepts as the thought that aRb. So the polemical situation is as follows. If you are a connectionist who accepts systematicity, then you must argue either that systematicity can be explained without compositionality, or that connectionist architecture accommodates compositional representation. So far as we can tell, Smolensky vacillates between these options; what he calls 'weak composi-

tionality' favors the former and what he calls 'strong compositionality' favors the latter.

We emphasize this distinction between systematicity and compositionality in the light of some remarks by an anonymous *Cognition* reviewer: 'By berating the [connectionist] modelers for their inability to represent the common-sense [uncontextualized] notion of "coffee" . . . Fodor and McLaughlin are missing a key point – the models are not supposed to do so. If you buy the . . . massive context-sensitivity . . . that connectionists believe in.' Our strategy is *not*, however, to argue that there is something wrong with connectionism because it fails to offer an uncontextualized notion of mental (or, *mutatis mutandis*, linguistic) representation. Our argument is that if connectionists assume that mental representations are context sensitive, they will need to offer some explanation of systematicity that does not entail compositionality *and they do not have one.*

We do not, therefore, offer direct arguments for context-insensitive concepts in what follows; we are quite prepared that 'coffee' should have a meaning only in context. Only, we argue, *if* it does, then some non-compositional account of the systematicity of coffee-throughts will have to be provided.

2   Though we shall generally consider examples where complex symbols literally *contain* their Classical constituents, the present condition means to leave it open that symbols may have Classical constituents that are not among their (spatiotemporal) parts. (For example, so far as this condition is concerned, it might be that the Classical constituents of a symbol include the values of a 'fetch' operation that takes the symbol as an argument.)

3   We assume that the elements of propositions can include, for example, individuals, properties, relations and other propositions. Other metaphysical assumptions are, of course, possible. For example, it is arguable that the constituents of propositions include *individual concepts* (in the Fregean sense) rather than individuals themselves; and so on. Fortunately, it is not necessary to enter into these abstruse issues to make the points that are relevant to the systematicity problem. All we really need is that propositions have internal structure, and that, characteristically, the internal structure of complex mental representations corresponds, in the appropriate way, to the internal structure of the propositions that they express.

4   The following notational conventions will facilitate the discussion: we will follow standard practice and use capitalized English words and sentences as canonical names for mental representations. (Smolensky uses italicized English expressions instead.) We stipulate that the semantic value of a mental representation so named is the semantic value of the corresponding English word or sentence, and we will italicize words or sentences that denote semantic values. So, for example, COFFEE is a mental representation that expresses (the property of being) *coffee* (as does the English word 'coffee'); JOHN LOVES THE GIRL is a mental representation that expresses the

proposition that *John loves the girl*; and so forth. It is important to notice that our notation allows that the mental representation JOHN LOVES THE GIRL can be atomic and the mental representation COFFEE can be a complex symbol. That is, capitalized expressions should be read as the names of mental representations rather than as structural descriptions.

5   Smolensky apparently allows that units may have continuous levels of activation from 0 to 1. In telling the coffee story, however, he generally assumes bivalence for ease of exposition.

6   As we shall see below, when an activity vector is tokened, its component vectors typically are not. So the constituents of a complex vector are, *ipso facto*, non-Classical.

7   Notice that this micro-feature is 'off' in CUP WITH COFFEE, so it might be wondered why Smolensky mentions it at all. The explanation may be this: operations of vector combination apply only to vectors of the same dimensionality. In the context of the weak constituency story, this means that you can only combine vectors that are activity patterns *over the same units*. It follows that a component vector must contain the same units (though, possibly at different levels of activation) as the vectors with which it combines. Thus if GRANNY combines with COFFEE to yield GRANNY'S COFFEE, GRANNY must contain activation levels for all the units in COFFEE and vice versa. In the present example, it may be that CUP WITH COFFEE is required to contain a 0-activation level for GLASS CONTACTING WOOD to accommodate cases where it is a component of some other vector. Similarly with OBLONG SILVER OBJECT (below) since cups with coffee often have spoons in them.

8   Presumably Smolensky does not take this list to be exhaustive, but we don't know how to continue it. Beyond the remark that although the micro-features in his examples correspond to 'nearly sensory-level representation[s]' that is 'not essential', Smolensky provides no account at all of what determines which contents are expressed by micro-features. The question thus arises why Smolensky assumes that COFFEE is not itself a micro-feature. In any event, Smolensky repeatedly warns the reader not to take his examples of micro-features very seriously, and we don't.

9   They can't have both; either the content of a representation is context dependent or it's not. So, if Smolensky does think that you need strong compositional structure to explain systematicity, and that weak compositional structure is the kind that connectionist representations have, then it would seem that he *thereby* grants Fodor and Pylyshyn's claim that connectionist representations can't explain systematicity. We find this all very mysterious.

10 If they were necessary and sufficient, COFFEE wouldn't be context dependent.

11 The function of the brackets in a Classical bracketing tree is precisely to exhibit its decomposition into constituents; and when the tree is well formed this decomposition will be unique. Thus, the bracketing of '(John)

(loves) (the girl)' implies, for example, both that 'the girl' is a constituent and that 'loves the' is not.

12   It's a difference between psychology and physics that whereas psychology is about the causal laws that govern tokenings of *(mental) representations*, physics is about the causal laws that govern (not mental representations but) atoms, electrons and the like. Since *being a representation* isn't a property in the domain of physical theory, the question whether mental representations have constituent structure has no analog in physics.

13   More precisely: we take Smolensky to be claiming that there is some property D, such that if a dynamical system has D its behavior is systematic, and such that human behavior (for example) is caused by a dynamical system that has D. The trouble is that this is a platitude since it is untendentious that human behavior is systematic, that its causation by the nervous system is lawful, and that the nervous system is dynamical. The least that has to happen if we are to have a substantive connectionist account of systematicity is: first, it must be made clear what property D is, and second it must be shown that D is a property that connectionist systems can have by law. Smolensky's theory does nothing to meet either of these requirements.

14   Actually, Smolensky is forced to choose the second option. To choose the first would, in effect, be to endorse the Classical requirement that tokening a symbol implies tokening its constituents; in which case, the question arises once again why such a network isn't an implementation of a language of thought machine. Just as Smolensky mustn't allow the representations of roles, fillers and binding units to be sub-vectors of superposition vectors if he is to avoid the 'implementation' horn of the Fodor/Pylyshyn dilemma, so too he must avoid postulating mechanisms that make role, filler and binding units explicit (specifically, accessible to mental operations) whenever the superposition vectors are tokened. Otherwise he again has symbols with Classical constituents and raises the question why the proposed device isn't a language of thought machine. Smolensky's problem is that the very feature of his representations that make them wrong for explaning systematicity (viz. that their constituents are allowed to be imaginary) is the one that they have to have to assure that they aren't Classical.

15   Fodor and Pylyshyn were very explicit about this. See, for example, chapter 3, p. 132.

16   Terence Horgan remarks (personal communication) 'often there are two mathematically equivalent ways to calculate the time-evolution of a dynamical system. One is to apply the relevant equations directly to the numbers that are elements of a single total vector describing the initial state of the system. Another way is to mathematically decompose that vector into component normal-mode vectors, then compute the time-evolution of each [of these] . . . and then take the later state of the system to be described by a vector that is the superposition of the resulting normal-mode vectors.' Computations of the former sort are supposed to

be the model for operations that are 'sensitive' to the components of a mental representation vector without recovering them. (Even in the second case, it's the theorist who recovers them in the course of the computations by which he makes his predictions. This does not, of course, imply that the constituents thus 'recovered' participate in causal processes in the system under analysis.)

Reference

Smolensky, P. (1987) The constituent structure of connectionist mental states: a reply to Fodor and Pylyshyn. *Southern Journal of Philosophy* 26, 137–60.

6

Reply: Constituent Structure and Explanation in an Integrated Connectionist/Symbolic Cognitive Architecture

Paul Smolensky

1 Introduction

The relation between cognitive theories based on connectionist computation and those based on symbolic computation is a remarkably complex issue. This is perhaps surprising: the contrasts between the two computational paradigms are so great that it seems many fairly important points of difference should be obvious. Yet the terrain is strewn with claims that contradict each other in important ways. Progress seems to require that we avoid treating Connectionist or symbolic approaches each as monolithic; it is essential to identify within each approach multiple principles and assumptions, and to recognize the complexity of the pattern of logical relations among all these principles. In this chapter I present a new cognitive architecture based on a combination of principles, some derived from Connectionist theories, others from symbolic theories, and others representing a novel integration of the two. The new cognitive architecture is called ICS for 'Integrated Connectionist/Symbolic' architecture. My main claim is that the combination of principles defining ICS is coherent, that the ICS architecture is different from existing architectures in important ways, and that these differences allow the ICS architecture to achieve goals which are not simultaneously attainable by any single existing architecture, either symbolic or connectionist.

1.1 ICS

Several of the primary principles of ICS can be summarized as follows:

Principles of ICS

(1) Alg_{pdp}: In all cognitive domains, cognitive processes are described by algorithms for spreading activation between connectionist units.

(2) Rep_{pdp}: In all cognitive domains, representations are distributed patterns of activity.

(3) Rep_{sym}: In core parts of higher cognitive domains, representations are symbol structures.

(4) Sem_{sym}: The semantic interpretation of these symbolic representations are compositionally derived from their syntactic structure.

(5) Fun_{sym}: In core parts of higher cognitive domains, the input/output functions computed by cognitive processes are described by (recursive) symbolic functions.

Clearly, Alg_{pdp} and Rep_{pdp} derive from the parallel distributed processing (PDP) approach to connectionism, while Rep_{sym}, Sem_{sym} and Fun_{sym} derive from the 'Classical' symbolic approach. Crucially, the following two principles are *rejected* in ICS:

Principles rejected in ICS

(6) $Empiricism_{pdp}$: All important structure in connectionist networks arises from empiricist learning.

(7) Alg_{sym}: Higher cognitive processes are described by symbolic algorithms.

$Empiricism_{pdp}$ is a strongly (but often implicitly) held principle in much PDP research, and in ICS it must be rejected in order that networks may be given structure which supports symbolic representations. Alg_{sym} is a strongly (but sometimes implicitly) held principle in much symbolic cognitive research: symbolic AI consists almost entirely in the search for such algorithms, as does symbolic cognitive modeling and symbolic computational linguistics. The 'Classical' approach to cognitive architecture (e.g. Fodor and Pylyshyn, chapter 3)[1] explains basic properties of cognition by assuming that cognitive processes consist in algorithms that manipulate syntactic constituents, thereby endowing them with causal roles. That Alg_{sym} is rejected in ICS constitutes a crucial departure from symbolic theory across the entire spectrum of cognitive science. That Alg_{sym} fails to hold in ICS is a consequence of the way connectionist processes are used to support symbolic computation.

The negations of $Empiricism_{pdp}$ and Alg_{sym} are therefore central principles of ICS which put it in conflict with previous architectures:[2]

Further principles of ICS

(8) **Nativism$_{ics}$**: Some crucial structure in connectionist networks does *not* arise from learning ($= -$ $Empiricism_{pdp}$).

(9) **Alg$_{ics}$**: There are important higher cognitive processes which are *not* described by symbolic algorithms ($= -$ Alg_{sym}).

It is central to this paper that ICS adopts Rep_{sym}, Sem_{sym} and Fun_{sym}, but rejects Alg_{sym} in favor of its negation Alg_{ics}. This is a principal source of the novelty and power of ICS, but it also makes ICS difficult to grasp. For Rep_{sym}, Sem_{sym} and Fun_{sym} assert that higher cognitive representations, semantics and functions *are* symbolic, while Alg_{ics} says that cognitive algorithms are *not*. Symbols, and the rules governing them, therefore have a most curious status: they *are* real in the sense of governing the semantics and the functions computed, but *not* real in the sense of participating in a causal story, capturable as an algorithm,[3] of the internal mechanism which computes these functions. Of what possible theoretical use could such impotent symbols be? How could they possibly allow us to *explain* regularities in the cognitive system, if they are not part and parcel of the algorithms generating its behavior?

Answering such questions is the crux of the chapter: it requires most of the discussion, once the groundwork is laid by section 2.1. The answers are difficult to encapsulate in a few words, but they amount to this: algorithms are only *one* kind of structure that may exist in a processing system; there are other kinds of structure which also provide explanations of system behavior. The connections in the networks of the ICS architecture are governed by *structural principles* which entail that symbolic functions get computed, but not in virtue of instantiating a symbolic algorithm. The structure is defined over an abstract space which does not involve the kinds of space- and time-decompositions essential for defining symbolic algorithms. Designing such abstract structure is the key to designing ICS. The abstract structure which is crucial to cognitive explanation is one that makes it inappropriate to attribute causal roles to the symbols and the rules governing them.

1.2   Goals

In order that we may eventually more clearly assess the success of ICS (section 4.3), it is worth spelling out its goals explicitly at the outset.

226   PAUL SMOLENSKY

Goals of ICS

(10)   *Preservation*: Do not sacrifice the depth of explanation of higher cognition currently achieved by symbolic theory. This includes explanations of the basic cognitive properties put forth in F&P, most notably the productivity of higher cognition, as well as explanatory accounts of actual human linguistic competence.

(11)   *Reduction*: Explain how symbolic computation is built upon neural computation.

(12)   *Revision*: Use insights derived from the reduction of symbolic computation to lower-level principles to improve upon symbolic accounts of higher cognition.

(13)   *Integration*: Understand how symbolic computational principles which explain core parts of higher cognition integrate with computational principles which explain other aspects of cognition.

The new architecture ICS is needed because existing architectures – symbolic, connectionist or hybrid – are inadequate for simultaneously addressing all these goals. Before justifying this statement, I must digress momentarily to discuss reduction: it is the primary motivation for ICS, and a prerequisite for the other main goal, revision.

1.2.1   Reduction, neural nets and connectionist nets   It would be hard to find many cognitive scientists who reject physicalism, yet it is remarkable how many cognitive scientists have been content with a theory which is absolutely insensitive to knowledge of the physical substrate of cognition. In principle, symbolic theory unaided might offer opportunities for better understanding the relation of the virtual machine which is the symbolic architecture and lower-level cognitive machines, virtual or physical; yet in practice, for many decades, symbolic theory has been able to offer only Total Mystery as its account of the underpinings of symbolic computation. If we are to take reduction at all seriously, it appears to be a fact of life that we must look beyond the boundaries of Classical symbolic theory.

Going to the other extreme and developing computational accounts which slavishly reproduce in enormous detail all that we now know of the structure of the brain would be to guarantee failure, if the goal is in fact reduction – rather than elimination – of symbolic theory. To achieve reduction, it is necessary to find the right degree of preservation of principles of symbolic computation, and the right degree of preservation of principles of neural computation, so that a coherent theory can be constructed, and the next step taken towards a more thorough-going unification. I have argued elsewhere (*OPTC*, Section 4) that PDP connectionism preserves what currently appear to be the most fundamental principles of neural computation; it therefore provides a good starting point for seriously attempting reduction. While there are truckloads of facts about the nervous system which are ignored by PDP principles, it is nonetheless the case that a PDP architecture differs from a classical architecture in fundamental ways which make it much more deeply compatible with neural computation. While falling seriously short of a complete reduction to neural computation, a reduction of the symbolic architecture to a PDP architecture is a major step, and, I believe, historically quite unprecedented. It is just such a reduction which is the subject of this chapter.[4]

To put this argument more crudely: some dismiss PDP architectures because of the many facts about neural structure which are not taken into account. For experimental neuroscientists to adopt such a posture is hardly surprising. For those practicing Classical symbolic theory to do so, however, is preposterous. For while the principles of neural computation which shape PDP are few, they are absolutely fundamental, and they are ignored entirely by Classical theory. There is one and only one property of neural computation which is invoked in Classical theory: the brain is horrendously complex, and there is a lot going on in there which we do not understand. Of all the organs of the body, then, it is the perfect one to house the Classical theory of how mental computation is physically realized: the Total Mystery Theory.[5]

So if reduction is a serious goal, we must look beyond the confines of symbolic theory. Detailed, low-level neural modeling will not do, since it is currently hopeless to connect this to high-level symbolic computation. Eliminativist connectionism, also, clearly will not do the job, since the premise of reduction is that the symbolic architecture needs to be explained, and this is denied altogether by eliminativism. Hybrid architectures – in which a connectionist box somehow exchanges information with a symbol-manipulating box – do not address reduction at all. The remaining approach in practice is Implementationalist Connectionism.

Implementationalist Connectionism is, in a sense, as slavishly devoted to a detailed and literal interpretation of symbolic computation as low-level neural modeling is devoted to a faithful copy of every bump on the neuron. Strictly speaking, this approach seeks to literally *implement* symbolic computation in networks of connectionist units; such a network can then be described at two levels. At the lower level, there are algorithms for passing activity between units. At the higher level, there are symbolic representations and algorithms. Formal, precisely correct and complete descriptions are available at both levels. Such an inter-level reduction is what defines the implementation relation between the levels of description (or of virtual machines) in conventional computers.

The issue of implementation is taken up shortly, in Section 2.1; for now, the relevant point is that, by definition, Implementationalist Connectionism has rather limited prospects for achieving the goal of revision (12). The implementationalist strategy is heavily top-down; while much is made of opportunities for insights from symbolic computation to inform the design of lower-level connectionist networks, the result is that few opportunities arise for the power and novelty of connectionist computation to lead to new higher-level theory. I hasten to add, however, that to many connectionists, especially eliminativist- and empiricist-leaning ones, the ICS architecture has too much the flavor of Implementationalist Connectionism, and appreciating the senses in which ICS is *not* Implementationalism requires a certain degree of care. (Crucially, Alg$_{sym}$ (7) is a central tenet of Implementationalism but is rejected by ICS (9).) In Section 3.3, I argue that ICS enables new and important insights for the (higher-level) theory of grammar to bubble up rather directly from principles of connectionist computation, just the kind of progress which is impossible under Implementationalism. Rather than a literal implementation of symbolic computation, ICS relies on a *partial embedding* of symbolic computation in PDP networks.[6]

1.2.2 ICS strategies Before launching into the ICS story from its beginning, it is worth sketching briefly the ICS strategies for pursuing the goals (10)–(13), and how these strategies rely on exploiting principles from both symbolic and PDP connectionist computation.

ICS strategies for achieving goals (10)–(13)
(14) *Preservation*: Retain a higher level of computational description at which representations and functions have symbolic form to which basic cognitive principles may refer (Section 3).
(15) *Reduction*: Show how certain abstract global (higher-level) structure in distributed connectionist activity patterns can be formally described as (recursive) symbolic constituency (Section 2.1), and how certain abstract global (higher-level) structure in connection patterns entails that the functions computed are (recursive) symbolic functions (Section 2.2).
(16) *Revision*: Show how *optimization* principles of connectionist computation percolate up to the higher level to derive new organizational principles for grammar (Section 2.3) which can improve the explanatory power of linguistic theory (Section 3.3).
(17) Integration: The fundamental ICS computational principles which pertain to core higher cognition (and language in particular) and on which symbolic computation is built are special cases

of more general (and less structured) principles which underly many connectionist models of other cognitive domains (Section 4.3.1).

The plan for the chapter, then, is to explain the new ICS computational architecture in section 2, providing in section 2.2–3 the crucial discussion of how symbols and rules can play essential roles in computational explanations while not playing roles in a causal, algorithmic account of processing. These results on computational architecture are brought together into a theory of cognitive architecture in section 3, where I argue that not only is the new architecture *sufficient* to explain fundamental 'symbolic' cognitive properties, it is also able to *refine* symbolic theory in one of its strongest areas, generative grammar. In section 4 I argue that ICS is not less adequate than Classical theory in explaining the *necessity* of cognitive systems to display these 'symbolic' properties, and that, unlike existing symbolic or connectionist architectures, ICS has made meaningful contributions towards the realization of all these goals.

I may as well be up front about the fact that 'platitudinality' *is not* one of the goals of ICS. Some might feel that the right explanation of how symbolic computation can arise from neural computation is a story one should be able to discuss comfortably with Granny over tea and cookies. I confess to preferring other ways of enjoying Granny's company.[7]

2 Embedding Symbolic Computation in Connectionist Networks: The ICS Computational Architecture

2.1 Refining the problem

Our first step is to see how to partially embed symbolic computation in a PDP connectionist architecture. This matter is less obvious than it appears: two contradictory claims are pervasive. The first asserts that connectionist architectures are computationally much weaker than symbolic architectures; that connectionist computation is just association-ism, which is not structure-sensitive, and that it therefore falls far short of the computational power needed for symbolic structure processing.[8] On the other hand, it is frequently asserted that connectionism can be used to implement Turing machines, that neural nets are universal computers, and that there's nothing in conventional computing they can't emulate. Clearly, something is missing. A simple, but I believe basically sound, diagnosis of the problem is that two different notions of connectionist network are involved: 'weak' and 'strong' notions, the latter capable of structure processing, the former prima facie too weak to do so.

2.1.1   The power of PDP v. local connectionist networks

So to sort out these issues it is useful to distinguish two broad classes of connectionist architectures.[9] I'll call the 'weaker' networks 'PDP models' and the 'stronger' ones 'local connectionist networks'. In PDP models, information is represented by patterns of activity. There is a pattern encoding an input, and in the simplest case the activity that defines it flows through a set of connections to form a pattern encoding an output: the input/output mapping is done via simple associations between inputs and outputs. There seems to be no sense in which the input has *structure* corresponding to that of symbolic representations (constituents embedded within one another, for example), no sense in which the processes are structure-sensitive. Given that the strengths of the associative connections in PDP models are normally determined by some sampling of an 'environment' of input/output pairs, these connections normally constitute a measure of statistical correlations during experience, and so it is often claimed that the processing in such networks is *statistics- but not structure-sensitive*. Clearly, this is a most unlikely medium for implementing symbolic structure processing.

The story for local connectionist models, on the other hand, is quite different. In many cases, the units in these models are binary on/off units, each of which can be interpreted as the Boolean value true/false of some perhaps complex proposition. These units are typically connected to one another by carefully worked-out schemes, and their decision rules (about when to be on or off) equally carefully designed, so that the network as a whole computes the truth value of some set of propositions. One historically important example of such networks comprises those developed by McCulloch and Pitts (1943), whose work is usually regarded as playing an important role in the ultimate development of digital computers. Clearly, the relation between computation in such networks and symbolic computation is very tight. Another example of such networks is illustrated by a network in Minsky's (1967, s. 3.5) text which simulates a finite-state automaton. Each unit represents a combination of an input symbol and an internal machine state, and one unit is active at a time. Such a network could be the 'CPU' of a Turing machine, attached to a conventional Turing machine tape. Indeed, the tape itself could also be replaced by an unbounded set of local connectionist units, or even by a single unit with infinite precision activation value (Pollack, 1987). The theory of such local connectionist networks is so intimately associated with the classical theory of computation and automata that drawing any principled boundary between them may well be impossible.

So the situation, crudely, is really quite simple: local connectionist networks are, for all intents and purposes, a sub-part of conventional computation theory, and *modulo* the usual bookloads of technicalities (see, e.g., Smolensky et al., forthcoming), there are no fundamental differences between the computational power of these networks and that of Turing machines. Implementing symbolic computation in such networks can be done in a variety of ways, and is essentially unproblematic (if often unenlightening).

Implementing any interesting and powerful subset of symbolic computation with the other brand of connectionist system, PDP models, by contrast, seems rather impossible. Aside from the ICS architecture described here, I know of no principled and general approach. Thus it must be clearly understood that the *proposal under discussion in this chapter is a means of partially embedding symbolic computation in PDP models specifically*, not in 'connectionist networks' construed generally enough to include local connectionist models. Some of the crucial properties of ICS which make it a PDP approach to embedding symbolic computation are the following:

Symbol processing in ICS is PDP, not local connectionist

(18)   *Distributed:* A symbolic structure is represented by a pattern of activity over a set of units; each unit participates in the representation of a number (possibly all) of the constituents comprising this structure: Rep_{pdp} (2).

(19)   *Parallel:* When a structure is processed, all its constituents are processed simultaneously: Alg_{ics} (9).

(20)   *Continuous:* The patterns of activity comprising symbolic structures form a discrete subset of the points in a continuous space of patterns, all of which can be processed by the network; the pattern representing a structure is surrounded in this space by a continuum of nearby points which constitute similar but different patterns.

No other general theoretical approach to the connectionist realization of symbolic computation, as far as I know, possesses these properties; certainly local connectionist networks do not.[10]

Properly understanding the significance of property (18) is essential: this is the property of *distributed representation* which is the hallmark of PDP. Most people think of connectionist networks only in terms of individual *units;* the import of distributed representation is precisely that in PDP networks, a representation is not to be found at a unit, but in an *activity pattern.* Mathematically, an activity pattern is a *vector*, a list of numbers such as (0.3, −1.2, 0.9, . . .) giving the activity of all the units over which the pattern resides.[11] Thus a concise and, as we will see, quite fruitful way of encapsulating this crucial difference between local connectionist networks and PDP models is this:

Contrast between PDP and local connectionism: the essence distilled
(21)   (a)   In local connectionist networks, a representation is borne by a *unit.*
        (b)   In PDP models, a representation is borne by a *vector*.

And crucially, the units whose activities define the representational vector of *different* representations are the *same* units: different representations are different activity vectors over a fixed set of units, not activity over different units.

Thus in order to partially embed symbolic computation in a PDP model, the questions we must now address are precisely these:

The central questions in designing ICS
(22)   (a)   How can vectors be treated as symbol structures?
        (b)   How can PDP networks processing these vectors achieve structure-sensitive processing?

2.1.2   A Bit of Vector Space Theory   (21b) explains why the mathematics of vectors figures so prominently in PDP theory, and (22) explains why this mathematics enters crucially into the design of ICS. Vector operations are crucial, for example, in refining the question (22b) about PDP processing. Information processing in PDP networks is the spread of activation, usually involving the central operation of vector space theory, matrix multiplication. In most networks, matrix multiplication is the core of the processing, around which all sorts of more complicated operations take place. In its purest form, however, PDP processing simply *is* matrix multiplication. Since this fact figures centrally in ICS explanations, we must pause to spell this out.

The purest PDP model is the 'linear associator', which works as follows. There is a set of input units on which resides an activation vector i encoding some input. There is a set of output units which will host another activation vector o encoding the output associated with i, after activation has spread from the input units to the output units via a set of connections, each with its own strength or *weight*. If some input unit has activity value i and its connection to a particular output unit has weight w, then that ouput unit receives an amount of activation equal to wi (the numerical product of w and i) from that input unit. The output unit receives such activation from all the input units, and it simply adds all these contributions up to determine its own activation value o. To write this out explicitly, let the input units be labelled 1, 2, . . .; we'll use the variable α to denote any one of these input unit labels. The activity of input unit α will be denoted i_α. The total set of input activity values, the *input vector*, is then $\mathbf{i} = (i_1, i_2, \ldots, i_\alpha, \ldots)$. Using the variable β to denote the labels of the output units, and o_β to denote the activity of output unit β, we also have the corresponding *output vector* $\mathbf{o} = (o_1, o_2, \ldots, o_\beta, \ldots)$. The weight of the connection to output unit β from input unit α will be written $W_{\beta\alpha}$. The amount of activation that output unit β receives from input unit α is then $W_{\beta\alpha}i_\alpha$. The total activity of output unit β is then the sum of all such contributions:

$$(23) \quad o_\beta = W_{\beta 1}i_1 + W_{\beta 2}i_2 + \ldots + W_{\beta\alpha}i_\alpha + \ldots = \Sigma_\alpha W_{\beta\alpha}i_\alpha$$
$$\text{(for all output units } \beta)$$

The last expression denotes the sum over all values of α (Σ_α) of the weight to output unit β from input unit α $(W_{\beta\alpha})$ times the activity of input unit α (i_α). A compact way of writing equation (23) is:

$$(24) \quad \mathbf{o} = \mathbf{W} \cdot \mathbf{i}$$

which says that the vector $\mathbf{o}$ is simply the product of the matrix $\mathbf{W}$ and the vector $\mathbf{i}$. Here $\mathbf{W}$ is the *weight matrix* of the network, which is simply the set of all the weights $W_{\beta\alpha}$ between input and output units. The operation of matrix multiplication, here denoted by $\cdot$, is *defined* so that (24) is simply an abbreviation for (23).

2.1.3 The problem refined Let us then wrap up our clarification of the computational problems to which ICS is a proposed solution. In section 2.1.1 we saw that while realizing symbolic computation in local connectionist networks is no great problem, such a realization within PDP connectionism is not only much more difficult, it would appear impossible. The defining property of PDP was seen to be that representations are borne by activity vectors, so section 2.1.2 was dedicated to the rudiments of vector space theory. What is crucial for the argument in this chapter is that the core of processing in PDP models is multiplication of an activity vector by a connection weight matrix. We now bring these refinements to bear on the fundamental principles of ICS given in section 1.1 (1–5). The principles concerning representations (2, 3) are now:

The representational principles of ICS
(25) **Rep$_{pdp}$**: In all cognitive domains, representations are vectors ($\cong$ 2).
(26) **Rep$_{sym}$(HC)**: In core parts of higher cognitive domains, representations are symbol structures (= 3).

Our first sub-problem, question (22a) of section 2.1.1, is now therefore:

(27) **Q$_{rep}$**: How can Rep$_{pdp}$ and Rep$_{sym}$ be simultaneously correct? That is, how can one and the same computational data object be a vector of connectionist activations and a symbol structure?

The principles concerning processing (1, 5) are now:

The processing principles of ICS
(28) **Alg$_{pdp}$**: In all cognitive domains, cognitive processes are spreading activation algorithms (= 1) . . .
(29) **Alg$_{pdp}$(W)**: . . . the core operation of which is the multiplication of an input activation vector **i** by a weight matrix **W** to get the output vector:

$$o = W \cdot i \ (= 24).$$

(30) **Fun$_{sym}$(HC)**: In core parts of higher cognitive domains, the input/output functions computed by cognitive processes are described by (recursive) symbolic functions (= 5).

Our second sub-problem, question (22b), is:

(31) **Q$_{proc}$**: How can Alg$_{pdp}$(W) and Fun$_{sym}$ be simultaneously correct? That is, how can one and the same computation be a spreading activation process (e.g. matrix multiplication) and also the computation of a symbolic function – e.g. a function which takes inputs of the form [John [loves Mary]] and generates outputs of the form loves (John, Mary) (where the symbols John and Mary can be replaced by arbitrarily complex phrases)?

For answering these questions Q$_{rep}$ and Q$_{proc}$, and thereby partially embedding symbolic computation in a PDP model, all the work on implementing symbolic computation in local connectionist networks is, unfortunately, quite irrelevant.

2.2   Connectionist constituents?!?

In section 2.2.1 we see how vectors can have constituent structure. In section 2.2.2 we see how connectionist processing can possess an abstract structure which enables recursive functions to be computed over these constituents. In such processing, the constituents play roles in explanations but not in algorithms. In section 2.3, we extend the theory so it may apply to the domain of grammar.

2.2.1   Representations   The most basic question, Q_{rep} (27), asks how the kind of constituent structure so critical to symbolic representations can be embedded in the structure of vectors. What is at stake here is one of the most basic principles of cognitive science, the combinatorial strategy for explaining cognitive productivity.

2.2.1.1   THE COMBINATORIAL STRATEGY FOR EXPLAINING PRODUCTIVITY
Surely productivity is the most remarkable property of higher cognition, one which can fruitfully be idealized as the ability to correctly process a potentially infinite variety of inputs using only a finite store of knowledge. And Classical cognitive theory has a tremendously success-ful strategy for answering this question, in an impressive diversity of higher cognitive domains:

(32)   *The combinatorial strategy* explains productivity by assuming that mental representations, like the sentences of a language, consist of arrays of symbols that can be combined in a potentially infinite variety of ways, and that mental processes operating on recursive principles can correctly handle this potentially infinite combina-torial variation, using only finitely specified knowledge.

If we can answer Q_{rep} satisfactorily, then the ICS architecture will have at its disposal the prerequisite for deploying the combinatorial strategy: constituent structured representations. If not, some alternative strategy will be required for explaining productivity (or denying it). Eliminativist, empiricist connectionism attempts to respond to the challenge of productivity by showing that a connectionist network presented with a set of input/output examples from a function will learn to generalize to other novel examples. It may be that implicit in this work is a general and powerful explanation of the productivity of higher cognition, but at this early stage, the research is experimental rather than theoretical, and what is available is only a set of isolated examples of networks, most of which seem to elicit optimism that the approach will ultimately manage to explain productivity from eliminativist empiricist connectionists, but the contrary from others. In ICS, I avoid the approach of eliminativist empiricist connectionism, preferring to embrace the combinatorial strategy for explaining productivity in the absence of some well-defined theoretical alternative.

I hasten to add that, while ICS incorporates *part* of the Classical strategy for explaining productivity, it also *rejects* another part. The combinatorial strategy (32) does not specify what kind of (a) 'finitely specified knowledge' and (b) 'recursive principles' are employed; in the classical architecture, but not in ICS, these take the form of (a) a finite set of symbol manipulation rules, and (b) a recursive sequential process for applying these rules – in short, symbolic algorithms (7), which are not part of ICS (9). In both the classical and ICS architectures, mental representations (in core parts of higher cognition) have combinatorial constituent structure; in the classical, but not the ICS, architectures, these constituents have a causal role in processing. Let us move on, then, to define these vectorial constituents.

2.2.1.2   TENSOR PRODUCT REPRESENTATIONS   As in Classical theory, in ICS, mental representations can be formally described as a set of symbol structures whose semantics are recursively (compositionally) determined from their syntax (3, 4). In order to most straightforwardly manifest the recursive character of these symbol structures, since recursion is a central issue here, I will adopt the LISP convention in which all symbol structures are binary-branching trees. Thus the proposition *p* which is rendered in English by *Sandy loves Kim* will have the following symbolic representation:

(33)

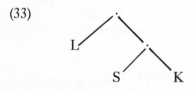

This tree (33) will be written[12] as [L, [S, K]]; this expression will sometimes be abbreviated by the predicate calculus notation L (S, K). The atomic symbols L, S, and K obviously denote the predicate and arguments which are referred to respectively by *loves*, *Sandy*, and *Kim*. In the Classical theory we stop here, and don't say anything further about how these individual symbols L, S, K are realized, and how these realizations are combined to form the realization of [L, [S, K]]. In ICS, we brazenly dare to commit to a theory of how such realization[13] takes place.

2.2.1.2.1   THE DEFINITION   In ICS, $p = [L, [S, K]]$ is realized as the following connectionist activity vector:

(34) $p = r_0 \otimes L + r_1 \otimes [r_0 \otimes S + r_1 \otimes K]$

I will explain the terms in this expression through comparison with their symbolic counterparts.

A symbolic representation like $[L, [S, K]]$ for the proposition p referred to by *Sandy loves Kim* depends on the arbitrary association of the predicate love and the arguments Sandy and Kim with the atomic symbols L, S, and K, respectively. In an exactly corresponding way, in ICS, the representation of p depends on an association of love, Sandy and Kim with the respective activity vectors L, S, and K.[14] Furthermore, the symbolic representation $[L, [S, K]]$ of the proposition p depends on an arbitrary association of the propositional arguments Sandy and Kim to the syntactic positions – first and second – of their corresponding symbols S and K in the syntactic structure.[15] Similarly, the ICS representation of p depends on the association of the argument Sandy to a vector r_0 which can be thought of as signifying 'left branch' of a binary-branching tree node; this association is manifest in the part $r_0 \otimes S$ of the ICS representation (34). Correspondingly, the other argument of p, Kim, is associated with a vector r_1 thought of as signifying 'right branch'. The two vectors r_0 and r_1 are the fundamental building blocks in terms of which the representations for all positions in binary trees are recursively defined, as we shortly see. Obviously, it will not do for r_0 and r_1 to be one and the same vector; we would have no way of distinguishing left from right in that case. Indeed, since we are working in a vector space, what is required is that r_0 and r_1 be *independent* as vectors: one cannot simply be a multiple of the other, as in $r_0 = 2 r_1$.

Clearly, it just invites confusion on crucial distinctions to say 'the proposition $R(a,b)$ is represented by the syntactic expression R(a,b)' – all the arbitrariness in the semantic mapping is thereby hidden. This is especially true if we are lazy with our typography, and just say 'the proposition R(a,b) is represented by the syntactic expression R(a,b)'! In the preceding discussion I have been at pains to take greater care. Having done so I will henceforth, when there is little risk of confusion, denote $[L, [S, K]]$ by the more customary L (S, K). Since the binary tree structure made explicit in the notation $[L, [S, K]]$ more clearly exhibits the recursive character of these syntactic structures than does the string notation L (S, K), I will treat the former as the 'real' symbolic structure, and the latter as simply a convenient abbreviation for it.

Having discussed the vectors r_0, r_1, L, S, and K appearing in (34), it remains to define the operations used to combine these vectors into the vector **p** representing the entire proposition *p*. These operations are + and $\otimes$: vector addition (superposition) and the tensor product. The + operation is used to combine the vectors representing sub-constituents into a vector representing a composite structure. Mathematically, vector addition is defined in the obvious element-by-element way: $(2, -3, 5) + (0, 3, -2) = (2, 0, 3)$. The first element in the list of numbers comprising the vector $\mathbf{x} + \mathbf{y}$ is just the numerical sum of the first element of **x** and the first element of **y**, and similarly for all the other elements. This operation is often called *superposition* because it is the way that waves superimpose upon each other in many physical media (e.g. sound waves). In the case at hand, **x** and **y** each represent patterns or 'waves' of activity over connectionist units, and $\mathbf{x} + \mathbf{y}$ is the pattern of activity arising from superimposing one pattern on top of the other. If $\mathbf{x}_0$ is the vector representing some sub-tree **x** placed in the 'left branch' role, and $\mathbf{y}_1$ is the vector representing another tree **y** placed in the 'right branch' role, then $\mathbf{x}_0 + \mathbf{y}_1$ is the vector representing the combined tree [**x**, **y**]. Each of $\mathbf{x}_0$ and $\mathbf{y}_1$ will be called an *(immediate) constituent (vector)* of their sum $\mathbf{x}_0 + \mathbf{y}_1$

'Placing a sub-tree in the left branch role' is achieved by the other vector operation $\otimes$, the tensor product. To 'place a sub-tree x in the left branch role', we take the vector representing **x**, **x**, and *bind* it to the vector $\mathbf{r}_0$ representing the 'left branch' role, by taking the tensor product:

(35) $\mathbf{x}_0 = \mathbf{r}_0 \otimes \mathbf{x}$

Arithmetically, the tensor product operation is defined as follows. Given two vectors such as $\mathbf{r} = (1\ 3\ 5)$ and $\mathbf{f} = (2\ 4)$, their tensor product is the vector containing all possible products of one element of **r** and one element of **f**: $\mathbf{r} \otimes \mathbf{f} = (2\ 6\ 10\ 4\ 12\ 20)$. Generally, given

$$\mathbf{r} = (r_1, r_2, \ldots, r_i, \ldots), \quad \mathbf{f} = (f_1, f_2, \ldots, f_j, \ldots)$$

then their tensor product is

(36) $\mathbf{r} \otimes \mathbf{f} = (\ldots, r_i f_j, \ldots)$

Clearly, if there are *n* elements in the **r** vector and *m* elements in the **f** vector, there will be *nm* elements in their tensor product. A critical property of the tensor product (which distinguishes it from its simpler counterpart in matrix algebra, the outer product) is that *tensor products can be embedded recursively*. Thus, in forming the tensor product $\mathbf{r} \otimes \mathbf{f}$, it may well be that the vector **f** is already itself a tensor product, say

$f = a \otimes b$; the result then is a three-way tensor product $r \otimes (a \otimes b)$; the elements of this third-order product vector are each the result of multiplying together *three* numbers, one from r, one from a, and one from b.

This recursive property of tensor products leads to the ability to recursively bind sub-trees to left/right branch roles, an ability already demonstrated in our example of p in (34), repeated here:

(37) $p = r_0 \otimes L + r_1 \otimes [r_0 \otimes S + r_1 \otimes K]$

The structure in this vector mirrors that of $p = [L, [S, K]]$ exactly. (The tree diagram of (33) may be helpful in following this explanation.) The left sub-tree of p is the symbol L; and one constituent of the vector p is $r_0 \otimes L$, the result of binding the left-branch role vector r_0 to the vector L. Superimposed on this constituent $r_0 \otimes L$ is another constituent which represents the right sub-tree $[S, K]$ of p: the vector $r_1 \otimes [r_0 \otimes S + r_1 \otimes K]$. This vector is the result of binding the right-branch role vector r_1 to the vector f which represents the sub-tree $[S, K]$; f is itself a tensor product representation with internal structure $f = [r_0 \otimes S + r_1 \otimes K]$. Recursively descending to examine f, we see exactly the same structure as for p: it is the superposition of two constituent vectors, one for the left sub-tree and the other for the right. This time, however, both sub-trees are simple symbols, so there is no further decomposition; the atomic sub-trees S and K are each directly represented by their corresponding vectors S and K.[16]

What we have just worked through is a particular case of the following general rule:

(38) *Recursive tensor product representations*: The realization of $[p, q]$, where p and q are any two symbolic sub-trees, is

$r_0 \otimes p + r_1 \otimes q$

where p and q are the respective realizations of p and q.

This concludes the definition of (recursive) tensor product representations.[17] The constituent structure present in these vectors is the solution that ICS provides to the question Q_{rep} (27). To formulate this as a principle:

(39) **Rep$_{ics}$ (HC)**: In core parts of higher cognitive domains, representations are vectors which have the structure of recursive tensor product representations.

Here and in the rest of the chapter, 'HC' is used to label the specialized versions of more general cognitive principles which are assumed to apply in higher cognitive domains.

2.2.1.2.2   SEMANTIC INTERPRETATION   So far, we've discussed the semantic relationship between vectors and propositions only in the direction from propositions to vectors: given a proposition, what vector represents it? A few new issues arise when we look at the question concerning the other direction.

Any vector like p of (34) can be expressed as the sum of other vectors in an infinite variety of ways. Thus it might be believed that there is some ambiguity in determining for a given vector such as p what its constituents are. To be concrete, let's take the simpler example of the r_1 sub-constituent of p:

$$q = r_0 \otimes S + r_1 \otimes K$$

This vector realizes the right sub-tree $q = [S, K]$ in the symbolic expression for p. Given the vector q, in order to determine that this vector realizes $[S, K]$ we need to recognize it as the sum of two vectors, one for each constituent S and K:

$$q = q_S + q_K$$

But if q, like any other vector, can be decomposed in any of an infinite number of ways into a sum of two other vectors, what singles out the *correct* pair of vectors q_S and q_K? Why can't q be decomposed into a sum of two vectors which represent the constituents Q and Z, leading us to mistakenly identify q as the realization of $[Q, Z]$? The answer is simply that for the purposes of semantic interpretation, not just *any* two vectors will do: one must be of the form $r_0 \otimes x$, the other of the form $r_1 \otimes y$, for some pair of vectors x, y. The fact that r_0 and r_1 are independent vectors makes it impossible for more than one such pair of vectors x, y to work in the decomposition of q. A simple proof may be found in the Appendix section A.1.[18]

To summarize, ambiguities will be rampant if r_0 and r_1 are equal, or are simple multiples of each other (that is, not independent vectors); but as long as this degenerate case is ruled out, there cannot be two semantic interpretations of a single vector. And, of course, comparable degeneracies must be ruled out of any representational scheme; for example, ambiguities would be unavoidable in a symbolic representational system in which the symbol representing Kim was identical to that representing Sandy, or in one which was so haplessly constructed that left and right arguments could not be consistently kept straight. Such problems are avoided in the tensor product representational scheme provided the relevant, vector space, notion of independence is respected.[19]

So an ICS activity vector cannot have more than one semantic interpretation. Could a vector have none? Indeed, it can. The *representations* are special vectors with semantic interpretations, those with tensor product form. Assuming a finite set of symbols, these form a discrete subset embedded in the continuous vector space of all activity patterns. The fact that many vectors have no semantic interpretation is in certain respects directly analogous to the fact that in symbolic representational schemes not all possible symbol structures have semantic interpretations; to take an extreme example, in a string-based predicate calculus representation,)K, (LS does not, even if L (K, S) does. This general topic will be revisited in section 4.3.2.

Are the constituents in a tensor product representation *really there?* Saying some fairly precise things about this quite vague question will occupy much of the rest of this chapter. There are some contradictory intuitions to contend with, to be sure. Since the individual constituents are superimposed when combined, they certainly do lose their individual identity in an intuitively compelling sense. It would be easy to object that: 'Aren't you really claiming that 2 and 4 are constituents of 6 just because $2 + 4 = 6$?'[20] On the other hand, I've already shown that the semantic interpretation process in ICS is unambiguous; while 6 could equally well be written as $5+1$, tensor product vectors cannot be semantically decomposed in more than one way, because of the distinguished status of the vectors r_0 and r_1 in determining which vector decompositions are relevant to semantic interpretation. To foreshadow an analogy soon to be developed in detail, the decomposition of tensor products into constituents is more correctly mapped onto the decomposition of a Gödel number $2^2 3^4$ into its 'constituents' 2 and 4. And for an intuition that lends some plausibility to the notion of vector constituents, consider superposition of sound waves: the pressure wave encoding *The Sounds of Silence* is, after all, a superposition which mixes up altogether the Simon and the Garfunkel constituents – yet we have no trouble believing that in a meaningful sense those constituents are real. This intuitive example is a much-corrupted version of many cleaner examples in physics in which scientific explanation is crucially dependent on the decomposition of waves of all kinds into constituents which are superimposed exactly as are those of tensor product representations.[21]

One final remark. In this section I have discussed the semantics of vectors in ICS in terms of propositions. This is actually just one of the ways that vectors are interpreted in ICS. In the work on grammar discussed in sections 2.3 and 3.3, tensor product representations are interpreted in terms of linguistic structures rather than propositions. In that context, the vector **p** we used as our pedagogical example would be interpreted as the tree structure p = [L, [S, K]] itself, rather than as a proposition (like *Sandy loves Kim*) which would be denoted by p in some symbolic representational system. Grammars are viewed as functions mapping symbolic input structures to symbolic output structures; these inputs and outputs are realized in ICS as tensor product representations, and connectionist processing is used to compute outputs from inputs.

2.2.2 Processing: non-algorithmic structure

2.2.2 Processing: non-algorithmic structure   One crucial test of the reality of the constituents of tensor product representations is whether it is possible for PDP connectionist networks to process them in such a way as to display structure sensitivity. In this section we see that indeed it is possible to design such networks while adhering to the principle Alg_{pdp} (28–29) of massively parallel processing. These networks display structure sensitivity without constituents having the kind of causal role that they have in Classical systems, where the system's internal behavior is governed by algorithms operating over constituents: extracting them, comparing them, rearranging them to construct new structures. The ICS networks achieve structure-sensitive processing – e.g. compute recursive functions – in a non-classical way which is quite difficult to grasp: non-Classical explanations of productive behavior seem patently impossible to many. As an aid to the intuition, I will begin the discussion of the ICS explanation with two analogies; in the first, the numerical vectors which form the representational medium of ICS are replaced by a more familiar representational scheme using single numbers.

2.2.2.1   THE GÖDEL BOX   Paleoroboticists in another possible world have unearthed a curious black box. It has a keypad and a display, several dials, a switch and a little red light. Several generations of graduate students exploring countless hypotheses about the box have at last arrived at a remarkable discovery. Seven keys on the keypad can be interpreted as the digits 0–6, and an eighth as an 'enter' key; a sequence of key presses can then be taken as a numeral in base 7 designating some number. This number in turn can be interpreted as the Gödel number of a binary tree with symbols at the nodes of the tree; the symbols can be taken to be S_1, S_2, . . ., each symbol S_k coded by the number k; and each possible position in the binary tree is coded by a prime number: the root node is coded by $2 \equiv p_0$, its left child node is coded by $3 \equiv p_{10}$, the right child of root is coded by $5 \equiv p_{11}$, and so on forever down to deeper and deeper levels of the tree. So the tree $[S_3, [S_2, S_6]]$ is encoded by the number $p_{10}{}^3 p_{110}{}^2 p_{111}{}^5 = 3^3 \, 13^2 \, 17^5$. A series of key presses ending in the 'enter' key therefore inputs a labelled binary tree to the Gödel box. The marks that then scroll across the display are a code for another labelled binary tree: again, the base-7 code of a Gödel number defined just as for the input (the marks corresponding to the digits 0–6 having been deciphered by the resourceful graduate students). Now the point of interpreting the key presses and displays as tree inputs and tree outputs is that, so interpreted, the students have determined that the input/output function computed by the box is a simple recursive function which rearranges the input tree in a determinate way to generate the output tree. In fact, different settings of the dials on the box lead it to compute different recursive functions. Finally, flipping a switch on the box puts it into a slightly different mode; now, the tree that is encoded by the input key presses either causes the little red light to come on, or it doesn't. The students have managed to determine that the light illuminates when the tree which has been input is a valid parse tree of a formal language, specified by a rewrite-rule grammar. Turning the dials on the box changes the grammar.

This triumph of descriptive generalization in hand, the students naturally move on to find the explanation of the remarkable behavior of the Gödel box. They propose that, in its first mode, the box takes the input Gödel number and extracts from it the symbols encoded, placing each into a memory register appropriately located in a binary tree data structure; it then sequentially, recursively, pulls out the appropriate parts of the tree for the recursive function being computed, recombines them to create another tree data structure, and finally steps through the nodes of the output tree computing the Gödel number which it then outputs to the display. In the second mode, the box starts off the same way, extracting the symbols from the input number and placing them at appropriate locations in the tree data structure; it then descends the tree from the root checking whether the symbol at each node, and those of its two children in the tree, match the left and right sides of one of the grammar rules. If all nodes match a rule, it turns on the light; otherwise it doesn't.

Shortly thereafter, the students finally find a way to open up the box. To their shock and dismay, they discover that in the first mode what the Gödel box does with its input number is to multiply it by 3249049379387, subtract 19384737, divide by 874987, take the remainder, multiply it by 108379174, and output the result. Turning the dials on the box simply changes the numbers used in this computation. In the second mode, the calculation performed inside the box is similar, except that at the end, if the resulting number is even, the red light is turned on; if odd, it's left off.

This gives several more generations of graduate students – in mathematics, this time – quite a puzzle, until ultimately a new branch of number theory emerges, full of remarkable theorems about the relation between powers of primes and arithmetic operations with certain combinations of numbers, theorems which make it possible to prove that the computations performed in the box in fact perform recursive functions on Gödel numbers of labelled binary trees.

2.2.2.2 THE VISA BOX   Inspired by my tale of the Gödel box, a friend of mine built a remarkable present for me. She knows that I hate computing tips in restaurants, since, never seeming to have more than $2.50 in cash on hand, I always have to pay by Visa, and I usually get slips which give me only my 'sub-total': the food bill and tax combined, with no breakdown. It violates my one religious conviction to give a tip on tax, and figuring out how much of the 'sub-total' is the food bill for the purpose of computing the tip is quite a drag. But after receiving my new Visa box I can now face going to restaurants again. You just set one dial to the local food tax rate, another to the tip rate you feel like giving that day; you type in the sub-total from your bill, and out pops the total to write on the bottom line of the Visa slip. The servers call on their personal incentive to back-compute their tip and write it in for you.

It seemed pretty obvious what goes on inside the Visa box. First, it takes the sub-total and extracts the food bill, using the setting on the tax-rate dial; it then extracts the tax. With the food and tax separately stored, it next takes the food bill and applies the setting on the tip-rate dial to determine the tip amount. Then it adds this to the food bill, and finally adds this to the tax, and displays the result.

Imagine my surprise when one night, desperate to evade the obligation to finish yet another too-long paper, I pried open the box, and discovered that it simply multiplies the input i by a number w and reads out the result o:

$$o = wi$$

With the tax/tip-rate dials set at 10%/15%, for instance, it just multiplies by 1.136. With the dials set at 7%/20%, it multiplies by 1.187. Calling upon my best empiricist efforts, I experimentally determined that, to an excellent approximation, the number it multiplies by is

$$w = (100 + x + p)/(100 + x)$$

where x and p are the tax and tip percentages, respectively. Since the paper still wasn't finished, I pondered this awhile. Calling upon my best mathematical efforts, I managed to work out the following explanation for why the Visa box gets the right answer:

tax = $(x/100)$ (food); tip = $(p/100)$ (food); sub-total = (food) + (tax)

∴ subtotal = (food) + $(x/100)$ (food) = $(1 + x/100)$ (food)

∴ food = (sub-total) / $(1 + x/100)$

∴ total = (food) + (tax) + (tip)

$\quad$ = (food) + $(x/100)$ (food) + $(p/100)$ (food)

$\quad$ = $(1 + x/100 + p/100)$ [food]

$\quad$ = $(1 + x/100 + p/100)$ [(sub-total) / $(1 + x/100)$]

$\quad$ = $(1 + x/100 + p/100)$ / $(1 + x/100)$ (sub-total)

$\quad$ = $[(100 + x + p) / (100 + x)]$ (sub-total)

$\quad$ = w (sub-total)

Not for the first time, I marveled at my friend's ingenuity.

As a final desperate move to escape my paper, I summoned up my best philosophical efforts and managed to generate a deep question (but, alas, not an answer): are the food and tax *really constituents* of the Visa box's internal representation of the sub-total? Surely, in some sense, they would be if the machine actually worked the way I'd expected, for the first thing the machine would have done would be to extract these constituents and then manipulate them according to the (obvious) algorithm I'd expected to see inside. I'd have seen little registers where the tax and food would get stored. But that isn't how it works. On the other hand, the very question my proof answers, 'how come the box computes the correct total, for all settings of the dials?', makes no sense without the notions of tax and food – for after all, the semantics of the first dial is the tax rate on the food, and of the second, the tip rate on the food portion alone. The 'correct total' is *defined* in terms of the tax and food; these must enter into the semantic characterization of the function the box computes, and in the proof/explanation of its correct performance.

Having nothing left to summon, I returned to finish the paper.

2.2.2.3 EXPLAINING PRODUCTIVITY IN ICS The kind of magical number-theoretic calculation at the heart of the Gödel box is strictly hypothetical. However, it has a direct counterpart in ICS in tensor-theoretic calculations. The reason the former are impossible, while the latter are surprisingly straightforward, is simply that representing complex structures in large vectors, as done in ICS, allows the structure to be accessible to simple operations in a way which is impossible when complex structures are encoded in a single number, as done in the Gödel box. And, surprisingly, the tensor-theoretic calculations of ICS are highly analogous to the simple arithmetic calculations in the Visa box. In short, ICS marries the rich structural semantics of the numbers manipulated in the Gödel box with the simple numerical operations which actually work in the Visa box, by scaling up from single numbers to vectors.

Here, then, is a sketch of the explanation in the ICS case:

ICS explanation of structure-sensitive recursive function computation

(40) The core connectionist processing operation is simply the multiplication of the input activity vector i by the matrix of connection strengths W; the output activity vector o is then simply:

$$o = W \cdot i$$

where $\cdot$ denotes matrix multiplication (29).

(41) Extracting the left or right sub-tree of a tree is a matrix operation; that is, if s is the vector realizing $[x, y]$, and x and y are the vectors realizing the left and right sub-trees x and y (in general, complex trees in their own right), then there are two matrices W^{ex}_0 and W^{ex}_1 such that:

$$x = W^{ex}_0 \cdot s \text{ and } y = W^{ex}_1 \cdot s$$

(42) Successively performing a sequence of two extraction operations – e.g. first extract the right child of s, getting t, then extract the left child of t, getting r – therefore produces the same ultimate result as successively multiplying s by a sequence of matrices:

$$t = W^{ex}_1 \cdot s$$

$$r = W^{ex}_0 \cdot t = W^{ex}_0 \cdot W^{ex}_1 \cdot s$$

Moreover, the matrix product of two matrices is another matrix; so

$$r = W^{ex}_{01} \cdot s$$

where the matrix W^{ex}_{01} is just defined as the product $W^{ex}_0 \cdot W^{ex}_1$. This can be recursively repeated to any depth. Thus the extraction of *any* sub-constituent, no matter how deep in the tree, is achieved by multiplication of a single appropriate matrix, a matrix which crucially has a special structure: that of a product of a sequence of copies of the fundamental matrices

W^{ex}_0 and W^{ex}_1.

(43) Like extraction of constituents from an existing tree, constructing new trees from existing constituents can be performed by simple matrix multiplications and additions, based on fundamental matrices W^{cons}_0 and W^{cons}_1.[22] Like extraction, sequences of construction operations can be combined into a single matrix operation, and indeed sequences of interleaved extraction and construction operations can be so combined.

(44) Thus a single matrix multiplication of an input vector s representing an arbitrarily complex tree s by a matrix W to produce an output vector r representing a tree r can compute a complex, structure-sensitive input/output function f which can also be characterized as the result of a sequence of extractions and recombination operations. Such a sequential algorithm characterizes the function f which is computed, but not the means by which it is computed. The fact that this function f is correctly computed by multiplying by W is explained by the fact that W possess certain global structure: it is a certain product and sum of fundamental matrices W^{ex}_0, W^{ex}_1, W^{cons}_0 and W^{cons}_1. This global form corresponds in a direct way to the steps of the sequential algorithm. For example, the following pseudo-LISP expression[23] describes a recursive function f which transforms structures of the 'English passive sentence' form s = [P, [[aux, V], [by, A]] (where P, V and A are arbitrarily complex sub-trees) to the 'propositional form' [V, [A, P]]:

(a) $f(s)$ = cons (ex$_1$ (ex$_0$ (ex$_1$ (s)))),
              cons (ex$_1$ (ex$_1$ (ex$_1$ (s)))), ex$_0$ (s))).

f is realized by the following weight matrix:

(b) W = W^{cons}_0 [W^{ex}_1 W^{ex}_0 W^{ex}_1] +
         W^{cons}_1 [W^{cons}_0(W^{ex}_1 W^{ex}_1 W^{ex}_1) + W^{cons}_1 (W^{ex}_0)].

(45) This multiplication by a single matrix W can be performed by the simplest connectionist operation of spreading activation: (40). Thus we have networks which compute symbolic (recursive) functions, where we can prove that they do indeed correctly

compute such functions, and therefore we can explain with complete precision how they do so – yet there is no symbolic algorithm operating on the constituents which governs the network. It is a simple one-step process, input vector to output vector, in which the equivalent of a complex set of extraction and construction operations on constituents are all performed simultaneously. Fun_{sym} (30) is a theorem.

(46)   Furthermore, the set of matrices $\mathbf{W}$ (or the set of networks they define) which compute such recursive functions can be very simply characterized:

$$\mathbf{W} = \mathbf{w} \otimes \mathbf{R}$$

Here, $\mathbf{w}$ is a *finite rearrangement* weight matrix, which rearranges symbols within some finite depth of the tree; it contains a finite number of weights which achieve this rearrangement (indeed, many interesting recursive functions involve small $\mathbf{w}$ matrices with very few weights). The *recursion matrix* $\mathbf{R}$ is a fixed unbounded matrix with an extremely simple form (all its elements are either 0 or 1).[24] $\mathbf{R}$ takes the finite number of elements in $\mathbf{w}$ which govern rearrangements near the tree root, and 'copies' them unboundedly to fill up $\mathbf{W}$, creating a matrix which recursively propagates the same rearrangement to unbounded depth in the tree. The idealization to unboundedly deep trees through unbounded (or infinite) networks or $\mathbf{W}$ matrices is immediate. The infinite behavior of recursive function evaluation is generated through the finite 'knowledge' $\mathbf{w}$. In sum, the computation of recursive functions follows from the following principle:

Alg_{ics} (HC,W): In core parts of higher cognitive domains, weight matrices have the form:

$$\mathbf{W} = \mathbf{w} \otimes \mathbf{R}$$

where $\mathbf{w}$ is a finite rearrangement weight matrix, and $\mathbf{R}$ is the recursion matrix.

The crucial difference between the ICS encoding of structure in tensor product vectors and the Gödel box encoding of structure in Gödel numbers lies in (41): in the former but not the latter case, constituents can be accessed or stored using simple multiplication and addition (just as in the Visa box, in fact – but multiplication and addition of matrices rather than single numbers); many such operations can be combined into a single operation of the same type. Thus the structure that governs the function computed is not a structure over operations, but a structure internal, as it were, to the single operation. The structure resides in the space of matrices which operate on tensor product vectors, and is an abstract structure governing the interrelation of all the connection weights.

Since step (41) is crucial to the entire explanation, section A.2 of the Appendix is devoted to showing why it is true. Further details of this explanation (40–46) are too technical and involved to be appropriate here; the reader is referred to Smolensky et al. (1992) and the references therein.

We can now see how the PDP properties of distributed, parallel and continuous processing (18–20) of section 2.1.1 are achieved in ICS. The representation is distributed: since the vectors realizing all the constituents in the structure are superimposed upon each other, each unit participates in the realization of many symbols. The processing is parallel: all the constituents in the input are simultaneously processed by multiplication by W, which also creates all the constituents in the output simultaneously (in a single 'associative' operation, in fact). Finally, the operations consist of numerical multiplication and addition, and these can be applied to any input vector in the space, not just the special discrete subset consisting of the vectors realizing symbolic structures.

Furthermore it is now clear that Alg_{sym} (7) fails, making its negation Alg_{ics} (9) the principle operative in ICS. The one-step matrix multiplication by which a recursive function is computed in ICS is in no sense a symbolic algorithm involving step-by-step extractions, comparisons, recombinations and insertions. The recursive functions computed in ICS can *also* be computed by such symbolic algorithms, but these algorithms have nothing to do with the causal story of how the behavior is generated in ICS. The structure which explains how it is that recursive functions get computed is not such symbolic algorithmic structure: rather it is the abstract structure of the weight matrix W, structure captured for example in equation (44b).[25] The structure critical to explaining higher cognitive behavior in ICS is abstract tensor product structure in spaces of activation and weight matrices. This tensor product structure has everything to do with constituent structure, as it has been defined here. Tensor product constituents play absolutely indispensable roles in the description and explanation of cognitive behavior in ICS. But these constituents do not have a *causal* role, in the sense of being the objects of operations in algorithms actually at work in the system. These constituents are in this sense *acausally explanatory*. But regardless of what we choose to call them, these constituents provide a novel, non-Classical explanation of the productivity of higher cognition.[26]

2.3   Language and grammar

Do tensor product representations *really* have syntactic structure? Can they *really* handle embedding and recursion? Since recursive syntactic structure is present in very pure form in formal language theory, of the many ways of making these questions more precise, one of the sharpest is to formulate them as follows: can tensor product representations be used in PDP connectionist systems to capture *formal languages*? If so, to what level in the Chomsky formal language hierarchy? Can such systems capture the entire hierarchy, making them as powerful as Turing machines in the languages they generate?

In this section I describe formal results showing that the answer to the last question is *yes*. This requires that a theory of languages and grammars be formulated within ICS. The central idea in this theory is that of *relative well-formedness* or *Harmony*. Well-formedness, of course, plays a central role in grammatical theory; in the case of a formal language, an absolute notion of well-formedness is what distinguishes the strings that are part of the language (those for which a well-formed parse, according to the grammatical rules, can be constructed) from those strings that are not in the language. What is less obvious is that a notion of well-formedness – which I've called 'Harmony' – also plays a central role in connectionist theory; what is even surprising is that by identifying connectionist well-formedness and linguistic well-formedness, a novel and quite powerful approach to grammar can be formulated.

2.3.1   Harmony of activation vectors   The Harmony of an activation vector in a connectionist network is a numerical measure of the degree to which that vector respects the constraints encoded in the connection matrix: the degree to which the vector is well formed, according to the connections. Explaining this sentence will take most of this section.

To begin at the beginning, consider a negative connection of weight, say, -0.8, from a unit α to a unit β. This connection has the following effect: if unit α is active, then unit β is inhibited by it: β receives negative activation from α. We can interpret this connection as implementing a little constraint, which says that if α is active, then β should not be active. This constraint has a strength: 0.8; if the connection weight were -8.0 instead, it would be implementing the same constraint, with ten times the strength. Of course, unit β may also have a positive connection from another unit γ, say, one of weight $+0.5$. This connection can be interpreted as implementing a constraint in the other direction: if unit γ is active, then β should be active too; this constraint has strength 0.5. If α and γ are both active, then β is subject to two conflicting constraints and (assuming for simplicity that the activation levels of α and γ are equal) it is the stronger one which wins: the negative activation received from the connection of weight -0.8 overcomes the positive activation received from the connection of weight $+0.5$.

With respect to the single connection to β from α, all activity patterns can be assessed according to how well they respect the constraint corresponding to that connection. Any activity pattern a which has both α and β simultaneously active – say, the activity of α is $a_\alpha = +0.7$, and that of β is $a_\beta = +0.4$ – violates the constraint. The constraint therefore assesses a with *negative Harmony*; the numerical quantity, for reasons to be clearer shortly, is computed as:

$$H_{\beta\alpha}(\mathbf{a}) = a_\beta \, W_{\beta\alpha} \, a_\alpha = (+0.4) \, (-0.8) \, (+0.7) = -0.224$$

The Harmony of an activity pattern a with respect to a connection to β from α is simply the three-way product of the activation value of unit β times the weight to β from α times the activation value of α. If the weight is negative, and both activations are positive, the result is a negative number, indicating the violation of the constraint corresponding to that connection. The greater the weight of the connection (i.e. the strength of the constraint), and the greater the positive activations, the more negative is the assessed Harmony.

Now suppose further that in the pattern a, the activation value of unit γ is $+0.7$. Then the same pattern a *satisfies* the constraint corresponding to the connection ($+0.5$) to β from γ; the harmony of a with respect to this constraint is positive:

$$H_{\beta\gamma}(\mathbf{a}) = a_\beta \, W_{\beta\gamma} \, a_\gamma = (+0.4) \, (+0.5) \, (+0.7) = +0.140$$

The net Harmony of a with respect to both these two connections combined is gotten simply by adding together the individual Harmony values:

$$H_{\beta\alpha}(\mathbf{a}) + H_{\beta\gamma}(\mathbf{a}) = (-0.224) + (+0.14) = -0.174$$

This is negative: a satisfies the weaker constraint, but violates the stronger constraint, leading to a net violation which is indicated by a negative combined Harmony value. This result comes out correctly because of the particular way the numerical magnitude of Harmony values is computed.

Let's compare the pattern a to another pattern a′ which is identical to a except that the activitation value of unit β is negative instead of positive: $a'_\beta = -0.4$, whereas $a_\beta = +0.4$. The new pattern a' now violates the weaker constraint (which says that γ is active so β should be too) while satisfying the stronger constraint (which says that α has positive activation so β should not). Reversing the sign of a_β to that of a'_β in the previous equations reverses the signs of all the Harmony values, so now the value of H (a') with respect to these two connections is *positive* (+0.174). More well formed than a with respect to these two connections is a': it conforms better to the set of two constraints. And, indeed, as we've already discussed, the activation flow into β from both α and γ combined would have the net effect of inhibiting β, not exciting it, so activation flow will tend to generate pattern a' rather than pattern a.[27] The result of activation flow of course depends on the particular rules governing activation spread in the network; however, as we see in a moment, for an important class of typical networks, the result of spreading activation will be to create a pattern of activity which has maximal Harmony. This pattern is the one which 'best satisfies' the pair of constraints corresponding to the pair of connections we've been considering. Thus activation spread is a process of *parallel soft-constraint satisfaction*; the constraints are 'soft' in the sense that each may be over-ruled by other constraints, and therefore violated in the final pattern – violation of a constraint is not impossible, as with 'hard constraints'. A soft constraint may be violated, but at a cost: the harmony is lowered, by an amount depending on the strength of the violated constraint.

In general, this account of activation spreading as a parallel soft-constraint satisfaction, or Harmony maximization, process applies not to a pair of connections, but to the complete set of connections in a network. The total Harmony of a pattern a in a network with connection weight matrix W is just the sum of the Harmony values of a with respect to all the individual connections. This can be written:

(47)   **Wf$_{pdp}$** (**Def.**): The well-formedness or *Harmony* of an activation
vector a is:

$$H\ (a) = \Sigma_{\beta\alpha}\ H_{\beta\alpha} = \Sigma_{\beta\alpha}\ a_\beta\ W_{\beta\alpha}\ a_\alpha = a^T \cdot W \cdot a$$

Here $\Sigma_{\beta\alpha}$ means 'sum over all pairs of units β, α', and the last expression is simply a compact expression for this sum using vector/ matrix multiplication ($\cdot$); this way of producing a number, $H(a)$, from a vector a and a matrix W is ubiquitous in vector space theory.

The reason for creating the concept of Harmony is that it figures into an important result from the theory of PDP computation: a theorem concerning Harmony maximization. Before stating this result, we need to give a high-level characterization of the kind of computation performed in PDP models. First, an input, encoded as an input vector **i**, is imposed on a set of input units, where it remains unchanged throughout the computation.[28] Then activation flows from the input units to other units; in many cases, this eventually 'settles' and the overall activation vector of the entire network, **a**, no longer changes. The input vector **i** is a part of the total activation vector **a**, since the input units are a part of the total population of units in the network. We will phrase this as follows: the total vector **a** is a *completion* of the input vector **i**. We can think of different networks as completing **i** in different ways. Part of the total activation vector **a** is also the output vector **o**: this is the part of **a** which lists the activity values of the output units. Thus, as the network computes a completion **a** of an input **i**, part of what it's doing is mapping the input **i** to a corresponding output **o**; this mapping of **i** to **o** is the function *f* computed by the network.

The remaining definition we need is of a central class of PDP networks:

(48)   *Harmonic nets (def.)*: A PDP network is *harmonic* if it possesses the following properties:

   (a) *Activation rule:* If the total activation flowing into the unit is positive, the activation will increase (or stay the same); if negative, decrease.

   (b) *Connectivity:* The connectivity pattern is either feedforward (no closed loops) or symmetrical feedback ($w_{\beta\alpha} = w_{\alpha\beta}$; the connection weight to β from α equals that to α from β).

   (c) *Updating:* Units change their activation values one at a time, or they change their activity by a very small amount at each update (ideally, continuously in time).

Now we can state the result:

(49)   *Harmony maximization (theorem)*.[29] In harmonic nets, at each moment of processing, the Harmony of the total activation vector increases (or stays the same). Furthermore, for a very wide set of activation rules,[30] the activation settles to a final vector which maximizes *H* (**a**), among the vectors **a** that are completions of the input **i**.

Harmony maximization is fundamental to ICS because it makes it possible to reason at a higher level of analysis than that of individual units, connections, activation rules, update rules, and on and on for all the details of the connectionist level of analysis. Harmony maximization enables most of this complexity to be encapsulated into a simple, yet powerful, principle which allows us to operate at higher levels; this principle is a further refinement of the most basic principle (1):

(50) Alg_{pdp}:   In all cognitive domains, cognitive processes are spreading activation algorithms (= 28 = 1) . . .

(51) $\text{Alg}_{\text{pdp}}(H)$:   . . . a core class of which are those operating in harmonic nets . . .

(52) $\text{Fun}_{\text{pdp}}(H)$:   . . . which perform parallel soft-constraint satisfaction; i.e., they complete input activation vectors to total activation vectors which maximize Harmony. (= 49: principle of Harmony maximization)[31]

As we have seen (49), (52) is a logical consequence of (51), and not an independent hypothesis of the theory. Indeed, the ability to derive the principle $\text{Fun}_{\text{pdp}}(H)$ governing the functions computed is a main motivation for hypothesizing that $\text{Alg}_{\text{pdp}}(H)$ holds of the algorithms doing the computing.

2.3.2   Harmony of symbol structures: Harmonic Grammar   The importance of the processing assumption $\text{Alg}_{\text{pdp}}(H)$ is that it allows Connectionist principles to inform analysis at a higher level. In higher cognitive domains, at such a level the representational assumption (39) $\text{Rep}_{\text{ics}}(\text{HC})$ applies: the vectors of interest have the form of tensor product representations. So what are the implications of having these two higher-level principles, harmony maximization and tensor product representation, both in force? The mathematical consequences are remarkably simple:

(53) **Wf$_{\text{ics}}$(HC) (theorem)**: Suppose **a** is a tensor product vector realizing a symbolic structure s with constituents c_i, according to $\text{Rep}_{\text{ics}}(\text{HC})$ (39).
(a) The harmony of this representation is:

$$H(\text{s}) \equiv H(\text{a}) = \Sigma_{ij}\, H(c_i,\, c_j).$$

(b) Equivalently, the harmony of s can be computed using the following rules:

R_{ij}: if s simultaneously contains the constituents c_i and c_j then   add the numerical quantity $H(c_i,\, c_j)$ to H.

Each R_{ij} is called a *soft rule*, and the collection of rules defines a *Harmonic Grammar*. To determine the Harmony of a structure s, we simply find all rules R_{ij} which apply to s and add up all the corresponding Harmony contributions $H(c_i \ c_j)$.

(c) Soft rules can be equivalently recast as soft *constraints*. If $H(c_i, c_j)$ is a negative value $-s_{ij}$, then R_{ij} is interpreted as the (negative) constraints:

C_{ij}: s *should not* simultaneously contain the constituents c_i, c_j (strength: s_{ij})

If $H(c_i, c_j)$ is a positive value $+s_{ij}$, then R_{ij} corresponds to the (positive) constraint:

C_{ij}: s *should* simultaneously contain the constituents c_i, c_j (strength: s_{ij})

$H(s)$ is computed by adding the strengths of all positive constraints which s satisfies and subtracting the strength of all the negative constraints which it violates.

(d) Viewed at the lower level of the connectionist network, each Harmony contribution $H(c_i, c_j)$ is a measure of the degree to which the pair of vectors $\mathbf{c}_i$, $\mathbf{c}_j$ realizing c_i, c_j conform to the soft constraints encoded in the weight matrix $\mathbf{W}$; it can be calculated according to the formula:

$$H(\mathbf{c}_i, \mathbf{c}_j) = \Sigma_{\beta\alpha} (\mathbf{c}_i)_\beta \ W_{\beta\alpha} \ (\mathbf{c}_j)_\alpha$$

Let me illustrate soft rules by discussing some which correspond to a conventional phrase structure re-write grammar rule:

(54) S $\rightarrow$ NP VP

Two corresponding soft rules, informally stated, are:

(55) (a) $R_{\text{S, NP}}$: If s contains a constituent labelled S and its left sub-constituent is labelled NP, then add $+2$ to H.

(b) $R_{\text{S, VP}}$: If s contains a constituent labelled S and its right sub-constituent is labelled VP, then add $+2$ to H.

That these rules instantiate the general soft-rule schema for $R_{i,j}$ is fairly obvious. In (55a), for example, the constituent c_i is an S at some node in the parse tree, while the second constituent c_j is an NP at a node which is the left child node of the S. The harmony contribution from this pair, $H(c_i, c_j)$, is $+2$; the fact that this quantity is positive means that this pair of constituents is well-formed according to the grammar.[32]

The principle (53) Wf_{ics} (HC) determines how the Harmony of a symbolic structure (e.g. a parse tree) s is computed in terms of its symbolic constituents. The computation is a simple one provided the quantities $H(c_i, c_j)$ are known; in that case, no reference to the connectionist level of activation vectors and weight matrices is required: the entire computation can be performed on the basis of the symbolic constituents alone. Evidently, to apply the rules $R_{S, NP}$ and $R_{S, VP}$ (55) we need only know about the location of S, NP, and VP labels in a parse tree: we need to know nothing about the activity vectors used to realize these constituents, and the connections used to process them, except for what is encapsulated in (55): that the aggregate effect of all the relevant activations and weights is to assess a Harmony of $+2$ to these arrangements of constituents in a structure.

Given the ability to assess the Harmony of any symbol structure, provided by principle (53) Wf_{ics} (HC), it is now (in principle) straightforward to determine the functioning of the grammar: apply principle Fun_{pdp} (*H*), as follows. Imagine the network receives a string of symbols, encoded as an input vector **i**, which it must parse according to its Harmonic Grammar. According to Fun_{pdp} (*H*), the net effect of the processing in the network is to complete this input vector into a total pattern of activity **a** which has maximum Harmony. This vector **a** is the parse of the input **i** according to the grammar encoded in the network's connections **W**.[33] That is, we have the following symbolic version of Fun_{pdp} (*H*):

(56) **Fun_{ics} (H):** Given an input symbolic structure i, the harmonic grammar assigns to i the output symbolic structure ('parse') s with maximal Harmony, among those which are completions of i. The higher the value of Harmony of this parse structure s, the more well formed the grammar judges the input (= 49: Harmony maximization).

The input is always part of the parse structure. For phrase structure grammars (context-free grammars), the parse is a tree whose terminal symbols give the input string, and whose structure shows how the input symbols are grouped into constituent phrases. For formal grammars, we can arbitrarily impose a cut-off of acceptable Harmony for the parse in order for an input string to be judged sufficiently well formed by the grammar to be admitted into the language. For instance, we may choose a cut-off of 0: inputs assigned parses with negative Harmony are then not in the formal language, while those with non-negative Harmony are.[34]

The utter simplicity of Harmonic Grammar may give the impression that it is quite a weak notion. Only pairs of constituents are examined. Each pair is crudely assigned a number, and these numbers are simply added up. Interactions would seem to be very weak. So it is reasonable to expect that this connectionist-derived linguistic formalism, Harmonic Grammar, is too weak to handle *real syntax* like that of phrase structure/ context-free grammars. This expectation is, however, demonstrably false.

(57) **Fun$_{ics}$(CFL) (theorem)**: Any context-free language can be specified by a Harmonic Grammar.

The proof of this theorem would take us too far afield; it may be found in Smolensky et al. (1992, s. 3.1.2). The idea of the proof is simple: context-free re-write rules like (54) are replaced by harmonic grammar soft rules like (55) which provide positive Harmony for legal dominations (constituent/sub-constituent relations); at the same time, a carefully designed set of rules like:

(58) R_S: If s contains a constituent S, add -3 to $H(s)$.

assess negative Harmony for all symbols (like S) which occur in the parse tree. The negative Harmony values in rules like (58) are designed so that if the symbol has a legal parent in the tree, and the full number of required legal children, then its negative Harmony will be just cancelled by the positive Harmony arising from all these legal dominations. The net result is that well-formed parse trees have 0 Harmony, while all other structures have negative harmony: so the formal language is, as required, all and only those input symbol strings whose maximum-Harmony parse tree has non-negative (indeed 0) Harmony.

Extending theorem (57) from context-free grammars to unrestricted grammars is straightforward; the only complication is that parse structures are no longer simply trees, but more complex symbolic structures whose realization in tensor products has not yet been attempted; I know of no reason to expect any difficulties, however, given the utter generality of the tensor product technique for representing arbitrary symbolic structures. As far as harmonic grammars at the symbolic level are concerned, however, there is no doubt: for any re-write rule grammar there is corresponding Harmonic Grammar which generates the same formal language (Smolensky et al., 1992, p. 28).

Unrestricted grammars are the formal-language equivalents of Turing machines: the former is the top of the Chomsky language hierarchy and the latter the top of the automaton hierarchy. Thus the power of the computational abstraction provided by ICS, Harmonic Grammars, is as great as that of Turing machines. In this sense, at least, the goal of realizing the power of symbolic computation in a PDP model has been achieved.

In order to avoid misunderstanding of this claim, it is important to make what is usefully viewed as a competence/performance distinction for ICS – different in important respects from Classical competence/ performance distinctions, but sharing enough central properties to justify the name.

2.3.3 A competence/performance distinction The competence/performance distinction at issue in ICS turns critically on the difference between an input/output *function*, and an *algorithm* for computing the function: this difference is marked on the labels for, on the one hand, (51), $\mathbf{Alg}_{pdp}(H)$, and, on the other, (52), $\mathbf{Fun}_{pdp}(H)$, and its special case for higher cognition, (56), $\mathbf{Fun}_{ics}(H)$.

A Harmonic Grammar specifies an input/output function, in terms of what is generally known as an *optimization* formulation: the output is that completion of the input which maximizes (or 'optimizes') the Harmony function; the output specified by the grammar is in this sense 'optimal' or most well formed.

How is this optimal output to be computed/constructed/found? This is the problem which a *parsing algorithm* must solve. It is not the job of grammars to *compute*: they are *functions*, and their job is to abstractly specify, for any input, its correct output/parse/structural description. And this a Harmonic Grammar does, using a novel means of specification: optimization.

This means of specifying a function is derived from the underlying connectionist processing: $\mathbf{Fun}_{pdp}(H)$ is a consequence of $\mathbf{Alg}_{pdp}(H)$, via the Harmony maximation theorem (49). Thus it should be possible to use the algorithms of harmonic nets (48) to compute the functions required by Harmonic Grammars. And, indeed, it is, although experience in doing so is extremely limited. But there is a gap between the connectionist algorithms of $\mathbf{Alg}_{pdp}(H)$ and the Harmonic Grammars of $\mathbf{Fun}_{pdp}(H)$ which must now be examined.

Optimization theory distinguishes two kinds of optima: *local* and *global*. A local optimum is a solution which is better than any of its 'neighbors': this notion is relative to some concept of 'neighborhood' in the space of possible solutions. In the PDP case, a local Harmony maximum is an activation vector **a** with the property that any small change in the activation of any of the units will lower the Harmony of the activity pattern. A global optimum is a solution which simply is better than *every* alternative. Thus a local Harmony maximum a may not be a global maximum because it may be that a set of large changes to the activations in a would result in a higher Harmony pattern.

Computing the global maximum of harmony functions is computationally intractable, and it is important to realize that neither connectionist networks nor any other known algorithm can exactly solve this problem efficiently, for arbitrary Harmony functions (that is, arbitrary weight matrices or arbitrary sets of soft rules in a Harmonic Grammar). There are two senses then in which the Harmony maximization theorem (49) holds. The first is that harmonic nets compute *local* Harmony maxima; this is true for a large variety of activation functions. For some special ones, a further result is true: there is a limit, which idealizes away from efficiency, in which the *global* maximum is computed. For example, the spreading activation algorithm employed in Harmony Theory (Smolensky, 1986a), also called 'simulated annealing', is a probabilistic algorithm with the property that the probability of computing the global maximum approaches 1 as the amount of processing time is allowed to grow without bound.

The Harmony maximum employed in Harmonic Grammar is the global maximum; at least as currently formulated, there is no notion of 'neighboring' parses and no meaning therefore to 'local maximum'. The function specified by a Harmonic Grammar according to $Fun_{ics}(H)$ constitutes a notion of *grammatical competence*. There is a gap between this and parsing algorithms governed by $Alg_{pdp}(H)$ which are potential models for *linguistic performance*. If rapid computation is required, the algorithms will compute local Harmony maxima rather than global maxima, leading to a kind of deviation from the competence theory which is as yet thoroughly unexplored. On the other hand, there is an idealization of a 'perfect grammar-using network' which is allowed unbounded time to compute the global maximum; in this limit, the PDP algorithm modeling performance computes the function specifying competence.

A second kind of idealization appeared in the discussion of productivity in section 2.2.2.3. The recursive tensor product representations used in ICS achieve perfectly umambiguous realization of symbolic structure but, to do so, sufficiently large networks must be employed to cope with the size of symbol structures required. In the idealization of infinite productivity – unboundedly large trees being evaluated by recursive functions, unboundedly long sentences in a formal language, unboundedly deep recursion – unboundedly large networks are required. As was already explained in (46), however, this idealization is very simply accommodated in ICS: these unboundedly large networks are unproblematically finitely specified.

2.3.4 On the psychological reality of Harmonic Grammar rules

We can now return to the main topic of the chapter: constituent structure and the explanatory and causal roles of constituents. The rules of a grammar are 'constituents' of mental knowledge, in some sense, and it is interesting to ask of them what we asked in section 2.2.2.3 of the constituents of mental representation: do they play essential roles in cognitive explanation? Do they enter into algorithms which generate cognitive behavior? These questions bear, of course, on the 'psychological reality' of the grammar rules, an issue of long-standing interest in cognitive science.

Consider first explanation. The theorem on formal languages (57) is proved entirely through the analysis of soft rule sets. In this proof, the individual rules play separable and ineliminable roles. Furthermore, the infinite, recursive nature of formal languages figures centrally in the general issue of productivity; harmonic grammar therefore offers further evidence that explanations of productivity are possible and powerful in ICS. And, indeed, in the next section we will see that Harmonic Grammar has led to developments in linguistic theory which strengthen the explanatory power of the theory of the grammar of human language. The explanatory power of soft rules in Harmonic Grammar is considerable.

Turning to causal roles and algorithms, however, we must draw the same conclusion for rules as knowledge constituents as we did for symbols as representation constituents. These rules do not figure into symbolic algorithms for linguistic performance in ICS. These algorithms are massively parallel PDP activation-spreading algorithms, defined over units and connections. Each Harmonic Grammar rule corresponds to a widely distributed pattern of connections, connections which also share in the realization of many other rules. An algorithmic description of this connectionist Harmony-maximization process is impossible – as far as we now know. The processing amounts to constructing the output parse structure in a continuous, non-discrete fashion, in parallel across the whole structure, satisfying all the constraints in the Harmonic Grammar simultaneously. The conclusion, again, is that there are no symbolic algorithms describing ICS processing: Alg_{sym} (7) fails, and its negation Alg_{ics} (9) holds.

These remarks have a mostly speculative status at present, however, since experience with such algorithms is almost nil, and much more study of the approach at the algorithmic level is necessary before definite assessment is possible.

3 The ICS Cognitive Architecture

The main focus in section 2 has been the construction of a novel and sufficiently powerful *computational* architecture, one which uses new linking principles to bring together computational principles from PDP connectionism and principles from Classical symbolic computation. Scattered throughout sections 1 and 2 are several principles of the ICS *cognitive* architecture. To begin, I simply assemble 14 of these in section 3.1. Then in section 3.2 I use these principles to assess the status in ICS of the general cognitive properties which form the center of F&P's critique of connectionism. Finally, in section 3.3 I consider the contribution of ICS to an area of empirical cognitive science central to the Classical approach: the theory of the grammar of human languages. The material in section 3 will serve as the basis of an assessment of ICS in section 4.

3.1 The principles of ICS

Representation

(59) Rep_{pdp}:   In all cognitive domains, representations are distributed patterns of activity. (= 2)

(60) Nativism_{ics}:   Some crucial structure in connectionist networks does *not* arise from learning. (= 8)

(61) $\text{Rep}_{ics}(\text{HC})$:   In core parts of higher cognitive domains, representations are vectors which have the structure of recursive tensor product representations. (= 39)

(62) ∴ $\text{Rep}_{sym}(\text{HC})$:   In core parts of higher cognitive domains, representations are symbol structures. (= 3)

(63) $\text{Sem}_{sym}(\text{HC})$:   The semantic interpretation of these symbolic representations are compositionally derived from their syntactic structure. (= 4)

Processing

(64) Alg_{pdp}:   In all cognitive domains, cognitive processes are spreading activation algorithms ... (= 1)

(65) $\text{Alg}_{pdp}(\text{W})$:   ... the core operation of which is the multiplication of an input activation vector i by a weight matrix **W** to get the output vector:

$$o = W \cdot i. \ (= 29)$$

(66) $\text{Alg}_{\text{ics}}(\text{HC,W})$:   In core parts of higher cognitive domains, weight matrices have the form:

$$W = w \otimes R$$

where w is a finite rearrangement matrix, and R is the recursion matrix. (= 46)

(67)∴ $\text{Fun}_{\text{sym}}(\text{HC})$:   In core parts of higher cognitive domains, the input/output functions computed by cognitive processes are described by (recursive) symbolic functions. (= 5)

(64) Alg_{pdp}:   In all cognitive domains, cognitive processes are spreading activation algorithms . . . (= 1)

(68) $\text{Alg}_{\text{pdp}}(H)$:   . . . a core class of which are those operating in harmonic nets . . . (= 51)

(69)∴ $\text{Fun}_{\text{pdp}}(H)$:   . . . which perform parallel soft-constraint satisfaction; i.e. they complete input activation vectors to total activation vectors which maximize Harmony H. (= 52)

(70)∴ $\text{Fun}_{\text{ics}}(\text{HC},H)$:   Given an input symbolic structure i, the Harmonic Grammar assigns to i the output symbolic structure ('parse') s with maximal Harmony, among those which are completions of i. The higher the value of Harmony of this parse structure s, the more well formed the grammar judges the input. (= 56)

(71)∴ $\text{Fun}_{\text{ics}}(\text{CFL})$:   Any context-free language can be specified by a Harmonic Grammar. (= 57)

(72)∴ $\text{Alg}_{\text{ics}}(\text{HC})$:   There are important higher cognitive processes which are *not* described by symbolic algorithms. (= 9)

The logical status of these principles is indicated in this list as follows: all have the status of axioms except those marked with '∴', which are theorems. We return to discuss this logical structure when we consider the goal of reduction (11) in section 4.

3.2   Status of the F&P properties in the ICS architecture

We first consider the properties pertaining to representation, then those concerning processing.

3.2.1 Representations: systematicity and compositionality   One consequence of the ICS principles yet to be discussed is:

(73)   **Systematicity(HC) (theorem):** In core parts of higher cognitive domains, the set of possible representations form a systematic set; for example, if it is possible to represent the proposition p referred to by *Sandy loves Kim*, then it is also possible to represent the proposition p' referred to by *Kim loves Sandy*.

This is, of course, little surprise, since at the higher level of description, the representiations of these propositions in ICS are the symbolic forms $p \equiv L(S, K)$ and $p' \equiv L(K, S)$; systematicity is one corollary of the fact that ICS realizes symbolic representations $\text{Rep}_{sym}(HC)$ (62) in higher cognitive domains. But it is worth showing this result explicitly.

According to $\text{Rep}_{ics}(HC)$ (61), in ICS higher cognitive representations have the form of tensor product representations which get their semantics compositionally, following $\text{Sem}_{sym}(HC)$. As explained at some length in section 2.2.1.2.1, the proposition p of (73) is represented by the vector (34):

$$p \equiv r_0 \otimes L + r_1 \otimes [r_0 \otimes S + r_1 \otimes K]$$

which realizes $p = L(S, K) \equiv [L, [S, K]]$. In order for a particular cognitive system to be able to represent p, then, it must have vectors L, S, and K with which to construct p. This means that in addition to p, the representational vector space must also contain the vector

$$p' \equiv r_0 \otimes L + r_1 \otimes [r_0 \otimes K + r_1 \otimes S]$$

which realizes $p' = L(K, S) \equiv [L, [K, S]]$ and which represents the proposition p'. This example illustrates that the space of tensor product vectorial representations possesses the same systematic structure as that of Classical symbol systems; of course, were this not so, there would be no way for tensor product vectors to realize symbol structures.[35]

While systematicity(HC) is a consequence of more basic ICS principles, compositionality of semantics in higher cognitive domains is simply an assumption: $\text{Sem}_{sym}(HC)$ (63). This fact will be discussed below in section 4.3.2.

3.2.2   Processes: productivity and inferential coherence   A worthy account of general inference, including the property F&P call 'inferential coherence', is an open problem for ICS, and for PDP modeling for that matter. There is little to say at this point; a few remarks of comparison to the Classical account will be offered in section 4.1.1.2.

Of all the F&P properties, the one which has been most central to the development of ICS has been producitivity, because of its fundamental and central role in cognitive science generally (as discussed in section 2.2.1.1). In ICS, the productivity of higher cognition is a logical consequence of more basic principles; two extremely general characterizations of productivity were derived. The first is $\text{Fun}_{\text{sym}}(\text{HC})$, (67), which asserts that recursive functions are computed; the explanation of how this follows from more fundamental principles was the subject of section 2.2.2.3. The second result was $\text{Fun}_{\text{ics}}(\text{HC},H)$ (70), which asserts that recursive formal languages can be specified by the grammar formalism, Harmonic Grammar, which follows from fundamental principles of ICS. The explanatory role of Harmonic Grammar rules was discussed in section 2.3.4.

Two major points have been made about the explanation of productivity in ICS. The first is that such explanation has not previously been possible within the confines of PDP models, as opposed to local connectionist networks (section 2.1.1). The fact that ICS uses PDP and not local connectionism has, of course, pervasive computational consequences; but it also has an important foundational consequence: the ICS explanation of productivity is non-Classical. Constituents in ICS do *not* play causal roles in the sense of participating in symbolic algorithms for generating productive behavior. How constituents can fail to play such roles while still explaining productivity is the central paradox resolved by ICS. As explained in some detail in section 2.2.2.3, the crucial observation is that there are other kinds of structure a processing system may possess besides the kind of structure which constitutes symbolic algorithms; certain abstract (tensor product) structure in the spaces of activity and connection patterns is what explains productivity in ICS, and constituents are part and parcel of this structure. Yet the algorithms actually responsible for generating behaviour do not operate over these constituents, but rather over their micro-structure; there is no symbolic algorithm which is at work manipulating these constituents, and no explanation based on such manipulations is possible.

3.3   Generative grammar

The adequacy of a proposed cognitive architecture such as ICS obviously needs to be assessed on many fronts, and most of these remain to be seriously examined. In addition to adequacy with respect to computational and foundational issues, considered in sections 2 and 3.2, the other area in which ICS has been tested is a more empirical domain, one which is also close to the heart of the classical architecture: the theory of grammar, taken as knowledge of human language.

In section 2.3, computational issues in language and grammar were taken up, and the resulting principles of Harmonic Grammar were applied to formal languages, which are usually considered part of the theory of computation. But Harmonic Grammar has also been applied to natural language, and it has led to new insights and developments in generative grammar; these are very briefly taken up in this section.

According to Harmonic Grammar, grammars are sets of simultaneous, conflicting, soft constraints, with conflicts resolved by recourse to a notion of relative strength. This differs from certain Classical conceptions of grammar in two important ways. First, in the notion of simultaneous constraint satisfaction, and, secondly in the idea that the constraints are soft.

Chomsky's earliest work on natural language grammar followed the lead of formal grammars in defining a language in terms of which strings could be generated by a set of sequential string-rewriting rules (phrase structure rules and transformations). In our discussion of formal languages in section 2.3, we saw how to recast such a notion of sequential rewriting with a Harmonic Grammar of simultaneous constraints. Such a transition, from viewing a grammar as a set of operations in a sequential algorithm to viewing it as a set of simultaneous well-formedness constraints, is one which occurred in generative grammar research on syntactic theory some 15 years ago. It is generally regarded as a major advance in syntactic theory, increasing the explanatory power of generative grammar dramatically.

Thus in the context of modern generative syntax, the first element of the Harmonic-Grammar conception is not revolutionary: the output assigned by a grammar to an input is not the result of a grammatically specified sequential algorithm but, rather, that completion of the input which simultaneously satisfies a set of grammatically specified constraints. On the other hand, the second element of Harmonic Grammar is novel: the idea that the constraints are 'soft – they are *conflicting*, so that many are often violated in the legal structures of the language, and conflicts are resolved by a notion of relative strength.

The power of this second element, *soft* constraints, to deal with complex constraint interaction in natural language was demonstrated in research in French syntax. A topic of considerable research in generative grammar is that of *split intransitivity*, in which different intransitive verbs pattern differently in various syntactic and semantic respects. Researchers have been strongly divided over whether the constraints which explain these phenomena are syntactic or semantic. The phenomena are ruled in large part by *tendencies* which have not been successfully capturable through hard constraints. A particularly challenging pattern of grammaticality judgements is presented by French split intransitivity phenomena. In our Harmonic Grammar account, we showed that this complex pattern could be explained by a set of *soft* constraints, some syntactic, some semantic, and some involving syntactic/semantic compatibility (see Smolensky et al. 1992, s. 3.1.5 and Appendix, and references therein.)

In relevant respects, the history of the phonological component of generative grammar has differed from that of the syntactic component. In syntax, the transition from conceiving a grammar as a sequential rewrite rule algorithm to viewing it as a set of parallel constraints significantly advanced the explanatory power of the theory, but in phonology, such a transition has been considerably more problematic. The sequential-algorithm conception is still dominant, with constraints hovering at the margins of the theory, resistant to attempts to promote them to the core. Harmonic Grammar is providing a significant instrument of change in this picture. It now appears that in phonology, successfully shifting to a conception of grammar based on constraints depends crucially on having a formal framework of *soft* constraints.

Phonological applications of Harmonic Grammar led Alan Prince and myself to a remarkable discovery: in a broad set of cases, at least, the relative strengths of constraints *need not be specified numerically*. For if the numerically weighted constraints needed in these cases are ranked from strongest to weakest, it turns out that each constraint is stronger than all the weaker constraints *combined*. That is, the numerical strengths are so arranged that *each constraint can never be over-ruled by weaker constraints, no matter how many*. This has led to a non-numerical successor to harmonic grammar, *Optimality Theory* (Prince and Smolensky, 1993), in which constraints are arranged in *strict dominance hierarchies*, each constraint strictly stronger than all the lower-ranked constraints (even when combined). In a variety of areas in phonology, Optimality Theory, for the first time, has made it possible to shift the formal framework of grammar completely away from that of a symbolic algorithm, to one of simultaneous soft-constraint satisfaction. The increased explanatory power is sometimes dramatic, significantly strengthening the theory of Universal Grammar.

For example, it becomes possible to identify a set of conflicting phonological constraints which all languages share, and which therefore form part of Universal Grammar. Individual grammars rank these universal constraints differently in their language-particular dominance hierarchies, so the conflicts among the universal constraints are resolved differently in different languages. This often gives rise to very different surface patterns in the different languages, but these can now be explained as arising from a common set of constraints. By analyzing the results arising from ranking the universal constraints in all possible dominance hierarchies, it becomes possible to deduce predictions/ explanations of which patterns are and are not possible in human languages. This approach to explaining typological variation has been carried out both within phonology (Prince and Smolensky, 1993) and within morphosyntax (Legendre, et al. 1993).

Optimality Theory can be viewed as resolving an artifact within generative grammar that is a relic of its Classical origins. The idea of a universal set of well-formedness conditions has a long history in linguistics, much of it characterized in terms of *tendencies* or *markedness*. Markedness is a notion of relative well-formedness which pervades informal linguistic theory but which has never been successfully adopted as a core concept at the center of a formal theory. In large part, this is because it is a notion fundamentally out of place in a formalism in which a grammar is a sequential algorithm for constructing an output from an input. Harmonic Grammar, on the other hand, **is** a formal theory of markedness, or can be so interpreted. Freeing linguistic theory from the demands of algorithm construction in the way that Harmonic Grammar and Optimality Theory do allows markedness-type notions to claim center stage; indeed, these now *become* the grammar.

Optimality Theory is a contribution to symbolic generative grammar which ICS gives rise to by allowing central concepts from PDP computation – parallel soft-constraint satisfaction – to rise up from the lower level and constructively engage with linguistic theories of symbolic representation.

4   Summary Assessment

It is now time to assess the degree to which ICS meets its goals and overcomes various objections.

4.1   The necessity objection

F&P make the following argument:

(74)   *The necessity objection* to connectionism: Of course, a connectionist net *can* be wired up in accordance with the F&P properties, but a connectionist network can also be wired up *not* to possess these

properties. Thus the connectionist architecture cannot, but the classical architecture does, explain why a cognitive system *must* possess these properties.

In this section we assess this objection, and show that with respect to ICS it fails: the Classical account is at least as stipulative and unexplanatory, by this criterion.

First, as shown in section 2.1.1, the opening 'of course' in the necessity objection reflects a basic confusion. As we saw, while it is in some sense unproblematic to 'wire up' local connectionst networks to implement symbolic computation and thereby exhibit the F&P properties, within the class of connectionist networks most often entertained as a candidate cognitive architecture, PDP models, just the opposite presupposition is warranted: that 'wiring them up'to display anything other than simple associationism is impossible. That is, when evaluating PDP models, before worrying about the necessity objection, we must satisfactorily address:

(75) *The sufficiency objection* to connectionism: Of course, a connectionist net *cannot* be wired up in accordance with the F&P properties, because connectionist networks just have unstructured representations, and just do statistical association, not structure-sensitive processing.

It is only after the development of PDP into ICS, as outlined in Sections 2–3, that the sufficiency objection can be put aside, and only then that the necessity objection merits any serious attention.

4.1.1 Necessity of the F&P properties in the classical architecture   In order to compare the level of explanation of the 'necessity' of the F&P properties obtained in ICS and in the Classical theory, let's start by collecting the Classical principles which have already been presented:

Principles of the Classical architecture
(76) **Rep$_{sym}$(HC):**   In core parts of higher cognitive domains, representations are symbol structures. (= 62 = 3)
(77) **Sem$_{sym}$(HC):**   The semantic interpretation of these symbolic representations are compositionally derived from their syntactic structure. (= 63 = 4)
(78) **Alg$_{sym}$(HC):**   Higher cognitive processes are described by symbolic algorithms. (= — 72 = 7)

(79) $\therefore$ $\mathbf{Fun_{sym}(HC)}$: In core parts of higher cognitive domains, the input/output functions computed by cognitive processes are described by (recursive) symbolic functions. (= 67 = 5)

Except for (78), which is explicitly rejected in ICS (72), the other three principles also hold in ICS.

Now let us consider the four F&P properties in turn, and compare the level of explanation achieved by the Classical theory and by ICS.

4.1.1.1 SYSTEMATICITY AND COMPOSITIONALITY

As stated, $Rep_{sym}(HC)$ (76) does not in fact entail systematicity. For the presence of one symbol structure, say L (S, K), does not entail the presence of another, say [L (K, S)]. In fact, what is required for a Classical account of systematicity is a stronger version of (76):

(80) $\mathbf{Rep_{sym}(HC)^*}$: In core parts of higher cognitive domains, the set of representations forms a symbol *system*.

And, of course, this assumption is frequently stated in terms of symbol systems. The point here is that *systematicity* is a basic part of the definition of a symbol *system*; the Classical theory gets systematicity by *assuming* it, not by deriving it from more fundamental principles. The necessity of systematicity is not *explained* by the Classical theory in any sense; it is simply *described* by it.[36]

The situation with compositionality is very simple: it is a bald assumption in both the Classical and ICS theories. Neither theory provides anything like an explanation of it.

4.1.1.2 PRODUCTIVITY AND INFERENTIAL COHERENCE

In the Classical theory, productivity – as captured, for example, in $Fun_{sym}(HC)$ (79) and denoted by the '$\therefore$' – is a theorem; this is the real locus of explanatory power in the Classical theory, as discussed in section 2.1.1. The explanation derives from a different source than in ICS: it is a consequence of symbolic algorithms $Alg_{sym}(HC)$ (78).

The Classical theory of inference is an impressive accomplishment, explaining how purely syntactic processes can be semantically truth-preserving. Questions of inference have not yet been explored seriously in ICS, so the issue has been neglected in this chapter. The Classical theory might be concisely expressed through the following pair of principles:

(81) $\text{Alg}_{sym}(\text{Inf})$:   Inference is performed by serially applying the symbol manipulation operation of resolution.

(82).∴ $\text{Fun}_{sym}(\text{Inf})$:   Inference is truth preserving: given representations the semantic interpretations of which are true, the same holds of the products of inference.

That (82) follows from (81) is an important result of modern symbolic logic; of course, the resolution rule of inference in (81) could be replaced by any other set of sound inference rules and the result (82) would still hold.

It should be noted that the level at which stipulation is necessary here, (81), is the level of specifying some set of inference rules which happen to be sound ones. The Classical theory explains why inference is semantically truth preserving on the assumption that a set of sound rules is applied during processing; its power to explain the necessity of such a property cannot go deeper, to answer the question, 'why *those* rules, and not other (unsound) ones?' In order to match the level of explanation provided by the symbolic theory, it suffices to stipulate some principle governing inference which is comparable to (81).

And indeed ICS could in theory accommodate the stipulation (81) without problem: since the ICS architecture realizes symbolic representations and functions – via $\text{Rep}_{sym}(\text{HC})$ (62) and $\text{Fun}_{sym}(\text{HC})$ (67) – the resolution rule of inference could be realized and used in various ways to perform inference. One way to do this would be to apply the rule serially, in which case $\text{Alg}_{sym}(\text{Inf})$ would hold for the ICS theory as well as the Classical: this would be to follow the implementationalist strategy (section 1.2.1); the Classical explanation would be taken over exactly. Nothing new would then be accomplished at the higher level of analysis – but it could not be claimed that ICS was disadvantaged with respect to the Classical theory as regards explaining inferential coherence. I have not codified this approach into ICS because I am confident that it is possible to do much better. In sum: if one were content to simply match the level of explanation of the Classical account of inference, this could in theory be done straight away; but since more attractive ICS approaches are almost certainly available, I prefer to wait.[37]

4.2   ICS v. the Classical theory on the F&P properties

We can now bring together the discussion of the explanation of the F&P properties in ICS (section 3.2) and in the Classical theory (section 4.1):

(83) *Systematicity:* In ICS, this is a derived consequence of more basic principles assumed to govern connectionist activation patterns. It is achieved by stipulation in the Classical theory, which, on principle, refuses to posit lower-level principles from which systematicity might be derived.

(84) *Compositionality:* Achieved by stipulation in both Classical theory and ICS.

(85) *Productivity:* Derived from more basic principles in both Classical theory and ICS. In the Classical theory, from the assumption that cognitive processes are symbolic algorithms operating on constituents. In ICS, from the lower-level assumption that cognitive processes are certain kinds of connectionist activation spreading algorithms which *cannot* be redescribed at the higher level as symbolic algorithms.

(86) *Inferential coherence:* In the Classical theory, truth preservation is a derived consequence of a more basic algorithmic assumption. The issue is not currently addressed in ICS. However, the Classical assumption could be adopted directly into ICS, achieving exactly the same explanation.

Thus we see that in no case is the level of explanation achieved in the Classical theory greater than that available in ICS. On the other hand, greater depth of explanation is offered by ICS for both systematicity and productivity. And in the latter case, the ICS explanation is clearly different from the Classical one.

Of the F&P properties, productivity stands out as the one the importance of which pervades cognitive science; this chapter has therefore focused on the ICS explanation of productivity. But there are several other goals for ICS, and we now take them up.

4.3 Evaluation relative to ICS goals

The goals set for ICS (10–13) were given in section 1.2; we now examine them in turn.

4.3.1 Preservation The goal here (10) is to preserve the depth of explanation of higher cognition already achieved by symbolic theory. In section 4.2 we saw that, with respect to the F&P properties of higher cognition, this goal has been met by ICS – and, for some properties, it has been exceeded.

Looking more widely across cognitive science, for instance to AI, linguistics and cognitive psychological modeling, it is clear that there are many open problems to solve before this goal can be fully achieved. A half-century of development of symbolic computation has obviously produced a tremendous richness of concepts and techniques; a great deal more research will be required before it is possible to determine the extent to which, and exactly how, this richness can be realized in ICS. But the ICS embedding of symbolic computation in PDP models outlined in this chapter seems to provide a solid foundation for such research.

4.3.2 Reduction Here, the goal (11) is to explain how symbolic computation is built upon neural computation. As argued in section 1.2.1, reduction of symbolic computation to PDP connectionism is one of the few feasible strategies, if not the only one, for pursuing this goal from our current position. The success of ICS in achieving such a reduction can be assessed by examining the principles of the ICS cognitive architecture (59–72). Those principles marked with '∴' are consequences of the other principles. There are three principles of symbolic computation which are targets for reduction: Rep_{sym} (HC) (62), Sem_{sym}(HC) (63) and Fun_{sym}(HC). Of these, two are flagged with '∴': Rep_{sym}(HC) and Fun_{sym}(HC) have been reduced to lower-level principles of PDP computation – the symbolic structure of representations and the recursive character of the functions computed over these representations have been reduced to tensor product structural properties of activation vectors (section 2.2.1.2) and connection weight matrices (section 2.2.2.3). Two open problems merit discussion: further reduction or explanation of the more fundamental PDP principles assumed here, and the lack of reduction of the compositionality of semantics: Sem_{sym}(HC).

The tensor product structure of activations and weights to which Rep_{sym}(HC) and Fun_{sym}(HC) have been reduced raises a number of open questions: is there some deeper explanation of the tensor product structure? By what means is the special structure of the vectors and matrices 'enforced'? Is it correct to assume that this structuring is innate, or could it in fact be learned? Is there an explanation from the connectionist level of why grammatical constraints so often have the special strict domination property developed and exploited in Optimality Theory?[38]

The fact that these questions arise, and can be framed with precision, is a hallmark of progress. Of course, the Classical theory escapes all comparable penetrating and difficult questions – they are all rendered unaskable – by invoking the Mystery Theory as its account of how human symbolic computation is realized.

On the other hand, ICS offers no progress on the reduction or explanation of compositional semantics. In the course of this chapter, the need for a stronger semantic theory in ICS has suggested itself in a few places. Here, it would constitute significant progress to be able to reduce $Sem_{sym}(HC)$ to more basic connectionist principles as we have done for the other two symbolic principles of ICS, $Rep_{sym}(HC)$ and $Fun_{sym}(HC)$. This would presumably involve a semantic theory which assigns interpretations to general activation vectors in the continuous vector space supporting PDP representations (20), and not just the special discrete subset with tensor product form (see discussion in section 2.2.1.2.2). The difficult task facing such a theory is to enable the compositionality of semantic interpretation for those vectors with tensor product form to be derived as a theorem. Development of such a theory in a completely general context seems unrealistic at present; what seems to be needed is a cognitive domain where a continuous space of semantic interpretations is available rather than a space of discrete propositions, for example. One possibility for such a domain which might make contact with existing linguistic theory within ICS is linguistic semantics: the theory of meaning of natural language sentences. Recent work on 'cognitive semantics' suggests ways in which discrete, proposition-like semantic interpretations might be embedded within a larger continuous space of interpretations. Another possible domain for exploration is perceptual/motor skill, used by Haugeland (1991) to illustrate his persuasive argument that a truly connectionist semantics must involve a continuous space of semantic interpretations.

Another issue which seems to deserve treatment in this future semantic theory is the choice of vectors to represent concepts or to realize symbols. Whereas atomic symbols form an unstructured set, the vectors realizing them do not: some sets of vectors are orthogonal to, or independent of, each other, others are not; some pairs of vectors are more similar to each other than are other pairs; and so forth. This structure is not exploited in ICS as it has been presented here, but it seems possible that the mutual relations of different activity vectors realizing atomic symbols can usefully be tied to the relations of their semantic interpretations. Clearly, enriching the semantic theory in ICS calls for a major research effort, and I will not attempt to predict the outcome of such an effort here.[39]

4.3.3 Revision   This goal (12) is to use insights derived from the reduction of symbolic computation to lower-level principles to improve upon symbolic accounts of higher cognition. I have argue that ICS achieves this in a core domain of higher cognition, grammatical theory (section 3.3). Optimization principles from PDP computation are brought up to the higher level, where they take the form of Harmonic Grammars: systems of simultaneous soft constraints. The subsequent grammatical formalism, Optimality Theory, significantly enhances the explanatory power of generative grammar.

4.3.4 Integration   The final goal (13) is to understand how symbolic computational principles which explain core parts of higher cognition integrate with computational principles which explain other aspects of cognition. In this connection it is significant that the basic principles of ICS which are assumed to hold in higher cognitive domains – and which entail the symbolic principles – are specializations of general PDP principles, with additional structure. $Rep_{ics}(HC)$ arises by taking the general principle Rep_{pdp} that representations are vectors, and adding tensor product structure. $Alg_{ics}(HC,W)$ is gotten from the general principle $Alg_{pdp}(W)$ that core connectionist processing is matrix multiplication by adding recursive tensor product structure. (As discussed in the previous section, there is unfortunately not yet a more basic, general principle 'Sem_{pdp}' from which to derive $Sem_{sym}(HC)$ – perhaps through '$Sem_{ics}(HC)$', a more structured specialization of Sem_{pdp}.) Thus ICS allows us to see precisely how the symbolic architecture of higher cognition is a consequence of specialized structure arising within the more general PDP cognitive architecture, which latter can naturally be applied to the modeling of a variety of lower-level cognitive phenomena which do not fall within the compass of the symbolic architecture. ICS also suggests ways that the symbolic character of 'core' higher cognition might interact with non-symbolic (perhaps continuous or ill-structured) aspects of 'non-core' higher cognition, for example aspects of language which are not well captured in symbolic theory. The connectionist algorithmic substrate suggests processing models for higher cognitive domains (e.g. language) which employ the same processing mechanisms as PDP models of lower cognitive domains (e.g. perception).

Even more speculatively, the embedding of a symbolic architecture within a PDP architecture raises the possibility of models of conceptual and grammatical development through PDP learning, and perhaps even exploration of the biological evolution of the symbolic architecture from less-structured PDP architectures in lower animals.

4.4   Conclusion

If the only goal of a cognitive architecture were preservation of the successes of Classical symbolic theory, the classical architecture would indeed be hard to beat. There are a number of other goals, however, including reduction to more fundamental principles which explain how the symbolic architecture is realized, revision of symbolic theory based on such explanations and integration of the symbolic architecture with other components of cognition. The integrated connectionist/symbolic cognitive architecture offers a number of contributions towards these other goals, preserving much of the explanatory power of symbolic theory at the same time. This is done by using connectionism to refine, rather than eliminate or replace, symbolic theory. Since the form of connectionism used to realize the symbolic architecture is PDP modeling, the lower-level computational principles involved are quite different from those of symbolic computation, and the result is a novel picture of cognition in which the constituents of mental representations and mental knowledge play crucial roles in explaining cognitive behavior, without having any roles in the algorithms which causally generate that behavior.

Acknowledgments

This research was partly supported by NSF Grant BS-9209265 and by a Faculty Fellowship from the University of Colorado. The research was carried out with the aid of Euclid, a software tool for supporting argumentation; Euclid was developed by Bernard Bernstein and Paul Smolensky under the support of NSF Grant IST-8609599, with additional support from Symbolics Inc. and Apple Computer.

Special thanks to my collaborators Géraldine Legendre, Yoshiro Miyata and Alan Prince for many discussions of these issues. Thanks for comments, discussions and encouragement to Rob Cummins, Dan Dennett, Jerry Fodor, Vinod Goel, Terry Horgan, Clayton Lewis, Mike Mozer, Georges Rey, Don Williams and the members of the Boulder Connectionist Research Group. Thanks also to audiences at Berkeley, Penn, the SUNY-Buffalo Conference on Cognition and Representation, and many others beyond my ever-diminishing memory span. Thanks to Dave Rumelhart for sharing many insights over the years, among them, the observation that Dukakis never had a chance in a popular election: his positions on the issues were complex, while his opponent had a remarkable gift for delivering utterly simple and appealing positions with transcendent confidence.

A   Appendix

Two more technical demonstrations omitted from the text are presented here.

A1   Proof of uniqueness of constituent decomposition (s. 2.2.1.2.2)

The notation is that of section 2.2.1.2.2. Suppose (for the purpose of deriving a contradiction) that constituent decomposition were not unique, i.e. that q could be written in two ways:

$$q = r_0 \otimes S + r_1 \otimes K$$

$$q = r_0 \otimes Q + r_1 \otimes Z$$

with either $S \neq Q$ or $K \neq Z$. Then it would follow by subtracting the two equations and rearranging that

$$r_0 \otimes [S - Q] = r_1 \otimes [Z - K]$$

Given the definition of the tensor product, in terms of components we would then have:

$$r_0 [S_i - Q_i] = r_1 [Z_i - K_i]$$

for each and every i. Now the supposed ambiguity exists because either $S \neq Q$ or $K \neq Z$. Suppose that $S \neq Q$; exactly analogous reasoning works if instead $K \neq Z$. Since $S \neq Q$, there is at least one component of the vectors which differs: call it i: $S_i \neq Q_i$. That means we can divide the last equation by $[S_i - Q_i] \neq 0$, giving

$$r_0 = r_1 [Z_i - K_i]/[S_i - Q_i].$$

This means that r_0 is a simple multiple of r_1 (the multiplier being $[Z_i - K_i]/[S_i - Q_i]$). This contradicts the independence of r_0 and r_1.

A2   Explanation of (41) (s. 2.2.2.3)

This can be seen with the help of a two-dimensional picture, if we take a simple enough case and break the problem into small enough pieces. Consider again the vector q representing $q = [S, K]$. The problem of extracting its left constituent S is the problem of computing from the vector

$$q = r_0 \otimes S + r_1 \otimes K$$

the vector S. Using the definition of the tensor product to rewrite this equation, the components of q are:

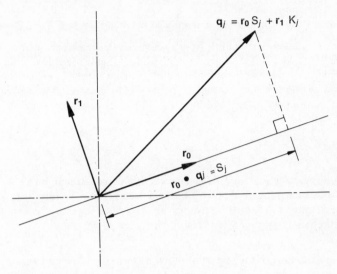

Figure 6.1   Extracting S_j from the vector $q_j = r_0 S_j + r_1 K_j$.

$q_{ij} = (r_0)_i S_j + (r_1)_i K_j$

If we put together all the components with a fixed j and different i values into a vector, we get:

$q_j = r_0 S_j + r_1 K_j$

Our problem is to compute S from q, which we do by computing each component S_j of S from q_j. How this is done is shown in figure 6.1 q_j is a weighted combination of the vectors r_0 and r_1, and we need to determine the weight of r_0, which is precisely S_j. But this can be done easily, using a basic vector operation: the dot product $\cdot$. Figure 6.1 illustrates the simplest case, when r_0 and r_1 are at right angles to each other and of length one. In this case we take the dot product of q_j with r_0, written $r_0 \cdot q_j$, and the result is exactly what we want: S_j. Geometrically, in this case, taking the dot product of q_j with r_0 amounts simply to determining the length of the perpendicular projection of q_j onto an axis running through r_0. Algebraically, taking the dot product $r_0 \cdot q_j$ is performing the following computation:

$$S_j = r_0 \cdot q_j = \Sigma_i (r_0)_i q_{ij} = \Sigma_{ik} [(r_0)_i \, \delta_{kj}] q_{ik} = (W^{(2)} \cdot q)_j$$

where the matrix $W^{(2)}$ has elements:

$$[\mathbf{W}^{(2)}]_{j,ik} \equiv (\mathbf{r}_0)_i \, \delta_{kj}$$

$\mathbf{W}^{(2)}$ creates a first-order vector $\mathbf{S}$ from a second-order tensor product vector $\mathbf{q}$, so its left matrix index is a single one ('j') while its right index is double ('ik'); the summation in the matrix multiplication '·' runs over this double-index. The symbol δ_{kj} denotes 1 if $k = j$ and 0 if $k \neq j$. The matrix of values $\{\delta_{kj}\}$ is therefore the identity matrix I of note 24. This means we can write $\mathbf{W}^{(2)}$:

$$\mathbf{W}^{(2)} = \mathbf{r}_0 \otimes I$$

The full recursive function which extracts the left sub-tree of a tree must be realized by a matrix which maps n^{th}-order tensor product vectors (for trees of depth $n-1$) into $n-1^{\text{th}}$-order tensor product vectors; $\mathbf{q}$ in our example just involves the case of $n = 2$. For each n, we have

$$\mathbf{W}^{(n)} = \mathbf{r}_0 \otimes I \otimes I \otimes \ldots \otimes I$$

with $n-1$ factors of I. The matrix $\mathbf{W}$ which realizes the recursive extract left sub-tree function is:

$$\begin{aligned} \mathbf{W} &= \mathbf{W}^{(1)} + \mathbf{W}^{(2)} + \ldots + \mathbf{W}^{(n)} + \ldots \\ &= \mathbf{r}_0 + \mathbf{r}_0 \otimes I + \ldots + \mathbf{r}_0 \otimes I \otimes I \otimes \ldots \otimes I + \ldots \\ &= \mathbf{r}_0 \otimes [1 + I + \ldots + I \otimes I \otimes \ldots \otimes I + \ldots] \\ &= \mathbf{r}_0 \otimes \mathbf{R} \end{aligned}$$

where $\mathbf{R}$ is the *recursion matrix* of (46), expressed in terms of I following note 24. This matrix illustrates the general case presented in (46):

$$\mathbf{W} = \mathbf{w} \otimes \mathbf{R}$$

where the finite rearrangement 'matrix' $\mathbf{w}$ is simply $\mathbf{r}_0$.

Notes

Upon rediscovering the paper 'Connectionism, computation and cognition' (in T. Horgan and J. Tienson (eds), *Connectionism and the Philosophy of Mind*, Kluwer, 1991), I see that Robert Cummins and Georg Schwarz employ a thought experiment about a calculator which is strongly reminiscent of (but rather less elaborate than) the thought experiments concerning the Gödel and

Visa boxes in section 2.2.2. Mine were almost certainly inspired by an earlier version of their paper, which I read circa 1987.

1 In this chapter, I use the following abbreviations: 'F&P' = Fodor and Pylyshyn (chapter 3); 'F&M' = Fodor and McLaughlin (chapter 5); '*OPTC* = 'On the proper treatment of connectionism', Smolensky (chapter 2); '*CCLOT* = 'Connectionism, constituency and the language of thought', Smolensky (chapter 4).

2 I use 'PDP' here rather than 'connectionism' because here and throughout much of this chapter what is true of PDP-style connectionism is not necessarily true of the other major style of connectionism, 'Local Connectionist Networks'. See section 2.1.1 and note 4 below.

3 Throughout this chapter, when I say that some elements (e.g. symbolic constituents) at the higher, symbolic level of description have no 'causal role', I mean exactly that there is no description of the internal state dynamics at the higher level which can be stated as an algorithm operating over these elements. The rejection of Alg_{sym} will mean that ICS is clearly non-'Classical' in the sense of F&P. On this F&M and I are apparently in agreement: 'We shall see that his architecture is genuinely non-Classical since the representations he postulates are not "distributed over" constituents in the sense that Classical representations are' (F&M, chapter 5, p. 200). 'We conclude that assuming that mental representations are activation vectors does not allow Smolensky to endorse the Classical solution of the systematicity problem. And, indeed, we think Smolensky would grant this since he admits up front that mental processes will not be causally sensitive to the strong compositional structure of mental representations' (F&M, chapter 5, p. 215). I agree with the last sentence under one interpretation, 'mental processes will not be algorithms processing constituents', but *not* under the interpretation, 'the outputs causally resulting from mental processes will not depend on the compositional structures of inputs.'

   In their concluding section, F&M (pp. 217–18) mistake my position on causality and reduction entirely. I am in complete agreement with them that lower-level (e.g. connectionist) accounts rarely replace higher-level (e.g. symbolic) ones: 'It is the view that successful microtheories always eliminate macrotheories from science that I referred to in the conclusion of the target article as "naive . . . eliminative reductionism" and Stich is right that the PTC view rejects the eliminative conclusion' (reply to commentary on *OPTC*, Smolensky 1988, p. 64). The basis on which I conclude that symbolic constituents do not play causal roles at the higher symbolic level in PTC or ICS is entirely different from that attributed to me by F&M; it is that there are no algorithms at this level operating on such constituents which govern the processing.

4 While the PDP approach to connectionism adopts the assumption of distributed representations, Rep_{pdp} (2), a competing connectionist approach rejects this assumption. This approach, lately going by the somewhat misleading name 'Structured Connectionism', is discussed

below in section 2.1 under the name 'Local Connectionist Networks'. This competing approach also claims to capture neural computational principles; see, e.g., Feldman (1989) and references therein.

5   Further evidence that connectionism is significantly more in contact with neuroscience than is Classical theory: during many decades of flourishing symbolic theory, 'theoretical neuroscience' remained a virtual oxymoron. Yet in the few years since the advent of PDP, computational insights deriving from PDP have nourished a great deal of progress in theoretical neuroscience (see any issue of the MIT Press journal, *Neural Computation*, or any of a dozen related journals which have appeared in the past half-decade). As predicted in *OPTC*, PDP has proved itself a fruitful level of computational abstraction between the symbolic and the neural; it serves not only to foster theories of how symbolic computation might be reduced, but also of how aspects of neural *structure* may in fact give rise to neural *computation*.

6   Requiring connectionism to follow either one or the other extreme paths of eliminativism or implementationalism was, of course, a major aspect of the argumentation strategy of F&P. The false dichotomy implicit in this argument is revealed by the existence of intermediate paths such as that pursued in ICS. However, it should be noted that since ICS is very much an integrated connectionist/symbolic architecture, it may well fall outside the scope of the category of 'connectionist cognitive architectures' targeted by F&P (although any coherent definition of the category which includes the two approaches they address, eliminativism and implementationalism, would seem forced to include ICS as well). The 'PTC' approach to connectionism advocated in *OPTC* uses connectionism to *refine* symbolic theory, rather than to eliminate or implement it. The rhetorical position adopted in *OPTC* apparently obscured for many readers the degree to which the PTC view necessitates a serious endorsement of symbolic theory (see my replies to peer commentary in Smolensky, 1988). In hopes of remedying this, I have given the PTC approach, as it has now been considerably further developed, a new name in which 'connectionist' and 'symbolic' have parity: Integrated Connectionist/Symbolic architecture, ICS.

It is a *fundamental mistake* to view PTC or ICS as constituting 'the connectionist competitor' to Classical theory. It is easy to see this debate as classicists *v.* connectionists, with Smolensky holding the flag for Team Connectionist; such interpretations are invited by phrases like 'As for Smolensky's "tensor product" defense of connectionism' (Fodor, 1991, p. 279). The truth is entirely different, and not as brutally simple-minded. PTC, and even more explicitly ICS, is committed to using connectionist concepts and techniques to explain and enrich symbolic theory. The subtleties and difficulties of ICS are not those which arise from denying all that is Classical – on the contrary, they are rather those which arise from trying to formally and precisely understand how Classical and connectionist ideas can *both* be correct, how they can effectively co-exist in a coherent and powerful theory. Much of the anti-connectionist argumentation in F&P and F&M are directed against *eliminativist* connectionism, and on many issues ICS and Classical theory take the same anti-eliminativist position. This point is especially important to appreciate in understanding the work discussed in section 3.3: research on connectionism and generative grammar which is collaborative work with Alan Prince, also noted for a highly influential critique (Pinker and Prince, 1988) commonly viewed as blanketly anti-connectionist. The cognitive architecture landscape is, fortunately, much richer than that presupposed by those viewing this debate as a classicist *v.* connectionist duel. For the comfort of such Boolean combat rituals, Monday night football rather than cognitive architecture is probably the sport of choice.

7   For further discussion, see Dennett (1991).

8   The list of fundamental elements of symbolic computation which have been alleged to be beyond the scope of connectionist computation is impressive: the type-token distinction, variables, variable binding, embedding, recursion, non-finite-state computation, etc.

9   Like most such broad distinctions, this one is not unproblematic. For our purposes, however, a coarse-grained distinction suffices.

10 In complex processing, there is a natural conflict between the distributed and the parallel properties. Existing PDP models which perform aspects of symbolic computation (e.g. Pollack, 1990; Touretzky, 1990) do so serially: since each unit is representing multiple constituents, these networks first pull out a single constituent and then perform some relatively complex 'symbolic' operation on it. These models give up on parallelism but retain distribution. The reverse is true of local connectionist networks (e.g. Feldman, 1989 and references; Touretzky and Wheeler, 1991), which often directly map, say, a symbolic tree structure onto a local connectionist network with matching tree *connection* structure; the physically separated constituents are then processed in parallel. Some 'connectionist' models have *neither* distribution *nor* parallelism (e.g Minsky's finite state machine simulator cited in the text).

11 The definition F&M give, 'A vector is, of course, a magnitude with a certain direction' (chatper 5, p. 204), is appropriate for vectors in physics or geometry. What is called for in connectionism is often a somewhat different conception of 'vector'; the most mundane, and usually perfectly adequate, conception is a simple list of numbers. Such a list *can* be visualized as a point in a large-dimensional space, with each number in the list being a coordinate of the point along one of the many coordinate axes in the space. An arrow extending from the coordinate origin in the space to this point is also a common conception for the vector – and such an arrow *can* sometimes be thought about in terms of a 'length' (or 'magnitude') and a 'direction', when a suitable notion of 'length' can be imposed on this space. (The technical concept of 'vector space' does not require a notion of 'length'.) For the purposes of this chapter, however, it will usually be best to think of the vectors under discussion as simple lists of activity values.

12 The traditional LISP notation for this tree would be (L . (S . K))

13 As discussed in section 1.2.1, the level of abstraction at which these symbols are 'realized' is closer to, but not equal to, the neural level.

14 Whether this association should be regarded as equally arbitrary is not clear until progress on the semantics of ICS is made; see section 4.3.2. For now, the association can be taken to be arbitrary.

15 Clearly, there is nothing in the *proposition p* – as opposed to its English rendition *Sandy loves Kim* – which determines that Sandy is in any sense *left-of* Kim.

16 I have ignored a minor complication needed to make this account formally correct. As the example of **p** shows, a symbol at depth one in the tree (L) will appear in a second-order tensor product, while a symbol at depth two (S) will appear in a third-order product. These vectors have different numbers of elements, and cannot be added according to the definition of + given in the text. This difficulty is immediately resolved: a representation of a tree is a vector comprised of sub-vectors, each listed one after the other: the first represents symbols at depth 0; the next, symbols at depth one; the next, symbols at depth two ... Each sub-vector has more elements than the one before. Constituent superposition is done separately in each sub-vector. Formally, the superposition operation required is the 'direct sum' ⊕ rather than the simple sum +. A representational scheme can be devised which does not separate the representations of different levels in the tree, but it is less simply defined; see Smolensky et al. (1992).

17 The units in connectionist networks supporting tensor product representations generally need to take on continuous, unbounded activation values in order to accommodate the results of the arithmetic operations which define these representations. (These units should not have activation values limited to the range 0 to 1, contrary F&M, chapter 3 p. 210.)

18 F&M raise this objection (pp. 212–13). The issue of uniqueness of semantic interpretation, under the label of 'faithfulness of representation', was a fundamental concern in the technical papers in which tensor product representations were defined and analyzed (the technical report, Smolensky, 1987b, and its published version, Smolensky, 1990). In this chapter I have gone into considerably more technical detail than in my earlier 'non-technical' papers because the effectiveness of those papers was diminished by my (in retrospect naive) assumption that someone seriously critiquing the proposal would look at the original technical papers actually containing the proposal. These original papers are not cited by F&M, and their characterization of my response to this objection reveals no impact of the analysis of these original papers. The demonstration of the uniqueness of *semantic* decomposition given in the present chapter is equivalent to ones provided in the original proposals of tensor product representations (e.g. s. 2.2.2 and theorem 3.1.1 of Smolensky 1987b, published as s. 2.2.2 and theorem 3.1 of Smolensky, 1990). F&M (chapter 5, p. 213) mischaracterize my response to the semantic uniqueness issue by citing an argument (about 'normal modes') from *CCLOT* (chapter 4, p.

189) which addressed a different but related question: how can the notion of 'vector constituent' appealed to in ICS, given the non-uniquess of vector decomposition, play any role in the *explanation of processing*? This is the subject of section 2.2.2 of the present chapter.

19 It might be wondered whether the 'bad' case of dependent vectors r_0 and r_1 is more or less 'special' than the 'good' case of independent vectors. If the vector space is one-dimensional (a single connectionist unit – 'vectors' degenerate to a single number) then of course independence is *impossible*; if the vector space is more than one-dimensional, then a set of *dependent* vectors is very 'special' or degenerate: it has measure 0. So if the two vectors were picked at random, say, among those vectors of length 1, then the probability that the two chosen vectors would be dependent would be 0. The 'bad' case is clearly the degenerate one.

20 See F&M (chapter 5, p. 214).

21 A very close physical analog of the tensor product representational notion of constituency is found in quantum physics, as explained in *CCLOT* (chapter 4, note 13). A less complete analog from classical physics is also presented in *CCLOT* (chapter 4, p. 189). 'The physics lesson is greatly appreciated; but it is important to be clear on just what it is supposed to show' (F&M, chapter 5, p. 214). Gratitude is always welcome, but in this case I'm afraid I'm not entitled to it, since F&M don't seem all that 'clear on just what it is supposed to show'. To wit, 'far from being an unnatural way to break up the part of a connectionist state vector that represents an input, decomposing the vector into components is exactly what we'd expect to need to do to explain the processing of that input ... in order to *understand and explain* the regularities in the network's behavior we will need to break the vector for the structure into the vectors for the constituents, and relate the processing of the whole to the processing of the parts' (*CCLOT*, chapter 4, pp. 189–90, emphasis original). F&M's 'reply' to the 'physics lesson' shows the lesson to have been a total loss; this 'reply' is the opening quote of note 26 in this chapter. Superposition in distributed representations, starting with a tutorial introduction to vectorial representations, was the subject of Smolensky (1986b), briefly discussed in *OPTC* (chapter 2, section 9.3); see also Smolensky (1989, s. 3.3) and van Gelder (1990).

22 If x and y are the vectors representing trees x and y, then the vector representing [x, y] is:

$$W^{cons}_0 \cdot x + W^{cons}_1 \cdot y$$

This equation is equivalent to (38); the matrices W^{cons}_0 and W^{cons}_1 are defined so that taking their *matrix* product with a vector achieves the same result as taking the *tensor* product with r_0 and r_1, respectively.

23 The function call cons (p, q) creates the pair [p, q] from arbitrary trees p and q; written (cons p q) in LISP. The function call ex_0 (s) extracts the left sub-tree of a tree s; written (car s) in LISP. ex_1(s) extracts the right sub-tree of s; written (cdr s) in LISP.

24   R is given by the simple formula:

$$R = 1 + I + I \otimes I + I \otimes I \otimes I + \cdots$$

where I is the identity matrix in the vector space containing the role vectors r_0 and r_1: the matrix which all elements are 0 except those on the diagonal, which are 1.

25   The symbolic expression (44a) for f can be interpreted as describing an algorithm for how a designer constructs the *network* (the weight matrix W: (44b)) for computing f – not an algorithm for how the network constructs the *output* $o = f(i)$ from the input i.

26   '[T]he constituents of complex activity vectors typically aren't "there", so if the causal consequences of tokening a complex vector are sensitive to its constituent structure, that's a miracle' (F&M chapter 5, p. 215). We have seen that indeed, the causal consequences of tokening such representations *are* sensitive to constituent structure: but (a) the constituent vectors *are* 'there' in the relevant sense, and (b) the causal consequences are not mediated by Classical algorithms operating over the constituents. The sense (a) in which the constituent vectors are 'there' is just that the activity vector contains them, in a superposition, and the weights that process the activity vector have a corresponding structure which responds to the constituents in a structure-sensitive way. Is it so incomprehensible that Simon's and Garfunkel's voices each have causal consequences, despite the fact that neither are '*there*' when you *naively* look at the pressure wave realizing *The Sounds of Silence?*

27   In some networks, activation values cannot be negative, but this should not obscure the point here. Instead of choosing $a'_\beta = -a_\beta$, let a'_β be *any* value less than a_β; then it will still follow that $H(a') > H(a)$. The lower the activation value of unit β, the more well formed the pattern. So the most harmonic pattern will be the one with the lowest activation value for β that is allowed in the particular network (this lower limit varies from network to network).

28   This way of presenting an input to a network, 'clamping', is not the only way, but it is the one overwhelmingly used, at least in cognitive modeling.

29   The generality of this result has emerged through the work of many people; for references, see Smolensky et al. (1992, p. 14).

30   (47) gives the core of the Harmony function needed in (49) for a large variety of networks; additional terms get added which are idiosyncratic to the particular activation function used by the units to compute their activation. Generally, (47) is the part of the Harmony function that depends on the weights – the knowledge – in the network; the additional terms usually do not. Furthermore, the simple case of a linear associator (29 = 40; the explanation in section 2.2.2.3) falls under the theorem (49); the additional term one needs to add to (47) in that case is just $- o^2/2$.

31   Harmony maximization is presumably just one of a whole family of principles waiting to be developed which allow higher-level analysis of

various types of networks. Harmony maximization represents one kind of analysis for dynamical systems like connectionist networks; dynamical systems theory has a number of more exotic analyses worthy of study.

32 A few remarks should be added. First, in these soft rules, the two constituents referred to as c_i, c_j can be the same, i.e. a rule can refer to only one constituent, as in the rule (58) below. Secondly, in tensor product representation, a 'constituent' is a structure bound to some particular structural role; so it is perfectly legitimate to refer to roles such as 'left sub-constituent', as in (55a). Finally, soft rules like (55) corresponding to re-write rules like (54) must be *embedding invariant*: the Harmony of an S, NP pair must not depend on the level of its embedding in the tree. (This is an important part of the recursiveness of the notion of well-formedness in formal languages.) Thanks to (53d), relating the Harmony of constituent pairs to the underlying weight matrix W, it can be proved that the condition $Alg_{ics}(HC, W)$ on W (46) *entails* embedding invariance (see Smolensky et al. 1992, s. 3.1.3).

33 The bottom-up form of the logic here, then, is: W determines the set of $H(c_i, c_j)$'s by (53d); these pair-wise Harmony values determine the soft rules R_{ij} by (53b); and these in turn determine which parse of an input has maximum Harmony and is therefore the correct parse, by (56).

34 All inputs, even ungrammatical ones, are assigned a parse (structural description) by the grammar; this is a familiar notion in generative grammar.

35 This discussion shows how completely irrelevant to ICS is one of the main arguments of F&P: 'since the semantics of connectionist nets reside in the complex structure of labels assigned to units, there is no explanation of systematicity.' This argument is in fact only relevant to certain local connectionist models in which entire propositions are represented by single units. Its irrelevance to PDP models generally was a main point of Smolensky (1987a), and the 'coffee story' developed therein and in Smolensky (chapter 4).

36 F&P and F&M are not exactly clear on what is premise and what conclusion in the Classical account. Consider, for example F&M (pp. 202–3; emphasis and subscripts added):

> These *assumptions₁* about the syntax and semantics of mental representations are summarized by condition (C) ... The Classical explanation of systematicity *assumes₂* that (C) holds by nomological necessity ... *It should be fairly clear₃* why systematicity is readily explicable on the *assumptions₄*, first, that mental representations satisfy (C), and secondly, that mental processes have access to the constituent structure of mental representations ... So, then, *assuming₅* that the processes that integrate the mental representations that express propositions have access to their constituents, *it follows that₆* anyone who can represent John's loving the girl can also represent the girl's loving John ... [a]nd *suppose₇* that the mental processes that mediate the drawing of inferences have access to the constituent structure of mental representations. Then *it should be no surprise₈* that anyone who can infer P from P&Q&R can likewise infer P from P&Q ... To summarize: the

> Classical solution to systematicity problem *entails₉* that (a) systems of mental representation satisfy (C) . . . and (b) mental processes are sensitive to the constituent structure of mental representations.

The summary conclusion of this passage is that (a) and (b) are *entailed₉* – but exactly these statements were introduced earlier in the passage as *assumption₁*, *assumption₂*, *assumption₄*, *assumptions₅* and *supposition₇*. The conclusion of systematicity introduced by '*follows that₆*' does not, in fact, follow from the preceding assumptions, as stated, whatever their number. What follows is that all the syntactic pieces which would be required to construct The girl loves John *must be present in the representation of* John's loving the girl; it does *not* follow that these pieces can necessarily be so reassembled. This conclusion *would* hold if condition(C) were phrased, as it often is, so that the representations were assumed to form a symbol system – in which case, to repeat the text, systematicity is a bald *assumption*, not something which *follows₆* from anything. Perhaps this explains the earlier hedged claim, that '*it should be fairly clear₃*' why systematicity holds. The even more dramatic hedge '*it should be no surprise₈*' which introduces the alleged conclusion of inferential coherence is compelled by the even more clear failure of all the stated assumptions to actually *entail* the alleged conclusion. For such inferential coherence to be an actual entailment obviously requires much less vague and casual *suppositions₇* about inferential processes than merely that they 'have access to the constituent structure of mental representation'. I certainly 'have access' to all the material in my dozens of computer manuals, and, for that matter, all the material in the Library of Congress. Would that it followed that I *can* do all that *could* be done with such information.

37 The real opportunities afforded by ICS for cognitive science are the incorporation of new conceptual and technical tools from continuous/ numerical mathematics, to complement the Classical set of almost exclusively discrete/symbolic mathematics. With representation and processing, as discussed in this chapter, this takes the form of exploiting vector and tensor calculus. For inference, the opportunity is to explore ways of integrating *symbolic* inference at the higher level with *probabilistic* inference at the lower level. Principles of probabilistic and statistical inference are fundamental to PDP connectionism; indeed, one place where they figure prominently is Harmony Theory (Smolensky, 1986a), the probabilistic aspects of which have yet to be incorporated in ICS. Just as discrete/symbolic representations may be embedded within continuous/ numerical/vectorial representations, so principles of symbolic inference should embed within principles of probabilistic inference: in many respects, the latter are just a special case of the former, when all probabilities are 0 or 1. It is clear that much work is waiting to be done, and I prefer to leave ICS open to accommodate such future developments.

38 A possible answer to this last question can be developed following a suggestion of David Rumelhart (personal communication). Suppose the PDP algorithm computes only local Harmony maxima (see section 2.3.3).

Suppose it is important for communication that language processing computes global harmony maxima fairly reliably, so different speakers are not constantly computing idiosyncratic parses which are various local Harmony maxima. Then this puts a (meta-)constraint on the Harmony function: it must be such that local maximization algorithms give global maxima with reasonably high probability. Strict domination of grammatical constraints appears to satisfy this (meta-)constraint. For a bit more discussion, see Smolensky et al. (1992, s. 3.3).

39   The distinction between the two notions I have dubbed 'weak' and 'strong' compositional structure in Connectionist vectorial representations (*CCLOT*, chapter 4) is relevant here. ICS as defined in this chapter appeals to the 'strong' notion: realization of symbolic representations via tensor products. The 'weak' notion has not yet been formalized, and is much more intuitively defined (see *CCLOT*, chapter 4, section 2.2). Developing the Connectionist semantics imagined in the text might well involve formalizing this 'weak' notion, but there are many problems to face in doing so (including perhaps the challenge of 'micro-features'). I agree with F&M's assessment that the notion must be regarded as problematic, at least until these problems are resolved, as a number of other comparable problems have been solved in the development of ICS. However, F&M are incorrect to say that 'It is claim (4) that distinguishes the strong from the weak notion of compositional structure: a representation has weak compositional structure if it contains context-dependent constituents' (chapter 5, pp. 204–5). The question of context dependence is really beside the point; what makes the compositional structure of tensor product representations *strong* is that the constituents are *strongly bound to specific structural roles*, through tensor products with role vectors. The sense in which these representations have *structure* is therefore much stronger than in the 'weak' case, where the constituents are simply simultaneously present, without being placed in articulated structural roles. There is a precise sense in which the 'weak' case only allows the realization of *sets*, while the 'strong' case allows the realization of recursive tree structures and, in fact, a tremendous variety of structures.

F&M's remark that 'Smolensky's views about "weak" compositional structure are largely inexplicit and must be extrapoated from his "coffee story"' (chapter 5, p. 203) is also rather dubious, given that *CCLOT* (chapter 4) contains an entire section (2.2.2) entitled 'Morals of the Coffee Story', which enumerates four quite *explicit* conclusions to be drawn from the 'weak' notion. The opening sentence of this section makes the crucial point, which F&M ignore: 'The first moral I want to draw out of this *coffee* story is this: unlike the ultra-local case . . . with distributed representations, complex representations *are* composed of representations of constituents' (chapter 4, p. 174, emphasis in original). The crucial point made by the 'weak' notion as illustrated by the 'coffee story' is that the entire PDP approach to cognitive architecture depends on the use of distributed representations, and to that entire approach, most of the F&P critique is simply *irrelevant* – because all of F&P is built on the premise that the connectionist representation of the proposition *A&B* is a unit labelled A&B. Section 2.2.2 of *CCLOT* proceeds directly from the first sentence quoted above to demonstrate the fallacy of F&P's argument that distributed representation is irrelevant. And while F&M pretend to miss the point of the 'weak' notion of connectionist compositional structure, the crucial premise of F&P, which the 'weak' notion renders irrelevant, makes not even a fleeting appearance in F&M.

F&P contains two distinct contributions. The first is a challenge to connectionism, one which I have found must instructive and constructive. The second is a purported demonstration of the impossibility of connectionism meeting this challenge. This demonstration, I have consistently argued, is relevant to local connectionist modeling but quite irrelevant to PDP models. Again, we see the importance of this distinction between these two conceptions of the connectionist architecture, a distinction emphasized in section 2.1.1 of this chapter.

References

Dennett, D.C. (1991) Granny's Campaign for safe science. In B. Loewer and G. Rey, (eds), *Meaning in Mind: Fodor and his Critics*, pp. 87–94. Cambridge, Mass., Basil Blackwell.

Feldman, J.A. (1989) Neural representation of conceptual knowledge. In L. Nadel, L.A. Cooper, P. Culicover and R.M. Harnish (eds), *Neural Connections, Mental Computation*, pp. 68–103. Cambridge, Mass., MIT Press/Bradford Books.

Fodor, J.A. (1991) Replies. In B. Loewer and G. Rey (eds), *Meaning in Mind: Fodor and his Critics*, pp. 255–319. Oxford: Blackwell.

Gelder, T. van (1990) Compositionality: a connectionist variation on a classical theme. *Cognitive Science* 14, 355–84.

Haugeland, J. (1991) Representational genera. In W. Ramsey, S. Stich and D. Rumelhart (eds), *Philosophy and Connectionist Theory*, pp. 61–90. Hillsdale, NJ, Erlbaum.

Legendre, G., Raymond, W. and Smolensky, P. (1993) An Optimality-Theoretic typology of case and grammatical voice systems. *Proceedings of the Nineteenth Annual Meeting of the Berkeley Linguistics Society*. Berkeley, Calif., February, pp. 464–78.

McCulloch, W. and Pitts, W. (1943) A logical calculus of the ideas immanent in nervous activity. *Bulletin of Mathematical Biophysics* 5, 115–33.

Minsky, M. (1967) *Computation: Finite and Infinite Machines*. Englewood Cliffs, NJ, Prentice Hall.

Pinker, S. and Prince, A. (1988) On language and connectionism: analysis of a parallel distributed processing model of language acquisition. *Cognition* 28, 73–193. Reprinted in S. Pinker and J. Mehler (eds), *Connections and Symbols*. Cambridge, Mass., MIT Press, 1988.

Pollack, J. (1987) On connectionist models of natural language processing. Unpublished PhD dissertation, Department of Computer Science, University of Illinois, Urbana, Illinois.

Pollack, J. (1990) Recursive distributed representations. *Artificial Intelligence* 46, 77–106. Reprinted in G. Hinton (ed.), *Connectionist Symbol Processing,* Cambridge, Mass., MIT Press/Bradford Books, 1991.

Prince, A. and Smolensky, P. (1993) Optimality Theory: constraint interaction in generative grammar. Technical Report CU-CS-696–93, Department of Computer Science, University of Colorado at Boulder, and Technical Report TR-2, Rutgers Center for Cognitive Science, Rutgers University, New Brunswick, NJ. April. To appear in the Linguistic Inquiry Monograph Series; Cambridge, Mass., MIT Press.

Smolensky, P. (1986a) Information processing in dynamical systems: foundations of Harmony Theory. In D.E. Rumelhart, J.L. McClelland and the PDP Research Group (eds), *Parallel Distributed Processing: Explorations in the Microstructure of Cognition.* Vol. 1: *Foundations,* pp. 194–281. Cambridge, Mass., MIT Press/Bradford Books.

Smolensky, P. (1986b) Neural and conceptual interpretations of parallel distributed processing models. In J.L. McClelland, D.E. Rumelhart and the PDP Research Group (eds), *Parallel Distributed Processing: Explorations in the Microstructure of Cognition.* Vol. 2: *Psychological and Biological Models,* pp. 390–431. Cambridge, Mass., MIT Press/Bradford Books.

Smolensky, P. (1987a) The constituent structure of connectionist mental states: a reply to Fodor and Pylyshyn. *Southern Journal of Philosophy,* 26 (suppl.), 37–63. Reprinted in T. Horgan and J. Tienson (eds), *Connectionism and the Philosophy of Mind,* pp. 281–308. Dordrecht: Kluwer, 1991.

Smolensky, P. (1987b) On variable binding and the representation of symbolic structures in connectionist systems. Technical Report CU-CS-355-87, Department of Computer Science, University of Colorado at Boulder, February.

Smolensky, P. (1988) Putting together connectionism – again. *Behavioral and Brain Sciences* 11, 59–74.

Smolensky, P. (1989) Connectionist modeling: neural computation/mental connections. In L. Nadel, L.A. Cooper, P. Culicover, and R.M. Harnish (eds), *Neural Connections, Mental Computation,* pp. 49–67. Cambridge, Mass., MIT Press/Bradford Books.

Smolensky, P. (1990) Tensor product variable binding and the representation of symbolic structures in connectionist systems. *Artificial Intelligence* 46, 159–216. Reprinted in G. Hinton (ed.), *Connectionist Symbol Processing.* Cambridge, Mass., MIT Press/Bradford Books, 1991.

Smolensky, P., Legendre, G. and Miyata, Y. (1992) Principles for an integrated connectionist/symbolic theory of higher cognition. Technical Report CU-CS-600–92, Department of Computer Science, University of Colorado at Boulder.

Smolensky, P., Mozer, M.C. and Rumelhart, D.E. (eds) (forthcoming) *Mathematical Perspectives on Neural Networks.* Hillsdale, NJ, Erlbaum.

290 PAUL SMOLENSKY

Touretzky, D. (1990) BoltzCONS: dynamic symbol structures in a connectionist network. *Artificial Intelligence* 46, 5–46. Reprinted in G. Hinton (ed.), *Connectionist Symbol Processing.* Cambridge, Mass., MIT Press/Bradford Books, 1991.
Touretzky, D. and Wheeler, D. (1991) Sequence manipulation using parallel mapping networks. *Neural Computation* 3, 98–109.

PART II
Subdoxastic Explanation II: Connectionism and Eliminativism

7

Introduction:
Connectionism and Eliminativism

Cynthia Macdonald

What kinds of descriptions will an adequate scientific psychology employ in its explanations? Will that science find room for intentional descriptions: descriptions of states with propositional content? Or will it ultimately reduce explanations employing such descriptions to others, or eliminate them altogether? And what other descriptions might that science employ? Will they be ones at the level of cognitive processing, which employ classical or connectionist architectures? Or will they be descriptions of the neurophysiological structures and connections in the brain that underlie cognition?

Since the work of David Marr, it has become customary for cognitive scientists to assume that a scientific psychology will employ descriptions of human cognition at many levels of explanation, and that these levels do not compete with, but rather supplement, one another. Marr's (1982) seminal work, *Vision*, is a classic example of a theory of visual perception that makes use of three distinct levels of description in its explanation of visual perception. The first, computational level, describes the function that the visual system computes (in human cognition, this level is often referred to as the semantic, or intentional, level). The second, algorithmic, level describes the means by which the function is computed. At this level, the function that the system carries out is further analysed into sub-functions whose execution enables the system to carry out that function. The third, implementation, level describes how the function is physically realized. On Marr's theory, an adequate account of visual perception describes *what* function is carried out by the visual system, *how* it is carried out, and the physical *means by which* it is carried out.

A computer can be described at each of these three levels. At the level of implementation, the computer's hardware is described. At the algorithmic level, facts about the way in which the system stores and processes data are described. This level of description abstracts from the physical details of the hardware. At the computational level, the descriptions are more abstract still. Here the functions computed at the algorithmic level are described in mathematically transparent terms which abstract from the ways in which the computer carries those functions out.

Human cognition can be described in similar terms. Language acquisition and production, for example, can be described at these three levels of analysis. At the level of implementation, the neurological system is described, whereas at the algorithmic level, the cognitive processes involved in language use and acquisition are described. At the computational level, the structural properties of language as a symbol system are described.

Marr's conception of the general form that a theory of cognition should take is widely accepted by cognitive scientists and cognitive psychologists. In particular, it is accepted by those whose views on cognitive architecture differ widely, such as Jerry Fodor, on the one hand, and Paul Smolensky and Andy Clark, on the other. These theorists disagree about which type of model, classical or connectionist, best models cognitive processes such as those involved in visual perception, language acquisition and production, and memory, at the algorithmic level. But theirs is a 'within-level' disagreement, since they all agree that an adequate overall psychology will make use of semantic or intentional, algorithmic and neurological descriptions. The semantic descriptions are typically taken by these theorists to be descriptions within common-sense or 'folk' psychology.

The debate between Fodor and Pylyshyn, Fodor and McLaughlin, and Smolensky in Part I of this volume concerned potential conflict at the algorithmic level between classical and connectionist models of cognitive processing. The debate in this Part, although it too involves connectionist and classical architectures, concerns a conflict of a different kind. Here the disagreement is a 'between-level' one. All of the theorists involved in the present debate agree that explanations at the algorithmic level describe a distinct level of cognition. Their disagreement concerns whether the explanations at the level of common-sense psychology are compatible with those at the level of cognitive processing. The question raised by William Ramsey, Stephen Stich and Joseph Garon (hereafter RS&G) in chapter 8 is whether the features possessed by intentional mental states, such as beliefs and desires, posited at the semantic, common-sense or folk psychological level conflict with those possessed by the states posited at the level of Connectionist theory. RS&G argue that the features of common-sense beliefs do conflict with the features of the states posited by a certain class of connectionist models of propositional memory, or belief, so that if these models are correct, then common-sense psychology is false. Further, they argue that if common-sense psychology is false, then eliminativism – the view that intentional states such as beliefs, desires etc. do not exist – follows.

Both Clark and Smolensky dispute the first part of RS&G's argument, although for different reasons. Clark (chapter 9) argues that common-sense psychology and Connectionist theory are not in conflict with one another. In his view, RS&G are mistaken about the nature of connectionist models, which can be seen to describe states that have the same features as those possessed by posits of common-sense psychology. Smolensky, too, believes that RS&G are mistaken about the nature of connectionist models. However, unlike Clark, Smolensky (chapter 10) freely admits that none of the states posited by Connectionist theory has all of the features possessed by the posits of common-sense psychology. Smolensky does not think that this shows that, if connectionist models of belief are right, then common-sense psychology is wrong. This is perhaps because, for him, the proper understanding of connectionism construes Connectionist theory as a refinement of the Classical view, which does posit states that have all of the features possessed by the posits of common-sense psychology. On this way of thinking, Connectionist theory does not show common-sense psychology to be *seriously* wrong. So whereas Clark and Smolensky both think that connectionist models of memory/belief do not show common-sense psychology to be seriously wrong, they think this for different reasons. Clark thinks that the posits of Connectionist theory do have the same features as those possessed by the posits of common-sense psychology; Smolensky does not.

RS&G go on to argue that, if common-sense psychology is seriously wrong, eliminativism follows. Here again, Clark's and Smolensky's responses are different. Clark believes if common-sense psychology were to be shown by Connectionist theory to be seriously wrong, then common-sense psychology would be threatened with eliminativism. Smolensky, however, thinks otherwise. Since Connectionist beliefs have most but not all of the features possessed by the beliefs of common-sense psychology, Connectionist theory does show common-sense psychology to be wrong. But just as of a false theory does not thereby entail eliminativism for the posits of that theory, Connectionist theory, being a refinement of the classical view, does not entail eliminativism with regard to the posits of common-sense psychology.

In their final reply (Chapter 11), Stephen Stich and Ted Warfield agree with Smolensky that eliminativism does not follow from the claim that common-sense psychology is serious wrong. However, for them, this is because the move from the claim that common-sense psychology is false to the conclusion that there are no beliefs, desires and the like, requires additional premises, and they consider the two most likely candidates to be highly problematic. So, although they agree with Smolensky that Connectionist theory does not entail eliminativism, they do so for different reasons.

The arguments of RS&G, and the replies of Clark, Smolensky, and Stich and Warfield, raise a number of interesting and important issues. One is what the nature of the conflict is between Connectionist theory and common-sense psychology. Is the conflict real or merely apparent? Does it only arise as a result of a misunderstanding of how connectionist models work, as Clark thinks? Or does it arise, as RS&G, and Stich and Warfield believe, because the features of Connectionist beliefs really do conflict with those of the beliefs of common-sense psychology? If so, how radical a conflict is it?

This last question raises another issue that is central to the debate, viz. the issue of how radical a theory conflict must be to justify the eliminativist conclusion. Is it enough that Connectionist beliefs do not share *all* of the features the beliefs of common-sense psychology? Or are some of these features more important than others to the question of elimination? If Connectionist beliefs were to lack all of the features possessed by the beliefs of common-sense psychology, would the elimination of common-sense psychology be justified? And if not, why not?

The questions raised above can be grouped into two categories: the first concerns the relation between connectionist models of belief and common-sense psychology, and their respective posits and associated features; and the second concerns the ramifications of a conflict between connectionist models of belief and common-sense psychology for the issue of eliminativism. We briefly discuss these in turn.

Common-sense Psychology and Connectionist Models of Belief: Do they Conflict?

RS&G argue that it is central to a certain class connectionist models of belief that the units on which algorithms are defined lack three features possessed by the beliefs of common-sense psychology. These features are:

1 Semantic interpretability.

2   Functional discreteness.
3   Causal efficacy.

First, beliefs, desires and the like have propositional content, content that is semantic in being representational and truth-evaluable. Further, common-sense psychology treats the predicates expressing propositional content, such as 'believes that cats have paws', as projectable – as capable of figuring in causal laws – and the properties expressed by these predicates as natural psychological kinds.

Secondly, beliefs and the like are functionally discrete. It is not exactly clear what RS&G mean by this, but their illustration is that it makes sense to say that an individual has acquired or lost a single belief independently of all other intentional states. This is taken to require that each belief be encoded in a system by a sub-structure that is distinct from the sub-structures encoding other beliefs, so that the addition or removal of a single sub-structure does not disturb others in the system.[1]

Thirdly, beliefs and the like are causes of behaviour. Further, it makes sense to say, of a pair of beliefs that an agent has, that one rather than the other caused the agent to act. So beliefs are causally discrete states.

These three features are given the name 'propositional modularity'. RS&G argue that certain connectionist networks lack the final two of these three features. The networks in question are ones in which representations are widely rather than locally distributed. Such networks may be capable of semantic interpretation. It is true that individual units in these networks are not semantically interpretable; information is distributed throughout the network rather than being encoded in individual nodes or units. However, as RS&G point out, 'it is often plausible to view such networks as collectively or holistically encoding a set of propositions' (chapter 8, p. 322). The activity patterns, or activity vectors, of which Clark and Smolensky speak, for example, may be semantically interpretable. What is significant for RS&G's argument is that, in such networks, there is no comfortable semantic interpretation of the individual weights and units of the network; and so it is not possible to localize a particular propositional representation in the weights and units of the network. This bears directly on the second feature of propositional modularity, that of functional discreteness. Consider two widely distributed networks, A and B, the first of which encodes 16 propositions and the second of which encodes those 16 plus one further proposition (figures 8.5 and 8.8 in chapter 8). How are we to make sense of the claim that network B has acquired a new belief? Since information is distributed throughout the network, although A and B may differ greatly, there is no functionally distinct sub-structure in B that can be identified with the representation of that new proposition: no sub-structure whose addition to or removal from the network does not disturb others in the network. In a network such as this, there are no functionally discrete, semantically interpretable states; and so, from the point of view of Connectionist theory, there are no commonalities describable in the language of that theory that are projectable. Thus, whereas the predicates of common-sense psychology are projectable and the content properties expressed by them are treated as genuine kinds, Connectionist predicates are not projectable and Connectionist beliefs do not form a single kind. Common-sense psychology treats the belief that cats have paws as a natural kind; Connectionist theory treats the class of models of a being who believes that cats have paws as a 'chaotically disjunctive set'. This point will be important to the discussion of Smolensky's reply. Finally, these networks lack the third feature. Given that the same units or nodes are capable of participating in many different activity patterns, and given that information encoded in the network is distributed across many units, no single unit, or any aggregate of them, is capable of a single, fixed semantic interpretation. As a result, 'it simply makes no sense to ask whether or not the representation of a particular proposition plays a causal role in the network's computation, (chapter 8, p. 327).

RS&G argue that because the models they describe are intended to be interpreted as models of *cognition* rather than as models of neural implementation, Connectionist beliefs are incompatible with the beliefs of common-sense psychology. They further claim that since the beliefs of common-sense psychology cannot be identified with Connectionist beliefs, one or the other of Connectionist theory or common-sense psychology must be rejected if the other is true. In their view, it is not possible to retain both, since Connectionist theory construes beliefs as radically different from the beliefs of common-sense psychology. It is true that not all cases of theory conflict are ones that justify the eliminativist conclusion. In certain cases, say, in the case of the conflict between the Ptolemaic and Copernican theories of the planets, despite the conflict, the falsity of one theory is not taken to justify the claim that the entities posited by that theory do not exist. In these cases, we are prepared to say that the false theory is false, not because there are no ϕs, but because the ϕs do not have the properties the theory attributes to them. The difference between these two types of theory change, according to RS&G, is that between 'ontologically conservative' and 'ontologically radical' theory change. The eliminativist conclusion is justified in cases of ontologically radical theory change, and the change from common-sense psychology to Connectionist theory is this kind of theory change.

In sum, RS&G argue that Connectionist beliefs lack two of the three features of propositional modularity possessed by the beliefs of common-sense psychology. This, they argue, makes the difference between common-sense psychology and Connectionist theory a case of radical theory change. They further argue that, since the elimination of common-sense psychology is justified in cases of radical theory change, if connectionism is true, then eliminativism with regard to the posits of common-sense psychology follows.

However, both Smolensky and Clark deny that there is a radical shift between common-sense and Connectionist conceptions of belief. Clark denies this because he thinks RS&G neglect a level of description of connectionist models, viz. one at which their activity patterns are semantically clustered, which shows Connectionist beliefs to possess all three features of propositional modularity. At this level of description, not only are Connectionist beliefs semantically interpretable, but they have the same cluster profiles, which shows Connectionist beliefs to be natural kinds.[2]

Smolensky too thinks that RS&G neglect a level of description of certain connectionist models, viz. one which describes patterns of activity, or activity vectors. At this level, certain connectionist systems can be semantically interpreted and their states are functionally discrete (although not causally efficacious), and Smolensky argues that it is both justifiable and necessary to ascribe to these systems beliefs. Smolensky's system, which he calls $RSGnet_0$, is one which takes propositions as input and 'judges' them to be true or false.[3] $RSGnet_0$ has a number of input units with a degree of activation, $a_1, a_2, \ldots, a_n$, which encode a given proposition, p, as well as a set of weights, $w_1, w_2, \ldots, w_n$, each of which connects a single input unit to output unit o (figure 10.1), which is interpreted as a judgement, for the input proposition p, that p is true/false. The output o of $RSGnet_0$ is a product of $a_1, a_2, \ldots, a_n$ and $w_1, w_2, \ldots, w_n$, or more simply, a product of the weight vector $\mathbf{w}$ (= $w_1, w_2, \ldots, w_n$) and the activity vector $\mathbf{a}$ (= $a_1, a_2, \ldots, a_n$). It is at the level of vectors that the question of semantic interpretability, hence of a Connectionist notion of belief, arises.

Smolensky defines two rather different notions of belief for the connectionist system he describes: C-beliefs, which are the result of weight analysis on the behaviour of the network, and L-beliefs, which are the result of learning analysis on the behaviour of the network. Intuitively, given a system with fixed weights, that system has a C-belief just in case the activation input is associated with any positive weight. In the case of weight analysis, the weight vector $\mathbf{w}$ is known, and the result of weight analysis is to determine how a network with $\mathbf{w}$ will respond to different activity inputs $\mathbf{a}$ (= $a_1, a_2, \ldots, a_n$). Since $\mathbf{w}$ by definition in

300 CYNTHIA MACDONALD

RSGnet$_0$ is positive, the system will determine a positive output (the judgement, true) when the activity vector **a** (the input vector encoding a given proposition p) is positive, a negative output (the judgement, false) when **a** is negative, and no output at all if **a** is neither positive nor negative.

In geometrical terms, **w** can be viewed as arrows leading from the point of origin of an n-dimensional state space to the point with coordinates $(w_1, w_2, \ldots, w_n)$ (and similarly for **a** and $(a_1, a_2, \ldots, a_n)$) (see figure 10.2a of chapter 10). The arrow, **w**, cuts the state space into two half-spaces by means of a plane which is perpendicular to **w** and which passes through the point of origin. **W**, by definition, lies in the positive half of this state space, and, depending on where each activity vector **a** lies, an output o will be determined (see figure 10.2b). For each proposition p, RSGnet$_0$ has a C-belief that p is true (false) if the encoding input **a** of p lies in the positive (negative) half-space determined by the weight vector **w**.

The second, rather different, notion of belief that Smolensky introduces is that of L-belief. In this situation one wants the system to learn, i.e. to come to believe, a set of propositions. The idea is that one gets the system to do this by getting it to settle on a weight which will be positive for each activity pattern associated with a proposition in the set that one wants it to learn. Training RSGnet$_0$ produces a weight vector **w** that correctly associates each proposition with its correct truth value. Each component of **w** will be a weight vector associated with a particular proposition, say p, in the training set. This weight vector is the encoding of the L-belief that p has a certain truth value (true, in this case). The result of training is to produce, for each proposition p in the training set, the 'belief' that p is true/false. L-beliefs are encoded in weight vectors that determine outputs interpretable as correct judgements as to the truth or falsity of particular propositions in the training set.

In geometrical terms, each activity vector **a**, encoding a proposition p, determines a positive and a negative half-space in the wame way that **w** does: the arrow through the point of origin to the coordinates $(a_1, a_2, \ldots, a_n)$ in an n-dimensional space has a plane perpendicular to it that divides the **a**-space into two half-spaces. The half-space in which **a** lies is the positive half-space, and the other is the negative half-space. For each **a** encoding a proposition p, if **w** lies in the half-space in which arrow **a** does, then the system correctly judges p true. If **w** lies in the negative half-space determined by **a**, the system correctly judges p to be false (see figure 10.2c in chapter 10).

What is the relation between C-beliefs and L-beliefs? Whereas C-beliefs are associated with whole weight space regions, L-beliefs are associated with particular vectors in those weight space regions. As Smolensky says. 'The C-belief that p is false is a large region of weight space p^- in which w must lie for the net to judge p false. The L-belief that p is false is one particular vector $-p^*$ in this large region, (chapter 10, p. 372).

Unlike Clark, Smolensky gives a precise and careful account of the sense in which a certain connectionist model is capable of description in semantic terms, and the sense in which its vectors are functionally discrete. There are, however, questions concerning whether Smolensky's C- and L-beliefs are legitimately so-called. Stich and Warfield do not appear to question their semantic interpretability (although, as chapter 1 of this volume, introducing the classicism/connectionism debate, shows, there are important questions to be asked about this).[4] Nor do Stich and Warfield question Smolensky's claim that C- and L-beliefs are not causally efficacious, and that they therefore lack a fundamental feature that the beliefs of common-sense psychology possess. In fact, because Stich and Warfield accept this claim of Smolensky's, they do not construe his reply as taking issue with their claim that, if connectionist models of belief are correct, common-sense psychology is seriously wrong (although Smolensky himself does).

Stich and Warfield argue that there are problems with both (a) Smolensky's and Clark's claim that Connectionist beliefs are natural kinds, and predicates expressing their propositional contents are projectable; and (b) Clark's claim that Connectionist beliefs are discrete, causally active states.[5] With regard to (a) they argue that the fact that *some* connectionist systems have a level of description (at the patterns of activity, or vector, level) at which commonalities, even semantic ones, emerge, does not establish that connectionist beliefs are natural kinds. Connectionist systems such as NETtalk can be characterized in two ways. One way is to characterize them functionally or behaviourally in terms of their input/output relations. Characterized in this way, a NETTALKER is a system trained to transform text to speech. Another way to characterize them is structurally, in terms of their architecture. Characterized in this way, NETtalk is a NETTALK system with a specific structure. According to Stich and Warfield, what Clark shows at most is that one type of connectionist model (NETTALKER with a specific architecture (i.e. one with NETtalk structure) exhibits the same cluster profile on analysis. This not only does not show that *other* types of connectionist models (ones that are not NETTALKERS) exhibit these commonalities; it does not even show that other NETTALKERS with an architecture or structure that differs from NETtalk (in, say, having more hidden units) will exhibit these commonalities. And what Smolensky shows is that *some* connectionist systems, such as RSGnet$_0$

and RSGnet, exhibit commonalities describable as C- and L-beliefs. By his own admission, this claim may not generalize to other connectionist systems and so these features may not be projectable. So it cannot threaten RS&G's claim that Connectionist beliefs are not natural kinds.

Although Stich and Warfield (chapter 11) are not explicit about this, they take their arguments to show that, since the commonalities that emerge from cluster analysis, learning analysis and weight analysis on connectionist systems with specific structures or architectures are not projectable, Connectionist beliefs are not functionally discrete. Quite apart from their arguments, however, it is unclear why Smolensky claims that his L-beliefs are functionally discrete in $RSGnet_0$ and RSGnet. On the characterization given earlier, in order for a belief to be functionally discrete, it must be encoded in a sub-structure of the system that is distinct from the sub-structures that encode other beliefs in the system. But Smolensky's L-beliefs do not seem to meet this requirement (although it seems likely that his C-beliefs do). It is true that there will be many differences between network A, which processes 16 propositions, and network B, which processes those 16 propositions plus one other, and these differences may be describable at the level of vector analysis. But this does not show that the encoding of a given proposition (say, the 17th one) is independent of the encoding of others. Moreover, Smolensky himself appears to concede this when he says,

> Functional discreteness can be seen via L-beliefs as well, although greater caution is required. For, assuming Nets A and B to have been trained according to (7), their weight vectors w_A and w_B are given by (6) as:
>
> (11)   A $w_A = tr\,(p)p^* + tr(q)q^* + tr(r)r^* + \ldots$
>   B $w_B = tr(p)p^* + tr(q)q^* + tr(r)r^* + \ldots + tr(z)z^*$
>
> where z is the extra (17th) proposition on which Net B is trained. It is important to remember that the * operation depends on the training *set*, so that *in fact* the vector denoted p^* in (11A) *and that denoted* p^* *in (11B) are, in general, somewhat different vectors.* (Chapter 10, p. 375; emphasis added)

Since the weight vector p^* is the 'pure encoding of the belief that p is true', it seems that the sub-structure encoding the belief that z is *not* distinct from the sub-structures encoding other beliefs in the system. If it was, we should expect that the vector which encodes the belief that p to remain constant from A to B despite the encoding in B of the additional 17th proposition, which it does not.

With regard to (b) Stich and Warfield take issue with Clark's claim that Connectionist beliefs are discrete, causally active states. The problem that connectionism faces is how one can make sense of the idea that one rather than another of two beliefs an agent has, both of which are equally apt to cause the same behaviour in a particular case, actually caused that behaviour. Clark's solution is to identify two sorts of beliefs in connectionist models: enduring ones, which he identifies with dispositions to produce activation patterns, and transient ones, which are causally efficacious in producing behaviour. His claim is that the dispositional states produce activation patterns that produce outputs, which are then fed back into the system (by the process of back propagation) so that they can play a role in inferences that lead to behaviour. Stich and Warfield argue that this account cannot explain how even modestly complex patterns of inference produce behaviour. (This is because Clark's models have no short-term memory.)[6] Smolensky's C- and L-beliefs are in a worse position still. Smolensky takes beliefs to be dispositions to produce activity patterns. However, he expressly denies that they are causally efficacious. If he is correct about this, his account is incapable of delivering an answer to the above question.

Smolensky concedes this, although it is not clear why he should (again, see chapter 1). If one accepts Stich and Warfield's argument from the non-projectability of C- and L-beliefs to their non-functional discreteness, it seems that Smolensky's C- and L-beliefs lack two of the three features of propositional modularity attributable to common-sense beliefs.

Connectionism and Eliminativism

This raises the issue of how radical a theory conflict must be to generate the question of elimination. RS&G argue that it is enough to justify the eliminativist conclusion that the theory conflict is radical, although they note that there is no simple answer to the question of what makes for a radical theory conflict. Some guidelines exist, however, and here the notable one is that if the posits of one theory strike us as fundamentally unlike the posits of another, the conflict is radical. RS&G argue that Connectionist beliefs *are* fundamentally different from the beliefs of common-sense psychology, and so the eliminativist conclusion is justified.

This is where the importance of the issue aired above, concerning whether there is a conflict between common-sense and Connectionist concepts of belief, emerges. In Smolensky's opinion, that C- and L-beliefs possess two of the three features of propositional modularity is enough to block the eliminativist conclusion; and elsewhere (in Chapter 2) he argues that Connectionist psychology is properly viewed as a *refinement* of Classical psychology (which construes beliefs as having the three features of propositional modularity). As he sees it, just as quantum mechanics is a refinement of classical mechanics, and their posits do not compete with one another, Connectionist psychology is a refinement of Classical psychology, and their posits do not compete with one another. Similarly, Copernican astronomy is properly viewed as a refinement of Ptolemaic astronomy, since both theories are theories of the planets. Theory refinement does not lead to elimination, although it may lead to a quite different conception of the nature of the posits of the original theory. Connectionist beliefs are different from the beliefs of common sense, which the Classical view endorses; but they are still recognizably *beliefs*.

Smolensky and RS&G disagree about whether the shift from common-sense to Connectionist psychology is ontologically radical. This way of viewing the debate concerning connectionism and eliminativism would seem to put Smolensky in the weaker position, given that C- and L- beliefs lack two of the three features of propositional modularity. However, Stich and Warfield's reply (chapter 11) represents a change in view from RS&G's paper on the relation between ontologically radical theory change and eliminativism. Unlike RS&G, Stich and Warfield maintain that no amount of radical theory shift justifies the eliminativist conclusion: Connectionist beliefs could lack *all three* features of propositional modularity and still the eliminativist conclusion would not follow. They argue that a further premise is necessary to get from the claim that a theory change is ontologically radical to the eliminativist conclusion, and that the two most frequently relied on in arguments for eliminativism are highly problematic.

The first is a claim about how the references of terms in a theory are fixed. The claim is that, associated with each theoretical term is a set of descriptions that fixes or determines the reference of that term. If, for each theoretical term, all or most of the descriptions associated with it are satisfied by some one entity or kind, then the term refers to that entity or kind; otherwise the term has no referent. In a case where all or most of a theory's theoretical terms have no referents, the appropriate conclusion is that the entities posited by the theory do not exist. Stich and Warfield argue that the description theory of reference embodied in this premise is controversial and problematic, and many have argued forcefully and persuasively that it is false. The dominant alternative to it is the causal/historical view, according to which the reference of a term is determined by a causal chain which connects the term, via others' uses of it, to an object in whose presence the term was originally introduced. This alternative they consider to be particularly appealing in accounting for the references of theoretical terms, since it can easily explain how people can refer to an object or kind despite having radically mistaken beliefs about it.

The second is a claim about how certain features of an entity or kind are related to it. The claim is that such features are 'conceptually necessary', in the sense that it is part of the concept of that entity or kind that it have those features. So, for example, one might claim that it is part of the concept of a belief that it possess the features of propositional modularity. Stich and Warfield point out that this view appears to require commitment to the analytic/synthetic distinction – to the view that certain sentences are 'true in virtue of meaning alone' whereas others are true or false in virtue of facts about the world – and that this distinction has been shown, notably by Quine (1953), to be highly dubious.

Of both candidates for premises, Stich and Warfield claim that because they are highly problematic, anyone wishing to rely on them cannot simply take them for granted. Arguments are needed for them, and they will not be easy to come by. This, of course, does not establish that the eliminativist conclusion cannot be justified, nor do Stich and Warfield suppose that it does. What they are concerned to establish is that no theory change, however radical, can alone justify eliminativism. If they are right, then they and Smolensky are in agreement, but once again, for different reasons. Smolensky thinks that eliminativism does not follow from the falsity of common-sense psychology because Connectionist theory does not show common-sense psychology to be *seriously* wrong, or wrong *enough*. But Stich and Warfield think that, even if Connectionist theory showed common-sense psychology to be wrong about *all* of the features of propositional modularity that common sense takes beliefs to have, the eliminativist conclusion would still not follow.

The question remains as to how, given that there *are* cases of radical theory change that have led to elimination, the eliminativist conclusion in these cases is to be justified. Stich and Warfield argue that it will take some pretty fancy argument to defend the description theory against its alternative, the causal/historical view, particularly since the latter can readily explain the fact that a person can refer to an object or kind despite having wildly mistaken beliefs about it. However, the causal/historical view is tailor-made primarily for names, and by extension, for terms for *certain sorts* of objects or kinds, namely, ones that are capable of being referred to ostensively, such as 'cat', 'magnet', and 'water'.

This raises the question of how the references of terms in a theory for objects or kinds that are not capable of being referred to ostensively – theoretical terms such as 'electron', for example – are fixed.[7] A natural extension of the causal/historical view would be to construe such terms as referring to whatever it is that is responsible for the phenomena scientists are attempting to explain. But this seems to get some important facts wrong. On this view of reference, the reference of 'phlogiston' would be taken to be that substance, whatever it is, that is responsible for combustion. But then scientists using the term 'phlogiston' would have been referring to *oxygen*, since it is oxygen and not phlogiston that is responsible for combustion, and falsely attributing to it certain properties (e.g. that it does not sustain life). This gets things wrong because, by Stich and Warfield's own lights, the phlogiston/oxygen case is a case of theory replacement by elimination, not one of theory change where the original posits are retained.

So it seems that the causal/historical view is not well suited to explaining how the references of terms whose referents are not capable of being referred to ostensively are determined. It has difficulties, as the description theory does not, explaining why certain cases of theory falsification lead to elimination. A better story might begin along the causal/historical lines, but then depart from it by moving the burden of reference from the name or expression initially used to fix the reference of the substance or kind to the predicates associated with properties which are, subsequent to the introduction of the term, taken to constitute the object or kind. Thus, suppose that a group of scientists intent on explaining a set of phenomena, P, come to think that a single substance or kind is responsible for P, and they introduce a term with which to 'baptize' this substance or kind, such as 'whatever is responsible for P'. As time goes on, various hypotheses about the properties that constitute this substance or kind are formulated, in order to give an explanatory role to the term. The explanatory role of the term in the theory depends on these individual or kind-constituting properties associated with the term. If these properties are sufficient to explain P, the burden of reference will be taken over by the predicates associated with these properties, and will no longer be associated with the term 'whatever is responsible for P'.

This account gives a plausible explanation, as the causal/historical account does not, of why the phlogiston/oxygen case is one of theory replacement by elimination, viz. that the properties that were taken to constitute the kind were found not to be satisfied by any kind. Moreover, it provides a plausible explanation in general of the introduction of non-ostensive (or theoretical) terms into a theory. Applied to the case of common-sense psychology, it might be taken to justify the eliminativist conclusion in a situation such as the one Stich and Warfield envisage. Suppose that terms for states with propositional content are treated as non-ostensive and that their referents are taken to be responsible for phenomena such as purposive behaviour. Terms for such states may be introduced as terms for states with propositional content, but it may be no part of the reference-fixing story that these states have the features constitutive of propositional modularity. However, the burden of reference, on the present account, comes to be taken over by the predicates associated with properties taken to constitute the kind, the features of propositional modularity. If, as in the situation envisaged by Stich and Warfield, it is found that no states satisfy the predicates associated with these kind-constituting properties, then the appropriate conclusion should be that there are no intentional states, not that there are intentional states whose properties are radically different from those of propositional modularity.[8]

This account brings out a point about the relation between an object or kind and its individual or kind-constituting properties, a point that connects with Stich and Warfield's discussion of the second candidate for a premise in the argument for eliminativism. Stich and Warfield suppose that the relation between a theoretical term and its associated properties needed to justify the eliminativist conclusion is one of 'conceptual necessity', whereby it is part of the concept of the object or kind that it have the properties specified by its associated descriptions. However, as the account above suggests, the relation between a kind and its kind-constituting properties may be such that truths expressing this relation are synthetic and necessary *a posteriori*, rather than necessary *a priori*. As Enc (1976, p. 279) puts it:

the central sentences are privileged in that as long as the theory is in currency, they are regarded as expressing truths about *x*. (I do not mean that they are analytic. I mean that *x*, in every possible world in which it exists, is the kind of thing the central sentences assert it to be.)

Against this construal of the second candidate for a premise, the arguments by Quine against the analytic/synthetic distinction have no force. Other arguments of Quine's, in particular, his arguments against the essence/accident distinction, may be relevant, but that is another matter.

Acknowledgement

I am indebted to Stephen Laurence for discussions on issues involved in this debate.

Notes

1 This lack of clarity in the discussion of functional discreteness by RS&G infects Stich and Warfield's discussion of Smolensky's position in their final reply in chapter 11. There they seem to associate projectability, not with semantic interpretability as here, but with functional discreteness (see chapter 8, p. 316 and pp. 328–9 and chapter 11 pp. 399–400). Clark's reading of RS&G also clearly associates projectability with semantic interpretability.

RS&G point out that they do not see functional discreteness as conflicting with the view that propositional states are often acquired in clusters, or with the view that having a particular belief presupposes a system of other related beliefs. Their point is that once this system is fixed, it makes sense to suppose that one can acquire or lose a single belief without disturbing others in the system. Moreover, they claim that this is 'radically inconsistent' with the holistic nature of connectionist systems. John Heil (1991) contests this claim. He points out that many, notably Donald Davidson (1970, 1987), hold that the domain of propositional attitudes is itself holistic, rather than consisting of discrete, sentence-like states, and that this conception of propositional attitudes is not radically at odds with Connectionist theory. Further, he argues that the holistic nature of propositional attitudes need not imply that beliefs cannot be acquired or lost by a system singly – only that this cannot happen without other changes occurring in the system. This opens up another avenue of defence for those anti-eliminativists who believe that connectionist architectures are not radically at odds with common-sense psychology. We do not pursue this line here, however, since it plays no role in the debate below.

2 Cluster profiles are the result of a technique known as *cluster analysis*, a technique of statistical analysis of the behaviour of a network (i.e. its activity patterns). The result of such analysis, Clark tells us, is a tree structure which gives us information about which inputs/groups of inputs are treated similarly to others.

> For NETtalk it works like this: first, give the network a variety of inputs and record the hidden unit activations and output caused by each. Now gather together all the inputs which yielded a given output phoneme, and find an *average* mediating hidden unit activation vector. Do this for each phoneme. Now use hierarchical clustering analysis to pair up the most similar vectors. Find an average for each pair, and repeat the process (thus yielding pairs of pairs, pairs of pairs of pairs, and so on). The result is a tree structure which displays the way in which the network has learnt to structure the space of weights so as successfully to solve the problem. (chapter 9, p. 346)

At the bottom level, for instance, NETtalk grouped together 'p' and 'b' inputs; and further up, it grouped together 'o' sounds.

3   In fact, the network Smolensky employs to argue that, when weight analysis and learning analysis are performed on it, C- and L-beliefs emerge, is much simpler than RS&G's network, notably in that, whereas the latter has hidden units, Smolensky's network has none. However, Smolensky argues that his conclusions generalize to RS&G's network.

4   Here again, however, there is some obscurity, due to the association in RS&G of projectability with semantic interpretability and not functional discreteness (see note 5).

5   Stich and Warfield (chapter 11) seem to suggest that the argument against Smolensky's Connectionist beliefs being projectable is an argument against their being functionally discrete. But this is obscure given RS&G's characterization of functional discreteness and semantic interpretability, where projectability is associated with semantic interpretability and not functional discreteness. So it looks like Stich and Warfield still owe us an argument from the non-projectability of Connectionist beliefs to the non-functional discreteness of Connectionist beliefs (see note 1).

6   Cf. William Bechtel and Adele Abrahamsen (1991, p. 64): 'in connectionist networks, remembering is carried out by the same means as making inferences; the system fills in missing pieces of information. As far as the system's processing is concerned, there is no difference between reconstructing a previous state, and constructing a totally new state.' Stich and Warfield's point is that, without any short-term memory, there is no way for Clark's system to input $p\&q$ in order to get from $\mathbf{p}^*$, $\mathbf{q}^*$, $\mathbf{p}^*->p$, $\mathbf{q}^*->q$, and $p\&q ->r$ to r. Stich and Warfield also argue that implicit in Clark's account is a concept of propositional modularity that is much too weak (see chapter 11, p. 402).

7   The account described here is developed in detail by Berent Enc (1976). He notes that the ostensive/non-ostensive distinction is a relative one. Before microscopes were invented, molecules might not have been capable of being referred to ostensively. After this time, they were. The ostensive/non-ostensive distinction is introduced by him in order to avoid the problematic distinction between observational and theoretical terms.

8   The story here might be further refined and elaborated upon with the aid of a distinction, due to Adrian Cussins (1993) between *conflated concepts* and *misconceived composites*. A conflated concept is a conflation of two or more concepts from the same explanatory domain which subserve the function or functions of the original concept. An example is that of weight, which is a conflation of the concepts of mass and force, concepts that are from the same explanatory domain and subserve the function served by the concept of weight. From the point of view of the underlying theory, the concept of weight is imprecise, perhaps, but it is not misconceived: it is a conflation of two other, perfectly respectable concepts whose functions subserve the function of the original concept. A misconceived composite, on the other hand, brings together concepts none of which falls into the same explanatory domain and subserves the function served by the original concept. Examples of misconceived composites given by Cussins include

those of phlogiston and caloric fluid. Misconceived composites are candidates for elimination, whereas conflated concepts are not.

Armed with this distinction, connectionists such as Smolensky, who argue that the features of propositional modularity are in fact preserved in connectionist models, *but not by one and the same kind of entity* appear to be in a strong position to defend the view that the concept of propositional modularity is a conflated concept, not a misconceived composite. From the point of view of Connectionist theory, they might argue, activity vectors are semantically evaluable and functionally discrete, whereas the individual activity values that comprise these vectors are causally efficacious. So the concept of propositional modularity is subserved by concepts from the same explanatory domain that subserve the function served by the original concept of propositional modularity. (Of course, the success of this defence from the point of view of the present debate depends on whether activity vectors in connectionist systems are functionally discrete. Note also that Cussins himself employs the conflated concept/misconceived composite distinction to argue *for* the eliminativist conclusion.)

References

Bechtel, W. and Abrahamsen, A. (1991) *Connectionism and the Mind*. Oxford, Basil Blackwell.

Cussins, A. (1993) Nonconceptual content and the elimination of misconceived composites! *Mind and Language* 8 (2), 234–52.

Davidson, D. (1970) Mental events. Reprinted in D. Davidson, *Essays on Actions and Events*, pp. 207–25. Oxford, Oxford University Press, 1980.

Davidson, D. (1987) Knowing one's own mind. *Proceedings and Addresses of the American Philosophical Association* 60, 441–58.

Enc, B. (1976) Reference of theoretical terms. *Nous*, 10 (3), 261–82.

Heil, J. (1991) Being indiscrete. In John D. Greenwood (ed.), *The Future of Folk Psychology*, pp. 120–34. Cambridge, Cambridge University Press.

Marr, D. (1982) *Vision*. New York, W.H. Freeman.

Quine, W.V.O. (1953) Two dogmas of empiricism. In *From a Logical Point of View*. Cambridge, Mass., Harvard University Press.

8

Connectionism, Eliminativism and the Future of Folk Psychology

William Ramsey, Stephen Stich and Joseph Garon

1 Introduction

In the years since the publication of Thomas Kuhn's *The Structure of Scientific Revolutions* (1962), the term 'scientific revolution' has been used with increasing frequency in discussions of scientific change, and the magnitude required of an innovation before someone or other is tempted to call it a revolution has diminished alarmingly. Our thesis in this chapter is that if a certain family of connectionist hypotheses turn out to be right, they will surely count as revolutionary, even on stringent pre-Kuhnian standards. There is no question that connectionism has already brought about major changes in the way many cognitive scientists conceive of cognition. However, as we see it, what makes certain kinds of connectionist models genuinely revolutionary is the support they lend to a thoroughgoing eliminativism about some of the central posits of common-sense (or 'folk') psychology. Our focus in this chapter will be on beliefs or propositional memories, though the argument generalizes straightforwardly to all the other propositional attitudes. If we are right, the consequences of this kind of connectionism extend well beyond the confines of cognitive science, since these models, if successful, will require a radical reorientation of the way we think about ourselves.

Here is a quick preview of what is to come. Section 2 gives a brief account of what eliminativism claims, and sketches a pair of premises that eliminativist arguments typically require. Section 3 says a bit about how we conceive of common-sense psychology, and the propositional attitudes that it posits. It also illustrates one sort of psychological model that exploits and builds upon the posits of folk psychology. Section 4 is devoted to connectionism. Models that have been called 'connectionist' form a fuzzy and heterogeneous set whose members often share little more than a vague family resemblance. However, our argument linking connectionism to eliminativism will work only for a restricted domain of connectionist models, interpreted in a particular way; the main job of section 4 is to say what that domain is and how the models in the domain are to be interpreted. In section 5 we will illustrate what a connectionist model of belief that comports with our strictures might look like, and go on to argue that if models of this sort are correct, then things look bad for common-sense psychology. Section 6 assembles some objections and replies. The final section is a brief conclusion.

Before plunging in we should emphasize that the thesis we propose to defend is a *conditional* claim: *if* Connectionist hypotheses of the sort we will sketch turn out to be right, so too will eliminativism about propositional attitudes. Since our goal is only to show how connectionism and eliminativism are related, we will make no effort to argue for the truth or falsity of either doctrine. In particular, we will offer no argument in favor of the version of connectionism required in the antecedent of our conditional. Indeed our view is that it is early days yet – too early to tell with any assurance how well this family of connectionist hypotheses will fare. Those who are more confident of connectionism may, of course, invoke our conditional as part of a larger argument for doing away with the propositional attitudes.[1] But, as John Haugeland once remarked, one man's ponens is another man's tollens. And those who take eliminativism about propositional attitudes to be preposterous or unthinkable may well view our arguments as part of a larger case against connectionism. Thus, we'd not be at all surprised if trenchant critics of connectionism, like Fodor and Pylyshyn (chapter 3), found both our conditional and the argument for it to be quite congenial.

2   Eliminativism and Folk Psychology

'Eliminativism', as we shall use the term, is a fancy name for a simple thesis. It is the claim that some category of entities, processes or properties exploited in a common-sense or scientific account of the world do not exist. So construed, we are all eliminativists about many sorts of things. In the domain of folk theory, witches are the standard example. Once upon a time witches were widely believed to be responsible for various local calamities. But people gradually became convinced that there are better explanations for most of the events in which witches had been implicated. There being no explanatory work for witches to do, sensible people concluded that there were no such things. In the scientific domain, phlogiston, caloric fluid and the luminiferous ether are the parade cases for eliminativism. Each was invoked by serious scientists pursuing sophisticated research programs. But in each case the program ran aground in a major way, and the theories in which the entities were invoked were replaced by successor theories in which the entities played no role. The scientific community gradually came to recognize that phlogiston and the rest do not exist.

As these examples suggest, a central step in an eliminativist argument will typically be the demonstration that the theory in which certain putative entities or processes are invoked should be rejected and replaced by a better theory. And that raises the question of how we go about showing that one theory is better than another. Notoriously, this question is easier to ask than to answer. However, it would be pretty widely agreed that if a new theory provides more accurate predictions and better explanations than an old one, and does so over a broader range of phenomena, and if the new theory comports as well or better with well-established theories in neighboring domains, then there is good reason to think that the old theory is inferior, and that the new one is to be preferred. This is hardly a complete account of the conditions under which one theory is to be preferred to another, though for our purposes it will suffice.

But merely showing that a theory in which a class of entities plays a role is inferior to a successor theory plainly is not sufficient to show that the entities do not exist. Often a more appropriate conclusion is that the rejected theory was wrong, perhaps seriously wrong, about some of the properties of the entities in its domain, or about the laws governing those entities, and that the new theory gives us a more accurate account *of those very same entities*. Thus, for example, pre-Copernican astronomy was very wrong about the nature of the planets and the laws governing their movement. But it would be something of a joke to suggest that Copernicus and Galileo showed that the planets Ptolemy spoke of do not exist.[2]

In other cases the right thing to conclude is that the posits of the old theory are reducible to those of the new. Standard examples here include the reduction of temperature to mean molecular kinetic energy, the reduction of sound to wave motion in the medium, and the reduction of genes to sequences of polynucleotide bases.[3] Given our current concerns, the lesson to be learned from these cases is that even if the common-sense theory in which propositional attitudes find their home is replaced by a better theory, that would not be enough to show that the posits of the common-sense theory do not exist.

What more would be needed? What is it that distinguishes cases like phlogiston and caloric, on the one hand, from cases like genes or the planets on the other? Or, to ask the question in a rather different way, what made phlogiston and caloric candidates for elimination? Why wasn't it concluded that phlogiston is oxygen, that caloric is kinetic energy, and that the earlier theories had just been rather badly mistaken about some of the properties of phlogiston and caloric?

Let us introduce a bit of terminology. We will call theory changes in which the entities and processes of the old theory are retained or reduced to those of the new one *ontologically conservative* theory changes. Theory changes that are not ontologically conservative we will call *ontologically radical*. Given this terminology, the question we are asking is how to distinguish ontologically conservative theory changes from ontologically radical ones.

Once again, this is a question that is easier to ask than to answer. There is, in the philosophy of science literature, nothing that even comes close to a plausible and fully general account of when theory change sustains an eliminativist conclusion and when it does not. In the absence of a principled way of deciding when ontological elimination is in order, the best we can do is to look at the posits of the old theory – the ones that are at risk of elimination – and ask whether there is anything in the new theory that they might be identified with or reduced to. If the posits of the new theory strike us as deeply and fundamentally different from those of the old theory, in the way that molecular motion seems deeply and fundamentally different from the 'exquisitely elastic' fluid posited by caloric theory, then it will be plausible to conclude that the theory change has been a radical one, and that an eliminativist conclusion is in order. But since there is no easy measure of how 'deeply and fundamentally different' a pair of posits are, the conclusion we reach is bound to be a judgment call.[4]

To argue that certain sorts of connectionist models support eliminativism about the propositional attitudes, we must make it plausible that these models are not ontologically conservative. Our strategy will be to contrast these connectionist models, models like those set out in section 5, with ontologically conservative models like the one sketched at the end of section 3, in an effort to underscore just how ontologically radical the connectionist models are. But here we are getting ahead of ourselves. Before trying to persuade you that connectionist models are ontologically radical, we need to take a look at the folk psychological theory that the connectionist models threaten to replace.

3 Propositional Attitudes and Common-sense Psychology

For present purposes we will assume that common-sense psychology can plausibly be regarded as a theory, and that beliefs, desires and the rest of the propositional attitudes are plausibly viewed as posits of that theory. Though this is not an uncontroversial assumption, the case for it has been well argued by others.[5] Once it is granted that common-sense psychology is indeed a theory, we expect it will be conceded by almost everyone that the theory is a likely candidate for replacement. In saying this, we do not intend to disparage folk psychology, or to beg any questions about the status of the entities it posits. Our point is simply that folk wisdom on matters psychological is not likely to tell us all there is to know. Common-sense psychology, like other folk theories, is bound to be incomplete in many ways, and very likely to be inaccurate in more than a few. If this were not the case, there would be no need for a careful, quantitative, experimental science of psychology. With the possible exception of a few die-hard Wittgensteinians, just about everyone is prepared to grant that there are many psychological facts and principles beyond those embedded in common sense. If this is right, then we have the first premise needed in an eliminativist argument aimed at beliefs, propositional memories and the rest of the propositional attitudes. The theory that posits the attitudes is indeed a prime candidate for replacement.

Though common-sense psychology contains a wealth of lore about beliefs, memories, desires, hopes, fears and the other propositional attitudes, the crucial folk psychological tenets in forging the link between connectionism and eliminativism are the claims that propositional attitudes are *functionally discrete, semantically interpretable*, states that play a *causal role* in the production of other propositional attitudes, and ultimately in the production of behavior. Following the suggestion in Stich (1983, pp. 237 ff.), we'll call this cluster of claims *propositional modularity*. (The reader is cautioned not to confuse this notion of propositional modularity with the very different notion of modularity defended in Fodor, 1983.)

There is a great deal of evidence that might be cited in support of the thesis that folk psychology is committed to the tenets of propositional modularity. The fact that common-sense psychology takes beliefs and other propositional attitudes to have semantic properties deserves special emphasis. According to common sense:

1   When people see a dog nearby they typically come to believe *that there is a dog nearby*.

2   When people believe *that the train will be late if there is snow in the mountains*, and come to believe *that there is snow in the mountains*, they will typically come to believe *that the train will be late*.

3   When people who speak English say 'There is a cat in the yard', they typically believe *that there is a cat in the yard*.

And so on, for indefinitely many further examples. Note that these generalizations of common-sense psychology are couched in terms of the *semantic* properties of the attitudes. It is in virtue of being the belief *that p* that a given belief has a given effect or cause. Thus common-sense psychology treats the predicates expressing these semantic properties, predicates like 'believes *that the train is late*', as *projectable* predicates – the sort of predicates that are appropriately used in nomological or law-like generalizations.

Perhaps the most obvious way to bring out folk psychology's commitment to the thesis that propositional attitudes are *functionally discrete* states is to note that it typically makes perfectly good sense to claim that a person has acquired (or lost) a single memory or belief. Thus, for example, on a given occasion it might plausibly be claimed that when Henry awoke from his nap he had completely forgotten that the car keys were hidden in the refrigerator, though he had forgotten nothing else. In saying that folk psychology views beliefs as the sorts of things that can be acquired or lost one at a time, we do not mean to be denying that having any particular belief may presuppose a substantial network of related beliefs. The belief that the car keys are in the refrigerator is not one that could be acquired by a primitive tribesman who knew nothing about cars, keys or refrigerators. But once the relevant background is in place, as we may suppose it is for us and for Henry, it seems that folk psychology is entirely comfortable with the possibility that a person may acquire (or lose) the belief that the car keys are in the refrigerator, while the remainder of his beliefs remains unchanged. Propositional modularity does not, of course, deny that acquiring one belief often leads to the acquisition of a cluster of related beliefs. When Henry is told that the keys are in the refrigerator, he may come to believe that they haven't been left in the ignition, or in his jacket pocket. But then again he may not. Indeed, on the folk psychological conception of belief it is perfectly possible for a person to have a long-standing belief that the keys are in the refrigerator, and to continue searching for them in the bedroom.[6]

To illustrate the way in which folk psychology takes propositional attitudes to be functionally discrete, *causally active* states, let us sketch a pair of more elaborate examples.

In common-sense psychology, behavior is often explained by appeal to certain of the agent's beliefs and desires. Thus, to explain why Alice went to her office, we might note that she wanted to send some e-mail messages (and, of course, she believed she could do so from her office). However, in some cases an agent will have several sets of beliefs and desires each of which *might* lead to the same behavior. Thus we may suppose that Alice also wanted to talk to her research assistant, and that she believed he would be at the office. In such cases, common-sense psychology assumes that Alice's going to her office might have been caused by either one of the belief/desire pairs, or by both, and that determining which of these options obtains is an empirical matter. So it is entirely possible that on *this* occasion Alice's desire to send some e-mail played no role in producing her behavior; it was the desire to talk with her research assistant that actually caused her to go to the office. However, had she not wanted to talk with her research assistant, she might have gone to the office anyhow, because the desire to send some e-mail, which was causally inert in her actual decision-making, might then have become actively involved. Note that in this case common-sense psychology is prepared to recognize a pair of quite distinct semantically characterized states, one of which may be causally active while the other is not.

Our second illustration is parallel to the first, but focuses on beliefs and inference, rather than desires and action. On the common-sense view, it may sometimes happen that a person has a number of belief clusters, any one of which might lead him or her to infer some further belief. When he or she actually does draw the inference, folk psychology assumes that it is an empirical question what he or she inferred it from, and that this question typically has a determinate answer. Suppose, for example, that Inspector Clouseau believes that the butler said he spent the evening at the village hotel, and that he said he arrived back on the morning train. Suppose Clouseau also believes that the village hotel is closed for the season, and that the morning train has been taken out of service. Given these beliefs, along with some widely shared background beliefs, Clouseau might well infer that the butler is lying. If he does, folk psychology presumes that the inference might be based either on his beliefs about the hotel, or on his beliefs about the train, or both. It is entirely possible, from the perspective of common-sense psychology, that although Clouseau has long known that the hotel is closed for the season, this belief played no role in his inference on this particular occasion. Once again, we see common-sense psychology invoking a pair

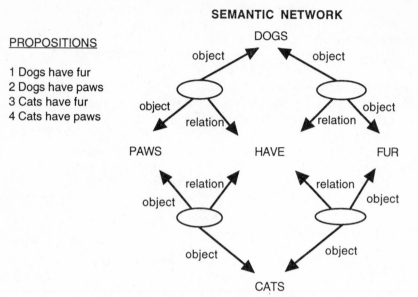

SEMANTIC NETWORK

PROPOSITIONS

1 Dogs have fur
2 Dogs have paws
3 Cats have fur
4 Cats have paws

Figure 8.1   A semantic network representation of memory in the style of Collins and Quillian (1972).

of distinct propositional attitudes, one of which is causally active on a particular occasion while the other is causally inert.

In the psychological literature there is no shortage of models for human belief or memory which follow the lead of common-sense psychology in supposing that propositional modularity is true. Indeed, prior to the emergence of connectionism, just about all psychological models of propositional memory, save for those urged by behaviorists, were comfortably compatible with propositional modularity. Typically, these models view a subject's store of beliefs or memories as an interconnected collection of functionally discrete, semantically interpretable states which interact in systematic ways. Some of these models represent individual beliefs as sentence-like structures – strings of symbols which can be individually activated by transferring them from long-term memory to the more limited memory of a central processing unit. Other models represent beliefs as a network of labeled nodes and labeled links through which patterns of activation may spread. Still other models represent beliefs as sets of production rules.[7] In all three sorts of models, it is generally the case that for any given cognitive episode, like performing a particular inference or answering a question, some of the memory states will be actively involved, and others will be dormant.

In figure 8.1 we have displayed a fragment of a 'semantic network'

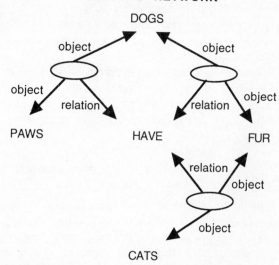

PROPOSITIONS

1 Dogs have fur
2 Dogs have paws
3 Cats have fur

Figure 8.2   Semantic network with one proposition removed.

representation of memory, in the style of Collins and Quillian (1972). In this model, each distinct proposition in memory is represented by an oval node along with its labeled links to various concepts. By adding assumptions about the way in which questions or other sorts of memory probes lead to activation spreading through the network, the model enables us to make predictions about speed and accuracy in various experimental studies of memory. For our purposes there are three facts about this model that are of particular importance. First, since each proposition is encoded in a functionally discrete way, it is a straight-forward matter to add or subtract a *single* proposition from memory, while leaving the rest of the network unchanged. Thus, for example, figure 8.2 depicts the result of removing one proposition from the network in figure 8.1. Secondly, the model treats predicates expressing the semantic properties of beliefs or memories as *projectable*.[8] They are treated as the sorts of predicates that pick out scientifically genuine *kinds*, rather than mere accidental conglomerates, and thus are suitable for inclusion in the statement of law-like regularities. To see this, we need only consider the way in which such models are tested against empirical data about memory acquisition and forgetting. Typically, it will be assumed that if a subject is told (for example) that the policeman arrested the hippie, then the subject will (with a certain probability) remember *that the policeman arrested the hippie* (see, for example, Anderson and Bower, 1973). And this assumption is taken to express a nomological generalization – it captures something law-like about the way in which the cognitive system works. So while the class of people who *remember that the policeman arrested the hippie* may differ psychologically in all sorts of ways, the theory treats them as a psychologically natural kind. Thirdly, in any given memory search or inference task exploiting a semantic network model, it makes sense to ask which propositions were activated and which were not. Thus, a search in the network of figure 8.1 might terminate without ever activating the proposition that cats have paws.

4   A Family of Connectionist Hypotheses

Our theme, in the previous section, was that common-sense psychology is committed to propositional modularity, and that many models of memory proposed in the cognitive psychology literature are comfortably compatible with this assumption. In the present section we want to describe a class of connectionist models which, we will argue, are *not* readily compatible with propositional modularity. The connectionist models we have in mind share three properties:

1   Their encoding of information in the connection weights and in the biases on units is *widely distributed*, rather than being *localist*.
2   Individual hidden units in the network have no comfortable symbolic interpretation; they are *sub-symbolic*, to use a term suggested by Paul Smolensky.
3   The models are intended *as cognitive* models, not merely as *implementations* of cognitive models.

A bit later in this section we will elaborate further on each of these three features, and in the next section we will describe a simple example of a connectionist model that meets our three criteria. However, we are under no illusion that what we say will be sufficient to give a sharp-edged characterization of the class of connectionist models we have in mind. Nor is such a sharp-edged characterization essential for our argument. It will suffice if we can convince you that there is a significant class of connectionist models which are incompatible with the propositional modularity of folk psychology.

Before saying more about the three features on our list, we would do well to give a more general characterization of the sort of models we are calling 'connectionist', and introduce some of the jargon that comes with the territory. To this end, let us quote at some length from Paul Smolensky's lucid overview.

Connectionist models are large networks of simple parallel computing elements, each of which carries a numerical *activation value* which it computes from the values of neighboring elements in the network, using some simple numerical formula. The network elements, or *units*, influence each other's values through connections that carry a numerical strength or *weight* . . .

In a typical . . . model, input to the system is provided by imposing activation values on the *input units* of the network; these numerical values represent some encoding, or *representation*, of the input. The activation on the input units propagates along the connections until some set of activation values emerges on the *output units*; these activation values encode the output the system has computed from the input. In between the input and output units there may be other units, often called *hidden units*, that participate in representing neither the input nor the output.

The computation performed by the network in transforming the input pattern of activity to the output pattern depends on the set of connection strengths; *these weights are usually regarded as encoding the system's knowledge* [emphasis added]. In this sense, the connection strengths play the role of the program in a conventional computer. Much of the allure of the Connectionist approach is that many connectionist networks *program themselves*, that is, they have autonomous procedures for tuning their weights to eventually perform some specific computation. Such *learning procedures* [emphasis added] often depend on training in which the network is presented with sample input/output pairs from the function it is supposed to compute. In learning networks with hidden units, the network itself 'decides' what computations the hidden units will perform; because these units represent neither inputs nor outputs, they are never 'told' what their values should be, even during training. (Smolensky, Chapter 2, pp. 28–9).

One point must be added to Smolensky's portrait. In many connectionist models the hidden units and the output units are assigned a numerical 'bias' which is added into the calculation determining the unit's activation level. The learning procedures for such networks typically set both the connection strengths and the biases. Thus in these networks the system's knowledge is usually regarded as encoded in *both* the connection strengths and the biases.

So much for a general overview. Let us now try to explain the three features that characterize those connectionist models we take to be incompatible with propositional modularity.

(1) In many non-connectionist cognitive models, like the one illustrated at the end of section 3, it is an easy matter to locate a functionally distinct part of the model encoding each proposition or state of affairs represented in the system. Indeed, according to Fodor and Pylyshyn, 'conventional [computational] architecture requires that

there be distinct symbolic expressions for each state of affairs that it can represent' (Chapter 3, p. 139). In some connectionist models an analogous sort of functional localization is possible, not only for the input and output units but for the hidden units as well. Thus, for example, in certain connectionist models, various individual units or small clusters of units are themselves intended to represent specific properties or features of the environment. When the connection strength from one such unit to another is strongly positive, this might be construed as the system's representation of the proposition that if the first feature is present, so too is the second. However, in many connectionist networks it is not possible to localize propositional representation beyond the input layer. That is, there are no particular features or states of the system which lend themselves to a straight-forward semantic evaluation. This can sometimes be a real inconvenience to the connectionist model builder when the system as a whole fails to achieve its goal because it has not represented the world the way it should. When this happens, as Smolensky notes,

> [I]t is not possible to localize a failure of veridical representation. Any particular state is part of a large causal system of states, and failures of the system to meet goal conditions cannot in general be localized to any particular state or state component. (Chapter 2, p. 64).

It is connectionist networks of this sort, in which it is not possible to isolate the representation of particular propositions or states of affairs within the nodes, connection strengths and biases, that we have in mind when we talk about the encoding of information in the biases, weights and hidden nodes being *widely distributed* rather than *localist*.

(2)   As we've just noted, there are some connectionist models in which some or all of the units are intended to represent specific properties or features of the system's environment. These units may be viewed as the model's symbols for the properties or features in question. However, in models where the weights and biases have been tuned by learning algorithms, it is often not the case that any single unit or any small collection of units will end up representing a specific feature of the environment in any straightforward way. As we shall see in the next section, it is often plausible to view such networks as collectively or holistically encoding a set of propositions, although none of the hidden units, weights or biases is comfortably viewed as a *symbol*. When this is the case we will call the strategy of representation invoked in the model *sub-symbolic*. Typically (perhaps always?) networks exploiting sub-symbolic strategies of representation will encode information in a widely distributed way.

(3)   The third item on our list is not a feature of connectionist models themselves, but rather a point about how the models are to be interpreted. In making this point we must presuppose a notion of theoretical or explanatory level which, despite much discussion in the literature, is far from being a paradigm of clarity.[9] Perhaps the clearest way to introduce the notion of explanatory level is against the background of the familiar functionalist thesis that psychological theories are analogous to programs which can be implemented on a variety of very different sorts of computers.[10] If one accepts this analogy, then it makes sense to ask whether a particular connectionist model is intended as a model at the psychological level or at the level of underlying neural implementation. Because of their obvious, though in many ways very partial, similarity to real neural architectures, it is tempting to view connectionist models as models of the implementation of psychological processes. And some connectionist model builders endorse this view quite explicitly. So viewed, however, connectionist models are not *psychological* or *cognitive* models at all, any more than a story of how cognitive processes are implemented at the quantum mechanical level is a psychological story. A very different view that connectionist model builders can and often do take is that their models are at the psychological level, not at the level of implementation. So construed, the models are in competition with other psychological models of the same phenomena. Thus a connectionist model of word recognition would be an alternative to – and not simply a possible implementation of – a non-connectionist model of word recognition; a connectionist theory of memory would be a competitor to a semantic network theory, and so on. Connectionists who hold this view of their theories often illustrate the point by drawing analogies with other sciences. Smolensky, for example, suggests that connectionist models stand to traditional cognitive models (like semantic networks) in much the same way that quantum mechanics stands to classical mechanics. In each case the newer theory is deeper, more general and more accurate over a broader range of phenomena. But in each case the new theory and the old are competing at the same explanatory level. If one is right, the other must be wrong.

In the light of our concerns in this chapter, there is one respect in which the analogy between connectionist models and quantum mechanics may be thought to beg an important question. For while quantum mechanics is conceded to be a *better* theory than classical mechanics, a plausible case could be made that the shift from classical to quantum mechanics was an ontologically *conservative* theory change. In any event, it is not clear that the change was ontologically *radical*. If our central thesis in this chapter is correct, then the relation between connectionist

Table 8.1   Propositions Network A and Network B

Proposition		Input	
1	Dogs have fur	11000011 00001111	1 true
2	Dogs have paws	11000011 00110011	1 true
3	Dogs have fleas	11000011 00111111	1 true
4	Dogs have legs	11000011 00111100	1 true
5	Cats have fur	11001100 00001111	1 true
6	Cats have paws	11001100 00110011	1 true
7	Cats have fleas	11001100 00111111	1 true
8	Fish have scales	11110000 00110000	1 true
9	Fish have fins	11110000 00001100	1 true
10	Fish have gills	11110000 00000011	1 true
11	Cats have gills	11001100 00000011	0 false
12	Fish have legs	11110000 00111100	0 false
13	Fish have fleas	11110000 00111111	0 false
14	Dogs have scales	11000011 00110000	0 false
15	Dogs have fins	11000011 00001100	0 false
16	Cats have fins	11001100 00001100	0 false

Added proposition

17	Fish have eggs	11110000 11001000	1 true

models and more traditional cognitive models is more like the relation between the caloric theory of heat and the kinetic theory. The caloric and kinetic theories are at the same explanatory level, though the shift from one to the other was pretty clearly ontologically radical. In order to make the case that the caloric analogy is the more appropriate one, it will be useful to describe a concrete, though very simple, connectionist model of memory that meets the three criteria we have been trying to explicate.

5   A Connectionist Model of Memory

Our goal in constructing the model was to produce a connectionist network that would do at least some of the tasks done by more traditional cognitive models of memory, and that would perspicuously exhibit the sort of distributed, sub-symbolic encoding described in the previous section. We began by constructing a network, we'll call it Network A, that would judge the truth or falsehood of the first 16 propositions displayed in table 8.1. The network was a typical three-

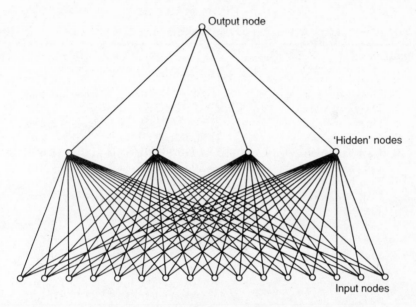

Figure 8.3 Typical three-tiered feed-forward network with 16 input units, four hidden units and one output unit.

tiered feed-forward network consisting of 16 input units, four hidden units and one output unit, as shown in figure 8.3. The input coding of each proposition is shown in the center column in table 8.1. Outputs close to 1 were interpreted as 'true' and outputs close to zero were interpreted as 'false'. Back propagation, a familiar connectionist learning algorithm, was used to 'train up' the network thereby setting the connection weights and biases. Training was terminated when the network consistently gave an output higher than 0.9 for each true proposition and lower than 0.1 for each false proposition. Figure 8.4 shows the connection weights between the input units and the leftmost hidden unit in the trained up network, along with the bias on that unit. Figure 8.5 indicates the connection weights and biases further upstream. Figure 8.6 shows the way in which the network computes its response to the proposition *Dogs have fur* when that proposition is encoded in the input units.

There is a clear sense in which the trained up Network A may be said to have stored information about the truth or falsity of propositions (1)–(16), since when any one of these propositions is presented to the network it correctly judges whether the proposition is true or false. In this respect it is similar to various semantic network models which can be constructed to perform much the same task. However, there is a

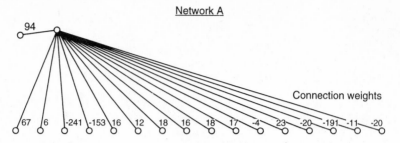

Figure 8.4   Input weights and bias to first hidden node in network with 16 propositions.

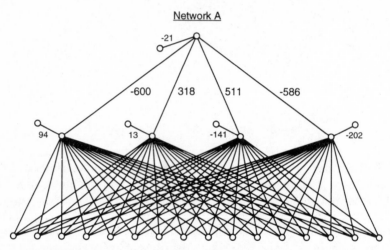

Figure 8.5   Weights and biases in network with 16 propositions.

striking difference between Network A and a semantic network model like the one depicted in figure 8.1. For, as we noted earlier, in the semantic network there is a functionally distinct sub-part associated with each proposition, and thus it makes perfectly good sense to ask, for any probe of the network, whether or not the representation of a specific proposition played a causal role. In the connectionist network, by contrast, there is no distinct state or part of the network that serves to represent any particular proposition. The information encoded in Network A is stored holistically and distributed throughout the network. Whenever information is extracted from Network A, by giving it an input string and seeing whether it computes a high or a low value for the output unit, *many* connection strengths, *many* biases and *many* hidden units play a role in the computation. And any particular weight or unit

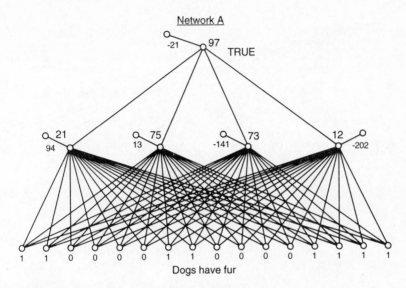

Figure 8.6 Network's response to the proposition *Dogs have fur.*

or bias will help to encode information about *many* different propositions. It simply makes no sense to ask whether or not the representation of a particular proposition plays a causal role in the network's computation. It is in just this respect that our connectionist model of memory seems radically incongruent with the propositional modularity of common-sense psychology. For, as we saw in section 3, common-sense psychology seems to presuppose that there is generally some answer to the question of whether a particular belief or memory played a causal role in a specific cognitive episode. But if belief and memory are subserved by a connectionist network like ours, such questions seem to have no clear meaning.

The incompatibility between propositional modularity and connectionist models like ours can be made even more vivid by contrasting Network A with a second network, we'll call it Network B, depicted in figures 8.7 and 8.8. Network B was trained up just as the first one was, except that one additional proposition was added to the training set (coded as indicated in table 8.1). Thus Network B encodes all the same propositions as Network A plus one more. In semantic network models, and other traditional cognitive models, it would be an easy matter to say which states or features of the system encode the added proposition, and it would be a simple task to determine whether or not the representation of the added proposition played a role in a particular episode modeled by the system. But plainly in the connectionist network

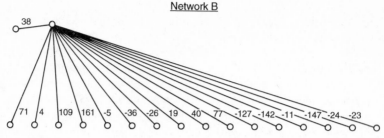

Figure 8.7   Input weights and bias to first hidden node in network with 17 propositions.

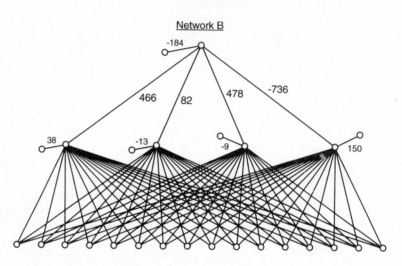

Figure 8.8   Weights and biases in network with 17 propositions.

those questions are quite senseless. The point is not that there are no differences between the two networks. Quite the opposite is the case; the differences are many and widespread. But these differences do not correlate in any systematic way with the functionally discrete, semantically interpretable states posited by folk psychology and by more traditional cognitive models. Since information is encoded in a highly distributed manner, with each connection weight and bias embodying information salient to many propositions, and information regarding any given proposition scattered throughout the network, the system lacks functionally distinct, identifiable sub-structures that are semantically interpretable as representations of individual propositions.

The contrast between Network A and Network B enables us to make our point about the incompatibility between common-sense psychology and these sorts of connectionist models in a rather different way. We noted in section 3 that common-sense psychology treats predicates expressing the semantic properties of propositional attitudes as projectable. Thus 'believes that dogs have fur' or 'remembers that dogs have fur' will be projectable predicates in common-sense psychology. Now both Network A and Network B might serve as models for a cognitive agent who believes that dogs have fur; both networks store or represent the information that dogs have fur. Nor are these the only two. If we were to train up a network on the 17 propositions in table 8.1 plus a few (or minus a few) we would get yet another system which is as different from Networks A and B as these two are from each other. The moral here is that though there are *indefinitely* many connectionist networks that represent the information that dogs have fur just as well as Network A does, these networks have no projectable features in common that are describable in the language of Connectionist theory. From the point of view of the connectionist model builder, the class of networks that might model a cognitive agent who believes that dogs have fur is not a genuine kind at all, but simply a chaotically disjunctive set. Common-sense psychology treats the class of people who believe that dogs have fur as a psychologically natural kind; Connectionist psychology does not.[11]

6 Objections and Replies

The argument we've set out in the previous five sections has encountered no shortage of objections. In this section we will try to reconstruct the most interesting of these, and indicate how we would reply.

Objection (1): Models like A and B are not serious models for human belief or propositional memory.

Of course, the models we've constructed are tiny toys that were built to illustrate the features set out in section 4 in a perspicuous way. They were never intended to model any substantial part of human propositional memory. But various reasons have been offered for doubting that *anything like* these models could ever be taken seriously as psychological models of propositional memory. Some critics have claimed that the models simply will not scale up – that while teaching a network to recognize 15 or 20 propositions may be easy enough, it is just not going to be possible to train up a network that can recognize a few thousand propositions, still less a few hundred thousand.[12] Others have objected that while more traditional models of memory, including those based on sentence-like storage, those using semantic networks, and those based on production systems, all provide some strategy for *inference* or *generalization* which enables the system to answer questions about propositions it was not explicitly taught, models like those we have constructed are incapable of inference and generalization. It has also been urged that these models fail as accounts of human memory because they provide no obvious way to account for the fact that suitably prepared humans can easily acquire propositional information one proposition at a time. Under ordinary circumstances, we can just *tell* Henry that the car keys are in the refrigerator, and he can readily record this fact in memory. He doesn't need anything like the sort of massive retraining that would be required to teach one of our connectionist networks a new proposition.

Reply: If our aim was to defend connectionist models of propositional memory, we would have to take on each of these putative shortcomings in some detail. And in each instance there is at least something to be said on the connectionist side. Thus, for example, it just is not true that networks like A and B don't generalize beyond the propositions on which they've been trained. In Network A, for example, the training set included:

Dogs have fur   Cats have fur
Dogs have paws   Cats have paws
Dogs have fleas   Cats have fleas

It also included

Dogs have legs

but not

Cats have legs

When the network was given an encoding of this last proposition, however, it generalized correctly and responded affirmatively. Similarly, the network responded negatively to an encoding of

Cats have scales

though it had not previously been exposed to this proposition.

However, it is important to see that this sort of point by point response to the charge that networks like ours are inadequate models for propositional memory is not really required, given the thesis we are defending in this chapter. For what we are trying to establish is a *conditional* thesis: *if* connectionist models of memory of the sort we describe in section 4 are right, *then* propositional attitude psychology is in serious trouble. Since conditionals with false antecedents are true, we win by default if it turns out that the antecedent of our conditional is false.

Objection (2): Our models do not really violate the principle of propositional modularity, since the propositions the system has learned are coded in functionally discrete ways, though this may not be obvious.

We've heard this objection elaborated along three quite different lines. The first line – let's call it Objection (2a) – notes that functionally discrete coding may often be *very* hard to notice, and cannot be expected to be visible on casual inspection. Consider, for example, the way in which sentences are stored in the memory of a typical von Neumann architecture computer – for concreteness we might suppose that the sentences are part of an English text and are being stored while the computer is running a word-processing program. Parts of sentences may be stored at physically scattered memory addresses linked together in complex ways, and given an account of the contents of all relevant memory addresses one would be hard put to say where a particular sentence is stored. But none the less each sentence is stored in a *functionally discrete* way. Thus, if one knew enough about the system, it would be possible to erase any particular sentence it is storing by tampering with the contents of the appropriate memory addresses, while leaving the rest of the sentences the system is storing untouched. Similarly, it has been urged, connectionist networks may in fact encode propositions in functionally discrete ways, though this may not be evident from a casual inspection of the trained up network's biases and connection strengths.

Reply (2a): It is a bit difficult to come to grips with this objection, since what the critic is proposing is that in models like those we have constructed there *might* be some covert functionally discrete system of propositional encoding that has yet to be discovered. In response to this we must concede that indeed there might. We certainly have no argument that even comes close to demonstrating that the discovery of such a covert functionally discrete encoding is impossible. Moreover, we concede that if such a covert system were discovered, then our argument would be seriously undermined. However, we're inclined to

332   WILLIAM RAMSEY, STEPHEN STICH AND JOSEPH GARON

think that the burden of argument is on the critic to show that such a system is not merely possible but *likely*; in the absence of any serious reason to think that networks like ours do encode propositions in functionally discrete ways, the mere logical possibility that they might is hardly a serious threat.

The second version of Objection (2) – we'll call it Objection (2b) – makes a specific proposal about the way in which networks like A and B might be discretely, though covertly, encoding propositions. The encoding, it is urged, is to be found in the pattern of activation of the hidden nodes, when a given proposition is presented to the network. Since there are four hidden nodes in our networks, the activation pattern on presentation of any given input may be represented as an ordered 4-tuple. Thus, for example, when network A is presented with the encoded proposition *Dogs have fur*, the relevant 4-tuple would be (21, 75, 73, 12), as shown in figure 8.6. Equivalently, we may think of each activation pattern as a point in a four-dimensional hyperspace. Since each proposition corresponds to a unique point in the hyperspace, that point may be viewed as the encoding of the proposition. Moreover, that point represents a functionally discrete state of the system.[13]

Reply (2b): What is being proposed is that the pattern of activation of the system on presentation of an encoding of the proposition *p* be identified with the belief that *p*. But this proposal is singularly implausible. Perhaps the best way to see this is to note that in common-sense psychology beliefs and propositional memories are typically of substantial duration; and they are the sorts of things that cognitive agents generally have lots of even when they are not using them. Consider an example. Are kangaroos marsupials? Surely you've believed for years that they are, though in all likelihood this is the first time today that your belief has been activated or used.[14] An activation pattern, however, is not an enduring state of a network; indeed, it is not a state of the network at all except when the network has had the relevant proposition as input. Moreover, there is an enormous number of other beliefs that you've had for years. But it makes no sense to suppose that a network could have many activation patterns continuously over a long period of time. At any given time a network exhibits at most one pattern of activation. So activation patterns are just not the sorts of things that can plausibly be identified, with beliefs or their representations.

Objection (2c): At this juncture, a number of critics have suggested that long-standing beliefs might be identified not with activation patterns, which are transient states of networks, but rather with *dispositions to produce activation patterns*. Thus, in Network A, the belief that dogs have fur would not be identified with a location in activation hyperspace but with the network's *disposition* to end up at that location when the proposition is presented. This *dispositional state* is an enduring state of the system; it is a state the network can be in no matter what its current state of activation may be, just as a sugar cube may have a disposition to dissolve in water even when there is no water nearby.[15] Some have gone on to suggest that the familiar philosophical distinction between dispositional and occurrent beliefs might be captured, in connectionist models, as the distinction between dispositions to produce activation patterns and activation patterns themselves.

Reply (2c): Our reply to this suggestion is that while dispositions to produce activation patterns are indeed *enduring* states of the system, they are not the right sort of enduring states – they are not the discrete, independently causally active states that folk psychology requires. Recall that on the folk psychological conception of belief and inference, there will often be a variety of quite different underlying causal patterns that may lead to the acquisition and avowal of a given belief. When Clouseau says that the butler did it, he may have just inferred this with the help of his long-standing belief that the train is out of service. Or he may have inferred it by using his belief that the hotel is closed. Or both long-standing beliefs may have played a role in the inference. Moreover, it is also possible that Clouseau drew this inference some time ago, and is now reporting a relatively long-standing belief. But it is hard to see how anything like these distinctions can be captured by the dispositional account in question. In reacting to a given input, say p, a network takes on a specific activation value. It may also have dispositions to take on other activation values on other inputs, say q and r. But there is no obvious way to interpret the claim that these further dispositions play a causal role in the network's reaction to p – or, for that matter, that they do not play a role. Nor can we make any sense of the idea that on one occasion the encoding of q (say, the proposition that the train is out of service) played a role while the encoding of r (say, the proposition that the hotel is closed) did not, and on another occasion, things went the other way around. The propositional modularity presupposed by common-sense psychology requires that belief tokens be functionally discrete states capable of causally interacting with one another in some cognitive episodes and of remaining causally inert in other cognitive episodes. However, in a distributed connectionist system like Network A, the dispositional state which produces one activation pattern is functionally inseparable from the dispositional state which produces another. Thus it is impossible to isolate some propositions as causally active in certain cognitive episodes, while others are not. We conclude that reaction pattern dispositions won't do as belief tokens. Nor, so far as we can see, are there any other states of networks like A and B that will fill the bill.

7   Conclusion

The thesis we have been defending in this chapter is that connectionist models of a certain sort are incompatible with the propositional modularity embedded in common-sense psychology. The connectionist models in question are those which are offered as models at the *cognitive* level, and in which the encoding of information is widely distributed and sub-symbolic. In such models, we have argued, there are no discrete, semantically interpretable states that play a causal role in some cognitive episodes but not others. Thus there is, in these models, nothing with which the propositional attitudes of common-sense psychology can plausibly be identified. If these models turn out to offer the best accounts of human belief and memory, we will be confronting an ontologically radical theory change – the sort of theory change that will sustain the conclusion that propositional attitudes, like caloric and phlogiston, do not exist.

Acknowledgments

Thanks are due to Ned Block, Paul Churchland, Gary Cottrell, Adrian Cussins, Jerry Fodor, John Heil, Frank Jackson, David Kirsh, Patricia Kitcher and Philip Kitcher for useful feedback on earlier versions of this chapter. Talks based on the chapter have been presented at the UCSD Cognitive Science Seminar and at conferences sponsored by the Howard Hughes Medical Foundation and the University of North Carolina at Greensboro. Comments and questions from these audiences have proved helpful in many ways.

Notes

1   See, for example, Churchland (1981, 1986), where explicitly eliminativist conclusions are drawn on the basis of speculations about the success of cognitive models similar to those we shall discuss.

2   We are aware that certain philosophers and historians of science have actually entertained ideas similar to the suggestion that the planets spoken of by pre-Copernican astronomers do not exist. See, for example, Kuhn (1970, ch. 10) and Feyerabend (1981, ch. 4). However, we take this suggestion to be singularly implausible. Eliminativist arguments can't be that easy. Just what has gone wrong with the accounts of meaning and reference that lead to such claims is less clear. For further discussion on these matters see Kuhn (1983), and Kitcher (1978, 1983).

3 For some detailed discussion of scientific reduction, see Nagel (1961), Schaffner (1967); Hooker (1981) and Kitcher (1984). The genetics case is not without controversy (see Kitcher, 1982, 1984).

4 It's worth noting that judgments on this matter can differ quite substantially. At one end of the spectrum are writers like Feyerabend (1981), and perhaps Kuhn (1962), for whom relatively small differences in theory are enough to justify the suspicion that there has been an ontologically radical change. Toward the other end are writers like Lycan, who writes:

> I am at pains to advocate a very liberal view . . . I am entirely willing to give up fairly large chunks of our commonsensical or platitudinous theory of belief or of desire (or of almost anything else) and decide that we were just wrong about a lot of things, without drawing the inference that we are no longer talking about belief or desire . . . I think the ordinary word 'belief' (qua theoretical term of folk psychology) points dimly toward a natural kind that we have not fully grasped and that only mature psychology will reveal. I expect that 'belief' will turn out to refer to some kind of information bearing inner state of a sentient being . . . but the kind of state it refers to may have only a few of the properties usually attributed to beliefs by common sense. (Lycan, 1988, pp. 31–2)

On our view, both extreme positions are implausible. As we noted earlier, the Copernican revolution did not show that the planets studied by Ptolemy do not exist. But Lavosier's chemical revolution *did* show that phlogiston does not exist. Yet on Lycan's 'very liberal view' it is hard to see why we should not conclude that phlogiston really does exist after all – it's really oxygen, and prior to Lavosier 'we were just very wrong about a lot of things.'

5 For an early and influential statement of the view that common-sense psychology is a theory, see Sellars (1956). The view has also been defended by Churchland (1970, 1979, chs 1 and 4); and by Fodor (1987, ch. 1). For the opposite view, see Wilkes (1978), Madell (1986) and Sharpe (1987).

6 Cherniak (1986, ch. 3) notes that this sort of absent mindedness is commonplace in literature and in ordinary life, and sometimes leads to disastrous consequences.

7 For sentential models, see John McCarthy (1968, 1980, 1986) and Kintsch (1974). For semantic networks, see Quillian (1966), Collins and Quillian (1972), Rumelhart et al. (1972), Anderson and Bower (1973) and Anderson (1976, 1980, ch. 4). For production systems, see Newell and Simon (1972), Newell (1973), Anderson (1983) and Holland et al. (1986).

8 For the classic discussion of the distinction between projectable and non-projectable predicates, see Goodman (1965).

9 See Broadbent (1985), Rumelhart and McClelland (1985), McClelland et al. (1986), Rumelhart et al. (1986, ch. 4), and chapters 2 and 3 of this volume.

10   The notion of program being invoked here is itself open to a pair of quite different interpretations. For the right reading, see Ramsey (1989).

11   This way of making the point about the incompatibility between connectionist models and common-sense psychology was suggested to us by Jerry Fodor.

12   This point has been urged by Daniel Dennett, among others.

13   Quite a number of people have suggested this move, including Gary Cottrell and Adrian Cussins.

14   As Lycan notes, on the common-sense notion of belief, people have lots of them 'even when they are asleep' (Lycan, 1988, p. 57).

15   Something like this objection was suggested to us by Ned Block and by Frank Jackson.

References

Anderson, J. (1976) *Language, Memory and Thought.* Hillsdale, NJ, Erlbaum.

Anderson, J. (1980) *Cognitive Psychology and Its Implications.* San Francisco, W.H. Freeman.

Anderson, J. (1983) *The Architecture of Cognition.* Cambridge, Mass., Harvard University Press.

Anderson, J. and Bower, G. (1973) *Human Associative Memory.* Washington, D.C., Winston.

Broadbent, D. (1985) A question of levels: comments on McClelland and Rumelhart. *Journal of Experimental Psychology: General* 114, 189–92.

Cherniak, C. (1986) *Minimal Rationality.* Cambridge, Mass., MIT Press/ Bradford Books.

Churchland, P. (1970) The logical character of action explanations. *Philosophical Review* 79, 214–36.

Churchland, P. (1979) *Scientific Realism and the Plasticity of Mind.* Cambridge, Cambridge University Press.

Churchland, P. (1981) Eliminative materialism and the propositional attitudes. *Journal of Philosophy* 78, (2), 69–90.

Churchland, P. (1986) Some reductive strategies in cognitive neurobiology. *Mind* 95, 281–309.

Collins, A. and Quillian, M. (1972) Experiments on semantic memory and language comprehension. In L. Gregg (ed.), *Cognition in Learning and Memory.* New York, Wiley.

Feyerabend, P. (1981) *Realism, Rationalism and Scientific Method: Philosophical Papers,* Vol. 1. Cambridge, Cambridge University Press.

Fodor, J.A. (1983) *The Modularity of Mind.* Cambridge, Mass., MIT Press.

Fodor, J.A. (1987) *Psychosemantics: the Problem of Meaning in the Philosophy of Mind.* Cambridge, Mass., MIT Press/Bradford Books.

Goodman, N. (1965) *Fact, Fiction and Forecast.* Indianapolis, Bobbs-Merrill.

Holland, J., Holyoak, K., Nisbett, R. and Thagard, P. (1986) *Induction: Processes of Inference, Learning and Discovery.* Cambridge, Mass., MIT Press/ Bradford Books.

Hooker, C. (1981) Towards a general theory of reduction. Parts I, II and III. *Dialogue* 20, 496–529.

Kintsch, W. (1974) *The Representation of Meaning in Memory*. Hillsdale, NJ, Erlbaum.

Kitcher, P. (1978) Theories, theorists and theoretical change,' *Philosophical Review* 87, 519–47.

Kitcher, P. (1982) Genes. *British Journal for the Philosophy of Science* 33, 337–359.

Kitcher, P. (1983) Implications of incommensurability. In P. Asquith and T. Nickles (eds), *Proceedings of the 1982 Biennial Meeting of the Philosophy of Science Association*, Vol. 2. East Lansing, Philosophy of Science Association.

Kitcher, P. (1984) 1953 and all that: a tale of two sciences. *Philosophical Review* 93, 335–373.

Kuhn, T. (1962) *The Structure of Scientific Revolutions*. Chicago, University of Chicago Press. 2nd edn, 1970.

Kuhn, T. (1983) Commensurability, comparability, communicability. In P. Asquith and T. Nickles (eds), *Proceedings of the 1982 Biennial Meeting of the Philosophy of Science Association*, Vol. 2. East Lansing, Philosophy of Science Association.

Lycan, W. (1988) *Judgement and Justification*. Cambridge, Cambridge University Press.

McCarthy, J. (1968) Programs with common sense. In M. Minsky (ed.) *Semantic Information Processing*. Cambridge, Mass., MIT Press.

McCarthy, J. (1980) Circumscription: a form of non-monotonic reasoning. *Artificial Intelligence*, 13, 27–39.

McCarthy, J. (1986) Applications of circumscription to formalizing common-sense knowledge. *Artificial Intelligence* 28, 89–116.

McClelland, J.L., Rumelhart, D.E. and the PDP Research Group (eds) (1986) *Parallel Distributed Processing: Explorations in the Microstructure of Cognition*. Vol. 2: *Psychological and Biological Models*. Cambridge, Mass.: MIT Press/ Bradford Books.

Madell, G. (1986) Neurophilosophy: a principled skeptic's response. *Inquiry* 29, 153–169.

Nagel, E. (1961) *The Structure of Science*. New York, Harcourt, Brace and World.

Newell, A. (1973) Production systems: models of control structures. In W. Chase (ed.), *Visual Information Processing*. New York, Academic Press.

Newell, A. and Simon, H. (1972) *Human Problem Solving*. Englewood Cliffs, NJ, Prentice Hall.

Quillian, M. (1966) *Semantic Memory*. Cambridge, Mass., Bolt, Branak and Newman.

Ramsey, W. (1989) Parallelism and functionalism. *Cognitive Science* 13, 139–144.

Rumelhart, D. and McClelland, J. (1985) Level's indeed! A response to Broadbent. *Journal of Experimental Psychology: General* 114, 193–7.

Rumelhart, D., Lindsay, P. and Norman, D. (1972) A process model for long term memory. In E. Tulving and W. Donaldson (eds), *Organization of Memory*. New York, Academic Press.

Rumelhart, D., McClelland, J.L. and the PDP Research Group (eds), (1986) *Parallel Distributed Processing: Explorations in the Microstructure of Cognition*. Vol. 1: *Foundations*. Cambridge, Mass., MIT Press/Bradford Books.

Sellars, W. (1956). Empiricism and the philosophy of mind. In H. Feigl and M. Scriven (eds), *Minnesota Studies in the Philosophy of Science*, Vol. 1 Minneapolis, University of Minnesota Press.

Schaffner, K. (1967) Approaches to reduction. *Philosophy of Science* 34.

Sharpe, R. (1987) The very idea of folk psychology. *Inquiry*, 30.

Stich, S. (1983) *From Folk Psychology to Cognitive Science*. Cambridge, Mass., MIT Press/Bradford Books.

Wilkes, K. (1978) *Physicalism*. London, Routledge and Kegan Paul.

9

Connectionist Minds

Andy Clark

Introduction

If the mind turns out to be as connectionism paints it, would the folk be refuted? Less cryptically, could the empirical discovery that the mind is a computational system of the kind known variously as connectionist or PDP (parallel distributed processing)[1] systems be in tension with any of the crucial assumptions underlying our daily use of belief and desire citing explanations?

In a lucid and provocative paper, Ramsey, Stich and Garon (chapter 8) claim to highlight just such a tension. They argue explicitly for a conditional of the form 'if a certain style of connectionist model proves psychologically accurate, then some of the central assumptions of folk psychology prove unfounded.' To be blunt, there seems to be an argument from connectionism to eliminativism about the propositional attitudes.[2]

In what follows I shall display this argument, and try to show that it depends crucially on a somewhat blinkered analysis of the processing of the computational systems concerned. In effect, I shall argue that the eliminativist argument only looks compelling if we artificially restrict the types of description of the network which we are willing to consider. There is, of course, a deeper question hereabouts. The question is, could *any* conditional which purports to take us from empirical discoveries to the falsity of the folk conception of mind turn out to be correct? I consider this question in the final section, in the context of a brief discussion of the role of conscious awareness of contentful states in folk psychology.

The strategy of the chapter is as follows: in section 1 I display some putative commitments of folk psychology. Section 2 runs through the eliminativist arguments which cite connectionism as a potential cause of the folk's fall from grace. In section 3 I look at a famous connectionist network called NETtalk and introduce the idea of higher levels of description of connectionist systems. Section 4 uses the lessons of NETtalk to dissolve the foundations of the eliminativist conditional. I end (section 5) by raising the more general issue of the tenability of *any* such conditional in the face of facts concerning our conscious experience of acting for reasons.

1   What the Folk Think

Ramsey, Stich and Garon, in chapter 8 (henceforth RS&G), depict the common-sense understanding of belief as involving a crucial commitment to what they call *propositional modularity*. The thesis of propositional modularity claims that propositional attitudes are: '*functionally discrete, semantically interpretable*, states that play a *causal role* in the production of other propositional attitudes, and ultimately in the production of behaviour' (chapter, p. 315). The attitudes are functionally discrete in so far as we are happy to speak of agents gaining or losing individual beliefs (chapter 8, p. 316). They are semantically interpretable in so far as folk psychology condones generalizations based on the semantic properties of beliefs. We group people together as all believing that so-and-so, and expect lawful regularities in their behaviour to be captured as a result. The predicate 'believes that P' is thus meant to be *projectable* in the sense of Goodman (1965). Finally, these functionally discrete, semantically interpretable states are said to play a role in the production of behaviour. An individual belief can be cited as the cause of a particular action. It is this last requirement which, in the end, turns out to afford the best chance of supporting the eliminativist case. It will be wise, then, to cite their own examples in a little detail.

The first concerns Alice, who wishes to send some e-mail, and believes she can do it from her office. She *also* wants to speak to her research assistant and believes she can do this at her office. But, and here is the crux, she *might* (according to folk psychological views about belief) go to the office as a result of *just one* of these two belief/desire complexes, both of which she possesses, and either (or both) of which would be sufficient to yield the behaviour (Chapter 8, p. 317).

The second example concerns Inspector Clouseau. Suppose Clouseau believes that the butler said that he spent the evening at the village hotel, and that he took the morning train home. And suppose Clouseau also believes (a) that the hotel is closed and (2) that the morning train is not running. Then Clouseau *could* infer (given his knowledge of what the butler said) that the butler is lying. And he could do so by either or both of two routes. He could spot the inconsistency over the hotel, or the train, or both. But it *at least makes sense*, on the folk psychological conception, to imagine that he *in fact* draws the conclusion solely by reflection on one of the two pieces of evidence. In short, 'we see common-sense psychology invoking a pair of distinct propositional attitudes, one of which is causally active on a particular occasion while the other is causally inert (Chapter 8, pp. 317–18).

In what follows, I shall use a different example which I find clearer, and which preserves all the essential structure of the authors' own cases. Consider Lesley. Lesley has the following two desires:

She desires a pint of Coopers
She desires to sit near an open fire

She also has the following long-standing beliefs:

She believes that the Dingo and Whistle serves draught Guinness
She believes that the Dingo and Whistle has an open fire

One night, while out walking, she reads and understands the pub sign 'Dingo and Whistle'. She goes in. And yet, it *makes sense* to suppose that she went in *solely* because of her desire for an open fire, *even though* the desire for Coopers, on its own, would have been sufficiently potent to cause her to enter.

The general form of the claim, then, is that someone might believe all of:

$$P, P \to Q, Q \to S, P \to R, R \to S$$

but on a given occasion *happen* to use only the Q-information in coming to the conclusion that S.

Traditional AI models, such as production systems and semantic networks, are (RS&G claim) visibly compatible with the thesis of propositional modularity. In a semantic network, for example, distinct propositions will be represented as distinct node-and-link patterns. The compatibility is even more apparent where there is storage of sentence-like symbol structures. But with highly distributed sub-symbolic connectionist models, according to RS&G, the compatibility disappears.

It would be unduly repetitious to spend much time describing this style of connectionist model here (it is done at length by Smolensky in chapter 2; see also Clark, 1989). But a few facts will help. First, the models in question represent data using densely connected networks of simple processing units connected in parallel by positively and negatively weighted links. Secondly, the *style* of representation involves *distributed superpositional* storage. Distributed here means that what might look like one item of information in a public formalism (e.g. 'Fido is a dog') is stored as a set of weights across many units, and these are sensitive to semantic regularities which are finer-grained than the public symbols. Thus 'dog' might be a pattern across banks of units which represent colour, eating habits, size, sound and so on. As representations become more and more distributed, the interpretability of individual units decreases until at the limit we cannot say what feature they encode. The use of distributed representations makes superpositional storage easy. For what this means is that *one* set of units and weights can be finely tuned so that it is able, upon being given appropriate inputs, to call up many different patterns of activation which code for various items, e.g. a network which stores 'dog' as a distributed pattern of size, sound and eating habit features could find *one* set of weights which can give appropriate patterns to represent dog, cat, calf and so on. It could also store quite orthogonal patterns (e.g. for 'bagel') (see McClelland et al., 1986, ch. 17).

Connectionist systems thus *encode* knowledge as complex patterns of positive and negative weights linking up simple processing units. These units are often arranged into three functional layers. An input layer, in which the network can be given a cue for a particular act of recall or processing; a hidden unit layer, in which the complex pattern of weights is further choreographed by units with activation thresholds which then pass activation values to a final layer of output units which express the system's considered response to the input. The system thus *expresses* its knowledge as a pattern of activation consequent upon a given input.

What is it, then, that the folk are meant to find embarrassing?

2   Two Eliminativist Arguments

RS8G offer two main arguments whose purpose is to highlight an alleged incompatibility between connectionist storage and representation and the assumptions of propositional modularity. These are:

1   An argument concerning superpositional storage and discrete causal efficacy.
2   An argument concerning natural kinds.

Let us rehearse these in turn.

Superpositional storage

We are asked to consider a network (called Network A) whose task is to answer yes or no to 16 questions. The questions are posed by giving the network a coding for a proposition as input (e.g. dogs have fur) and reading off a yes/no answer by consulting a single output unit which is interpreted to mean 'yes' if it comes on, and 'no' if it stays off. It is a simple matter to deploy a standard connectionist learning algorithm to train a network to succeed in this task. The trained network will take a vector of values across input units to code up the proposition and learn[3] a set of weights leading to and from the hidden units which will mediate just the input–output profile we desire. Thus, suppose we have 16 input units and code 'dogs' as the pattern 11000011 across the first eight and code 'have fur' as the pattern 00001111 across the last eight. The system learns to take input 1100001100001111 and give output 1 (i.e. 'yes') at the sole output unit. The learnt weights connect the 16 input units to a layer of four hidden units and on to the output unit. The important fact is that this *single* array of weights must be subtly adjusted (via an automatic learning algorithm) so as to work not just for *one* proposition but for all 16. The knowledge is thus stored superpositionally in a single, subtly orchestrated, set of weights.

At this point we are *already*, according to RS&G, starting to cross swords with folk psychology. For the folk would like to say that it is the belief that dogs have fur which causes them to say yes to the question 'do dogs have fur?' But *if* our memory was organized in the superpositional connectionist style, it seems unclear that it makes sense to say that it was *that* particular piece of stored information (rather than the rest) which caused the output. As they put it:

> The information encoded in Network A is stored holistically and distributed throughout the network. Whenever information is extracted ... *many* connection strengths, *many* biases and *many* hidden units play a role in the computation. And any particular weight or unit or bias will help to encode information about *many* different propositions. It simply makes no sense to ask whether or not the representation of a particular proposition plays a causal role in the network's computation. (chapter 8, pp. 326–7)

In other words, it is meant to be no more the case that it was the network's knowledge that dogs have paws that caused the 'yes' output than it was the case that its knowledge that, say, cats have fur, caused it. For it is all stored in a single set of weights.

Natural kinds

The second argument of RS&G I dub 'the argument from natural kinds'. It goes like this. Suppose you train a second network (B) on 17 propositions (the same 16 as network A, plus an extra one). Network B will learn a set of weights which are *globally* different from those of network A. This is because the use of superpositional storage means that the *way* you encode a proposition is crucially dependent on what *other* knowledge the network has to store.[4] The result is that a 17 proposition network must store *all 17* propositions in a way subtly different from the way the 16 proposition network stores its 16, *even if the 16 are a subset of the 17.* Contrast this with the more conventional procedure of adding a declarative representation (e.g. a sentence) to a list structure. The *lists*

List 1	List 2
dogs have fur	dogs have fur
cats have fleas	cats have fleas
	cats have fur

have a common typographic subset. And such commonality can be preserved in traditional symbolic models. But it seems to disappear in superpositional connectionist storage.

The conclusion which this is meant to force on us is that where folk psychology finds a natural psychological kind (all the believers that dogs have fur) Connectionist psychology does not – for the units-and-weights description of all the various networks which might encode such knowledge need have no common sub-part. As RS&G put it:

> The moral here is that though there are *indefinitely* many connectionist networks that represent the information that dogs have fur just as well as Network A does, these networks have no projectible features in common that are describable in the language of Connectionist theory [thus] the class of networks that might model a cognitive agent who believes that dogs have fur is not a genuine kind at all, but simply a chaotically disjunctive set. (Chapter 8, p. 329)

Finally, let us note that the examples of Alice, Clouseau and (in our case) Lesley are used to highlight the tension already suggested in Argument 1 by stressing the folk's apparent commitment to what I shall call the equipotency claim, viz.

Equipotency claim: An agent may have two long-standing beliefs which are both equipotent (both apt to cause the same piece of behaviour on a given occasion) AND YET the agent may *as a matter of fact* act on the basis of only *one* of the two beliefs.

The worry is that, given the facts about superpositional storage chronicled in Argument 1, it seems to make no sense to suppose that one of the beliefs rather than the other is active at a given moment.

I think we can capture the spirit of the eliminativist arguments in a simple picture. Imagine the following two ways of storing sentences. In the first way, you keep a discrete token of each sentence on a slip of paper in a drawer. It is then easy to see how to *use* the tokens one at a time. In the second way, you token each sentence as a pot of coloured ink. You then take a vat of water and throw in all the pots. It is now not easy to see how to use the colours separately. And worse still, the resultant overall colour will vary according to the global set of pots of ink put in. The commonality between various tokeners of the same sentence now seems lost to view. The question then is: how could a vat-and-inks (read 'superpositional connectionist') style of storage be compatible with the assumption of propositional modularity?

There are three ways out. We might just *deny* that the folk care about propositional modularity. I shan't do this. Or we might try to show that propositional modularity is safe *whatever* turns up in the head. I don't have a satisfactory way of doing that, though I discuss the matter a little in section 5. Finally, we might argue that distributed, sub-symbolic, superpositional connectionist models are actually more structured than RS&G think, and hence visibly compatible with the requirements of propositional modularity. To this end we might question the choice of a units-and-weights description as the sole description of a network for the purposes of a scientific psychology. That sounds like a good idea, and I pursue it in the next two sections.

3   The Analysis of NETtalk

Consider NETtalk. NETtalk is a connectionist network trained to negotiate the domain of text-to-speech transformations. More accurately, it takes a window of text and, letter by letter, yields a coding for phonemes which is then fed to a speech synthesizer which produces the spoken sounds. The network itself is fairly large, comprising 309 units and 18,629 connectors. The units include 80 hidden units and 55 output units corresponding to distinct phonemes (data drawn from Arbib, 1989). Network A in chapter 8, by contrast, involved only 21 units, of which four were hidden units and just one an output unit. This difference will prove important later on.

NETtalk learnt to negotiate the domain very successfully. In itself, however, such a discovery is of little value to a cognitive psychology. All we have learnt is that training can induce competence in the domain. But that much was already obvious. (After all, *children* learn to perform the task all the time!) In this sense, Connectionist cognitive science is methodologically inverted with respect to Classical AI. In Classical AI, ideally you begin by doing a thorough task analysis, and go on to construct an algorithm. Normally by the time you have an up and running system, you at least know how it works! The connectionist, by relying on training by examples, is often faced with an up and running system while still having no clear idea of how exactly it is doing the job. Connectionists, as a result, are driven to engage in a great deal of *post hoc* analysis of their networks.

Such analysis can take many forms. It may simply involve recording and pondering the spread of activation given specific inputs. It may involve artificially lesioning the networks (destroying units and/or connections) to see what patterns of disorder result. Or it may involve various kinds of statistical analysis of network activity (a nice summary of some of the techniques available is given in Smolensky, 1990). One such technique is *cluster analysis*. For NETtalk it works like this: first, give the network a variety of inputs and record the hidden unit activations and output caused by each. Now gather together all the inputs which yielded a given output phoneme, and find an *average* mediating hidden unit activation vector. Do this for each phoneme. Now use hierarchical clustering analysis to pair up the most similar vectors. Find an average for each such pair, and repeat the process (thus yielding pairs of pairs, pairs of pairs of pairs, and so on). The result is a tree structure which displays the way in which the network has learnt to structure the space of weights so as successfully to solve the problem. What is revealed is, to use Paul Churchland's phrase (Churchland, 1989) the 'similarity metric' which the weight space embodies. That is to say, which inputs, and which groups of inputs, are treated most similarly to other inputs, and other groups of inputs. The result, in the case of NETtalk, is striking. At the bottom level it grouped together items such as 'p' and 'b' inputs. A little higher up, we find a grouping of all the various soundings of 'o'. At the very top we find the system has divided the space into two large sectors, one corresponding to vowels and the other to consonants.

One further fact before we return to the arguments in RS&G: NETtalk, in common with most such systems, begins its training sequence with a random pattern of weights which are slowly corrected by the learning algorithm. The authors of NETtalk (Sejnowski and Rosenberg, 1986) gave an identical training sequence to a number of networks which began with *different* assignments of random weights. Since these in effect amount to 'knowledge already stored' (even though it's nonsense relative to the new task) the difference in random initial weights affected *how* the networks stored the learnt material. This is the same effect as was mentioned in the discussion of Network A's and Network B's storage of a particular proposition. Like Network A and Network B, the various trained-up versions of NETtalk had very different descriptions at the units-and-weights level of analysis. None the less, it turned out that all the versions of NETtalk yielded pretty much the *same* clustering profile when subjected to *post hoc* statistical analysis. In short, it was possible to discover a scientifically respectable higher level of description which unified what had seemed, *at the units-and-weights level, to be a chaotic disjunction of networks*.

The moral is that there may be higher-level descriptions which are both scientifically well grounded[5] and which capture commonalities between networks which are invisible at a units-and-weights level of analysis.

It is worth stressing that the availability of a higher level of description does not directly imply that a network is a mere implementation of a classical symbolic system. For the fact of distributed, sub-symbolic[6] encoding can still bite in so far as a system retrieves data, generalizes, interpolates and produces some error patterns (e.g. cross-talk when sub-symbolic encodings are very similar) in ways which are explicable only by appeal to its distinctively connectionist style of encoding and retrieval. In short, a network may have a cluster analysis which merits *symbolic labels* without itself being a processor of *symbols* in the Classical sense.

4 Eliminativism Revisited

Recall the argument from superpositional storage. The question was how can it make sense, given that many weights are active in causing an output and each weight participates in the storage of many items of data, to highlight a particular belief as causing an output?

Now let us shift our attention a little. Let us focus not on the active weights but upon what they are geared to *do*. What they are geared to do is to generate a pattern of hidden unit activity which then causes the output.

Consider further the *kind* of output we expect a real-belief encoding system to drive. Such a system must drive a large and subtle set of behaviours. In effect, it will be more like NETtalk (which has a large bank of output units) than the Networks A and B (which have only one unit, with two degrees of freedom). Such a system is very likely to succumb to some form of *post hoc* analysis.

Suppose it does so. In fact, let's suppose that it succumbs to a cluster analysis whose labels involve semantic entities. In such a case, we are able to untangle the superpositional storage by recourse to the higher-level descriptions of the hidden unit activation states. Thus if, on being given a certain input, the network goes into a hidden unit activation state which falls squarely into a cluster we have found reason to label 'dogs have fur', we would be warranted (*regardless* of superpositional storage) in saying that it gave a certain output because at that moment it believed that dogs have fur.

These are, of course, big ifs: if the network succumbs to such an analysis and *if* it warrants labels like 'dogs have fur'. But the move is dialectically sound. For RS&G purport to argue directly from distributed, sub-symbolic storage and representation to eliminativism. The mere *possibility* of a cluster analysis turning out as I've suggested shows that there is no direct inference of the kind claimed. For it should be obvious that if we can unpick the superpositional storage as suggested, then the arguments from natural kinds and equipotency are immediately undermined.

Thus consider once again the argument from natural kinds. The pivotal fact was the lack of any units-and-weights kind uniting nets A, B and so on. But we can now see that RS&G being unduly reductionist about well-motivated kinds. The fact that networks which are quite various at the units-and-connectivity level of description are treated as instances of a psychological kind need occasion no more surprise than the fact that an Amstrad and an Atari may, subject to running the right software, be treated as instances of a computational kind (e.g. as instantiations of a certain word-processing package). All that the variety-of-networks point establishes is that Connectionist *psychology* may need at times to avail itself of higher-level descriptions than units, connections and weights descriptions. But the example of cluster analysis shows that it is possible to reveal that a whole set of networks fall into an equivalence class defined by the way their various assignments of weights divide the spacing of possible input patterns into significant sub-spaces. Thus it would be perfectly legitimate (given the common clustering profile) to assign all the instances of NETtalk to a psychological kind *even though* they look very different at the units-and-weights level. Such a grouping might help us explain some shared error patterns and the relative difficulty of processing various inputs. Of course, as Churchland (1989) points out, for *some* explanatory purposes (e.g. predicting how future learning will affect weight distributions) the differences will make a difference. My point is only that there may be some legitimate psychological-explanatory interests which call for the higher-level grouping provided by the cluster analysis.

The basic philosophical point here is a very familiar one. Good explanations may demand the grouping together of systems which, at a low enough level of physical description, form a 'chaotically disjunctive set'. Thus economics may group an earth community and an anti-matter-earth community together as instantiating Keynesian economic systems. And we are probably all familiar with Putnam's peg-and-hole example (see Putnam, 1981) in which the explanation of variously constituted square pegs passing through square holes is to be given in terms of common higher-level properties of rigidity, solidity and so on.

Finally, there was the matter of equipotency. The worry, recall, was that it seemed to make no sense to suppose that an agent could have two beliefs, each capable of causing a given action, and yet only one of which did, as a matter of fact, cause the action. But now consider the case of Lesley's two beliefs (one about Coopers, one about the open fire). It is a simple matter to establish that the system must *in general* be capable of action which is appropriate to each belief individually (e.g. it must be capable of *some range* of actions which are beer-related and *not* fire-related). For otherwise the description of the network as knowing the two facts would be unwarranted. But this requires that the system be capable of a set of hidden unit activation patterns which are associated with the beer-belief, and a *different* (perhaps partially overlapping) set capable of powering different outputs, and associated with the fire-belief. So we can say that one belief rather than the other was active just in case, for example, we found an instance of activation in the beer-cluster and not in the fire-cluster (this kind of response, in RS&G, is accredited to Adrian Cussins and Gary Cottrell).

RS&G respond by saying that it is a mistake to identify the belief state with the transient activation state. Thus they write that:

in common-sense psychology beliefs and propositional memories are typically of substantial duration . . . An activation pattern, however, is not

an enduring state of a network . . . [for example] there is an enormous
number of . . . beliefs that you've had for years. But it makes no sense to
suppose that a network could have many activation patterns continuously
over a long period of time. At any given time a network exhibits at most
one pattern of activation. (Chapter 8, p. 331)

Suppose we accept this. The next obvious move is to suggest that we
might identify the belief not with the *transient* activation pattern but with
the long-standing *disposition* to produce that activation pattern in a given
circumstance. This move in the dialectic is credited to Ned Block and
Frank Jackson. The trouble is, of course, that it is not obvious that the
various dispositions said to correspond to various beliefs are sufficiently
extricable from one another, *qua* subvening states of the system, to
count as the 'discrete, independently causally active states that folk
psychology requires' (Chapter 8, p. 333).

But this just muddies the waters unnecessarily. Beliefs need to be
long-standing states, yes. And a belief-in-action needs to be capable of
having a functionally discrete realization, yes. But the folk are nowhere
committed to the view that the belief-in-action and the long-standing
stored state must be *physically identical*. The long-standing stored state
may be the disposition, given inputs *A–F* to propagate activation so as to
yield a pattern of hidden unit activation *P* which falls within a cluster
appropriate to 'believing that the pub has Coopers'. And the discrete
causal potency of that belief may be the power of that class of hidden
unit activation states to cause a distinctive kind of output. So we have
long-standing states and a degree of causal discretion. But what has
causal discretion is not the long-standing state but the state of activation
to which it gives rise.

Someone might, I suppose, worry that *being in a certain cluster* cannot,
properly speaking, be a cause. Thus, they might insist that what actually
does the causing must always be a *particular* hidden unit activation
pattern and hence that, if we have to appeal to clusterings of such
patterns to find analogues for semantic items, the semantic items cannot
figure in the real causal story.

But this is surely a dangerous move. For it places the philosophical
feet on a slippery slope to physics worship (and fundamental physics
worship at that). And this is radically revisionary. Chemistry, for
example, is generally regarded as a respectable special science, and yet
it is concerned to group different physical structures as instances of
chemical types and to define causal laws which apply to those types. So
unless the sceptic is willing is give up the causal efficacy of chemical
properties too, he or she would be unwise to object to the very *idea* of
higher-level constructs figuring in genuine causal claims.

In general, then, it seems as if the invocation of higher-level descriptions of hidden unit activity patterns may provide for the kind of causal discretion RS&G require. There is, however, a class of cases (invoked in a dialectic towards the end of Chapter 8), which may still look problematic. These are the cases (call them lemma-belief cases) where a particular belief is said to cause a particular belief, which in turn causes an action.

The trouble here is simple. Our account provides a single locus of discrete, causally-active belief states, viz. the locus consisting of a hidden unit activation pattern. But in some cases we seem to want two (or more) such loci. Thus consider the case of Clouseau who has the long-standing beliefs (dispositionally analysed)

$$p \rightarrow q, q \rightarrow s$$
$$p \rightarrow r, r \rightarrow s$$

and learns that p. Suppose we want to say of Clouseau that:

(a) he infers s using *only* the q-information;
and
(b) his belief that s then causes him to perform an action A.

It now looks as if the hidden unit states resulting from input p need to fall simultaneously into the q-cluster and the s-cluster variety. But the network cannot be in both states at once.

The answer here is to introduce a notion of *recurrency*. A recurrent network is one which can cycle an output state back as an input state and continue processing. Now *any* good model of the belief system must allow that belief can play two roles. One is to mediate between perception and action. The other is to mediate between belief and belief. This means that the output states and input states must be capable of taking belief states as *data* too. In which case the answer to the single locus worry is to invoke a single locus used twice in a serial process. Thus in the Clouseau case we would have input p yielding hidden unit activation falling into the q-cluster sector, which causes output meaning *that* q. This is then cycled back as input which yields activation falling into the s-sector and causing action A.

In sum, it seems that, contrary to the eliminativists' conditional argument, distributed sub-symbolic models *can* allow for individual beliefs to be discretely active[7] in causing behaviour and other beliefs. They can do so if we adopt the following analysis:

1   Long-standing states of believing that p = the networks disposition, given apt input, to produce hidden unit activation states falling into a cluster[8] which warrants the label p.
2   Active states of believing that p = patterns of hidden unit activation falling into the p-cluster.
3   Active lemma-belief states = as (2) but realized in a recurrent network.

5   Semantic Facts, Consciousness and Fodor's Metaphysical Prejudice

The bulk of this chapter has amounted to an unabashed empirical bet that any system complex enough to count as a believer will reveal (under some *post hoc* analysis) semantically clustered patterns of activation. Such reasonably complex models as we have available (e.g. NETtalk) lend support to this contention.

But suppose I were to lose the empirical bet? Suppose that, as it happens, there is NO well-motivated non-semantic level of description of the belief encoding networks which unearths a scientific kind in any way corresponding to any of the semantic kinds fixed on by belief-ascriptions. Then we've got trouble. There are (as far as I can see) just three options. Either we accept eliminativism (there are no beliefs and desires), or we accept a modified eliminativism (the belief/desire classificatory scheme has value in our daily lives, but beliefs are not *really* causes), or we attempt some sort of radical defence in which the *purely semantic* shows up as genuinely causal.

For a pure semantic fact (the fact that F believes that P) to be genuinely causal it must be the case that there can be true causal explanations which cite the belief despite there being no projectible non-semantic description of the system in which some internal state turns out to *be* the system's belief that P, and to have causal powers in the usual, non-semantic way.

(Notice that considerations concerning the holism of belief and desire, though persuasive and important, do nothing to establish this radical possibility. We can accept that an internal state can *count* as the belief that P only in the context of other possible beliefs (and even world states) and *still* insist that to have causal powers that belief requires a causally active token which is also identifiable as a token of some non-semantic kind.)

One philosopher who is explicitly opposed to the possibility of purely, semantic facts is Jerry Fodor. He writes:

I'd better 'fess up to a metaphysical prejudice ... I don't believe that there are intentional mechanisms. That is, I don't believe that contents *per se* determine causal roles. In consequence it's got to be possible to tell the whole story about mental causation (the whole story about the implementation of the generalizations that belief-desire psychologies articulate) without referring to the intentional properties of the mental states that such generalizations subsume. (Fodor, 1987 p. 139)

Such opposition seems plausible (a display of solid, materialist common sense) at least until we reflect that the semantic (intentional) properties of some mental states *seem* to have their causal powers in virtue of entering into our conscious awareness. Thus, often enough I perform some action consequent upon rehearsing a reason 'in my head'. The idea I wish to flirt with is then this: that beings capable of the conscious rehearsal of reasons have available a resource (viz. that conscious rehearsal) which can allow for the discrete causal efficacy of beliefs *regardless* of any stories about the underlying mode of storage and retrieval of data. Dualists (to take an extreme case) could hold both that spirit is undifferentiated *and* that individual consciously rehearsed beliefs are discrete causes of actions! In short, what makes it the case that my belief that *P* caused action *A* might be that it was my consciousness of *P*, *however realized*, that led to my *A*-ing.

Likewise, regarding the issue of psychological kinds, a friend of consciousness might say that the commonality between all the variously constituted believers that *P* just *consists in* the fact that an otherwise wild disjunction of physical constitutions all share the property of presenting the world to the beings concerned as being *P*-ish.

The appeal to consciousness threatens, however, to overvalue our conscious claims about our own reasons for acting. We do not want to find ourselves forced to say that the alcoholic, who sincerely insists that she went into the pub purely on the basis of her belief about the fire, is thereby *right*. I do not know how to deal with cases of self-deception. A second reason for being dissatisfied with the appeal to consciousness is that it will not do if we seek causal discretion for belief contents which are not consciously rehearsed.

What should NOT incline us to reject the account, surprisingly, is any bed-rock commitment to a materialistic worldview. For we may grant that conscious contents can provide a locus of causal discretion while still expecting, from a mature cognitive science, an account of how conscious awareness of reasons is possible. The materialistic account of the causal discretion of reasons may thus rest on an explanatory dog-leg. But this is hardly tantamount to giving up on materialism itself.

The attraction of the invocation of consciousness is that it rules out eliminativism at a stroke. But the drawbacks are still considerable. It *feels* deeply unexplanatory; it does not account for the causal discretion of non-conscious contentful states; it seems impotent in the face of self-deception. But the only *other* sure-fire way of ruling out eliminativism is (as Martin Davies, 1991, likes to remind us) to endorse some form of behaviourism. This option often seems less attractive than the eliminativism it is meant to exorcize.

Conclusions

RS&G claim that a certain class of connectionist model is not compatible with propositional modularity. The distinguishing features of this class are (a) the distributed encoding of information across many weights; (b) the lack of symbolic interpretation of individual hidden units; and (c) the models' intended status as distinctive cognitive models (see chapter 8, p. 320). But the alleged incompatibility of such models with the central (discrete causal efficacy) assumption of propositional modularity may, we argued, be an artefact of a restricted descriptive vocabulary. If we are forced to consider only a units-and-weights style description of networks, the compatibility is indeed elusive. But well-motivated higher levels of description are not only possible, they are, as the case of NETtalk shows, actual. To generate even a *prima facie* tension with propositional modularity, RS&G would need to demon-strate that a network, complex enough to count as encoding beliefs, would not succumb in any semantically structured way to such higher-level analysis. We found no reason to believe this, and some reason to disbelieve it.

The shadow of eliminativism, however remains. For as philosophers we can always ask: well, just *suppose* that mental processing turned out to be completely resistant to all attempts to find a well-motivated scientific description which follows the lines of the folk individuation of mental states. In such a case I am currently unsure what to say. It is just possible that an appeal to the conscious experience of the believer might save the day. But I can find no fully satisfactory version of such an argument.

What, then, of the eliminativist's conditional claim? The claim was that '*if* connectionist hypotheses of the sort we will sketch turn out to be right, so too will eliminativism about propositional attitudes' chapter 8, p. 312. And the answer can now be seen to depend on how we read the phrase 'of the sort we will sketch'. If this means 'distributed, superpositional networks intended as cognitive models', then the conditional fails. For some such models (viz. those which succumb to higher-level analyses such as cluster analysis) need be in no way suggestive of eliminativism. But if it really means 'networks in which *no* non-semantic description traces the lines of our folk individuation of mental states', we can do no better than an open verdict.

Acknowledgements

Thanks to Martin Davies and Michael Morris for useful comments on earlier versions of this chapter. The present text was prepared during a visiting fellowship in the Department of Philosophy, The Research School of Social Sciences, Australian National University and was presented at a meeting of the Aristotelian Society held at 5–7 Tavistock Place, London WC1, on 15 January 1990. I am especially grateful to Frank Jackson, Kim Sterelny and Fiona Cowie for their helpful comments.

Notes

1 The classic account of these models is given in McClelland et al. (1986) and Rumelhart et al. (1986). An influential account of the meta-theory and broader implications of the models is found in Smolensky chapter 2. Classical critical commentaries are Fodor and Pylyshyn chapter 3 and Pinker and Prince (1988). A relatively accessible treatment of all these developments is Clark (1989).

2 Of course, any such argument could equally be used (if we are sure that folk psychology is correct) as an *a priori* argument *against* connectionism.

3 Connectionist systems are often trained on examples rather than explicitly programmed. That is, instead of the theorist setting all of the many inter-unit weights, the system learns (by various automatic procedures) to assign weights which will generate the input-output profile suggested by the training examples.

4 This is really quite intuitive. The network must learn a single set of weights capable of driving all the required behaviour. One option, given enough hidden units, is to learn a kind of look-up table with unique sets of weights implicated in each piece of behaviour. But in general it is better to restrict the number of hidden units, hence forcing the network to use overlapping processing routes. The overlap means that the learnt weights must be carefully orchestrated in a way dictated by the global behaviour required. The result is that a net storing 17 propositions exhibits small but widely distributed weight differences to one storing 16, or 18, or 19 and so on.

5 As Graham Priest has pointed out, one can always find *some* mathematical function which will group together, in a principled way, any arbitrary set of states. But the point about cluster analysis is that it groups network states *by causal powers*. For it groups hidden unit activity patterns by reference to what outputs (phonemes) they produce.

6   NETtalk is not the best example here, since the symbolic/sub-symbolic distinction is elusive if we are not representing ordinary semantic items (like dogs, cats and bagels). But the general point is unaffected.

7   Notice that the account proposed does not establish the *other* part of the propositional modularity claim, viz. that beliefs can be acquired and lost individually. Perhaps this is all to the good, for it is less clear, as David Lewis has pointed out, that the folk are really committed to this. Lewis here suggested the example of geographical beliefs which, when gained, seem to have simultaneous effects upon other geographical beliefs.

8   Or some other construct used for the *post hoc*, higher-level analysis of networks. For a run down of the possibilities see Smolensky (1990).

References

Arbib, M.A. (1989) Notes from lectures on brain theory and artificial intelligence. Excerpted from *The Metaphorical Brain: an Introduction to Schema Theory and Neural Networks*. New York, Wiley.

Churchland, P. (1989) On the nature of theories: a neurocomputational perspective. In *The Neurocomputational Perspective*. Cambridge, Mass., MIT Press.

Clark, A. (1989) *Microcognition: Philosophy, Cognitive Science and Parallel Distributed Processing*. Cambridge, Mass., MIT Press/Bradford Books.

Davies, M. (1991) Aunty's own argument of the language of thought'. In W. Ramsey, D. Rumelhart and S. Stich (eds) *Philosophy and Connectionist Theory*. Hillsdale, NJ, Erlbaum.

Fodor, J.A. (1987) *Psychosemantics*. Cambridge, Mass., MIT Press.

Goodman, N. (1965) *Fact, Fiction and Forecast*. Indianapolis, Bobbs-Merrill.

McClelland, J.L., Rumelhart, D.E. and the PDP Research Group (eds) (1986) *Parallel Distributed Processing: Explorations in the Microstructure of Cognition*. Vol. 2: *Psychological and Biological Models*. Cambridge, Mass., MIT Press/ Bradford Books.

Pinker, S. and Prince, A. (1988) On language and connectionism. *Cognition* 28, 73–193.

Putnam, H. (1981) Reductionism and the nature of mental states. In J. Haugeland (ed.), *Mind Design*. Cambridge, Mass., MIT Press.

Rumelhart, D.E., McClelland, J.L. and the PDP Research Group (eds) (1986) *Parallel Distributed Processing: Explorations in the Microstructure of Cognition*. Vol. 1: *Foundations*. Cambridge, Mass., MIT Press/Bradford Books.

Sejnowski, T. and Rosenberg, C. (1986) NET talk: a parallel network that learns to read aloud. Johns Hopkins University, Electrical Engineering and Computer Science Technical Report, JHU/EEC-86/01.

Smolensky, P. (1990) Representation in connectionist networks. *Intellectica* 9–10, 127–65.

10

On the Projectable Predicates of Connectionist Psychology: A Case for Belief

Paul Smolensky

1 The Projectable Features of Connectionist Psychology

The moral here is that though there are *indefinitely* many connectionist networks that represent the information that dogs have fur just as well as Network A does, these networks have no projectable features in common that are describable in the language of Connectionist theory. From the point of view of the connectionist model builder, the class of networks that might model a cognitive agent who believes that dogs have fur is not a genuine kind at all, but simply a chaotically disjunctive set. Commonsense psychology treats the class of people who believe that dogs have fur as a psychologically natural kind; Connectionist psychology does not. (chapter 8, p. 329)

1.1   The false presupposition

In this passage, Ramsey, Stich and Garon (chapter 8, henceforth RS&G) make a pivotal claim, in terms they credit to Jerry Fodor. Lurking within is a false presupposition which is embraced by proponents of two opposite viewpoints on the relation of Connectionist to Classical psychology – by RS&G, endorsing eliminativism, and by Fodor and Pylyshyn (F&P, chapter 3), endorsing implementationalism. When the false presupposition is exposed and pursued in the context of RS&G's argument, the result is evidence for neither extreme view, but rather for a more complex and interesting position.

The mistaken presupposition in the passage from RS&G is revealed in the phrases 'projectable features . . . describable in the language of Connectionist theory'; 'not a genuine kind . . . but a chaotically disjunctive set'; not a 'natural kind' in 'Connectionist psychology'. At least to someone who has been actively involved for years in the effort to construct referents worthy of the names 'Connectionist theory' and 'Connectionist psychology', to penetrate the mysterious workings of connectionist networks and uncover their 'projectable features', to design more sophisticated networks embodying more cognitively power-ful and relevant 'natural kinds' – at least to such a reader, it comes rather as a shock to hear that one can already *presuppose* such notions, that one can simply display a connectionist network and presume to immediately glean from its surface the notions Connectionist theory does and doesn't provide to Connectionist psychology. Even a casual acquaintance with the connectionist literature must raise the worry that such a presupposition might be rather a dangerous one. As RS&G themselves urge: 'it is early days yet' (p. 312) – not just for the empirical discipline of Connectionist psychology, but also for the formal theory of connectionist computation.

Indeed, RS&G themselves identify my line of objection:

> *Objection (2):* Our models do not really violate the principle of propositional modularity, since the propositions the system has learned are coded in functionally discrete ways, though this may not be obvious.

> We've heard this objection elaborated along three quite different lines. The first line – let's call it Objection (2a) – notes that functionally discrete coding may often be *very* hard to notice, and cannot be expected to be visible on casual inspection . . .
> *Reply (2a):* It is a bit difficult to come to grips with this objection, since what the critic is proposing is that in models like those we have constructed there *might* be some covert functionally discrete system of propositional encoding that has yet to be discovered. In response to this we must concede that indeed there might. We certainly have no argument that even comes close to demonstrating that the discovery of such a covert functionally discrete encoding is impossible. Moreover, we concede that if such a covert system were discovered, then our argument would be seriously undermined. (chapter 8, p. 33)

Indeed, the point of this chapter is precisely to show explicitly that not only does such a 'covert' system of encoding exist – it is in fact just what is required to *explain* the behavior of the kind of networks that RS&G

consider. In order to uncover this covert system, we need to take due mathematical consideration of the following central principle (Smolensky, 1986, and chapter 2 of this volume), which will be invoked frequently in this paper:

Semantic level principle: Semantically interpretable aspects of distributed connectionist models reside at the higher level defined by activation *patterns* or *vectors*, and weight vectors – not at the lower level of individual units and connections. That is, semantic elements are *non-local*: individual semantic elements are defined over shared, spatially distributed, regions of the network.

In this chapter, I will show how, when this principle is applied to the network on which RS&G base their case, a 'covert' knowledge representation system emerges. I will argue, with Objection (2), that while it is not at all obvious from staring at individual units and connections, analyzing these networks at the higher level of activation and weight vectors leads to a Connectionist version of the notion of belief. And this notion has some, but not all, of the critical properties of *propositional modularity* which RS&G argue are just the features of folk psychological beliefs that render them targets for elimination by Connectionist psychology. (This notion can in fact be viewed as a specific formalization of an idea which RS&G articulate as Objection (2c): Connectionist beliefs are dispositions to produce activation patterns.)

The semantic level principle asserts that semantic notions in connectionist networks are abstract notions that must be formulated in terms of activation and weight *vectors*. The Connectionist notion of belief we will develop exemplifies this principle nicely. In its first formalization, *C-belief*, a Connectionist belief will be specified by a region within the space of weight vectors: a network holds a C-belief if its weight vector lies in that region. Whether a network holds a particular C-belief is, in general, dependent on *all* the individual weights in the network: on the entire weight vector. Different C-beliefs reside in the same vector of weights. In the second formalization, *L-belief*, one particular weight vector in the region defining a C-belief is singled out; a network holding this L-belief has this particular vector as one of the components of that network's weight vector. Both the notions of C-belief and L-belief possess one of RS&G's crucial properties of propositional modularity: functional discreteness. Different C- or L-beliefs have discrete identities – not in the sense of being physically localized to different parts of the network, but in the sense of being discretely identifiable and combinable *in the more abstract space of weight vectors* where semantically interpretable elements must be sought, according to the semantic level principle. On the other hand, C- and L-beliefs do not individually play the kind of *casual* role that their Classical counterparts do.

Pressure to develop Connectionist theoretical constructs to do at least some of the work of Classical beliefs also stems from another objection to RS&G's argument, one which they curiously don't address. RS&G's claim is that if a class of connectionist models is correct, then they constitute an ontologically radical theory shift in which folk psychological belief is eliminated. But *eliminated in favor of what?* The parade examples of eliminativism are cases where a notion such as caloric was eliminated in favor of a much richer and more formally elaborated set of concepts such as those of the kinetic theory of heat. With such admirable scientific progress as our guiding inspiration, we are led to expect that the primitive notion of folk psychological belief is to be eliminated in favor of a rich and formally elaborated set of concepts, concepts providing a more adequate explanation of basically the same problems that were formerly solved by Granny's humble folk psychology. These new concepts define the 'projectable features of Connectionist theory' and the 'natural kinds of Connectionist psychology'. *Where are they?* They are certainly not easily found in RS&G, and, I maintain, for very good reason – by and large, such concepts are only now being developed. Presumably, to Fodor, 'Connectionist psychology' co-refers with 'Humean associationism', and the projectable features of Connectionist theory are basically those recognized by Hume. This is not the image of glorious scientific progress evoked by the parade examples for eliminativism. So presumably RS&G envision some other concepts embodied in connectionist psychology. RS&G don't say what these concepts are, just what they are not: folk psychological beliefs, as characterized by the properties of propositional modularity.

My reply takes as its starting point not the shared presupposition of RS&G and Fodor – that we know what the projectible predicates of Connectionist theory are – but precisely its negation. In effect, I ask not what Connectionist theory can do for (to?) belief, but what belief can do for Connectionist theory. At least in the class of networks RS&G consider, I show that Connectionist theory *requires* a concept like belief, and that indeed such a concept can be constructed using existing theory.

What's at stake in this argument is the nature of the relation between the connectionist and classical cognitive architectures. If RS&G's argument were correct, the results, as they point out (p. 312), would be (a) that proponents of the cognitive architecture represented by the connectionist models RS&G consider should accept the eliminativist conclusion, at least as regards Classical belief, and (b) that those who find such an eliminativist conclusion untenable should reject this connectionist cognitive architecture and accept instead, for example, the implementationalist conclusion that the only viable connectionist architecture is one which implements the classical architecture.

However, the particular way that RS&G's argument will be shown to fail will lead to quite a different conclusion. Both the eliminativist and implementationalist conclusions will turn out to be unwarranted. *Contra* RS&G-style eliminativism, the concept of Connectionist belief we will construct will share several important properties of propositional modularity with its folk psychological cousin, and the theory shift is therefore not ontologically radical in the sense claimed by RS&G. *Contra* implementationalism, the Connectionist notion of belief will differ none the less in important ways from its Classical relative. *Contra* both eliminativism *and* implementationalism, the result will be that, by taking seriously a Classical notion, we actually advance connectionist theory – and at the same time, connectionist theory substantially revises that Classical notion. And when the relation between the connectionist and Classical notion of belief is examined in more detail, the relation between the connectionist and classical cognitive architecture which is exemplified will turn out to be the intermediate position between eliminativism and implementationalism proposed as 'The Proper Treatment of Connectionism' in chapter 2, adding new support for recent developments in that theoretical framework.

RS&G's argument resides in the philosophy of (cognitive) science; it purports to analyze the nature of a shift from folk psychological to Connectionist theory. Thus it should come as no surprise that the central concern in this chapter is with the actual content of Connectionist theory. The overarching fact is that developing a satisfactory theory of connectionist computation is extremely difficult, and while some progress has been made, such a theory still seems far off. Thus, for most kinds of connectionist networks, it is *impossible* to determine how Connectionist theory relates to Classical theory, simply because the theory of that kind of network is so weak. So it becomes critical what kind of connectionist model we choose to base our assessment of RS&G on. If we choose state-of-the-art connectionist cognitive models, the theory is so underdeveloped that no conclusions are possible. In order to have anything interesting to say, we must turn to simpler models where there is at least *some* existing theory. This would appear to be the spirit in which RS&G chose their model, although their argument is in fact oblivious to what Connectionist theory actually has to say concerning their model. As we will see, their model falls on the current frontier of network theory, and to the extent that the theory exists, it would seem to argue the incorrectness of RS&G's conclusions.

For a more definitive result, I prefer to focus on a model slightly simpler than RS&G's, a kind of network for which the theory is now quite complete. There, where we actually *have* a Connectionist theory on which to test RS&G's analysis, we can clearly identify its failures. Whether the conclusions based on Connectionist theory that actually exists are likely to survive in the face of future developments in Connectionist theory is a subject of speculation taken up in the conclusion (section 5).

1.2 Plan of the chapter

RS&G's argument hinges on a connectionist model which I'll call *RSGnet*. In my reply, I will study a simplification of RSGnet called *RSGnet$_0$*, defined in section 3. My reply depends crucially on *explaining* the behavior of networks like RSGnet; developing the necessary explanatory notions of *C-belief* and *L-belief* is much more straightforward for the simplified network RSGnet$_0$. The Appendix explicitly analyses the original RSGnet, showing how to apply the notions of C- and L-belief in explaining the more complex network (a *complete* explanation is not carried out, and is probably not possible until further progress has been made in Connectionist theory).

My argument develops as follows; each claim is labelled by the number of the section where it is presented:

2   Connectionist explanation requires *some* technical notion to do the work of belief. Two strategies exist for deriving such a notion: weight analysis and learning analysis.

3   Pursuing these two strategies within Connectionist theory, through analysis of the simplified network RSGnet$_0$, leads to derivation of two Connectionist formalizations of the notion of belief: C-belief and L-belief.

4   C- and L-beliefs possess some, but not all, of RS&G's properties of propositional modularity.

5   *Conclusion:* C- and L-beliefs show that RS&G have actually set up an argument supporting the 'proper treatment of connectionism', not eliminativism or implementationalism.

6   P.S. 1, response to a worry: It *is* legitimate to replace RSGnet by RSGnet$_0$; RSGnet$_0$ is just as valid as RSGnet as an illustration of RS&G's class of connectionist models.

7   P.S. 2, Appendix: C- and L-beliefs also play important roles in explaining RSGnet, although current theory may not suffice to fully explain RSGnet.

2 The Need for Connectionist Belief

RSGnet correctly judges the truth values of a set of (encoded) propositions. Now to what extent is this an *explanation* of a cognitive capacity? On the face of it, we have replaced one black box – the human reasoner we want to understand – with another black box, RSGnet. This constitutes progress to the extent that we can better inspect and understand RSGnet – which, after all, we designed ourselves – than we can the original human subject. As McCloskey (1992) argues, in this important respect, connectionist models are like animal models in biology. But the model then constitutes an *object* of analysis, not an analysis in and of itself; the network plays the role not of *explanans*, but rather of *explanandum* – a much simpler one, of course, than the original human case. The question then is, how can we *explain* the fact that RSGnet correctly judges the truth values of a set of propositions?

The pretheoretic instinct is to stare at the weights in RSGnet in search of the explanation: after all, it is these weights that encode the network's knowledge. RS&G encourage this instinct through illustrations such as their figures 8.4–8.8, each of which provides plenty of weights for contemplation. The result of such an atheoretic adventure is, of course, obvious at the outset: mystery and wonder that the network behaves correctly – not the least glimmer of insight.

So let's get serious. There is no need for pretheoretic eye-glazing given that the theory of computation in such networks has been underway for several decades; indeed, were this not the case, the technical means for actually creating RSGnet in the first place would not have existed. The business of section 3 is to bring to bear rather simple mathematical analysis of the weights in networks such as RSGnet, enabling the desired explanation. This explanatory strategy will be called *weight analysis*. But first we must consider an appealing alternative strategy.

Rather than turning to the weights themselves for explanation, we might turn to the learning process which produced those weights. This *learning analysis* would proceed to explain the behavior of RSGnet as follows: RSGnet was trained by presenting a set of propositions as input, each together with its correct truth value. The back-propagation learning algorithm was used to slowly move the initial weights to a set of final numerical values which associate the correct output to each of the training inputs. This explains the ultimate performance of the network.

There are two shortcomings of this putative explanation by learning analysis. The first, of course, is that it just propagates the burden of explanation back from the weights in RSGnet itself to the general learning algorithm, back-propagation, which produced them. We need now to explain why, in general, back-propagation produces weights which correctly associate outputs to inputs. Unfortunately – very unfortunately! – no such explanation is to be had; – this despite the truly remarkable success of back-propagation which rightfully earns it the status of a technical revolution in Connectionist theory (Chauvin and Rumelhart, forthcoming). For it is theoretically impossible for a learning algorithm to possess the power to train *any* network to correctly associate *any* set of inputs and outputs. For any given network architecture (set of units and connections with unspecified weights), there are always sets of input/output pairs which cannot possibly be correctly computed by that network: – no learning procedure can generate a correct set of weights, because no such weights exist. Thus there is no sound explanation of RSGnet which adverts only to properties of its training. At the very least, it must be shown that the training patterns and network architecture are *compatible*: that there is some correct set of weights for back-propagation to produce. And this in turn requires weight analysis. In fact, while such a demonstration of compatibility is *necessary*, it is unfortunately not *sufficient*, since, in networks like RSGnet with hidden units, back-propagation is not guaranteed to find a correct set of weights even when such weights provably exist. The same is true of every other algorithm for training networks with hidden units, as far as I know. So learning analysis is doubly difficult to carry through. First one needs to do weight analysis anyway, to demonstrate the compatibility of the network and training patterns; then, one needs to show that the network/training pattern combination is one for which back-propagation will succeed in constructing a correct set of weights. I am not aware of *any* means for actually carrying out the second step; if at all possible, it is surely extremely difficult.

In addition, learning analysis has another deficiency: even if successfully carried through, by itself, it would only explain why the network correctly performs *on its training set*. But in general, we also need to explain the network's performance on inputs it was *not* trained on – its generalization capacity. RS&G point out, for example, that RSGnet correctly generalizes to two propositions it was not trained on (chapter 8, p. 330) – *prima facie* evidence, at least, of some capacity for inference, as opposed to mere memorization. Explaining generalization capacity via the learning strategy is even more difficult than explaining correct behavior on the training set. There exist powerful methods for estimating the *probability* of correct generalization, but these techniques cannot explain particular patterns or instances of correct or incorrect generalization, for examples, why RSGnet correctly generalizes in the particular case of the two propositions RS&G cite: yet such explanation seems critical for claims of what knowledge is actually present in RSGnet. And, as we will see, weight analysis does provide means for studying generalization.

The strategy of weight analysis will provide considerable explanatory power, but like learning analysis, it is difficult to carry out. The purpose of the preceding remarks is simply to dispel any hopes that learning analysis can finesse the difficulties with a wave of a magic back-propagation wand. Weight analysis is difficult enough: learning analysis is even worse.

3   Deriving Connectionist Belief in RSGnet$_0$

I now develop the technical core of my argument: that when weight and learning analysis are employed to *explain* the behavior of nets like RSGnet, two Connectionist formalizations of the notion of belief emerge: C-belief and L-belief. Since the construction of these notions takes the semantic level principle as its starting point, C- and L-belief must be defined using notions from vector space theory (for basic tutorials on the use of vector concepts in Connectionist theory, see Jordan, 1986; Smolensky, 1986).

3.1   Weight analyis and C-beliefs

We will start this analysis by simplifying RSGnet in three ways, yielding a net we'll call *RSGnet$_0$*. In the original RSGnet, propositions are judged true or false if the output is sufficiently close to 1 or 0, respectively; our first modification is simply to adopt the interpretation that a proposition is judged true or false by RSGnet$_0$ if its output is positive or negative, respectively. (For technical reasons, this actually makes the transition back to RSGnet easier.) The second simplification is to eliminate the hidden units and connect each input unit directly to the output unit. The final simplification is to replace RSGnet's non-linear output unit with a simpler, linear unit, which computes its activation value simply by adding up, for each input unit, the activation of that input unit times the weight of its connection to the output unit. The result is a simple network illustrated in figure 10.1.

The output of RSGnet$_0$ is easily written down as a function of its input. Let n denote the number of input units, and let the activities of

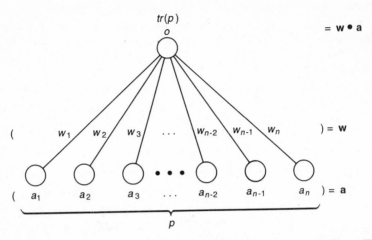

Figure 10.1   RSGnet$_0$, a simplification of RS&G's network RSGnet. The input is an activity vector **a** representing a proposition p, the output o is interpreted as a truth value, the correct value of which is $tr(p)$. The output is computed from **a** and the weight vector **w** as $o = \mathbf{w} \cdot \mathbf{a}$.

these input units be denoted $a_1, a_2, \ldots, a_n$. Each of the input units has a connection to the output unit, and the weights[1] of these connections will be denoted by $w_1, w_2, \ldots, w_n$. The output unit's value, o, is then given by the following equation:

(1) $o = w_1 a_1 + w_2 a_2 + \ldots + w_n a_n$

Equation (1) can be written even more transparently by grouping together all the weights into the *weight vector* $\mathbf{w} = (w_1, w_2, \ldots, w_n)$ and all the activities into an *activity vector* $\mathbf{a} = (a_1, a_2, \ldots, a_n)$. Now equation (1) can be rewritten:

(2) $o = \mathbf{w} \cdot \mathbf{a}$

The right-hand-side of (2) is nothing but an abbreviation defined by the right-hand-side of (1). But (2) is important because it is both conceptually and technically essential to reason about connectionist networks at the level of the *vectors* **w** and **a**, for it is at this higher level of aggregation, not the level of individual connections w_i and activations a_i, that the semantically relevant properties of connectionist networks lie, according to the semantic level principle. Henceforth, *all* analysis will concern the vectors **w** and **a** – their individual elements w_i and a_i will not figure at all.

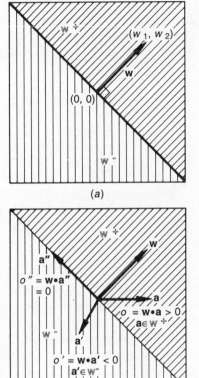

(a)

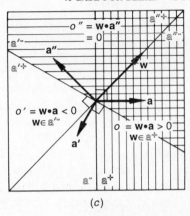

(c)

(b)

Figure 10.2 Diagrams of the state space of $RSGnet_0$ in the visualizable, two-dimensional case of two input units ($n = 2$). (a) The weight vector **w** separates space into two half-spaces $\mathbf{w}^+$ and $\mathbf{w}^-$. (b) The net with weight vector **w** produces a positive output given the input **a** since $\mathbf{a} \in \mathbf{w}^+$; negative for $\mathbf{a}'$; and 0 for $\mathbf{a}''$. (c) The same results as in (b), but with the roles of **w** and **a** reversed: the output for **a** is positive since $\mathbf{w} \in \mathbf{a}^+$, etc.

We can think of both the vectors **w** and **a** as points in an n-dimensional *state space*; **w**, for example, is the point with coordinates (w_1, w_2, . . ., w_n). Alternatively, it is sometimes useful to think of **w** as the *arrow* leading to the point (w_1, w_2, . . ., w_n) from the origin (0, 0, . . ., 0). This arrow cuts the entire state space into two half-spaces, as follows. There is a plane through the origin which is perpendicular to **w**.[2] The arrow **w** lies on one side of this plane; the half-space on the same side of this plane will be called the *positive half-space* determined by **w**, written $\mathbf{w}^+$. The other side of the plane is analogously the negative half-space $\mathbf{w}^-$ (see figure 10.2a).

With these higher-level concepts, we can give the expression **w·a** in (2) a revealing geometrical characterization. It turns out that **w·a** (and hence o) is positive if **a** lies in the positive half-space determined by **w**, $\mathbf{w}^+$; **w·a** is negative if **a** lies in the negative half-space determined by **w**, $\mathbf{w}^-$; and **w·a** is zero exactly when **a** lies on the plane separating these two half-spaces, the plane through the origin perpendicular to **w** (see figure 10.2b). This is useful for understanding how a network with a given weight vector **w** responds to different input activity vectors **a**.

An alternative perspective is useful for analyzing learning, where $\mathbf{w}$ is unknown while the training activity patterns $\mathbf{a}$ are given. The operation $\mathbf{w} \cdot \mathbf{a}$ is symmetric in the two vectors $\mathbf{w}$ and $\mathbf{a}$ ($\mathbf{w} \cdot \mathbf{a} = \mathbf{a} \cdot \mathbf{w}$), as is obvious from its definition (1). Thus, reversing the roles of $\mathbf{w}$ and $\mathbf{a}$, we can alternatively characterize the output $o = \mathbf{w} \cdot \mathbf{a}$ as positive or negative depending on whether $\mathbf{w}$ lies in the positive or negative half-space $\mathbf{a}^+$ or $\mathbf{a}^-$ determined by $\mathbf{a}$ (see figure 10.2c).

Now we can consider RSGnet$_0$ as an evaluator of propositions. Let a proposition p be encoded as an input activation vector $\mathbf{p}$. Then RSGnet$_0$'s output is, by (2), $o = \mathbf{w} \cdot \mathbf{p}$. If o is positive, p is judged true; if o is negative, false; if o is 0, then RSGnet$_0$ refuses to decide. Given the geometric interpretations of the two preceding paragraphs, we have:

(3)   The proposition p is judged true if its encoding $\mathbf{p}$ lies in $\mathbf{w}^+$, or, equivalently, if $\mathbf{w}$ lies in $\mathbf{p}^+$; p is judged false if $\mathbf{p}$ lies in $\mathbf{w}^-$, or, equivalently, if $\mathbf{w}$ lies in $\mathbf{p}^-$.

Given a set of training propositions $P = \{p, q, r, \ldots\}$, and a corresponding set of truth values $\{\text{tr}(p), \text{tr}(q), \text{tr}(r), \ldots\}$, (3) now clearly tells us what is required for RSGnet$_0$ to correctly judge each proposition π in P as having the truth value $\text{tr}(\pi)$: the weight vector $\mathbf{w}$ encoding the network's knowledge must simultaneously meet all the following conditions:

(4) $\mathbf{w}$ must lie in the positive half-space $\pi^+ =$ if $\text{tr}(\pi) = $ TRUE, and in the negative half-space π^- if $\text{tr}(\pi) = $ FALSE. (There is one such requirement for each proposition $\pi = p, q, r, \ldots$ in the training set P.)

Let's call the intersection of all the half-spaces referred to in (4) the *solution space*. If the solution space is non-empty – if all the half-spaces $\pi^{\pm}$ in (4) have a proper intersection – then the set of training propositions P with their corresponding truth values are *compatible* with RSGnet$_0$'s architecture, in the sense defined in section 1 above: there is some set of weights $\mathbf{w}$ which correctly judges the truth of all the training propositions. Otherwise no such set of weights exists (see Figure 10.3).

If the solution space is non-empty and more than one-dimensional, then there will be many inequivalent sets of weights which all correctly judge the training propositions, but which differ in their judgements on other propositions – that is, they generalize differently. The alternative patterns of generalization can be mapped out by studying the solution space, using (3) as follows. Let x be a proposition not in the training set, and consider the two half-spaces $\mathbf{x}^+$ and $\mathbf{x}^-$. Every weight vector $\mathbf{w}$ in

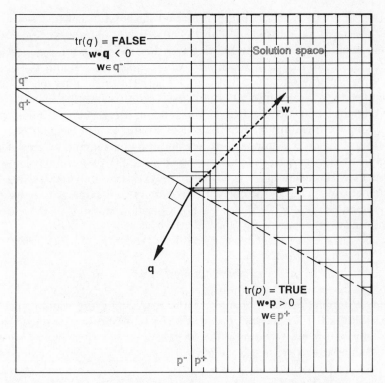

Figure 10.3   Given the training vectors **p**, **q** representing propositions for which $tr(p)$ = TRUE, $tr(q)$ = FALSE, the solution space is the intersection of the two half-spaces **p**⁺, **q**⁻. One arbitrarily chosen weight vector **w** in the solution space is shown.

the solution space which falls in **x**⁺ is one that generalizes or 'infers' that x is true; those with **w** falling in **x**⁻ 'infer' that x is false. Those with **w** falling in the plane separating **x**⁺ from **x**⁻ simply refuse to judge x.

With this analysis in hand, we adopt the following definition:

(5)   RSGnet₀ *has the C-belief that* π *is true (or false)* if **w** lies in π⁺ (or π⁻).

That is, a C-belief is specified by a region of state space (a half-space, π⁺ or π⁻, in fact), and to say that a network holds a C-belief is to say that the weight vector **w** that encodes its knowledge lies in that region. Successful training of a network on a set of propositions is achieved when the weights have been placed so that the network has all the training C-beliefs. When a network holds a C-belief about a proposition not in the training set, it can be said to 'infer' that C-belief. Depending on the network and the training set, it may or may not be possible to simultaneously hold all the training C-beliefs. When it is possible, there may be many alternative networks which hold the training C-beliefs, and these alternative networks may make different inferences about propositions outside the training set.

Suppose now that in RS&G's argument, we replace RSGnet with RSGnet$_0$, providing it with a weight vector $\mathbf{w}$ which enables it to correctly judge the propositions in some training set, and to draw some reasonable inferences. We can now formulate the following explanation of why RSGnet$_0$ behaves as it does: because, examining $\mathbf{w}$, we see that the network holds all the correct C-beliefs. That is, one by one, we can mathematically verify (5): for each proposition π, $\mathbf{w}$ is in the correct half-space π^+ or π^-.

3.2   Learning analysis and L-beliefs

For RSGnet$_0$, learning analysis, while requiring more caution, is also feasible and fruitful. Under a number of conditions, to be discussed shortly, the result of training RSGnet$_0$ is a weight vector $\mathbf{w}$ which can be illuminatingly written as follows:[3]

(6) $\mathbf{w} = tr(p)\mathbf{p}^* + tr(q)\mathbf{q}^* + tr(r)\mathbf{r}^* + \ldots$

In this equation, as before, $\mathbf{p}$ is the activity vector encoding the proposition p, and similarly for the other training propositions encoded as the vectors $\mathbf{q}, \mathbf{r}, \ldots$; the truth value of p is here encoded as $tr(p) = +1$ if p is true, $tr(p) = +1$ if p is false. The vector operation $*$ is discussed below.

The conditions under which (6) holds are as follows:

(7)   (a) The weights are all zero when training begins.
      (b) The learning algorithm is the Delta Rule, with the target output for input π being $tr(\pi)$, and with sufficiently small learning rate to ensure convergence.

The Delta Rule is a simplified version of back-propagation (which was originally dubbed the *Generalized Delta Rule*: Rumelhart et al., 1986b); it is appropriate for networks with no hidden units (for discussion and references, see Rumelhart et al., 1986a). It will converge to a correct set of weights when such weights exist. Such weights always exist in the case when the training patterns $\mathbf{p}, \mathbf{q}, \mathbf{r}, \ldots$ are *linearly independent*, that is, when none of them can be expressed as a weighted sum of the others. In this case, the * operation can be defined as follows. The vector $\mathbf{p}^*$ is the vector which is perpendicular to all the other training patterns $\mathbf{q}, \mathbf{r}, \ldots$ and which has $\mathbf{p} \cdot \mathbf{p}^* = +1$. This is a vector in the positive half-space $\mathbf{p}^+$ and in the plane separating the positive and negative half-spaces of all the other propositions $\pi = q, r, \ldots : \pi \cdot \mathbf{p}^* = 0$. The existence of such a vector $\mathbf{p}^*$ is guaranteed by the assumed linear independence of all the propositions.[4]

It is important to remember that the * operation is defined in terms of an entire training *set*. Repeated presentation of this entire set during network training is required for the learning algorithm to gradually evolve what amounts to the * operation, by incrementally taking into account the similarity of the patterns in the training set. The simple formula (6) which describes the *result* of this process hides the considerable computational subtlety of actually *deriving* all the vectors π^* from the training set.

Given the weight vector $\mathbf{w}$ of (6), it is now elementary to verify that for the input $\mathbf{p}$, and analogously for any other input training proposition, $RSGnet_0$ correctly produces the output value $tr(p)$:

$$(8) \quad o = \mathbf{w} \cdot \mathbf{p} = [tr(p)\mathbf{p}^* + tr(q)\mathbf{q}^* + tr(r)\mathbf{r}^* + \ldots] \cdot \mathbf{p}$$
$$= tr(p)\mathbf{p}^* \cdot \mathbf{p} + tr(q)\mathbf{q}^* \cdot \mathbf{p} + tr(r)\mathbf{r}^* \cdot \mathbf{p} + \ldots$$
$$= tr(p)$$

since by the definition of the * operation, $\mathbf{p} \cdot \mathbf{p}^* = +1$ and $\pi^* \cdot \mathbf{p} = 0$ for $\pi = q, r, \ldots$

An informal version of this simple argument goes as follows. For each proposition p, there is a weight vector $\mathbf{p}^*$ which is a 'pure' encoding of the belief that p is true: when the weights are set equal to $\mathbf{p}^*$, the network outputs TRUE ($o = +1$) for input $\mathbf{p}$, but refuses to judge all the other propositions $\mathbf{q}, \mathbf{r}, \ldots$ in the training set (it outputs $o = 0$). The weight vector $-\mathbf{p}^*$ is a corresponding pure encoding of the belief that p is false ($o = -1$). Thus $tr(p)\mathbf{p}^*$ is a pure encoding of the correct belief about p; let's name it as follows:

(9)   Given a proposition p in a training set, call the weight vector $tr(p)\mathbf{p}^*$ the *L-belief that p has truth value tr(p)* (NB: $\mathbf{p}^*$ is defined relative to the training *set*)

To handle the multiple beliefs in the training set, we can simply *add up*, that is, *superimpose*, all these L-beliefs, getting the total weight vector $\mathbf{w}$ of (6). This vector $\mathbf{w}$ has one *component* $tr(\pi)\pi^*$ – an L-belief – for each training proposition π. This weight vector $\mathbf{w}$ correctly judges all the training propositions, because when the proposition **p** is presented as input, one component of **w**, the L-belief for p, $tr(p)$**p***, yields the correct judgement $tr(p)$, while the remaining components $tr(\pi)\pi$* all refuse to pass judgment. Thus superimposing or adding together all the judgments gives the correct truth value.

The relation between the C-beliefs arising from weight analysis and the L-beliefs arising from learning analysis is this. The C-belief that p is false is a large region of weight space **p**⁻ in which **w** must lie for the net to judge p false. The L-belief that p is false is one particular vector −**p*** in this large region, a vector which is singled out only when the rest of the training set is specified (for only then can we define **p*** as that vector perpendicular to all the other training propositions). To correctly encode all the beliefs in a training set, **w** must lie in the intersection of all the training C-beliefs: the solution space. In the general case for which the solution space is non-empty – where the training proposition vectors are linearly independent – and the net is trained in accordance with (7), we can say that the particular vector **w** resulting from training is that vector (6) which is a sum of component vectors, one per training proposition: each such component is the corresponding L-belief. This vector lies in the solution space, as verified in (8).

So suppose we have a set of linearly independent training propositions, on which RSGnet$_0$ has been trained according to (7). Then the explanation of why RSGnet$_0$ behaves correctly which comes from our learning analysis runs as follows. The weight vector **w** encoding the net's knowledge can be decomposed into a superposition of components, each of which is an L-belief in one of the training propositions. That the network performs correctly on the training set is a direct consequence of this structure in **w**, as explained formally in (8) and informally in the subsequent paragraph. The L-beliefs are *constituents* of the network's knowledge, in a sense discussed below in section 5.

Equation (6) lets us determine how the network judges a proposition x not in the training set, in terms of the 'similarity' of the novel proposition to the training ones. For by (2) and (6), the output produced when **x** is input is:

$$(10) \quad o = \mathbf{w} \cdot \mathbf{x} = [tr(p)\mathbf{p}^* + tr(q)\mathbf{q}^* + tr(r)\mathbf{r}^* + \ldots] \cdot \mathbf{x}$$
$$= tr(p)\mathbf{p}^* \cdot \mathbf{x} + tr(q)\mathbf{q}^* \cdot \mathbf{x} + tr(r)\mathbf{r}^* \cdot \mathbf{x} + \ldots$$
$$= tr(p) \, sim(\mathbf{p}^*, \mathbf{x}) + tr(p) \, sim(\mathbf{q}^*, \mathbf{x}) + tr(p) \, sim(\mathbf{r}^*, \mathbf{x}) + \ldots$$

The 'similarity' function $sim(\mathbf{p}^*, \mathbf{x})$ is simply defined by **p***·**x**. It is a useful common connectionist practice to interpret **p***·**x** as the similarity between the patterns **p*** and **x** because it amounts to a correlation between the elements of the two patterns. For example, if the elements of the patterns $\mathbf{p}^*$ and $\mathbf{x}$ are all 1s and 0s (as in the input patterns to RSGnet), then it is a simple consequence of its definition (1) that $\mathbf{p}^*\cdot\mathbf{x}$ is just the number of places in which both vectors have a 1; if '1' is interpreted as the presence of some feature or property, as is not uncommon in Connectionist representations, then $\mathbf{p}^*\cdot\mathbf{x}$ is just the number of properties present in both $\mathbf{p}^*$ and $\mathbf{x}$ – one measure of their similarity.

What (10) says is that the response of the net to a novel input $\mathbf{x}$ is a weighted sum or superposition of its response to all its training propositions π, each such response weighted by the similarity of the novel input $\mathbf{x}$ to the training example π^*.

3.3   Summary: C- and L-beliefs in RSGnet$_0$

The strategies of weight analysis (section 3.1) and learning analysis (section 3.2) have each provided us with some important projectable predicates: C-beliefs and L-beliefs, respectively. The statements of Connectionist theory characterizing the conditions under which a network will correctly judge a proposition, and the result of learning, are stated directly in terms of C- and L-beliefs. These projectable predicates are not noticeable on casual inspection of the network, and are defined only at the level of activation and weight vectors. To stare at individual activities and weights in search of semantically meaningful predicates is as pointless as looking at individual bits in a digital computer memory.

We have derived C- and L-beliefs from the analysis of RSGnet$_0$, a simplification of the original RSGnet. One might worry that shifting attention from RSGnet to RSGnet$_0$ is unjustifiable. However, RS&G's claim concerns the implications of an entire *class* of connectionist networks, of which RSGnet is but one possible example, and it is easily seen that RSGnet$_0$ is also an equally valid example of the same class of models, a class I will refer to as *PTC models*: those embodying the 'proper treatment of connectionism'. This sub-argument justifying the legitimacy of RSGnet$_0$ for a reply to RS&G is postponed until section 6, in order to minimize distraction from the main line of argument.

4 C-beliefs and Propositional Modularity

We now move on to the crucial question: do the notions of C- and L-belief possess any of the three properties of propositional modularity which RS&G claim make Classical belief a target for elimination by the PTC form of connectionism? Let's consider these three properties in turn.

Semantic interpretability

Clearly both C-beliefs and L-beliefs involve semantic interpretation. The fundamental principle driving the analysis we have developed is the semantic level principle, which asserts that *semantically interpretable aspects of connectionist networks lie at the higher level of activation and weight vectors, and not at the lower level of individual units and connections*. To make claims about semantic properties of connectionist networks based on staring at individual units and connections is to make a fundamental category error. In the absence of something like weight and learning analysis, carried out at the vector level – in the absence of *some* understanding of what is going on at this higher level of description – no sound claims about any semantic properties are possible. But concepts such as C- and L-beliefs, and others that reside at the higher level, *do* exist, and do make it possible to explain the behaviors of connectionist networks in semantically interpretable terms.

Functional discreteness

RS&G's discussion of functional discreteness centers on the relation between their Network A – successfully trained on a set of 16 propositions – and Network B – successfully trained on this same set with an additional 17th proposition added. We can apply the notions of C- and L-beliefs to understand the relation between Net A and Net B, which are analogous to RS&G's except the network architecture is that of $RSGnet_0$ rather than that of RSGnet. The C-beliefs of Net B include the 17 it was trained on, 16 of which are also held by Net A. That means the weight vector w_B of Net B must lie in a solution space S_B that is smaller than the solution space S_A containing w_A: S_A is defined as the intersection of 16 half-spaces, while S_B is the intersection of these 16 with an additional 17th half-space. Despite the fact that the C-beliefs are not *physically localizable* to different spatial sub-regions of the networks, there is none the less a more abstract but perfectly well-defined sense in which the 17 beliefs are functionally discrete: the projectable predicates in terms of which we describe the knowledge-encoding vectors w_A/w_B are just the 16/17 C-beliefs. The sensible thing to say about these nets, *as far as actual Connectionist theory is concerned*, is precisely that there is a particular additional C-belief in the second net as compared to the first. Furthermore, if some process were to disturb the weight vector $\mathbf{w_B}$, so that it moved out of the solution space S_B while still remaining within the larger solution space S_A, it would make perfectly good sense to say that the second net had 'lost' or 'forgotten' the 17th belief, while retaining the other 16. The sensibleness of talking of one belief coming or going independently of others is the focus of RS&G's characterization of functional discreteness (chapter 8, p. 316).

Functional discreteness can be seen via L-beliefs as well, although greater caution is required. For, assuming Nets A and B to have been trained according to (7), their weight vectors $\mathbf{w_A}$ and $\mathbf{w_B}$ are given by (6) as:

(11)   A $\mathbf{w_A} = tr(p)\mathbf{p}^* + tr(q)\mathbf{q}^* + tr(r)\mathbf{r}^* + \ldots$
      B $\mathbf{w_B} = tr(p)\mathbf{p}^* + tr(q)\mathbf{q}^* + tr(r)\mathbf{r}^* + \ldots + tr(z)\mathbf{z}^*$

where z is the extra (17th) proposition on which Net B is trained. It is important to remember that the * operation depends on the training *set*, so that in fact the vector denoted $\mathbf{p}^*$ in (11A) and that denoted $\mathbf{p}^*$ in (11B) are, in general, somewhat different vectors.[5] Thus we can analyze $\mathbf{w_A}$ and $\mathbf{w_B}$ as containing 16 and 17 L-beliefs, respectively. In this case, the L-belief that p has truth value $tr(p)$ is in general somewhat different in the two networks.

Thus our excursion into basic Connectionist theory shows the falsehood of RS&G's crucial claim, part of which was cited in section 1 as the primary impetus behind this reply:

The contrast between Network A and Network B enables us to make our point about the incompatibility between common-sense psychology and these sorts of connectionist models in a rather different way. We noted in section 3 that common-sense psychology treats predicates expressing the semantic properties of propositional attitudes as projectable. Thus 'believes that dogs have fur' or 'remembers that dogs have fur' will be projectable predicates in common-sense psychology. Now both Network A and Network B might serve as models for a cognitive agent who believes that dogs have fur; both networks store or represent the information that dogs have fur. Nor are these the only two. If we were to train up a network on the 17 propositions in table 8.1 plus a few (or minus a few) we would get yet another system which is as different from Networks A and B as these two are from each other. The moral here is that though there are *indefinitely* many connectionist networks that represent the information that dogs have fur just as well as Network A does, these networks have no projectable features in common that are describable in the language of Connectionist theory. From the point of view of the connectionist model builder, the class of networks that might model a cognitive agent who believes that dogs have fur is not a genuine kind at all, but simply a chaotically disjunctive set. Common-sense psychology treats the class of people who believe that dogs have fur as a psychologically natural kind; Connectionist psychology does not. (chapter 8, pp. 328–9)

Causal role

While C- and L-beliefs possess the first two properties of propositional modularity, the same is not true of the final property. The modular causal roles of the beliefs of folk psychology are illustrated by RS&G as follows: it makes sense to say (a) that a particular instance of an action taken by an agent was caused by a particular belief/desire pair and not another, even though both pairs are held by the agent and both pairs rationally entail taking the given action; (b) that a particular instance in which an agent infers a conclusion was caused by one set of beliefs and not another, even though both sets are held by the agent and both sets logically entail the given conclusion (pp. 317–18). Focusing on the most relevant case (b), we must conclude that there is no corresponding sense for $RSGnet_0$ that some set of relevant C-beliefs are causally implicated in an inference on a particular occasion, while another set of relevant C-beliefs are not causally implicated on that occasion, but might be on another.

That this property fails for $RSGnet_0$ is probably clearest from learning analysis. As explained in (10) above, when a proposition x is presented to be judged, the net computes its judgment by superimposing its response to all the training patterns π, each such response weighted by the similarity of x to π^*. When this similarity is 0 – when $x \cdot \pi^* = 0$, i.e. when the L-belief $tr(\pi)\pi^*$ concerning π produces no judgment of x as true or false – then the effect of the training pattern π on the judgment of x is nil. (Thus, for example, if the truth value of π, $tr(\pi)$, were reversed prior to training the net, this would have no effect on the judgment of x.) In such a case it could be reasonably said that this L-belief is not relevant to x and has no 'causal role' in the judgment of x. On the other hand, if the similarity of x to π^* is non-zero, then the L-belief about the truth value of π is relevant, and it plays a causal role in the net's judgment of x. There is no meaningful sense in which a relevant belief might play a causal role in judging x on one occasion, but not another; all relevant beliefs always have the same causal role.

5 Conclusions

It is no accident that the two particular properties possessed by C- and L-beliefs are semantic interpretability and functional discreteness, while the property not holding of C- and L-beliefs is causal role. This splitting of the three properties of propositional modularity is a special case of a much more general pattern inherent in the PTC view of the relation between connectionist and Classical theory. To see how, the three properties should be classified as follows:

Semantic interpretability	Property of vector level of analysis
Functional discreteness	Property of function computed
Causal role	Property of algorithm

C-beliefs have the property of semantic interpretability by design: they are defined at the level of analysis where semantic properties reside in PTC models in general: the higher level of weight and activity vectors. Functional discreteness is a possible PTC property for a Connectionist notion like C-beliefs because it is a property of the *function computed* by the network, rather than of the *algorithm for carrying out the computation*. In general, Classical notions are far more relevant to the functions computed by PTC connectionist models (as characterized at the semantically relevant, higher level of vectors) than to the algorithms used to compute these functions (Smolensky et al. 1992). A C-belief is specified by a region in weight space, which amounts to a means of specifying a particular class of *functions* (those computed by the networks with weights lying in that region). On the other hand, beliefs having modular causal roles is a property of a class of *algorithms*, for example, those in which different beliefs can be meaningfully distinguished as falling in different parts of a memory (e.g. the nodes in the semantic network of RS&G's figure 8.1, or the members of a list of propositions), and for which it is meaningful to say that certain (logically relevant) parts of that memory are accessed during a particular inference process and other (logically relevant) parts are not.

This distinction between properties of functions and properties of algorithms plays a central role in Marr's (1982) three-level analysis of computational/cognitive systems. Properties of the function computed characterize his *computational level*; beneath this is the *algorithmic level*, and below that the *implementational level*. Marr's distinction between the computational and algorithmic levels, or the distinction between properties of cognitive functions and algorithms, provides a useful way of distinguishing the PTC position on the relation between Classical and Connectionist theory from the implementationalist and eliminativist positions. On the implementationalist view, connectionist networks serve only as a new implementation of the classical architecture; both the classical functions computed and the classical algorithms for computing them remain intact. On the eliminativist view, no sufficiently faithful counterparts of Classical notions can be found in Connectionist theory, so the Classical notions are eliminated altogether, from description of both function and algorithm. On the PTC view, however, the situation is more complex. Classical notions retain important roles in the description of cognitive functions, but not algorithms. Connectionist and Classical theory involve common concepts at Marr's computational level, but not at the algorithmic level. This situation can be illustrated as follows; an 'x' indicates commonality between Connectionist and Classical theory:

Marr's level	Implementationalist	PTC	Eliminativist
Computational (function)	x	x	
Algorithmic	x		
Implementational			

RS&G claim to show that *if* PTC-type connectionist models of inference are correct, *then* the Classical notion of belief is eliminated; therefore, by *modus ponens*, advocates of such models should endorse eliminativism, and, by *modus tollens*, advocates of Classical belief should reject such models and prefer, say, the implementationalist view of connectionism. But the analysis in this chapter has shown that, on the contrary, *if* PTC-type models of inference are correct, *then* what follows is neither support for eliminativism nor support for implementationalism, but rather support for the intermediate PTC position: the properties of Classical belief lying at Marr's computational level – semantic intepretability and functional discreteness – are retained by Connectionist theory, while those at the algorithmic level – modular causal roles – are abandoned. Thus the correct moral following from RS&G's argument is quite different from the ones they draw.

RS&G *talk about* 'Connectionist theory', claiming that it simply provides nothing which can redeem the folk psychological notion of belief. In fact, however, they do not avail themselves of any of the actual content of Connectionist theory, and do not have any means at all of explaining the behavior of RSGnet; they do not therefore have any explanation to offer of the ability to judge propositions, and little that should count as 'Connectionist psychology'. What they have is simply a network. When we turn to actual Connectionist theory to explain this network's behavior, to see what explanatory notions are thereby made available to Connectionist psychology, we see that in fact these notions *do* redeem Classical belief – partly. The part redeemed is just that which relates to specifying the *cognitive function* which is computed; the part rejected is that which relates to the *algorithm* used to compute that function. And this constitutes precisely the PTC position on the relation between Classical and Connectionist theory, as it has been further developed (Smolensky et al., 1992).

The correct conclusion of the line of argument established by RS&G is corroborated by other recent results within the PTC framework, which is now developing into an integrated Connectionist/symbolic cognitive theory. These corroborating results derive from three sources (Smolensky et al., 1992). First, in the area of grammar, it is shown how a Connectionist-grounded theory of grammar – Harmonic Grammar – instantiates the situation described above, in which certain symbolic theories of linguistic representation and grammatical constraints are adopted to a large extent at the computational level, but novel connectionist processing occurs at the algorithmic level. Secondly, it is shown how abstract structure processing is possible, where the function computed is describable using a symbolic programming language, but where the algorithm for computing the function is massively parallel connectionist spreading activation. Thirdly, the challenge of Fodor and Pylyshyn (see chapter 3) is met by showing how tensor product representations endow connectionist models with mental representations possessing constituent structure at the computational level, but purely connectionist, non-symbolic processing at the algorithmic level (see Smolensky, chapter 6). Indeed, the sense in which tensor product mental representations contain constituents at the computational level is formally identical to the sense, derived here in section 3.2, in which $RSGnet_0$'s knowledge – its weight vector $\mathbf{w}$ – contains individual L-beliefs as constituents. That is, the L-beliefs developed here describe the constituent structure of a network's *weight* pattern or *knowledge* – where the constituents are individual beliefs – in formally the same way as tensor product representations describe the constituent structure of a network's *activation* pattern or *data* – where the constituents correspond to those of a symbolic data structure, such as a parse tree. The crucial ingredient in all this work is the semantic level principle, which forces us to work at the level of weight and activity vectors, and to seek constituency in the structure of these vectors.

Finally, I want to consider the issue of the adequacy and complexity of the connectionist models discussed here. The central notions of this chapter, C- and L-beliefs, were developed for the simplest of all connectionist architectures, that of $RSGnet_0$. In the Appendix (section

7), I show how these notions extend to the more complex architecture of RSGnet. The further complexity of RSGnet calls for additional concepts, not all of which are as yet sufficiently well developed to enable a complete explanation of the behavior of RSGnet. Yet RSGnet is a very simple network by today's standards. And even the most sophisticated current networks are still far short of supplying anything like a satisfying model of human inference and belief.[6] It is certainly pertinent to ask whether the conclusions drawn here on the basis of RSGnet$_0$ and (to a less complete extent) RSGnet are likely to survive in the face of progress in connectionist modeling.

My answer relies heavily on the distinction drawn in section 2 between connectionist *networks*, which play the role of explanandum, and Connectionist *theory*, which plays the role of explanans. The term 'model' encourages us to blur this distinction. It seems safe to say that connectionist *networks* will always outrun Connectionist *theory*: there will always be many networks in use which are, for the moment at least, too complex to analyze, and these will provide important *questions* about what makes certain connectionist networks exhibit interesting behaviors; but Connectionist theory will not (yet) have the answers. Just the same, Connectionist theory is very likely to continue its current rapid rate of advancement for some time (e.g. Smolensky et al. forthcoming), and explanatory notions richer, more powerful and more cognitively relevant than C- and L-beliefs will emerge. Whether the new notions will support the conclusions drawn here from C- and L-beliefs is impossible to know in advance. Yet it is important to recognize that it is these theoretical notions, rather than the networks outrunning them, that define the state of the art in Connectionist *psychology*, as opposed to connectionist network design. I would argue, in fact, that it is the power of these same theoretical notions that will also ultimately set the limits to the success of connectionist network design: that, in the long run, the powerful networks are those which are *designed* to instantiate powerful analytic concepts. In the area of connectionist *cognitive* modeling, I believe many of the analytic concepts enabling the design of more powerful networks will, for some time yet, be begged, borrowed, or stolen from Classical theory. Thus I expect the conclusions drawn here *will* recur as more sophisticated Classical notions make their way (perhaps quite indirectly) into more sophisticated connectionist models.

This concludes the main line of argument. The following two sections address two postponed questions concerning the relation of the net studied here, RSGnet$_0$, to the net originally offered by RS&G, RSGnet. Section 6 shows that RSGnet$_0$ is just as valid as RSGnet as an illustration of the class of PTC-style connectionist models, the subject of RS&G's conclusion. And section 7 shows that the ideas of C- and L-beliefs developed for explaining $RSGnet_0$ also have important roles to play in explaining RSGnet.

6 A Worry: Adequacy of $RSGnet_0$ as an Illustrative Example

In this section I argue that it is legitimate to replace RSGnet with $RSGnet_0$ in replying to RS&G. As shown in the Appendix (section 7), the particular scheme RS&G use to encode propositions into activation vectors, together with the particular set of propositions and truth values of their training set, are not compatible with the simple architecture of $RSGnet_0$; that is, for these input patterns, the solution space is empty: there is no weight vector w which will allow $RSGnet_0$ to correctly judge RS&G's particular encoded training propositions; no way for it to simultaneously hold all those training C-beliefs. But the analysis of section 7 will also reveal *why* this incompatibility exists, and we will see that nothing relevant to RS&G's argument is involved. If a different encoding of the same training propositions had been selected (or a different set of propositions), there is no reason whatever that $RSGnet_0$ could not serve just as well as the original RSGnet as an illustrative model for examination. So in adopting $RSGnet_0$ as our example, we must assume that the particular encoded beliefs rather arbitrarily chosen by RS&G have been replaced by a set of encoded beliefs which are compatible with the architecture of $RSGnet_0$; when we speak of $RSGnet_0$ we will assume it to have been successfully trained on such an appropriate set of encoded beliefs.

Now it *is* true that the class of networks which, like $RSGnet_0$, lack hidden units is less computationally powerful than the class of networks which, like RSGnet, possess hidden units. Thus we expect realistic cognitive models to have hidden units. But RSGnet hardly counts as a realistic cognitive model; it is deliberately simplified in order to serve as an instructive example, so the additional instructiveness afforded by the additional simplicity of $RSGnet_0$ is indeed a virtue for our purposes. What RS&G claim is that it is the *general properties* of connectionist models which RSGnet illustrates, rather than RSGnet itself, which entail an eliminativist conclusion; so the crucial question is whether $RSGnet_0$ possesses these general properties.

In their section 4, RS&G characterize the class of connectionist models of relevance to their argument by three general properties. Starting with the last one, RS&G describe their third characteristic in the following terms:

Because of their obvious, though in many ways very partial, similarity to real neural architectures, it is tempting to view connectionist models as models of the implementation of psychological processes ... A very different view that connectionst model builders can and often do take is that their models are at the psychological level, not at the level of implementation. (Chapter 8, p. 323)

Certainly our interpretive position here regarding $RSGnet_0$ is the same as RS&G's regarding RSGnet, so there can be no worry about their third characteristic.[7]

Of greater concern are the first two general properties that RS&G identify: the *widely distributed* (1) and *sub-symbolic* (2) nature of the representations. With respect to (1) they state:

It is connectionist networks of this sort, in which it is not possible to isolate the representation of particular propositions or states of affairs within the nodes, connection strengths and biases, that we have in mind when we talk about the encoding of information in the biases, weights and hidden nodes being *widely distributed* rather than *localist*. (p. 322)

And with respect to (2):

it is often plausible to view such networks as collectively or holistically encoding a set of propositions, although none of the hidden units, weights or biases is comfortably viewed as a *symbol*. When this is the case we will call the strategy of representation invoked in the model *sub-symbolic*. (p. 322)

It is clear that when the input patterns constitute a widely distributed encoding of propositions, then $RSGnet_0$ illustrates the sub-symbolic strategy. When we consider it in some detail in section 7, we will see that RS&G's representation of propositions is in fact fairly weakly distributed, and since we are assuming for $RSGnet_0$ an alternative encoding of their training propositions anyway (one which is compatible with the $RSGnet_0$ architecture) we ought as well to consider a *fully distributed* input representation, so that $RSGnet_0$ becomes a better illustration of (1) and (2) than is the original RSGnet itself. A fully distributed representation of the propositions is one in which all connectionist units participate directly in the representation of all the constituents of the proposition. A systematic study of such representations, and their formal relation to less distributed forms of Connectionist representation (such as the 'semi-local' input representation of RSGnet) was presented in Smolensky (1987, 1990a). The Connectionist representational framework introduced there, *tensor product representations*, is sufficiently mathematically analyzable that it is possible to formally characterize conditions in which such representations (say, fully distributed ones) are compatible with the architecture of RSGnet$_0$; the theory is in place for systematically constructing an entire family of fully distributed encodings of RS&G's propositions with the property that RSGnet$_0$ can learn all the training beliefs.

The most important point is that – unless the input representation is 'hyper-local', where each input proposition is represented by its own dedicated unit, – the notions of C- and L-beliefs we have developed above are *non-local*: a single connection is involved in multiple C- and L-beliefs concerning different propositions. With fully distributed input representations, in fact, *every* connection is part of the C- or L-belief for *every* proposition. With a less distributed representation, such as that actually employed by RS&G, most connections are involved in several (but not all) beliefs. In this crucial respect, there is no difference at all between RSGnet$_0$ and RSGnet.

The salient difference between RSGnet and RSGnet$_0$ that the former possesses four hidden units and the latter none – does not bear on whether representation is widely distributed (1) or sub-symbolic (2). RS&G's initial statement of (2) – 'individual hidden units, in the network have no comfortable symbolic interpretation; they are *sub-symbolic*' (p. 320) refers to hidden units, but the concept of sub-symbolic representation, as we've already concluded, does not depend on the existence of hidden units. Given that the *input* representation of RSGnet is not in fact very widely distributed (as we see in section 7), the addition of the four hidden units to RSGnet serves to make its total representation more distributed than it would have been if the representation were carried entirely by the input units. But as a means of better illustrating sub-symbolic representation, adopting a fully distributed *input* representation for RSGnet$_0$ is *at least* as effective as adding a few hidden units to a weakly distributed input representation in RSGnet. One sense in which the former strategy is more satisfactory than the latter is that in at least some studies (e.g. Sanger, 1989, 1990) hidden representations trained by back-propagation, when examined in mathematical detail, have proved to be much *less* distributed than has commonly been assumed *a priori*. What the exact case might be in RSGnet is not clear, prior to analysis by some technique such as Sanger's *contribution analysis*, which turns out to be quite complex.

Thus, there is no reason to prefer RSGnet over RSGnet$_0$ as an illustration for the purposes of RS&G's argument. However, it is worth pursuing the notions of connectionist belief developed here a bit further, making contact with the original illustration, RSGnet. This is done in the following Appendix, the bottom line of which is that the presence of hidden units in RSGnet doesn't *eliminate the C- and L-beliefs which we have derived from its simpler cousin RSGnet$_0$; the hidden units just obscure* and *complicate* the C- and L-beliefs. This conclusion is worth some further analytic effort because it is of interest to know whether concepts such as C- and L-beliefs apply to more complex networks than RSGnet$_0$, and for this purpose RSGnet serves as a useful example. At the same time, the analysis of the Appendix should put to rest any lingering doubts about whether some trick has been played by studying RSGnet$_0$ rather than RSGnet. The question of whether notions such as C- and L-beliefs will apply to 'realistic' connectionist cognitive models which are considerably more complex than RSGnet was already taken up in section 5.

7   Appendix: Belief in RSGnet

The goal of this Appendix is to show that the same concepts and techniques that illuminate RSGnet$_0$ also shed light on RSGnet, although the greater complexity of RSGnet calls for additional techniques that go beyond the scope of this chapter and which in fact touch on open issues in Connectionist theory. Our first step is to formally characterize the input-to-output function which RSGnet computes, f. We begin at the semantic level, characterizing f in terms of propositions and truth values; then we examine the Connectionist representation RS&G employ, and rephrase f in terms of connectionist activations.

7.1   The function to be computed: semantic form

At the semantic level, the function f assigns truth values to propositions like dogs have fur with the form 'Xs have Ys' or have (X,Y). In RS&G's propositions, the X's can be categorized by the predicate mammal, and the Ys by the predicate mammal-part, so that the function f is in fact:

(12) f(have(X,Y)) = [mammal(X) & mammal-part(Y)]

   OR

   [— mammal(X) & — mammal-part(Y)]

In RS&G's examples, mammal(X) is TRUE for $X \in \{$dogs, cats$\}$ and FALSE for $X \in \{$fish$\}$; mammal-part(Y) is TRUE for $Y \in \{$fur, paws, fleas, legs$\}$ and FALSE for $Y \in \{$scales, fins, gills, eggs$\}$. An alternative form of (12) is useful:

(13) $f(\text{have}(X,Y)) = \text{mammal}(X) \ \text{XOR} \ \neg \, \text{mammal-part}(Y)$

The connective XOR is defined as follows: p XOR q is TRUE iff exactly one of p and q are TRUE; that is

(14) $p \ \text{XOR} \ q = [p \ \& \ \neg \, q] \ \text{OR} \ [\neg p \ \& \ q]$

Substituting from (13) $p = \text{mammal}(X)$ and $q = \neg \, \text{mammal-part}(Y)$ into (14) yields (12).

The paraphrase of f in terms of XOR (13) is useful because XOR is well known to be the simplest function whose computation in connectionist networks requires hidden units.[8] Thus we do not expect that the particular function f that RS&G have chosen for their example is in fact computable by networks such as RSGnet$_0$ which lack hidden units.[9] At the same time, elementary solutions to XOR using two hidden units are also classic, and we will make use of one of them.

7.2   The function to be computed: activation form

Now before seeing just how f can be computed by a connectionist network with two hidden units, we need to attend to the way the propositions have(X,Y) are encoded as activity vectors in RSGnet, as specified in RS&G's table 8.1. Overviews of relevant issues in Connectionist representation may be found, for example, in Hinton et al. (1986) and Smolensky (1986, 1990a, b).

RSGnet has 16 input units, so the activity vectors encoding input propositions consist of 16 numbers. We can throw away most of these without loss, however. Units 1 and 2 are always on; they carry no information and thus can be eliminated. The same is true for units 9 and 10. Units 3 and 4 are perfectly redundant with each other, they always have the same value. So we can keep unit 3 and throw away unit 4. In fact such adjacent pairs of units *all* have this property, so we can throw out all the even-numbered units.[10] We are left now with only six units, which divide into two sets: 3, 5, 7; and 11, 13, 15. The first three units represent X and the second three Y in the proposition have (X,Y).

The representation of X in units 3, 5, 7 is a local one: unit 3 represents fish; unit 5 represents cat; unit 7, dog. That is, the value of

X is determined by which one of these three units has activity 1; the others then have activity 0. Since dog and cat are isomorphic, we shall now ignore unit 5 (cat); everything we learn about unit 7 (dog) will apply as well to unit 5.

The local representation of X makes it easy to compute the term mammal(X) in f (12) using connectionist activity:

(15)   mammal(X) = [activity of unit 7 > 1]

The representation of Y is a bit more complicated. When only one of the units 11, 13, 15 is active (activity = 1), then the value of Y is, respectively, scales, fins, gills. If two of these units are active, then the value of Y is fur, paws or legs, depending on whether the *inactive* unit is 11, 13 or 15, respectively. Finally, if all three of these units are active, then Y = fleas. The crucial point about the representation of Y is this:

(16)   mammal-part(Y) = [total activity of units 11, 12, 15 >1]
                       = [TA > 1]

where TA is an abbreviation for the total activity of units 11, 12, 15.
Now it is easy to rewrite f (12) in terms of activations:

(17) f(have (X,Y)) = [mammal(X) & mammal-part (Y)]
                  OR
                  [$\neg$ mammal(X) & $\neg$ mammal-part(Y)]
              = [activity of unit 7 > 1] & [TA > 1]
                  OR
                  $\neg$ [activity of unit 7 > 1] & $\neg$ [TA >1]

7.3   C- and L-beliefs in RSGnet$_2$

This last expression (17) can be directly mapped into a connectionist network with one hidden unit computing each disjunct, and the output computing the OR of the two hidden units. Such a network, which adapts one of the standard solutions to XOR to the current case, is shown in figure 10.4. I will call this network RSGnet$_2$, the '2' indicating the number of hidden units.[11]

RSGnet$_2$ exactly computes RS&G's function f; it uses the same input as RSGnet, with irrelevant units ignored, and the same output, but the hidden layer has two rather than four units. The network can be completely understood. Let us now explicitly construct an explanation of how this network correctly evaluates propositions.

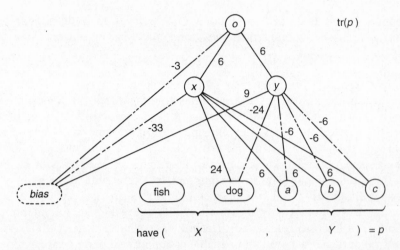

Figure 10.4   RSGnet$_2$, a version of RSGnet with two hidden units and with extraneous input units removed. Excitatory connections are shown with solid lines, inhibitory with broken lines. The 'bias unit' has constant activity value 1.

The output unit is the OR of the hidden units; the network judges a proposition TRUE if either of the hidden units becomes active when that proposition is represented on the input units. Thus we can in fact regard each hidden unit as also judging the input propositions; one unit specializes in spotting true propositions about mammals, the other about non-mammals (fish, actually). If either specialist declares an input true, so does the net as a whole; if neither specialist can certify the input's truth, the net judges it false.

So, our explanation of how this network correctly judges propositions is now pushed back to explaining how each hidden unit, each specialist, correctly judges the inputs; we can now focus on each hidden unit in isolation. *And this puts us in exactly the same position as explaining RSGnet$_0$:* the hidden unit on which we now focus plays the role of the output unit of RSGnet$_0$, which is directly connected to the input units. We can now bring to bear the same concepts and techniques of weight analysis and even learning analysis which we developed for RSGnet$_0$. Thus, for example, to explain how the first hidden unit correctly identifies the true propositions about mammals, we can say that Subnet$_{mammals}$ – the sub-network consisting of this hidden unit, the input units, and the connections between them – holds those C-beliefs from the training set which pertain to mammals. The particular weight vector $W_{mammals}$ of Subnet$_{mammals}$ – the vector of weights from the input units to the first hidden unit – can even be derived using learning analysis in terms of L-beliefs, given that the first hidden unit behaves as it does: judging propositions concerning mammals; we omit this computation due to space limitations.[12]

What is *much* more difficult, however, is explaining why training might produce *this* particular hidden unit behavior (specialists for mammals and non-mammals), as opposed to the infinity of other hidden unit behaviors which would also allow f to be correctly computed. The particular weights in RSGnet$_2$ illustrated in figure 10.4 were *designed* to directly compute the particular expression (17) for f; if, instead, all the weights were a result of (successful) learning, then the behavior of the hidden units would almost certainly not be expressible in such simple semantic terms. None the less, there are means of explaining the behavior of networks with trained hidden units (see, for example, Sanger, 1989 and references therein). As a whole, these methods are not yet sufficiently powerful to enable complete and precise explanation. Most networks of cognitive interest are considerably more complex than RSGnet, and in such cases the shortcomings of current explanations are generally substantial.

One way in which hidden unit behaviors can be analyzed is by redescribing them so that they reduce to semantically transparent, fully explainable networks, such as RSGnet$_2$. It often happens that a significant number of hidden units play virtually no role in the relevant network behaviors, and can be ignored. It may also happen that the work done by the two hidden units in RSGnet$_2$ are distributed over several hidden units in a trained network with additional hidden units; in this case, a 'rotation' of the space of hidden units may permit the behavior to be redescribed directly in terms formally equivalent to that of the two hidden units in RSGnet$_2$.[13] It is quite likely that such methods, if applied to RS&G's original four-hidden unit network RSGnet would allow us to explain its behavior by reducing it to RSGnet$_2$, or an equally transparent alternative two-hidden unit network for computing XOR.

Other methods exist which do not involve redescribing the hidden layer in terms of equivalent units with natural individual interpretations. In contribution analysis (Sanger, 1989), for example, *patterns* of hidden unit activity are identified which are responsible for the correct output being computed from an identified class of inputs. The hidden unit patterns and input classes are automatically extracted from the weights, and are not the result of *a priori* analysis of the function being computed. Hidden units often participate in more than one such pattern. Using contribution analysis, it might will be possible to extend to nets with hidden units the notions of C- and L-beliefs which we developed in section 3 for networks without hidden units; a C-belief, for example, would be determined by a region in weight space more complicated than a half-space, and depending both on hidden unit/ input unit weights and on hidden unit/output unit weights.

A final issue to revisit is that of the 11 extraneous input units in RSGnet which we discarded early in our analysis. For each of the five input units in our reduced networks $RSGnet_0$ and $RSGnet_2$, there is a *pair* of isomorphic units in the original network RSGnet. There is no *justified* basis for having different weights associated with the two identical units in each pair; indeed back-propagation will, on each training episode, make identical changes in the weights from each of two isomorphic units. Inspection of RS&G's figure 8.4, however, shows that the two units in isomorphic pairs do not have identical weights. This can be due only to differences in the (presumably random) initial weights on these pairs of units prior to learning. Whatever random differences there may be in the initial state are preserved during learning, since the *changes* to isomorphic weights are always identical at each step of training.

It is important to have random initial weights to break symmetries, especially between hidden units; for example, if the initial weights are all zero, then the hidden units start off indistinguishable and, as just emphasized, they must therefore stay identical throughout training. However, it is often useful to incorporate weight decay in networks so that the randomness that is important in the initial state will decay away in time; then random differences in the initial state do not persist when they are computationally spurious, as here.

Thus, we see that the mystery that RS&G confront us with in the form of RSGnet arises from a number of sources which are quite irrelevant to RS&G's argument:

(18) (a) The input is stretched from five to 16 input units by throwing in 11 extraneous units each of which is individually redundant with the essential five.

(b) Spurious random differences in the initial weights are allowed to persist indefinitely, so that the final network weights obscure the fact that only five of the 16 input units are independent, and that therefore many fewer weights than are shown in the RS&G figures are actually essential.

(c) A set of propositions and encoding of those propositions is chosen which embodies an XOR problem, thereby requiring hidden units.

(d) The hidden layer is chosen to contain four hidden units when only two would do.

Each of (18a–d) significantly complicates the explanation of how RSGnet manages to successfully judge propositions, and together they conspire to obscure the basic connectionist issues involved, which are cleanly exemplified by $RSGnet_0$. None the less, the C-beliefs and L-beliefs that explain $RSGnet_0$'s capacity for judging propositions are at work in RSGnet as well, as we have seen by successively stripping away the irrelevant complications in pushing the explanation of RSGnet back to $RSGnet_2$, and then finally back to $RSGnet_0$.

Notes

1   On p. 321, RS&G add to my brief characterization of connectionist nets the concept of *bias* of a unit. Actually, there is a standard trick, which I adopt here, that eliminates any need for biases: among the input units we assume is included a special 'bias unit' which always has activity 1. A weight b from the bias unit to another unit is formally identical to a bias b on the second unit. Now all the knowledge in the network is uniformly embodied as weights; there is no need to bother with a separate category, biases. In RSGnet, in fact, biases are particularly redundant, since the input units to the net already include not one but *two* bias units (the first two units; see RS&G's table 8.1).

2   This 'plane' is actually an $n-1$-dimensional 'hyperplane'.

3   This expression can be derived from more standard results which express $\mathbf{w}$ in terms of the vector $\mathbf{y}$ of output values ($tr(p)$, $tr(q)$, . . .) and the matrix $\mathbf{X}$ whose columns are the input vectors $\mathbf{p}$, $\mathbf{q}$, . . . For example, Kohonen (1977, p. 114) gives the result (given (7a)): $\mathbf{w} = \mathbf{y}^T(\mathbf{X}^T\mathbf{X})^{-1}\mathbf{X}^T$. The pseudo-inverse matrix $\mathbf{X}^* = (\mathbf{X}^T\mathbf{X})^{-1}\mathbf{X}^T$ has rows $\mathbf{p}^*$, $\mathbf{q}^*$, . . . as seen by the fact that $\mathbf{X}^* \mathbf{X} = \mathbf{1}$, which is equivalent to the definition below of $\mathbf{p}^*$ as the vector satisfying: $\mathbf{p}^* \cdot \mathbf{p} = \mathbf{1}$; $\mathbf{p}^* \cdot \boldsymbol{\pi} = 0$ for all training vectors $\boldsymbol{\pi} \neq \mathbf{p}$; and $\mathbf{p}^* \cdot \mathbf{v} = 0$ when $\mathbf{v}$ is perpendicular to all the training vectors (note 4; note $\mathbf{X}^* \mathbf{v} = 0$). While the pseudo-inverse expressions for $\mathbf{w}$ are well known in the literature (e.g. also Stone, 1986), I am not aware of previous presentations of the much more transparent form (6).

4   See, e.g., the discussion of dual bases in Smolensky (1987). To uniquely specify $\mathbf{p}^*$ in the case when there are vectors $\mathbf{v}$ perpendicular to the whole training set, we also require that $\mathbf{p}^*$ be perpendicular to all such vectors $\mathbf{v}$.

5   If $\mathbf{z}$ happens to be perpendicular to the 16 other propositions, then in fact the same * operation applies in both (11A) and (11B), and thus, in particular, the two $\mathbf{p}^*$s are identical.

6   In the spirit of RS&G I have played along with the rather preposterous suggestion that generalization in RSGnet can be regarded as a model of folk psychological-style inference from beliefs. As we saw clearly in (10), however, generalization in these kinds of networks is driven by *similarity*, and it is therefore quite unacceptable to regard this as an even remotely plausible model of true inference. This kind of objection was identified by

RS&G as Objection (1); their reply is that, since they are making a conditional claim, even if the objection is granted, it serves simply to deny the antecedent of their claim, making the conditional true, and then 'we win by default' (p. 331). But surely to grant the *vacuity* of their conclusion is hardly to defend it.

7   I would, however, like to object to a possible reading of RS&G's position on the status of a particular connectionist model relative to implementation of a particular psychological theory. This is not a matter of *interpretation* but of *fact*. A particular connectionist model such as $RSGnet_0$ either *is* a lower-level implementation of a psychological theory of belief which involves propositional modularity, or it is not. That is, a formal higher-level description of $RSGnet_0$ possessing the three properties defining propositional modularity either exists or fails to exist. One cannot reverse the fact of the matter by some choice of interpretation. I presume that RS&G have no quarrel on this score, but their emphasis on the *interpretative* character of (3) might invite a reading on the implementationalism issue which fails to do justice to the *factual* question.

8   Intuitively, the reason that XOR cannot be computed from the inputs p and q without hidden units is that the input p can neither directly excite nor inhibit the output: in cases when q is FALSE, p should excite the output unit, but in cases where q is TRUE, p should inhibit it. A direct influence from p to the output must be either excitatory or inhibitory, once and for all; but XOR requires that the influence of p reverse depending on the value of q. The network presented below (figure 10.4) is an adaptation for RSGnet of an XOR solution shown in Rumelhart et al. (1986a, p. 64); p excites one hidden unit, and inhibits the other; both these excite the output unit: q is connected in the opposite manner to the hidden units, so that p can only succeed in activating the hidden unit it excites when q is off, and therefore not inhibiting that hidden unit.

9   The reason for the hedge 'we do not expect' is that p XOR q *is* computable without hidden units if the input pair (p, q) is appropriately encoded in the input. The basic requirement for such computability is that the input encode something amounting to the *conjunction* of the truth values of p and q. Such 'conjunctive encodings' (Hinton et al. 1986) arise naturally out of a number of general considerations concerning connection representations, and are central to tensor product representations (Smolensky, 1990b). As a result, many tensor product representations for RS&G's propositions *would* result in those propositions being simultaneously learnable without hidden units, as claimed in section 6. On the other hand, the simple kind of representation adopted by RS&G leads to a version of the XOR problem which *does* require hidden units.

10   This is true for the 16 propositions on which Network A is trained. The 17th proposition, for Network B, violates this generalization slightly in the way it introduces a new value for Y, eggs; this is represented almost exactly like fins and, if necessary, slight weight modifications in the nets

392   PAUL SMOLENSKY

we consider below will suffice to ensure that eggs and fins are treated alike, as required by *f.*

11   Hidden unit *x* has a bias of −33, which can only be overcome if dog (= unit 7) is active (weight = +24) *and* if at least two of units *a, b,* and *c* (= units 11, 12, 15) are active (each weight = +6) – that is, when the first disjunct of (17) is TRUE. Hidden unit *y* has bias +9, which will be overcome by inhibition unless dog is not active (weight = −24) *and* not more than one of units *a, b,* and *c* are active weights = −6), that is, unless the second disjunct of (17) is TRUE. So if either of these disjuncts is TRUE, one or the other hidden unit will be active. The output's bias of −3 will be overcome if either hidden unit (weight = +6) is active. If neither disjunct in (17) holds, neither hidden unit will become active, and the output will be inactive. Here, following RS&G, 'active' and 'inactive' mean activations >0.9, and <0.1, respectively; the size of the weights are set so that net excitation and inhibition of hidden and output units is strong enough (magnitude > 2.2) to achieve activations >0.9 and <0.1 assuming these units have the standard logistic non-linear activation function σ of note 12 below.

12   The one remaining difference between the architectures of $RSGnet_0$ and $Subnet_{mammals}$ is that the output unit of the former network is linear, given by (1), while the output unit of the latter is the non-linear hidden unit of RSGnet. If *o* denotes the linear output, as in (1), then the non-linear output RS&G use is presumably the standard logistic sigmoid $\sigma(o) = 1/[1+e^{-o}]$. But this difference is easily accommodated. The output values for $RSGnet_0$ are +1,−1 for TRUE,FALSE; RS&G take the corresponding non-linear outputs to be 0.9,0.1. But when *o* = +2.2,−2.2, then σ(*o*) =0.9,0.1, so all we need to do in order to accommodate the non-linear output of $Subnet_{mammals}$ in our reduction of that net to $RSGnet_0$ is to replace the output values +1,−1 in our previous analysis of $RSGnet_0$ with the new values +2.2,−2.2; this change is trivial.

13   See, e.g, Munro (1991) for illustrations of rotations in the activity vector space of two hidden units for the 'encoder' task.

References

Chauvin, Y. and Rumelhart, D.E. (forthcoming) *Backpropagation and Connectionist Theory.* Hillsdale, NJ, Erlbaum.
Hinton, G.E., McClelland, J.L. and Rumelhart, D.E. (1986) Distributed representations. In D.E. Rumelhart, J.L. McClelland and the PDP Research Group (eds), *Parallel Distributed Processing: Explorations in the Microstructure of Cognition.* Vol. 1: *Foundations,* pp. 77–109. Cambridge, Mass., MIT Press/Bradford Books.
Jordan, M.I. (1986) An introduction to linear algebra in parallel distributed processing. In D.E. Rumelhart, J.L. McClelland and the PDP Research Group (eds), *Parallel Distributed Processing: Explorations in the Microstructure*

of Cognition. Vol. 1: *Foundations,* pp. 365–422. Cambridge, Mass., MIT Press/Bradford Books.

Kohonen, T. (1977) *Associative Memory: A System-theoretical Approach.* Berlin, Springer Verlag.

McCloskey, M. (1992) Network and theories: the place of connectionism in cognitive science. *Psychological Science* 2, 387–95.

Marr, D. (1982) *Vision.* San Francisco, W.H. Freeman.

Munro, P. (1991) Visualizations of 2-D hidden unit space. Technical Report LIS035/IS91003 School of Library and Information Science, University of Pittsburgh, Pittsburgh, Pennsylvania.

Rumelhart, D.E., Hinton, G.E. and McClelland, J.L. (1986a) A general framework for parallel distributed processing. In D.E. Rumelhart, J.L. McClelland and the PDP Research Group (eds), *Parallel Distributed Processing: Explorations in the Microstructure of Cognition.* Vol. 1: *Foundations,* pp. 45–76. Cambridge, Mass., MIT Press/Bradford Books.

Rumelhart, D.E., Hinton, G.E. and Williams, R.J. (1986b) Learning internal representations by error propagation. In D.E. Rumelhart, J.L. McClelland and the PDP Research Group (eds), *Parallel Distributed Processing: Explorations in the Microstructure of Cognition.* Vol. 1: *Foundations,* pp. 318–62. Cambridge, Mass., MIT Press/Bradford Books.

Sanger, D. (1989) Contribution analysis: a technique for assigning responsibilities to hidden units in connectionist networks. *Connection Science* 1, 115–38.

Sanger, D. (1990) Contribution analysis: a technique for assigning responsibilities to hidden units in connectionist networks. Unpublished PhD thesis, Department of Computer Science, University of Colorado at Boulder.

Smolensky, P. (1986) Neural and conceptual interpretation of parallel distributed processing models. In J.L. McClelland, D.E. Rumelhart and the PDP Research Group (eds), *Parallel Distributed Processing: Explorations in the Microstructure of Cognition.* Vol. 2: *Psychological and Biological Models,* pp. 390–431. Cambridge, Mass., MIT Press/Bradford Books.

Smolensky, P. (1987) On variable binding and the representation of symbolic structures in connectionist systems. Technical Report, CU-CS-355–87, Department of Computer Science, University of Colorado at Boulder.

Smolensky, P. (1990a) Tensor product variable binding and the representation of symbolic structure in connectionist networks. *Artificial Intelligence* 46, 159–216. Reprinted in G. Hinton (ed.), *Connectionist Symbol Processing.* Cambridge, Mass., MIT Press/Bradford Books, 1991.

Smolensky, P. (1990b) Representation in connectionist networks. *Intellectica* 9–10, 127–65.

Smolensky, P., Legendre, G. and Miyata, Y. (1992) Principles for an integrated connectionist/symbolic theory of higher cognition. Technical Report CU-CS-600–92, Department of Computer Science, University of Colorado at Boulder.

Smolensky, P., Mozer, M.C. and Rumelhart, D.E. (eds) (forthcoming) *Mathematical Perspectives on Neural Networks.* Hillsdale, NJ, Erlbaum.

Stone, G.O. (1986) An analysis of the delta rule and the learning of statistical associateions. In D.E. Rumelhart, J.L. McClelland and the PDP Research Group (eds), *Parallel Distributed Processing: Explorations in the Microstructure of Cognition*. Vol. 1: *Foundations*, pp. 444–59. Cambridge, Mass., MIT Press/Bradford Books.

11

Reply to Clark and Smolensky: Do Connectionist Minds Have Beliefs?

Stephen Stich and Ted Warfield

1 Introduction

In chapter 8 of this volume Ramsey, Stich and Garon (henceforth RS&G) argue for a conditional conclusion: '*if* Connectionist hypotheses of the sort we will sketch turn out to be right, so too will eliminativism about propositional attitudes' (p. 312). In the present chapter we will argue that this conditional is false. This, of course, constitutes a change in view for one of us, prompted in part by the good philosophical influence of the other. In the preceding chapters, both Andy Clark and Paul Smolensky also maintain that the conditional is false. So we all agree about the conclusion. But there is no real meeting of minds here. For though we agree on the conclusion, we disagree, at some points quite sharply, about the sorts of arguments that will support the conclusion.

The argument in RS&G (chapter 8) can be divided into two parts. The first of these contends that if certain Connectionist theories are correct, then folk psychology is pretty seriously mistaken. The second claims that if folk psychology is indeed seriously mistaken, then eliminativism follows. Clark (chapter 9), it seems, accepts the second part of this argument, while arguing against the first. But on our view, he has gotten things exactly wrong. The first part of the RS&G argument is *correct*. Clark's attempts to show that Connectionist hypotheses of the sort described in chapter 8 are compatible with folk psychology are both muddled and implausible. This will be our central theme in section 2. The real problem with the argument offered in RS&G comes in the second step. For the mere fact that folk psychology is mistaken does not *by itself* entail eliminativism about propositional attitudes; some further premise is needed. And it is our contention that none of the premises that have been relied on in the literature are at all plausible. In section 3 we will set out the two premises the seem to be most often invoked, and we will explain why both of them are beset with serious problems.

Our reaction to Smolensky's critique (chapter 10) is quite different. In chapter 8, RS&G claim that folk psychology is committed to a thesis that they label 'propositional modularity'. One of the central claims in Smolensky's chapter is that he has shown how to construct 'a Connectionist notion of belief' that has 'two of the three properties defining propositional modularity'. We are more than a bit skeptical about this claim, for reasons set out at the end of section 2.1. But even if Smolensky is right, his 'Connectionist notion of belief' lacks the third property defining propositional modularity. So if RS&G are right in claiming that folk psychology is committed to propositional modularity – and Smolensky gives no indication that he wishes to challenge the claim – then it seems he is *endorsing* the first step in the RS&G argument. For according to Smolensky, the 'Connectionist notion of belief' fails to have one of the three defining properties of propositional modularity that folk psychology endorses. So if the sorts of connectionist models that Smolensky considers give the right account about human propositional memory, then folk psychology is *wrong*.

Smolensky goes on to deny that this is enough to establish eliminativism. So, like us, he thinks that the second step in the RS&G argument is untenable. It is not clear to us exactly *why* Smolensky thinks that the second step in the RS&G argument doesn't work. Some of his comments suggest that, on his view, folk psychology hasn't turned out to be *wrong enough*. Two out of three features of propositional modularity is sufficient to stave off the eliminativist. But on our view the problem with the second step is much deeper than this. For, as we shall argue in section 3, even if the mechanism subserving human propositional memory lacked *all three* of the properties that define propositional modularity, we *still* could not draw an eliminativist conclusion without invoking premises that are, at a minimum, highly problematic.

2　Is Folk Psychology Compatible with Connectionist Models of Memory?

On Clark's reading (chapter 9), there are two main arguments in RS&G aimed at establishing the incompability between 'connectionist storage' and the cluster of claims about common-sense psychological states that

RS&G label 'propositional modularity'. One of these is '[a]n argument concerning superpositional storage and discrete causal efficacy; the other is '[a]n argument concerning natural kinds' (chapter 9, p. 343).

Clark thinks that both of these arguments are mistaken; we think it is Clark who is mistaken. Let's consider first the argument concerning natural kinds.

2.1 Natural kinds and 'higher levels of descriptions'

In RS&G a pair of networks (Network A and Network B) are described, each of which responds affirmatively to an input sequence that has been stipulated to code the proposition that dogs have fur. Both of these networks, it is claimed, 'might serve as models [albeit "tiny toy" models] for a cognitive agent who believes that dogs have fur; both networks store or represent the information that dogs have fur' (chapter 8, p. 329). When we look at the weights and biases in these two networks, however, they appear to have very little in common. Moreover, it is obvious that one could construct many other networks that store the information that dogs have fur, and that those would be

as different from Networks A and B as these two are from each other. The moral here is that though there are *indefinitely* many connectionist networks that represent the information that dogs have fur just as well as Network A does, these networks have no projectable features in common that are describable in the language of Connectionist theory. From the point of view of the connectionist model builder, the class of networks that might model a cognitive agent who believes that dogs have fur is not a genuine kind at all, but simply a chaotically disjunctive set. Common-sense psychology treats the class of people who believe that dogs have fur as a natural kind; Connectionist psychology does not. (Chapter 8, p. 329)

Clark disagrees. As he sees it, RS&G are being 'unduly reductionist' (p. 000) about the ways in which connectionists can characterize their kinds. There is, he claims, a 'higher level of description' (p. 347) that will unify what seems, '*at the units-and-weights level, to be a chaotic disjunction of networks*' (p. 347) To illustrate the sort of higher level of description that he has in mind, Clark sketches the sort of '*post hoc*' cluster analysis that Sejnowski and Rosenberg (1986) carried out on NETtalk. The crucial finding here is that, though different training runs led to versions of NETtalk that 'had very different descriptions at the units-and-weights level of analysis', it none the less 'turned out that all the versions of NETtalk yielded pretty much the *same* clustering profile when subjected to *post hoc* statistical analysis' (p. 347) 'The moral' that Clark would draw here is one we happily endorse: 'there may be higher-level descriptions which are both scientifically well grounded and which capture commonalities between networks which are invisible at the units-and-weights level of analysis' (p. 347).

But how, exactly, is this moral relevant to RS&G's natural kind argument? Apparently Clark thinks that just as various versions of NETtalk yield pretty much the same clustering profile so, too, various networks that model cognitive agents who share a given belief will also manifest higher-level commonalities that are invisible at the units-and-weights level of analysis. Indeed, according to Clark,

> the bulk of [his] chapter has amounted to an unabashed empirical bet that any system complex enough to count as a believer will reveal (under some *post hoc* analysis) semantically clustered patterns of activation. Such reasonably complex models as we have available (e.g. NETtalk) lend support to this contention. (chapter 9, p. 352)

We find this a deeply puzzling passage and, we must confess, we are not at all sure what it *means*. But on the most charitable interpretation we can come up with, Clark's 'unabashed empirical bet' strikes us as a sure loser. Indeed, it is our contention that the sort of higher-level commonalities that Clark's argument requires *aren't even there in the case of systems like NETtalk*. To see the point we have to get a bit clearer about *which* systems are alleged to have the 'higher-level' common properties.

One way of characterizing the relevant class of systems is behaviorally or functionally. 'NETtalk is a connectionist network trained to negotiate the domain of text-to-speech transformations. More accurately, it takes a window of text and, letter by letter, yields a coding for phonemes which is then fed into a speech synthesizer which produces the spoken sounds' (pp. 345–6). Let us use the term NETTALKER for any system that can carry out the appropriate text-to-speech transformations at a suitably impressive level of accuracy. Another way to characterize the relevant class of systems is by describing their architecture. 'The network [NETtalk] itself is fairly large, comprising 309 units and 18,629 connectors. The units include 80 hidden units and 55 output units corresponding to distinct phonemes' (p. 346). We will use the term NETtalk-structure for systems that fit this description and are otherwise similar to the network described by Sejnowski and Rosenberg (1986).

Now what Sejnowski and Rosenberg showed is that several different NETTALKERS *all of which had NETtalk-structure* 'yielded pretty much the *same* clustering profile when subjected to *post hoc* statistical analysis' (p. 347). On the basis of this it *might* be plausible to conjecture that all

NETTALKERS with a NETtalk-structure will yield much the same clustering profile. However, it is almost certainly the case that one could build lots of NETTALKERS that do not have anything resembling a NETtalk-structure. One can, in all likelihood, build NETTALKERS with 800 hidden units, or with 8,000. And, as Clark notes (note 4), when they are 'trained up' using back-propagation, systems with hidden units to spare tend to find strategies very different from those invoked by systems with fewer hidden units. The Sejnowski and Rosenberg cluster analysis was restricted to systems with a NETtalk-structure. Thus it provides no reason at all to suppose that *all* NETTALKERS, whatever their structure, will exhibit 'much the same clustering profile'. Indeed, it is far from clear that it even makes sense to compare the clustering profile of two NETTALKERS with radically different structures.

To see how all of this is relevant to RS&G's natural kind argument, let us return to Clark's 'unabashed empirical bet'. What Clark is betting is that 'any system complex enough to count as a believer' will manifest some higher-level commonalities with all other such systems. But now how does Clark propose to characterize the systems to which the bet applies? Plainly he doesn't want to restrict his claim to systems with structures like those of Network A and Network B, nor, for that matter, to networks with any other specific architectural features. Rather, the systems he's talking about are to be characterized behaviorally or functionally, in much the same way that the class of NETTALKERS was characterized a few paragraphs back. But, as we have just seen, there is not the slightest plausibility to the suggestion that all NETTALKERS exhibit similar or identical cluster profiles. And since Clark's 'bet' was based entirely on the analogy with NETtalk, it seems pretty clear that the smart money will bet against him.

Before leaving the natural kind argument, let us consider briefly how what we have said might apply to Smolensky's view. On what is perhaps the most natural reading, Smolensky's reply to RS&G's natural kind argument is rather similar to Clark's. For Smolensky, too, is urging that there are non-obvious 'higher-level' features shared by certain connectionist networks, though on casual inspection the networks appear to have little in common. The difference, of course, is that Smolensky does not rely on analogies; he explains in great detail how the putatively shared features (C-belief and L-belief) are to be defined.

Our problem with Smolensky's argument is that we are not at all sure *which* systems he thinks will manifest the common features that he characterizes. To see the point, let us return to the 'unabashed empirical bet' that is at the heart of Clark's argument. What Clark is betting is that 'any system complex enough to count as a believer' that *p* will manifest appropriate higher-level commonalities with any other system complex enough to count as a believer that p. And, indeed, this is exactly what is needed to rebut RS&G's natural kind argument. For what RS&G claim is that 'the class of networks that might model a cognitive agent who believes [that p] is not a genuine natural kind at all, but simply a chaotically disjunctive set' (chapter 8, p. 329). So if Smolensky is offering a serious rebuttal to RS&G's argument, he must be claiming that *any* connectionist network that would count as a model of a cognitive agent who believes that p would manifest the C-belief that p or the L-belief that p. However, if *this* is what Smolensky is claiming, then by his own admission his argument does not even come close to establishing his conclusion. For surely most, if not all, of the networks that we would take seriously as models of a cognitive agent who believes that p are going to be vastly more complex than either RSGnet or Smolensky's RSGnet$_0$. And far from giving us some reason to believe that *all* of these models have the C- or L-belief that p, Smolensky concedes that he does not even know how to define C- and L-belief for these more complicated systems. Now, of course, it may be unfair to Smolensky to attribute to him the claim that *all* networks that would count as a model of a believer that p will manifest the C- or L-belief that p. Certainly, he never explicitly makes such a claim. However, if he doesn't accept this claim, then it is hard to see how his sophisticated construction of C- and L-belief is at all relevant to RS&G's natural kind argument. RS&G claim that networks (*all* networks, of course, not *some* networks) that model agents who believe that p 'have no projectable features in common that are describable in the language of Connectionist theory' (Chapter 8, p. 329). So if we read Smolensky as claiming only that *some* networks that model agents who believe that p have the C- or L-belief that p, then he has simply failed to respond to RS&G's challenge.

At one point in chapter 10, Smolensky claims that it is 'likely' that 'explanatory notions [that are] richer, more powerful and more cognitively relevant than C- and L-beliefs will emerge' from Connectionist theory. Though he quite sensibly goes on to note that '[w]hether the new notions will support the conclusions drawn here from C- and L-beliefs is impossible to know in advance' (Chapter 10, p. 380). On the other side, RS&G cheerfully concede in their Reply (2a) that they have no argument demonstrating that it is impossible to discover the sort of 'covert functionally discrete . . . encoding' that folk psychology seems to require, and that 'if such a covert system were discovered, then [their] argument would be seriously undermined' (chapter 8, p. 331). So, though Smolensky's tone is perhaps a bit more optimistic than RS&G's, it seems to us that the difference between his position and RS&G's is all but indiscernible.[1]

2.2 Superpositional storage and discrete causal efficacy

The second argument in RS&G that Clark considers is the one he calls the argument from 'superpositional storage'. The essential claim in that argument is that, in networks like A and B, in which information 'is stored holistically and distributed throughout the network . . . [It] makes no sense to ask whether or not the representation of a particular proposition plays a causal role in the network's computation' (Chapter 8, p. 327). By contrast, common-sense psychology assumes that it typically *does* makes sense to ask whether a given belief played a role in a certain cognitive episode, or whether it was causally inactive in that episode. Moreover, common sense recognizes that in some cases '[a]n agent may have two long-standing beliefs which are both equipotent (both apt to cause the same piece of behaviour on a given occasion) AND YET the agent may *as a matter of fact* act on the basis of only *one* of the two beliefs' (Clark, chapter 9, p. 345). Clark labels this latter thesis the 'Equipotency claim'.

In responding to RS&G's argument, Clark's first move is to propose that we identify a belief with a certain pattern of hidden unit activation. If we do this, there will be no problem in saying whether or not a given belief plays a causal role in a particular computation that the network performs. But, as Clark goes on to note, this proposal was anticipated in RS&G, and criticized on the grounds that having a certain belief is typically a long-standing feature of a system, while being in a certain activation state is not an enduring state of the network.

Very well, Clark continues, '[s]uppose we accept this. The next obvious move is to suggest that we might identify the belief not with the *transient* activation pattern but with the long-standing *disposition* to produce that activation pattern in a given circumstance' (p. 350.) But, as Clark reports, this move, too was anticipated and criticized RS&G.

> The trouble is, of course, that it is not obvious that the various dispositions said to correspond to various beliefs are sufficiently extricable from one another, *qua* subvening states of the system, to count as the 'discrete, independently causally active states that folk psychology requires'. (p. 350)

'But', Clark continues,

> this just muddies the waters unnecessarily. Beliefs need to be long-standing states, yes. And a belief-in-action needs to be capable of having a functionally discrete realization, yes. But the folk are nowhere

committed to the view that the belief-in-action and the long-standing belief must be *physically identical*. The long-standing stored state may be the disposition [to produce an appropriate pattern of hidden unit activation]. And the discrete causal potency of that belief may be the power of that class of hidden unit activation states to cause a distinctive kind of output. (p. 350)

On our view, there are two rather different problems with this reply. First, the interpretation of the propositional modularity assumption that is implicit in the reply is much too weak; indeed, it is so weak that it renders the assumption completely trivial. For, on the interpretation of propositional modularity that Clark's argument requires, no deterministic system that stores propositional information could fail to satisfy propositional modularity. If this is right, there is nothing at all we could learn about the workings of such a system that would show that it violates propositional modularity. Secondly, as Clark himself concedes, his suggestion does not really address the problem posed by equipotency unless it is supplemented with an assumption about recurrency. But that assumption leads to models of cognitive activity that are both bizarre and unworkable. We'll elaborate on each of these problems in turn.

Imagine that you are given a black box which behaves just the way that RS&G's Network A does. Given any of the 16 coded sentences in table 8–1 of RS&G, it answers yes or no, and the answers are the same as the ones Network A would produce. Suppose further that we know the black box is a deterministic device: it responds the same way each time it is given an input of a particular type. Beyond this, we will assume we know nothing at all about how the device works.

Let's now ask whether the device respects the principle of propositional modularity. On Clark's interpretation of the principle, it would seem that the answer must be yes. For, every time the black box is given a particular input, it produces the same output. And there must be *some* pattern of internal states – simple or complex – which the system goes through in getting from the input to the output. So, following Clark, we can identify the 'belief-in-action' with this pattern of internal states, whatever it may be. Of course, this pattern is a transient state, not an enduring state of the system. So if we are looking for long-standing beliefs, it is not a good candidate. But this needn't worry us. For the system must have a long-standing disposition to produce the 'belief-in-action' pattern, and we can identify that disposition with the long-standing belief. Of course, the 'belief-in-action' is a very different state of the system from the long-standing belief. But, according to Clark, that's just fine. There is no need for the two to be identical. So it looks like our black box satisfies propositional modularity, as Clark would interpret it. And, since we know nothing about the box except that it is a deterministic device that responds appropriately, it looks like *any* deterministic device that can respond appropriately to various coded sentences must represent them in a propositionally modular fashion. On Clark's reading of propositional modularity, anything that behaves like a believer really is one.

Now we can imagine an opponent who would be quite happy with this result. The opponent we are imagining contends that common-sense psychology makes no really substantive claims about the mechanisms underlying behavior. There are passages in Dennett's work which appear to endorse such a view (see, for example, Dennett, 1987), and Jackson and Pettit (1990) also seem to flirt with this sort of neo-behaviorist account of belief. But this would be an odd position for Clark to endorse. A central theme in Clark's work is that if the scientific account of the mechanisms underlying behavior turn out to conflict with the common-sense account, 'then we've got trouble' (p. 352) since the eliminativist will have won the day. Since Clark is prepared to take this eliminativist threat seriously, he can't adopt the toothless interpretation of propositional modularity that his reply to RS&G requires. For, on that interpretation, any deterministic system that behaves like a believer automatically satisfies propositional modularity, and there is no possibility that a scientific account of the mechanisms underlying that behavior will conflict with propositional modularity.

Let's turn, now, to Clark's discussion of the equipotency problem. In the case sketched by RS&G, Clouseau has two long-standing beliefs each of which might contribute to his inference that the butler is lying. On Clark's proposal, both of these long-standing beliefs are dispositions of the belief-storage system. So how are we to tell which of them contributed to the inference? Clark's answer appeals to the notion of recurrence. In order to play a role in an inference, the dispositional state must first produce a hidden activation pattern, which causes an output; that output is 'then cycled back as input' to the storage system, which then yields the conclusion about the butler as a second output.

Perhaps the first thing to say about this proposal is that it hardly seems in the spirit of connectionism, since it ignores what ardent connectionists see as one of the most important virtues of their models: the capacity to simultaneously make use of a large number of facts or constraints. On Clark's account of inference, by contrast, each intermediate step in an inference must be individually activated and then cycled back as a premise in a new computational cycle.

But this is the least of the problems with Clark's proposal. A much more serious problem is that the idea just won't work when the logical forms of the conditionals involved in the inference are a bit more complex. Suppose, for example, that Clouseau has long-standing beliefs of the form:

If p^* then p
If q^* then q
and
If p & q then s

Now suppose he is informed that p^*. After a brief delay during which he may think about other matters, he is informed that q^*. How is he supposed to get to s? Well, as Clark tells the story, when he learns that p^*, he outputs p. At this point he might recycle p into the system. But it wouldn't produce s. Now q^* comes along. The system outputs q. Feeding this back as input won't yield s either. As far as we can see, there is *no* way for the system that Clark sketches to get from p^* and q^* to s. So, far from having the resources to handle cases of equipotence, the sort of system Clark proposes does not even have the capacity to handle simple inferences.

3 Does Eliminativism Follow From the Fact That Folk Psychology is Mistaken?

What we have been arguing thus far is that neither Clark nor Smolensky has provided any reason to question the first step in the argument set out in RS&G. That step claims if certain Connectionist theories about the mechanisms underlying human memory are correct, then folk psychology is mistaken. Smolensky, it seems, accepts this step, since he grants that the sorts of connectionist models he considers do not manifest the 'modular causal roles of the beliefs of folk psychology.' (chapter 10, p. 376). So if, as RS&G argue, folk psychology is committed to beliefs having modular causal roles, then, if Connectionist theories of the sort Smolensky and RS&G have in mind turn out to be correct, it follows that folk psychology is wrong – and wrong in a pretty serious way. Clark clearly does not accept the first step in the RS&G argument, and tries to argue that connectionist models of the appropriate sort are compatible with propositional modularity. But, as we have seen, his arguments just don't work.

In this section we propose to turn our attention to the second part of the RS&G argument, the one that claims that eliminativism follows if folks psychology turns out to be seriously mistaken. As noted earlier, it is our contention that this second part of the RS&G argument is untenable. Before setting out our reasons for rejecting this part of the argument, we would do well to remind ourselves what eliminativism is, and *isn't*. As used by RS&G, and by most of the other writers in the area, 'eliminativism' is a label for an *ontological* doctrine. What eliminativism about the propositional attitudes claims is that *there are no such things*. According to eliminativism, the beliefs, desires and other propositional attitudes invoked in common-sense explanations and predictions of behavior and action have the same ontological status as witches, caloric fluid and phlogiston: *they do not exist*. Eliminativism, at least as we use the term, is *not* the thesis that common sense makes many false claims about propositional attitudes. It is *not* the thesis that folk psychology is seriously mistaken. Of course, this latter thesis is invoked by those who wish to argue for eliminativism. But it surely is not the case that this latter thesis *by itself* entails eliminativism. To see the point we need only remind ourselves that the ancients held some wildly mistaken views about the sun, the stars, and even about the brain and other parts of their own bodies. But from the fact that ancient folk astronomy and ancient folk physiology were seriously mistaken, it surely does not follow that the sun, the stars and the brains that our ancestors were so wrong about did not exist. Analogously, there is a significant logical gap between the claim that folk psychology is seriously mistaken, and the claim that the propositional attitudes to which folk psychology appeals do not exist. How might this gap be filled?

There is remarkably little discussion of this question in the literature on eliminativism. However, it is our guess that most of those who are tempted to infer from the nonexistence of propositional attitudes the falsehood of folk psychology are tacitly assuming one of a pair of premises. Fleshed out in the right way, either one of the premises would be adequate to fill the logical gap. That's the good news for eliminativists. The bad news is that both of the premises are deeply problematic. We'll take them up one at a time.

3.1 Eliminativism and the description theory of reference

As Lycan (1988, p.4) has rightly noted, many eliminativists (and, indeed, many of their opponents) write as though they accepted some version of the description theory of reference for the theoretical terms employed in common-sense and scientific theories. Put very roughly, this account of reference claims that a term embedded in a theory refers to those things in the world that satisfy all (or most) of some special class of 'descriptions' (or open sentences) that the theory entails about the things. One particularly lucid and influential account along these lines was suggested by David Lewis (1970, 1972). According to Lewis (1972, p. 209), a theory typically provides an 'implicit functional definition' of the terms it introduces. Theoretical terms are 'defined as the occupants of the causal roles specified by the theory . . . as *the* entities, whatever those may be, that bear certain causal relations to one another and to the referents of the [observational] terms (Lewis, 1972, p. 211).[2] But what happens if the theory turns out to be false, if the pattern of causal relations specified by the theory doesn't really obtain? If this is the way things turn out, then, on Lewis's view, the theoretical terms would refer to nothing at all. Thus, for example, since the pattern of causal relations specified by phlogiston theory does not obtain, the term 'phlogiston' refers to nothing. Phlogiston does not exist. Analogously, '[i]f the names of mental states are like theoretical terms, they name nothing unless the theory . . . is more or less true' (Lewis, 1972, p. 213).

Obviously, if Lewis's account of the reference of theoretical terms is correct, it will provide just what the eliminativist needs to fill the logical gap noted above. For if Lewis is right, and if folk psychology turns out to be a seriously mistaken theory, then it will indeed follow that there are no such things as beliefs and desires. 'Belief,' 'desire' and the other theoretical terms of folk psychology will refer to nothing.

Unfortunately for the eliminativist, it is far from clear that Lewis is right, or indeed that any version of the 'description' theory gives the right account of reference for theoretical terms. In the two decades since Lewis's papers appeared there has been something of a sea of change in philosophical opinion on these matters. In response to the arguments and examples offered by Putnam, Kripke and others, most philosophers working in this area have concluded that description theories like the one elaborated by Lewis do not provide the correct account of the reference of terms used in a theory. The dominant contemporary view seems to be that some version of the causal/historical account of reference – something along the lines of the accounts sketched by Putnam (1975), Kripke (1972) and Devitt (see Devitt, 1981; Devitt and Sterelney, 1987) – will prove to be the correct account of the reference of most theoretical terms. According to these causal/historical accounts, the reference of a term is determined by a causal chain connecting users of the term with previous users from whom they acquired the term, and ultimately proceeding back to an event or series of events in which the term is introduced to refer to a certain object or kind.

One of the selling points of causal/historical theories is that they do a much better job of handling what Devitt and Sterenly (1987) call 'the problems of ignorance and error'. Causal/historical theories have a ready explanation for the fact that a person can refer to an object or kind despite having wildly mistaken views about that object or kind. Thus on the causal/historical theory it makes perfectly good sense to suppose that ancient star gazers and modern astronomers are talking about the very same heavenly bodies, even though the ancients thought that stars were holes in the celestial dome through which the light in the heavenly region beyond could penetrate. On description theories, by contrast, it is not at all obvious how it is possible for the ancients to be referring to anything at all.

All of this spells trouble for eliminativists. For if their strategy for filling the logical gap between the premise that common-sense psychology is seriously mistaken and the conclusion that the terms of common-sense psychology don't refer to anything is to invoke some version of the description theory of reference, then they are going to have to *defend* the theory and show that the competing causal/historical account is mistaken. We are more than a bit skeptical that this can be done. Indeed, one of us has argued elsewhere that there may be *no* correct theory of reference for terms embedded in a seriously false theory (see Stich, 1991, and forthcoming). But nothing in the current chapter turns on that rather radical view. Our point here is simply that the strategy for filling the gap that we've been considering is highly problematic. It is going to take some pretty fancy argument to make the description theory look plausible.

3.2   Eliminativism and 'constitutive' properties

In some of the literature in this area there are hints of a rather different strategy for filling the gap in the eliminativist argument. Rather than relying on the description theory of reference, this strategy invokes the notion of a conceptually necessary or 'constitutive' property. The basic idea is that some of our concepts require, as a matter of logical or conceptual necessity, that any object to which the concept applies must have certain properties. These properties are 'constitutive' of the concept. We would not apply the concept to an object, or count the object as falling within the category that the concept specifies, unless the object has the constitutive properties. Thus, for example, it might be urged that *being unmarried* and *being male* are constitutive properties for the concept of a bachelor, or that *having a negative charge* is constitutive for the concept of an electron. If something is not male and unmarried, we just would not classify it as a bachelor; if something does not have a negative charge, it would not count as an electron.

It is relatively easy to see how the notion of a constitutive property might be used to fill the logical gap in eliminativist arguments. If it can be shown that a certain property is constitutive for having propositional attitudes, then if science (or philosophical argument) can demonstrate that no one has that property, it follows that the no one has propositional attitudes. Thus, for example, if *having propositionally modular psychological states* is constitutive for having beliefs and desires, then if people do not have propositionally modular psychological states, then they do not have beliefs and desires. We are not at all sure that anyone really construes eliminativist arguments in this way, though there are a number of authors who sometimes write as though they take quite seriously the idea that certain properties are constitutive of the concept of belief, thus inviting this sort of eliminativist argument (see, for example, Evans, 1982, pp. 65, 104; Clark, 1989, pp. 146–50; 1991a, b, s.II; Davies, 1991, p. 239ff). The closer one gets to Oxford, the more fashionable this talk of 'constitutive' properties becomes. But if it is not clear that anyone actually interprets eliminativism in this way, it is clear that this strategy for filling the gap in the eliminativist argument faces some daunting difficulties.

The first difficulty is making a case for the claim that one or another property is in fact constitutive for having propositional attitudes. Thus, for example, the mere fact (if indeed it is a fact) that lots of people *think* or *presuppose* that beliefs are propositionally modular is surely not enough to establish that propositional modularity is constitutive for having beliefs. Nor would it be enough to show that many people would refuse to apply the term 'belief' to any state which is not propositionally modular. For it might simply be the case that most people (or indeed all people) happen to have some strongly held opinions about propositional attitudes, and that these opinions are false. There was, after all, a time at which most people would have refused to apply the term 'star' to an object that did not rotate around the earth. As we now know, they had some deeply entrenched false opinions about stars.

For those familiar with central themes in the philosophy of language during the past four decades, this first difficulty suggests a second. The whole idea of constitutive or conceptually necessary properties seems to presuppose that we can draw a distinction between analytic sentences (roughly those that are 'true in virtue of their meaning alone') and synthetic sentences (roughly those whose truth or falsity depends, in part, on the way the world is). If being unmarried is constitutive for being a bachelor, then presumably 'All bachelors are unmarried' is analytic. And if being propositionally modular is constitutive for being a belief, then 'All beliefs are propositionally modular' is analytic as well. But, of course, Quine and others have offered some enormously

influential arguments aimed at showing that there is no analytic/
synthetic distinction to be drawn (see, for example, Quine, 1953;
Harman, 1967). There are no sentences which are true solely in virtue
of their meaning. If this is right then there are no constitutive or
conceptually necessary properties.

We don't propose to review the arguments against the existence of
the analytic/synthetic distinction. Indeed, for current purposes we need
not even assume that the conclusion of those arguments is correct. All
that is needed for current purposes is the observation that the very
existence of analytic truths and thus of constitutive or conceptually
necessary properties is hotly disputed and highly problematic. Those
who want to fill the logical gap in the eliminativist argument by invoking
the idea of constitutive properties owe us some further argument. They
must, at least, make it plausible that the arguments against the analytic/
synthetic distinction are mistaken, and that the notion of constitutive
properties is defensible. If there are philosophers who choose to follow
this path, we wish them well. But we don't propose to hold our breath
until they succeed.

4 Conclusion

It's time to sum up. In chapter 8, RS&G claim that if certain sorts of
connectionist accounts of human memory turn out to be right, then so
too will eliminativism about the propositional attitudes. Their argument
has two parts. The first part maintains that if the connectionist theories
in question are right, then common-sense psychology has made some
major mistakes. As we read him, Smolensky agrees with this point,
though perhaps he does not regard the mistakes as *major* mistakes.
Clark, on the other hand, disagrees sharply with this part of the RS&G
argument. We side with RS&G and Smolensky, and against Clark. In
section 2 we set out some of the ways in which Clark's arguments are
muddled and unconvincing.

The second part of RS&G's argument maintains that if common-
sense psychology has made major mistakes, then eliminativism is
correct: there are no such things as beliefs and desires. Clark, it seems,
is happy enough with this part of the RS&G argument. But we are not.
It's our contention that there is no obvious way to get from the premise
that common-sense psychology is a seriously mistaken theory to the
conclusion that 'belief,' 'desire' and the other 'theoretical' terms of folk
psychology refer to nothing. In section 3 we considered two strategies

that might be invoked to get from the premise to the conclusion – the two that most writers seem to rely on – and we argued that both of them are extremely problematic. So unless there is some other way to fill the gap in the eliminativist argument, the bottom line is this: connectionism *might* show that commonsense psychology is wrong, but it lends no support whatever to the claim that common-sense psychological states do not exist.

Notes

1   One caveat is worth noting. Smolensky's notions of C- and L-beliefs only possess the first two properties of propositional modularity but not the third. It is not clear whether he expects that the 'richer, more powerful' explanatory notions that he hopes will emerge will have all three. If they don't, then they will not count as an adequate response to RS&G's challenge.

2   The locution that Lewis actually uses at the end of this quote is 'O-terms' not 'observational terms'. O-terms are 'original terms' which are understood prior to the introduction of the theory. The distinction, though an important one, is not relevant to our current concerns.

References

Clark, A. (1989) *Microcognition*. Cambridge, Mass., MIT Press/Bradford Books.

Clark, A. (1991a) Systematicity, structured representations, and cognitive architecture. In T. Horgan and J. Tienson (eds), *Connectionism and the Philosophy of Mind*. Dordrecht, Kluwer.

Clark, A. (1991b) Radical assent. *The Aristotelian Society* 65 (suppl.).

Davies, M. (1991) Concepts, connectionism and the language of thought. In W. Ramsey, S. Stich and D. Rumelhart (eds), *Philosophy and Connectionist Theory*. Hillsdale, NJ, Erlbaum.

Dennett, D. (1987) *The Intentional Stance*. Cambridge, Mass., MIT Press/Bradford Books.

Devitt, M. (1981) *Designation*. New York, Columbia University Press.

Devitt, M. and Sterelny, K. (1987) *Language and Reality*. Cambridge, Mass., MIT Press/Bradford Books.

Evans, G. (1982) *The Varieties of Reference*. Oxford, Oxford University Press.

Harman, G. (1967) Quine on meaning and existence (part I). *Review of Metaphysics* 21, 124–51.

Jackson, F. and Pettit, P. (1990) In defense of folk psychology. *Philosophical Studies* 59, 31–54.

Kripke, S. (1972) Naming and necessity. In D. Davidson and G. Harman (eds), *Semantics of Natural Language*. Dordrecht, Reidel.

Lewis, D. (1970) How to define theoretical terms. *Journal of Philosophy* 67, 427–46. Reprinted in *Philosophical Papers*. Oxford, Oxford University Press, 1983.

Lewis, D. (1972) Psychophysical and theoretical identifications. *Australasian Journal of Philosophy* 50, 249–58. Reprinted in N. Block (ed.), *Readings in Philosophy of Psychology*, vol. 1, pp. 207–15. Cambridge, Mass. Harvard University Press, 1980. (Page references are to the Block volume.)

Lycan, W. (1988) *Judgement and Justification*. Cambridge, Cambridge University Press.

Putnam, H. (1975) The meaning of 'meaning'. In K. Gunderson (ed.), *Language, Mind and Knowledge: Minnesota Studies in the Philosophy of Science* 7. Minneapolis, University of Minnesota Press.

Quine, W. (1953) *From a Logical Point of View*. Cambridge, Mass., Harvard University Press.

Sejnowski, T. and Rosenberg, C. (1986) NETtalk: a parallel network that learns to read aloud. The Johns Hopkins University, Electrical Engineering and Computer Science Technical Report, JHU/EEC-86/01.

Stich, S. (1991) Do true believers exist? *The Aristotelian Society* 65 (suppl.), 229–44.

Stich, S. (forthcoming) *Deconstructing the Mind*.

Index

Abrahamsen, Adele 309n
Ackley, D.H. 70, 74
activation evolution equation 40
activity vectors *see* vectors
ADDERS xii
AI *see* artificial intelligence
algorithmic level of description
  xii–xiii, 11, 293, 377–8; of
  computers 294; conflict at 294; of
  human cognition 294; of visual
  perception xii, 293
algorithms 12; constituents and 11;
  defined on superposition vectors 17;
  deterministic nature of symbol
  manipulation 4; ICS systems 17–18;
  simulated annealing 74, 259; Turing
  machine and 4
analytic/synthetic distinction 305, 307,
  408–9
Anderson, D.Z. 71
Anderson, J.A. 42, 189
Anderson, J.R. 29, 37, 38, 39, 69,
  319, 335n
Arbib, M. 78, 90, 346
Aristotle 166
artificial intelligence (AI) 30, 38, 182,
  341
Asanuma, C. 47
assignment of blame problem 64
associationism 164, 165, 166, 191

back-propagation 92, 364; Delta Rule
  370

Ballard, D.H. 29, 66, 83n, 91, 133,
  143, 153n, 170, 193n, 194n;
  implementational approach 147;
  Necker cube bi-stability 93, 94
Bayesian mechanism 140
Bechtel, William 309n
behavioural psychology xi
beliefs xi, xiv, 91; common-sense
  298–9, 303, 315–20, 349–50, 352;
  connectionist *see* connectionist
  beliefs; hidden unit activation
  348–52, 401; models of 318;
  transient activation state and 349–50,
  401
Berkeley, George 146
best fit principle 73
Black, I.B. 158n
Block, Ned 336n, 350
Bolinger, D. 145
BoltzCONS model 147
Boltzmann machine 70, 74, 83n, 84n,
  113, 195n
Bower, G. 319, 335n
brain xi, 46; causal transactions
  between processes of 5; damage to
  134, 138–9; as neural network xiii,
  9; noise sensitivity 134, 138–9; as
  semantic system 5
'Brain-State-in-a-Box' model 189
brain-style modelling 143–6
Broadbent, D. 95, 335n

Carroll, Lewis 142

causal efficacy xiv, 188–91, 215, 297, 315, 340, 376; L-beliefs 376; superpositional storage and 347–8, 401–4; of tensor product representations 20–2
center-embedding sentences 118
Chase, W.G. 133
Chauvin, Y. 364
Cherniak, C. 335n
Chomsky, Noam: formal language hierarchy 250; generative nature of linguistic competence 117; language hierarchy 258; natural language grammar 265; productivity argument 156n; statistical models of learning 145
Church, 44
Churchland, Paul M. 90, 334n, 335n, 349; similarity metric 346
Churchland, P.S. 90, 93
Clark, Andy 294, 301, 339–56, 395–404 passim; common sense psychology 295, 296, 297, 299; connectionist beliefs 302–3; equipotency 345, 349–51, 401, 403–4; hidden unit activation 348–52, 401; natural kinds argument 344–5, 348, 397– 400; NETtalk 301, 345–7, 397–9; semantic facts 352–4; superpositional storage 343–4, 347–8, 401–4
classicism xiii
classicism: active symbols 139–41; combinatorial syntax and semantics of representations xiii, 3, 98, 101–11, 112–13, 115, 116; complex mental representations 100–11; compositionality see compositionality of representations; computer metaphor see computer metaphor; computers 113; connectionism and xiv, 3–27, 97–115, 379; constituency 97, 201–2; constituents and 6, 8, 11, 22; continuous magnitudes 139–41; expressions 97; inference, systematicity of 129–31; language of thought xiii, 98, 112, 199; learning 113–14; linear associator model 232; machines 113; mental processes 6; mental representations 6; productivity of cognition 7, 116–19; refinement/

implementation debate 6, 8, 11–13, 146–8, 166–9, 304; rules, explicitness of 141–3; semantic content 97; semantic interpretation 10; semantic relations between symbols 4; semantics 202; 'soft' constraints 139–41; stochastic mechanisms 139–41; structure-sensitive operations 98, 111–15; symbol manipulation xiii, 9; syntax of mental representations 201–2; systematicity and xiii–xiv, 22–6, 119–23, 129–31, 191, 202–3, 220;Turing machine and 3–4; Turing machines see Turing machines; von Neumann machines see von Neumann machine
cluster analysis 308n, 346, 348–9, 355n, 397, 399
cluster profiles 299
coffee story 13, 66–7, 172–6, 177, 179, 203–10, 287n
cognition: algorithmic level 294; computational level 294; Computational Theory of Mind (CTM) 3, 6; implementation level 294; inferential coherence of see inferential coherence of cognition; language acquisition 294; Language of Thought Hypothesis (LOT) 3, 6; as network see networks; productivity of see productivity of cognition; Representational Theory of Mind (RTM) 3; as symbol manipulation xiii, 9, see also symbol manipulation; systematicity of see systematicity of cognition
cognitive science: birth of 4; Turing and 4
cognitive system 62; goal conditions 62–4; prediction goal 63–4, 73; prediction-from-example goal 63–4, 65, 73, 74
Cohen, M.S. 71
Collins, A. 318, 335n
common-sense psychology xi, xiv–xv 294–303; beliefs 298–9, 303, 315–20, 349–50; causal efficacy see causal efficacy; connectionism and xiv–xv, 295–338; connectionist model of memory and 396–404; desires xi,

xiv 341; eliminativism and xiv, 295–6, 298–9, 312–14, 395–6, 404–9; functional discreteness *see* functional discreteness; inference 317–18; memory, models of 318–20; ontologically conservative theory change 298, 314; ontologically radical theory change 298–9, 304, 314; propositional modularity *see* propositional modularity; semantic interpretability *see* semantic interpretability

competence theory 76

competence/performance distinction: ICS systems 258–60; sub-symbolic paradigm 76

compositionality of representations 7–8, 18, 123–9, 169–83, 218n; connectionism and 8; ICS systems and 18, 262–3, 269, 271; strong 8, 13–17, 177–83, 210–16, 219n; ultra-local case 169–71; weak 8, 13–17, 171–7, 203–10, 218n, *see also* systematicity of cognition

computation theory 111; effective procedures theory and 36; production system of 36, *see also* von Neumann machine

computational level of description xii–xiii 293, 377; of computers 294; of human cognition 294; of visual perception xii, 293

computational temperature 74

Computational Theory of Mind (CTM) 3, 6

computer metaphor 3–5; content-based retrieval 133; exceptional behaviour 133–4; graceful degradation, failure to display 135–6, 140; 'hundred step' constraint 133, 137; intuitive processes and 134; memory 134–5; mental symbols and 5; noise sensitivity and 134, 138–9; non-verbal processes and 134; parallel computation and 137–8; physical damage and 134, 138–9; problems with 133–6; rule-governed behaviour 133–4, 140; rules, explicitness of 141–3; semantics and 3, 4; speed of cognitive processes and 133, 137–8; storage 134–5; syntactic properties of

symbols 4; syntax and 3, 4, *see also* Turing machine

computers: algorithmic level 294; computational level 294; data processing 294; data storage 294; hardware 293; implementational level 293

conceptual unit hypothesis 41

conceptual-level 38; descriptions of intuition 73–80; schemata 78–9, 80; spreading activation 77–8, *see also* sub-conceptual level

conflated concepts 309n

connection evolution equation 40

connectionism: back-propagation 92, 364; belief *see* connectionist beliefs; brain and 9; brain-style modelling 143–6; causal connectedness 97; classicism and xiv, 3–27, 97–115, 379; common-sense psychology and xiv–xv 295–338, 396–404; complex mental representations 100–11; compositionality and *see* compositionality of representations; constituent structure of mental representations 6; constituents, context-dependency of 8, 13; continuity assumption 68–71; distributed representations 103–11, 169–83, 190; eliminativism and xiv, 303–7, 312; graph structures 102–3; ICS systems *see* Integrated Connectionist/Symbolic systems; labels, role of 101–2; language of thought and 164–97; learning and 10, 113–14; machines 113; memory and xiv, 117, 324–34; mental processes as representational 6; necessity objection to 267–70; NETtalk 301; networks *see* networks; non-verbal processes and 134; ontologically radical theory change 298–9, 304; pattern recognition 10, 92, 133; popularity of 132–6; productivity of cognition 7, 116–19; projectable feature of 357–62; Proper Treatment of Connectionism (PTC) 28–84, 165–6, 184–8, 191, 361, 377–81; propositional modularity and 321–2, 324–34; reasoning 114–15; refinement/implementation debate 6,

connectionism (*continued*)
8, 11–13, 146–8, 166–9, 304;
representationalism and 93–7;
representations as 'distributed' over
micro-features 103–11; semantic
content 97; semantic interpretation
10; statistical inference 182;
sufficiency objection to 268;
systematicity of cognition and xiv,
199–222; as theory of
implementation 146–8
connectionist beliefs   298–303, 304,
357–92, 395–410; causal efficacy and
376, 377; C-beliefs 299–301, 302,
303–4, 359–60, 362, 365–70, 373–6,
377, 379, 380, 383–4, 400;
functional discreteness and 374–6,
377; L-beliefs 299–301, 302, 303–4,
359–60, 362, 370–3, 377, 379, 380,
383–4, 400; learning analysis 363,
370–3; need for 363–5; propositional
modularity and 373–6, 402–3, 408;
semantic interpretability and 374,
377; weight analysis 363, 364,
365–70
connectionist dynamical system
hypothesis   40–1
conscious rule interpreter 36, 37, 52,
53, 197n; seriality and 57–8; skill
acquisition and 37; sub-symbolic
implementation of rule interpretation
58–9; sub-symbolic paradigm and
55–61; symbolic implementation of
rule interpretation 58–9; unconscious
rule interpretation hypothesis 38, 39
conservative theory change   298, 314
constituency: causal efficacy   188–91;
classical 97, 201–2; explanatory
relevance 188–91; vector
decomposition and 188–91
constituents 105–6; algorithms and 11;
causal role of 11; classical 6, 8, 11,
22; connectionist 6, 8, 11;
constituent structure of mental states
6, 13–17, 66–8; context-
independency 8, 13; decomposition
of 276; ICS systems 17–26; L-
beliefs and 379; real-constituency
106–7; role-dependent 14; semantic
evaluability of 11; of tensor product
representations 17–26, 241, 242, 249

constitutive properties: eliminativism
and   407–9
constraint propagation   135
context-dependence   8, 13, 60–1,
67–8, 207–10
continuous computation   68–71
Copernicus   298, 304, 313
Cottrell, Gary   336n, 349
Crick, F.   47
CTM *see* Computational Theory of
Mind
cultural knowledge   35–7, 56;
conscious rule interpreter 36; rules
36–7
Cummins, Robert   142, 193n, 278n
Cussins, Adrian   336n, 349; conflated
concepts 309n; misconceived
composites 309n

Davidson, Donald   308n
Davies, Martin   354, 408
Dell, G.S.   82n
Delta Rule   370
Dennett, Daniel   90, 281n, 336n, 403
Derthick,   84n
description theory of reference   304,
405–7
desires: common-sense psychology
and   xi, xiv, 341
determinism   135
Devitt, M.   406
discrete computation   71
Dolan, C.   178, 195n
Dreyfus, H.   90
Dreyfus, S.   90

effective procedures theory   36
eliminativism   93, 186, 235, 293–310,
347–52, 360, 361, 378; causal/
historical view of theory change
304–7, 406–7; common-sense
psychology and xiv, 295–6, 298–9,
312–14, 395–6, 404–9;
connectionism and xiv, 303–7, 312;
constitutive properties and 407–9;
description theory of reference and
405–7; meaning 312; natural kinds
argument 344–5, 348, 397–400;
ontologically conservative theory
change 298, 314; ontologically

radical theory change 298–9, 304–7, 314; phlogiston/oxygen theory change 306, 314, 406; propositional modularity and 297–9, 304, 315; superpositional storage 343–4, 347–8, 401–4
Enc, Berent 307, 309n
Evans, G. 408
excitatory connections 28
explanatory levels *see* levels of description

Fahlman, S.E. 90, 133, 134
Feldman, J.A. 29, 42, 78, 82n, 83n, 133, 150n, 194n, 280n, 281n; Necker cube bi-stability 93, 94
Feyerabend, Paul 334n, 335n
Fodor, J.D. 145
Fodor, Jerry A. xii, xiv 5, 91–160, 164–97 *passim*, 199–222, 223, 280n, 294, 312, 315, 321–2, 335n, 336n, 355n, 357, 360, 379; causal efficacy 190; on classicism 6; compositionality 7–8; Computational Theory of Mind (CTM) 3, 6; computer metaphor 3; constituent structure of mental states 6, 66; context-dependency of 8, 13; inferential coherence 7; language of thought 98; Language of Thought Hypothesis (LOT) 3, 6; necessity objection to connectionism 267–70; refinement/implementation debate 6, 8, 11–13, 146–8, 166–9, 304; Representational Theory of Mind (RTM) 3; semantic facts 352–3; semantic relations between symbols 4; superposition representations 18; symbolic paradigm in cognitive modelling 33; syntactic properties 4; systematicity 6–7; tensor product representations 16, 17–26; truth preservation 65
folk psychology *see* common-sense psychology
functional discreteness xiv, 297, 301, 315, 316–19, 331–3, 340, 374–6, 377, 378
functional discreteness: C-beliefs and 302, 374–6, 377; connectionist beliefs and 302; L-beliefs and 302, 374–6, 377

Galileo 313
Garon, Joseph 302, 303–4, 311–36, 339, 340–55, 357–90, 395–405, 409; common-sense psychology 294–300
Geach, P. 154n
Gelder, Tim van 196n, 283n
Geman, D. 72
Geman, S. 72
Generalized Delta Rule 370
generative grammar 264–7; split intransitivity 265–6
goal conditions 62–4
Gödel box 242–4, 245–6, 248, 278n
Gödel number 194n, 241
Goodman, N. 335n, 340
grammar: formal 265; generative 264–7; harmonic 254–8, 260, 265, 266, 267, 379; natural language 265
graph structures 102–3

Harman, G. 409
harmonic grammar 254–8, 265, 266, 267, 379; rules of, psychological reality of 260
harmony 250; of activation vectors 250–4; of symbol structures 254–8
harmony maximization 253–4
harmony theory 73–6; best fit principle 73; Boltzmann machine and 74; expert intuition 74; inference 73; model of expert intuition 74; prediction goal 73; prediction-from-examples goal 73, 74; schemata 78–9, 80
Hatfield, G. 90, 134–5, 141, 152n
Haugeland, John 54, 55, 273, 312
Hayes, P.J. 66, 170, 193n
Hebb, Donald 42, 132
Heil, John 308n
Hewett, C. 99, 138
Hillis, D. 138
Hinton, Geoffrey E. 29, 42, 63, 72, 83n, 84n, 90, 133, 134, 154n, 194n, 195n, 385; Boltzmann machine 70, 74; conjunctive coding 179, 391n; micro-features 172; non- verbal processes 134; role relations 157n
Hofstadter, D.R. 68, 141
Holland, J. 335n
Hooker, C. 335n
Hopcraft, J.E. 36

Horgan, Terence 221n, 278n
Hull, C.L. 132
Hume, David 146, 157n, 360

ICS systems *see* Integrated
    Connectionist/Symbolic systems
implementation: refinement/
    implementation debate 6, 8, 11–13,
    146–8, 166–9, 304
implementational level of
    description 293, 377; of computers
    293; of human cognition 294; of
    visual perception xii, 293
implementationalism 361, 378;
    methodological implications of 184–8
inference 5; common-sense
    psychology 317–18; harmony theory
    and 73; logical 74–7; soft constraints
    72; statistical 182; systematicity of
    129–31
inferential coherence of cognition xiii,
    6, 7
inferential coherence of cognition: ICS
    systems and 18, 263–4, 269–70,
    271
inhibitory connections 28
Integrated Connectionist/Symbolic
    (ICS) systems 8–9, 13–17, 224–88;
    algorithms of 17–18; cognitive
    architecture 261–7; combinatorial
    strategy for explaining productivity
    235–6; competence/performance
    distinction 258–60; compositionality
    and 18, 262–3, 269, 271;
    computational architecture 229–60;
    constituents 17–26; explaining
    productivity in 245–9; generative
    grammar 264–7; goals of 225–9,
    271–4; harmony maximization 253–4;
    inferential coherence and 18, 263–4,
    269–70, 271; Optimality Theory
    266–7; principles of 14, 224, 225,
    234, 261–2; principles rejected in
    224–5; processing principles of 234;
    productivity in 235–6, 245–9, 263–4,
    271; representational principles of
    234; representations in 14–17;
    structural principles 225; structure-
    sensitive recursive function
    computation 246–9; symbolic
    processing in 231–2; systematicity

22–6, 262–3, 269, 271; tensor
    product representations *see* tensor
    product representations; vectors
    14–16
intuition: conceptual-level descriptions
    of 73–80; expert 74; sub-symbolic
    paradigm and 39–42, 73–80
intuitive processor 37–8, 52, 58–9;
    conceptual unit hypothesis 41;
    connectionist architecture of 40;
    connectionist dynamical system
    hypothesis 40–1; natural language
    processes and 56; skill acquisition
    and 37; sub-conceptual level
    hypothesis 42; sub-conceptual unit
    hypothesis 42, 57; sub-symbolic
    hypothesis 42; sub-symbolic
    paradigm and 55–61, 73–80, *see also*
    sub-symbolic paradigm; symbolic
    paradigm

Jackson, Frank 336n, 350, 403
Jordan, M.I. 71, 365

Kant, Immanuel 78, 110–11
Katz, J.J. 154n
Kawamoto, A.H. 141, 156n, 179
Kintsch, W. 335n
Kirchoff's Law 75
Kitcher, P. 334n, 335n
knowledge: bootstrapping 36;
    conscious rule interpreter 36; context
    and 60–1; cultural 35–7, 56; domain
    35; effective procedures theory 36;
    encoding 342; formality 36;
    formalization of 35–44; individual
    37–8; innate 159n; intuitive 37–8,
    39–42; linguistic formulations of 36;
    logic 35; P-knowledge 59–60; public
    access to 35; reliability of 36; rules
    36–7; S-knowledge 59–60; scientific
    35, 36; soft constraints 72; in sub-
    symbolic systems 59–61; task 59–60;
    universality 36
Kosslyn, S.M. 90, 134–5, 141, 152n
Kripke, S. 406
Kuhn, Thomas 311, 334n, 335n

LADDERS xii
Laird, J. 140
Lakoff, G. 91
language acquisition 8, 294

language of thought xiii, 98, 112, 152n, 199
language of thought: connectionism and 164–97
Language of Thought Hypothesis (LOT) 3, 6
Larkin, J.H. 36
Lashley, K. 42
Lavoisier, Antoine L. 335n, *see also* phlogiston/oxygen theory change
learning: classical models 113–14; connectionist models 10, 29, 92, 113–14
learning analysis 363, 370–3
Legendre, G. 267
levels of description xii–xiii, 293, 301, 347, 377–8, 397–400
levels of description: of computers 294; conflict between 294; of human cognition 294; of visual perception xii, 293, *see also* algorithmic level of description; computational level of description; implementational level of description
Lewis, C.H. 38
Lewis, David 356n, 406, 410n
limitivism: methodological implications of 184–8
linear associator model 232
LISP 15, 30, 147, 159n, 183, 190, 217, 282n
logic systems 4–5; model-theoretic perspective 5; proof-theoretic perspective 5
logical inference *see* inference
LOT *see* Language of Thought Hypothesis
Lucretius 145
Lycan, W. 335n, 336n, 405

McCarthy, John 335n
McClelland, Jay L. 29, 82n, 83n, 135, 140, 141–2, 149–50, 151n, 156n, 179, 194n, 335n, 342, 355n
McClelland, J.L.: center-embedding sentences 118; on computer metaphor 159n; conjunctive coding 179; on connectionism as implementation 147, 159n; innate knowledge 158n; levels of organization 147; past-tense model

44–5, 60; productivity of cognition 118; 'proper description of processing' 30; recursion 118–19; representationalism 93, 94, 95
McCloskey, M. 363
McCulloch, W. 230
Macdonald, Cynthia 3–26, 293–310
Mackworth, A. 135
McLaughlin, Brian P. xii, 199–222, 294
McLaughlin, Brian P.: on classicism 6; constituents and 6, 13; pattern recognition 10; refinement/implementation debate and 8, 12; systematicity 7; tensor product representations 16, 17–26
Madell, G. 335n
Maratsos, M. 118
Marr, David 294, 377–8; levels of description xii–xiii, 293–4; visual perception xii, 293
memory xi
memory: brain damage and 134; connectionist models of xiv, 117, 324–34; models of 318–20
mental states: constituent structure of *see* constituents
mental symbols: semantic properties of 5; syntactic properties of 5
micro-features 103–11, 172, 207
Miller, George 107
Minsky, M. 70, 82n, 145, 230, 281n; assignment of blame problem 64
misconceived composites 309n
Mozer, M.C. 189
multi-dimensional scaling 46
Munro, P. 392n

Nagel, E. 335n
natural kinds argument 344–5, 348, 397–400
necessity objection to connectionism 267–70
NETtalk 301, 397–9; analysis of 345–7; cluster analysis 346
networks 102–3, 297–8; back propagation 92; connectionist model of memory 324–34; constituents, status of 8, 13; as dynamic systems 9; excitatory connections 28; feedback 10, 92, 114; ICS systems

networks (*continued*)
see Integrated Connectionist/
Symbolic (ICS) systems; inhibitory
connections 28; learning 10, 29, 92,
113–14; local connectionist 8, 230–2;
nodes xiii; pattern recognition 10;
recurrent 351; self-programming 29;
semantic evaluability 10; strongly
compositional 8, 13–17, 210–16;
superpositional storage 343–4,
347–8; units see units; weakly
compositional 8, 13–17, 203–10;
widely distributed 8
Neumann, von see von Neumann
neural architecture hypothesis 39
neural levels: sub-conceptual level and
46–51
Newell, A. 33, 91, 99, 140, 195n,
335n
Newtonian mechanics 12, 75–6
nodes 93, 97; causal connectedness
97; degrees of activation xiii, 9;
semantic content 97, see also
networks; units

Ohm's Law 74, 75
ontologically conservative theory
change 298, 314
ontologically radical theory
change 298–9, 304–7, 314
Optimality Theory 266–7; constraints
in 266
optimization theory 258
Osgood, Charles 132
Osherson, D. 143
oxygen/phlogiston theory change 306,
314, 406

Papert, S. 70, 145
parallel distributed processing (PDP)
see connectionism
parse trees 14, 15, 17, 379
past-tense model 44–5
pattern recognition 10, 92, 133
patterns of activity xiv, 10, 12, 301
'PDP': use of name 194n
PDP School 194n
Pearl, J. 72
performance theory 76
Pettit, P. 403

phlogiston/oxygen theory change 306,
314, 406
Pinker, S. 143, 150, 156n, 157n,
281n, 355n
Pitts, W. 230
Pollack, J.B. 82n, 231, 281n
Postal, P. 154n
prediction goal 63–4, 73
prediction-from-examples goal 63–4,
65, 73, 74
Priest, Graham 355n
Prince, Alan 143, 149–50, 266, 267,
281n, 355n
productivity of cognition xiii, 6, 7,
116–19, 269–70; combinatorial
strategy for explaining 235–6; ICS
systems and 235–6, 245–9, 263–4,
269–70, 271
proof theory 112
Proper Treatment of Connectionism
(PTC) 28–84, 165–6, 184–8, 191,
361, 377–81
propositional attitude psychology see
common-sense psychology
propositional content xi
propositional logic 4–5
propositional modularity xi, xiv–xv,
297–9, 304, 315–20, 340–2, 359,
360, 396, 402, 408; causal efficacy
see causal efficacy; C-beliefs and
373–6, 377; characterization of xv;
connectionism and xiv–xv, 321–2,
324–34; connectionist beliefs and
373–6, 402–3; functional
discreteness see functional
discreteness; L-beliefs and 373–6,
377; nature of xv; RTM and 3;
semantic interpretability see semantic
interpretability
propositional states see propositional
modularity
PTC see Proper Treatment of
Connectionism
Ptolemy 298, 304, 313
Putnam, H. 349, 406
Pylyshyn, Zenon W. xiv, 5, 91–160,
164–97 *passim*, 199, 200, 218, 221n,
223, 294, 312, 321–2, 355n, 356,
379; coffee story 13, 66–7, 172–6,
177, 179; compositionality 7–8; on
computer metaphor 159n; constituent

structure of mental states 6, 66; context-dependency of 8; inferential coherence 7; necessity objection to connectionism 267–70; refinement/ implementation debate 6, 8, 11–13, 146–8, 166–9, 304; semantic relations between symbols 4; superposition representations 18; symbolic paradigm in cognitive modelling 33; systematicity 6–7

quantum mechanics 12, 75–6, 191, 323
Quillian, M. 318, 335n
Quine, W.V.O.: analytic/synthetic distinction 305, 307, 408–9

radical theory change 298–9, 304–7, 314
Rakie, P. 158n
Ramsey, William 302, 303–4, 311–36, 339, 340–55, 357–90, 395–405, 409; common-sense psychology 294–300
rationality: in sub-symbolic paradigm 65–6
reasoning 114–15
recurrent networks 351
recursion 118–19
refinement/implementation debate 6, 8, 11–13, 146–8, 166–9, 304
relative well-formedness see harmony
Representational Theory of Mind (RTM) 3
representationalism 6, 93–7
representations 29; combinatorial syntax and semantics of xiii, 3, 98, 101–11, 112–13, 115, 116; complex 100–11; compositionality of see compositionality of representations; distributed 103–11, 169–83, 297–8, 342; as 'distributed' over micro-features 103–11; ICS systems and 235, 241, 262–3; tensor product 13, 14–15, 16–17, 178–83, 190, 212, 236, 239, 250, 379
Rey, Georges 194n
Riley, M.S. 73, 74
Rochester School 193n, 194n
Rosenberg, C.R. 50; cluster analysis 397, 399; NETtalk 347, 397, 398–9
RTM see Representational Theory of Mind

rule interpretation see conscious rule interpreter
rules 36–7, 38; conscious rule application 55–61; formulation of 37
Rumelhart, David E. 29, 41, 57, 82n, 83n, 96, 149–50, 151n, 194n, 286n, 335n, 355n, 364, 391n; Boltzmann machine 74; center-embedding sentences 118; on computer metaphor 159n; on connectionism as implementation 147, 159n; continuity assumption 70; Generalized Delta Rule 370; harmony theory 74; innate knowledge 158n; levels of organization 147; past-tense model 44–5, 60; productivity of cognition 118; 'proper description of processing' 30; recursion 118–19; representationalism 93, 94, 95; schemata 78

San Diego School 194n
Sanger, D. 383, 388
Schaffner, K. 335n
Schank, Roger 83n
schemata 78–9, 80
Schneider, W. 90
Schwarz, Georg 193n, 278n
scientific revolution 311
Sejnowski, T.J. 50, 63, 72, 82n, 83n, 90, 143; Boltzmann machine 70, 74; cluster analysis 397, 399; NETtalk 347, 397, 398–9
Sellars, W. 335n
semantic evaluability see semantic interpretability
semantic facts 352–4
semantic interpretability xiv, 11, 17, 296, 297–8, 301, 315, 340, 374, 377, 378; activity vectors 10; C-beliefs and 374, 377; classicism and 10; connectionism and 10; L-beliefs and 374, 377; patterns of activity 10; units and xiii, 10, 11
semantic relations between symbols 4–5
semantics: classical 202; combinatorial syntax and semantics of representations xiii, 3, 98, 101–11, 112–13, 115, 116; computer metaphor and 3, 4; semantic

semantics (*continued*)
properties of symbols 5; sub-conceptual/neural levels relationship and 47; sub-symbolic 64, 95; symbol manipulation and xiii
seriality: rule interpretation and 57–8
Sharpe, R. 335n
Shastri, L. 72, 82n
Shepard, R.N. 46
Simon, H.A. 33, 133, 195n, 335n
simulated annealing 74, 259
skill acquisition 37–8
Smolensky, Paul 28–84, 94, 143, 151n, 154n, 158n, 164–97, 199–222, 223–88, 294, 320–1, 322, 323, 342, 356n, 357–92, 395, 396, 399–400, 404, 409; activity vectors 10, 299–301; associationism 164, 165, 166, 191; C-beliefs 299–301, 302, 303–4, 359–60, 362, 365–70, 373–6, 377, 379, 380, 383–4, 400, 410n; on classicism 6, 7; coffee story 13, 172–6, 177, 179, 203–10, 287n; common-sense psychology and 295, 296, 297, 298, 299; compositionality 8, 13–17, 127, 128, 129, 203–16; conceptual unit hypothesis 41; conjunctive coding 179; connectionist belief *see* connectionist beliefs; connectionist dynamical system hypothesis 40–1; conscious rule interpretation 36–7; constituents and 6, 8, 17–26; cultural knowledge 35–7; Gödel box 242–4, 245–6, 248, 278n; ICS systems *see* Integrated Connectionist/Symbolic (ICS) systems; inferential coherence 18; intuitive processor *see* intuitive processor; knowledge, formalization of 35–44; L-beliefs 299–301, 302, 303–4, 359–60, 362, 370–3, 377, 379, 380, 383–4, 400, 410n; learning analysis 363–4, 370–3; network analysis techniques 346; non-verbal processes 134; ontologically radical theory change 304, 305; productivity of cognition 7; Proper Treatment of Connectionism (PTC) 28–84, 165–6, 184–8, 191, 361, 377–81; refinement/implementation debate 6, 8, 11–13, 146–8, 166–9, 304;

strongly compositional structure 8, 13–17, 210–16; sub-conceptual level *see* sub-conceptual level; sub-conceptual unit hypothesis 42, 57; sub-symbolic paradigm *see* sub-symbolic paradigm; systematicity 7, 199–222; tensor product representations 178–83, 190, 212, 236, 239, 379; ultra-local case 169–71; unconscious rule interpretation hypothesis 38, 39; vector as mental representation 13; Visa box 244–5, 248, 279n; weakly compositional structure 8, 13–17, 203–10; weight analysis 363, 364, 365–70
soft constraints 72, 73, 75, 139–41, 265–6
Sperber, 78
spin glasses 83–4
Stabler, E. 142
Sterelny, K. 406
Stich, Stephen 301, 302, 311–36, 339, 340–55, 357–90, 395–410; analytic/synthetic distinction 305; common-sense psychology 294–300; eliminativism 93; propositional modularity 315; radical theory shift 303–7
Stone, G.O. 390n
structure-sensitive operations 98, 111–15
sub-conceptual level 42; computation at 68–72, 77; continuity 68–71; methodologies 45–6; multi-dimensional scaling 46; neural levels and 46–51; past-tense model 44–5; principles 61–2; reduction of cognition to 51–5; representation at 44–6, *see also* conceptual-level
sub-conceptual level hypothesis 42
sub-conceptual unit hypothesis 42, 57
sub-symbolic hypothesis 42; connectionist dynamical system hypothesis 40–1; sub-conceptual hypothesis 42; sub-conceptual unit hypothesis 42, 57
sub-symbolic paradigm 33–4; best fit principle 73; competence/performance distinction 76; conscious rule application in 55–61;

continuity and 68–71; dimensional shifts 54; goal conditions 62–4; incompatibility with symbolic paradigm 43–4; intuitive processor *see* intuitive processor; knowledge in 59–61; prediction goal 63–4, 73; prediction-from-example goal 63–4, 65, 73, 74; rationality in 65–6; semantic shifts 54; semantics in 64; sub-symbolic hypothesis *see* sub-symbolic hypothesis, *see also* symbolic paradigm

sufficiency objection to connectionism 268

superposition representations 17, 18

superpositional storage 343–4, 401–4; causal efficacy and 347–8, 401–4

symbol manipulation: cognition as xiii, 9; deterministic nature of 4; in neural networks 12; syntax and semantics xiii; systematicity of cognition and xiv; Turing machine and 4

symbolic paradigm 33, 53; computation 71–2; conscious rule application 55; incompatibility with sub-symbolic paradigm 43–4; individual knowledge in 37–8; intentional instantiation 54; intuition in 37–8; skill in 37–8; systematic reductions 54, *see also* sub-symbolic paradigm

symbols: causal properties of 4, 5; mental 5; semantic properties of 5; semantic relations between 4–5; shape of 4; syntactic properties of 4, 5

syntax: classical 201–2; combinatorial syntax and semantics of representations xiii, 3, 98, 112–13, 115, 116; computer metaphor and 3, 4; sub-conceptual/neural levels relationship and 47; symbol manipulation and xiii; syntactic properties of symbols 4, 5

systematicity of cognition xiii, xiv, 6–7, 119–23, 199–222; classicism and xiii–xiv, 22–6, 119–23, 129–31, 191, 202–3, 269; connectionism and xiv, 199–222; ICS systems and 22–6, 262–3, 269, 271; problem of 200–3; symbol manipulation and xiv; tensor product representations and 22–6, *see also* compositionality of representations

systematicity of inference 129–31

systematicity of language comprehension and production 119–23

Tarski, Alfred 153n

tensor product representations 13, 14–15, 16, 178–83, 190, 212, 379; causal efficacy of 20–2; constituents of 17–26, 241, 242, 249; formal languages and 250–60; in ICS systems 236–9, 242; linguistic structures 241; recursive 239; systematicity and 22–6

theory: causal/historical view of change 304–7, 406–7; ontologically conservative change 298, 314; ontologically radical change 298–9, 304–7, 314; phlogiston/oxygen theory change 306, 314, 406; references of terms in 304–7; refinement of 304; scientific revolution 311

thought *see* cognition

Tienson, John 278n

Total Mystery Theory 227

Toulouse, G. 83n

Touretzky, David S. 66, 83n, 147, 195n, 281n

Turing, Alan xiii, 3, 4, 91, 133, 143, 166; algorithms 4; cognitive science and 3–4; computer metaphor 3–4; effective procedures theory 36

Turing machine 3–4, 30, 91, 97, 113, 143, 160n, 229, 230, 250, 258; algorithms 4; description of 4; deterministic nature of symbol manipulation 4; memory capacity 117; operation of 4; programs for 44; states of 4; symbol manipulation and 4

Ullman, J.D. 36

unconscious rule interpretation hypothesis 38, 39, 55

units xiii, 28, 91, 97, 146, 298, 321

units: circuit state feature 74; computational temperature 74;

units (*continued*)
degrees of activation xiii, xiv, 9, 28, 213; feature 74; filler 18, 19; in harmony networks 74; hidden 9, 10, 29, 45, 320, 321, 343, 346, 348–52, 364; input 9, 28–9, 321, 346; output 29, 321, 346; receptive field 91; semantic interpretability and xiii, 10, 11; similarity metric 346; simulated annealing 74, 259; stochastic 74, 91; superpositional storage 343–4, 347–8, 401–4; value units 91; vectors *see* vectors; weighted connections xiii, 9, 28, 29, 91, 113, 321, *see also* networks; nodes

VanLehn, Kurt 194n
VAX 137, 139, 144
vector space theory 232–3
vectors: activity xiv, 10, 12, 15, 16, 18, 19, 44, 67, 74, 213–15, 233, 237, 241, 250–4, 299–301, 359, 379; complex 15, 16; constituent structure 235–42; decomposition of 15, 17, 21, 24, 188–91, 241; definition 281n; evolution of 215; filled role 15; filler 14–15; functionally discrete 301; ICS systems 14–16; as mental representation 13; micro-feature 104; role 14–15; state 40; superposition 17, 18, 77, 179, 211–14; tensor

product 15, 16–17, 18, 20, 212–14, 248; weight 359, 379
virtual machine 36, 52–3, 158n, *see also* conscious rule interpreter
Visa box 244–5, 248, 279n
visual perception: algorithmic level xii, 293; computational level xii, 293; implementational level xii, 293
von Neumann machine 51, 52, 58, 91, 97, 113, 141, 160n; effective procedures theory and 36; programs for 43, 44; sub-conceptual levels and 55; VAX as 144

Waldrop, M.M. 83n
Waltz, D.L. 82n
Wanner, E. 118
Warfield, Ted 295, 296, 301, 302, 395–410; analytic/synthetic distinction 305; radical theory shift 303–7
Watson, J. 93
weight analysis 363, 364, 365–70
Wheeler, D. 281n
Wilkes, K. 335n
Wilson, 78
witches 312–13
Woods, W.A.

Ziff, P. 125